A Synthesis of Rese
Second Language V
English

MW00581089

"I applaud the authors for this sizeable undertaking, as well as the care exercised in selecting and sequencing topics and subtopics. A major strength and salient feature of this volume is its range: It will serve as a key reference tool for researchers working in L2 composition and in allied fields."

John Hedgcock, Monterey Institute for International Studies

"The authors command the field in ways that perhaps no one else does. Their vast collective knowledge shines on every page."

Barbara Kroll, University of Southern California

Synthesizing 25 years of the most significant and influential findings of published research on second language writing in English, this volume promotes understanding and provides access to research developments in the field. Overall, it distinguishes the major contexts of English L2 learning in North America; synthesizes the research themes, issues, and findings that span these contexts; and interprets the methodological progression and substantive findings of this body of knowledge. Of particular interest is the extensive bibliography, which makes this volume an essential reference tool for libraries and serious writing professionals, both researchers and practitioners, both L1 and L2.

This book is designed to help researchers become familiar with the most important research on this topic; to promote understanding of pedagogical needs of L2 writing students; and to introduce graduate students to L2 writing research findings.

Ilona Leki is Professor of English, directs the English as a Second Language program at the University of Tennessee, and is chair of the University's Interdisciplinary Program in Linguistics.

Alister Cumming is Professor and Head of the Modern Language Centre, Department of Curriculum, Teaching and Learning, Ontario Institute for Studies in Education, University of Toronto.

Tony Silva is Professor and Director of the ESL Writing Program, Department of English, Purdue University.

A Synthesis of Research on Second Language Writing in English

Ilona Leki
University of Tennessee

Alister Cumming
University of Toronto

Tony Silva
Purdue University

 Routledge
Taylor & Francis Group

NEW YORK AND LONDON

First published 2008
by Routledge
270 Madison Ave, New York, NY 10016

Simultaneously published in the UK
by Routledge
2 Park Square, Milton Park, Abingdon, Oxon OX14 4RN

Routledge is an imprint of the Taylor & Francis Group, an informa business

© 2008 Taylor & Francis

Typeset in Sabon by Prepress Projects Ltd, Perth, UK

Library of Congress Cataloging in Publication Data
Leki, Ilona.
A synthesis of research on second language writing in English/Ilona Leki, Alister Cumming and Tony Silva.
p. cm.
Includes bibliographical references and index.
ISBN 978–0–8058–5532–6 (hb: alk. paper) — ISBN 978–0–8058–5533–3 (pb: alk. paper) — ISBN 978–0–203–93025–0 (ebook: alk. paper) 1. English language—Study and teaching—Foreign speakers. 2. English language—Composition and exercises—Study and teaching—Foreign speakers. 3. Second language acquisition. I. Cumming, Alister H. II. Silva, Tony. III. Title.
PE1128.A2L383 2008
808'.0428—dc22
2007051687

ISBN 10: 0–805–85532–7 (hbk)
ISBN 10: 0–805–85533–5 (pbk)
ISBN 10: 0–203–93025–8 (ebk)

ISBN 13: 978–0–805–85532–6 (hbk)
ISBN 13: 978–0–805–85533–3 (pbk)
ISBN 13: 978–0–203–93025–0 (ebk)

To my beautiful and growing family
IL

To Razika
AC

To Nadine, Jack, Kathy, Claire, and Anthony
TS

Contents

Preface

A Synthesis of Research on Second Language Writing in English is a topical introduction to research in the explosively growing field of second language (L2) writing. The book is intended to provide access to the enormous and rapidly evolving research literature for specialist, veteran researchers, for graduate students new to the field, and for teacher educators and program administrators. The three such compendiums that exist for first language (L1) writing in English—covering 20 years each from 1942 to 1962 (Braddock, Lloyd-Jones, & Schoer, 1963), 1962 to 1982 (Hillocks, 1986), and 1983 to 2002, which includes for the first time a chapter on L2 writing (Smagorinsky, 2006)—have been essential reading for L1 writing professionals. With the present volume we hope to provide the same service to L2 writing professionals.

The book is a thematically organized synthesis of 20 years of published research on L2 writing in English, but it is neither a simple bibliography nor an annotated bibliography. Rather it is an interpretive, narrative synthesis of published research, that is, an analytical discussion of the most significant and influential findings of the past 20 years designed to promote understanding of L2 writing in English and to provide access to research developments in the field. It is intended for L2 writing researchers worldwide, L2 writing practitioners, graduate students in TESOL methods courses, L1 English writing professionals and practitioners, and graduate students in teacher education courses in literacy development, as well as writing centers serving the growing number of L2 writers using those services. Overall, the book distinguishes the major contexts of English L2 learning in North America, synthesizes the research themes, issues, and findings that span these contexts, and interprets the methodological progression and substantive findings of this body of knowledge.

Other compendium volumes provide different coverage of L2 writing research. Three bibliographies of L2 writing exist but are now more than a decade out of date: Schechter and Harklau (1991), Silva, Brice, and Reichelt (1999), and Tannacito (1995). Other overview books on the topic of L2 writing include Grabe and Kaplan (1996) and Casanave's

(2004) coverage of controversies in L2 writing, introductory textbooks for initial or inservice teacher education (e.g. Ferris & Hedgcock, 2005; Hedge, 1988; K. Hyland, 2003b; Leki, 1992; Reid 1993), edited collections of articles on distinct topics (e.g. Kroll, 2003; Matsuda, Cox, Jordan, & Ortmeier-Hooper, 2006; Silva & Matsuda, 2002), and studies of specialized subtopics related to L2 writing, including the recent University of Michigan Press series on L2 writing (e.g. Benesch, 2001, and Canagarajah, 2002a, on critical pedagogy; Casanave, 2004, on controversies in L2 writing; Connor, 1996, on contrastive rhetoric; D. Ferris, 2002, 2003, and L. Goldstein, 2005, on responding to writing; Johns, 1997, on genre; Liu & Hansen, 2002, on peer responding; Weigle, 2002, on assessment). In 2006 *Written Communication* published a summary of research articles on writing tallied by educational context, which combines L1 and L2 studies, over the past 5 years (vol. 23, no. 4). Both Norris and Ortega's (2006) and Cummins and Davison's (2007) edited volumes employ meta-analysis and other syntheses of research on L2 language teaching and learning more generally. By contrast, *A Synthesis of Research on Second Language Writing in English* contributes a comprehensive, topically focused, scholarly review of research on L2 writing, tracing the impact of significant research developments in the discipline. Of particular interest is the extensive bibliography, which we hope will make it an essential reference tool for libraries and serious writing professionals, both researchers and practitioners, both L1 and L2.

The synthesis is divided into three sections:

I   **Contexts for L2 Writing** reviews research on L2 writers' responses to the tasks confronting them in school settings from elementary through graduate school (chapters 1–4), outside school settings in the community, workplace, and professional environments (chapters 5–7), and in the context of the ideological issues surrounding and permeating L2 writing in English in North America (chapter 8).
II   **Instruction and Assessment** focuses on pedagogical issues grounded in theoretical foundations and teacher orientations (chapter 9) and on assessment issues within both courses and institutions (chapter 10).
III **Basic Research on Second Language Writing** reviews basic empirical research on L2 writers (chapter 11), their composing processes (chapter 12), their texts at the discourse level (chapter 13), and their texts at the sentence level (chapter 14).

A Note about Authorship

Given the different material treated, the approach taken to each section has necessarily varied. Section I provides a somewhat linear trajectory, moving from early descriptions of L2 writer needs to emerging understandings of the contexts of L2 writing. Section II provides a state-of-the-art approach grounded in consideration of the background to these current conditions. Section III leads researchers to published reports of research focused within particular parameters, dealing with particular focal areas, or coming to particular conclusions of interest to L2 writing researchers. Motivated in part by the quite disparate nature of the topics addressed in each section and our independent analyses of the pertinent research literature, we have not attempted to blend our distinctive writing styles in order to produce a single voice.

Acknowledgements

This volume grew out of an invitation to contribute a chapter on L2 writing for Peter Smagorinsky's *Research on Composition* (2006). Although we were most pleased to be able to participate in that work, as we prepared our chapter it became increasingly obvious that a single chapter could not do justice to the range and volume of research published on L2 writing in recent times. Thus, some of the research reviewed here was discussed in much reduced form in that volume. We would like to thank Peter both for his interest in including L2 writing for the first time in the substantive reviews of L1 writing research of which his edition was a continuation and for the inspiration to develop this one. We also thank three anonymous reviewers of our initial manuscript for providing especially appreciative, thoughtful, and useful analyses, which helped to shape the present version of the book. For help with collecting the research reviewed here, our thanks to Sue Chang, Tony Cimasko, Noke Glass, Tom Glass, Ethan Krase, Karyn Mallett, Robert Nelson, Laurel Reinking, Anne Snellen, and Yufeng Zhang. Our heartfelt thanks to Naomi Silverman, our editor at Routledge, for her limitless patience. And thanks to the support staff from Erlbaum and Routledge, particularly to Andrew R. Davidson for his painstaking care in copy-editing the volume.

Introduction

The field of L2 writing in English, while still relatively young, has clearly come of age. The last 25 years have seen several firsts in L2 writing research: the first journal devoted exclusively to L2 writing (the *Journal of Second Language Writing*); the first book linking L2 reading and writing (Carson & Leki, 1993); the first book focusing on adult education and L2 English (Burnaby & Cumming, 1992); the first book on what is being called Generation 1.5, that is, high school immigrant students (Harklau, Losey, & Siegal, 1999); the first bibliographies of published work (Silva, Brice, & Reichelt, 1999; Tannacito, 1995); the first conferences devoted exclusively to L2 writing (Purdue Symposium on Second Language Writing and others). Several accounts of the history of L2 writing pedagogy and of the discipline itself document the development and growing importance of L2 writing studies as a field of practice and investigation. (See for example Blanton, 1995; Cumming, 1998, 2001b; Kaplan, 2000; Matsuda, 1998, 1999, 2003c, 2003d; Matsuda, Canagarajah, Harklau, Hyland, & Warschauer, 2003; Raimes, 1991; Silva, 1990, 1993; Silva & Brice, 2004; Silva & Matsuda, 2002.)

So many L2 writing subfields have evolved, in fact, and with such rapidity that it has become difficult for area specialists to stay abreast of findings in subdisciplinary areas outside their expertise. As an obvious example, a great deal of L2 writing research has focused on aspects of undergraduate writing in English-medium institutions. Increasing numbers of these students in North America are immigrants and coming to university study as graduates of U.S. and Canadian high schools. Yet university researchers and practitioners are often not familiar with the research on L2 writing in, for example, secondary schools.

Writers for whom English is not their first or strongest language permeate North American society and respond to writing demands in contexts from kindergarten to graduate school and from professional publishing to community literacy and adult education programs. Research on these writers in North America was sporadic until the beginning of the 1980s. At about that time, the influence on L2 writing of audiolingual methods of teaching language, with their focus on grammatical patterns, had waned and been replaced by a pedagogy encouraging the examination and imitation of model texts. Thus, in terms of research into L2 writing what little there was consisted primarily of text analyses such as contrastive rhetoric studies, needs analyses, and error analyses.

Research into L1 student writing processes had been inaugurated with Emig's (1971) study of high school writers and began in L2 in the 1980s, in particular with Zamel's (1983) and then Raimes' (1985) "case studies" showing that, like L1 writers, L2 students also tried to and could express meanings rather than just manipulate language but struggled with writing, needing more time, more vocabulary, "more of everything" (Raimes, 1985, p. 250). In the meantime, interest in English for Specific Purposes (which has subsequently and partially morphed into an interest in genre studies) grew steadily (Horowitz, 1986a, 1986b), continuing the documentation of text, situation, and needs analyses to determine the types of tasks L2 writers would eventually face and studies of contrastive rhetoric aimed at discovering the different culturally determined rhetorical starting points from which L2 writers approached English texts.

One of the first book-length collections on L2 writing focused, as has the majority of research published since then, on L2 writers at the tertiary level and argued for the de-ghettoization of English as a Second Language (ESL) learners (Benesch, 1988); another, an ethnographic study, researched child bilingual writers, arguing for more respect and more meaningful writing opportunities for these children (Edelsky, 1986).

Around the early 1990s the number of published reports of research began to balloon. Early interest in needs analyses, instructional interventions, text analyses, and learner processes continued, but research concerns expanded toward writing construed both more broadly and more socially: studies of identity issues in relation to L2 writing, in particular learning to write in the former colonial language; of workplace writing; of writing by special populations such as children and graduate students (although high school students' writing has still received relatively little attention); of the effects of immigration (and interruptions to formal schooling for refugees during resettlement) on L2 writing development. More cognitively focused interests continued as well into research on such issues as the effect of L1 writing proficiency on L2 writing; of L1 literacy instruction on L2 literacy development; of L2 language proficiency on L2 writing; of knowledge storage in one language and knowledge retrieval in another.

A new thread was initiated, or at least brought into focus, by Santos' (1992) article discussing the absence in ESL and English as a Foreign Language (EFL) writing instruction of the political agenda so salient in L1 publications on writing. This observation brought swift counterassertions that ESL/EFL was inherently political and resulted in a foregrounding of the role of critical pedagogy in L2 writing (Benesch, 1993; Severino, 1993). The context for thinking about L2 writing expanded from determining how to develop and deliver instruction suitable for and useful to L2 learners to examining the effect of English language teaching (ELT) worldwide. The global ELT project came under critical scrutiny as researchers explored the (often negative) effects of the spread of English, driven in part by old colonialist structures, on other cultures, societies, and languages. And, as Kroll (2003) has argued, as English-dominant societies are increasingly driven by literacy and digital literacy, "the pursuit of English entails a pursuit of written English" (p. 1).

Nevertheless, pedagogical issues inevitably continue to direct much L2 writing research. Researchers hope to answer still unanswered questions about appropriate and effective responses to L2 writing; the role of culture and its influence on L2 writers; the role of L1 literacy development and language planning in countries worldwide in the development of L2 literacy; the emerging role of postmodernism, feminism, gay and lesbian studies, race studies, and class issues in the discipline; the question of imposing English-based literacy values, such as avoiding plagiarism and developing a personal voice and "critical thinking" in L2 writers.

Through this foment, L2 writing research has become progressively better informed, theoretically and methodologically. Researchers now typically use mixed designs (qualitative and quantitative), reflecting an increased breadth and depth of knowledge. Early interests in texts and cognitive processes have expanded from simple to more complex perspectives that consider broad-based, social understandings and more inclusive images of L2 writing and writers. As a result, our understanding of learning to write in a second language "has expanded and refined conceptualizations of (a) the qualities of texts that learners produce, (b) the processes of students' composing, and, increasingly, (c) the specific sociocultural contexts in which this learning occurs" and helped us to see the "multi-faceted nature of second-language writing and the extensive variability associated both with literacy and with languages internationally" (Cumming, 2001b, p. 1). As Silva and Matsuda (2002) noted, these understandings have inevitably entailed more complex and careful consideration of pedagogical and assessment issues in L2 literacy.

More broadly, understandings of literacy itself have become considerably more sophisticated. Cumming cites the work of Hornberger (1989) and Hornberger and Skilton-Sylvester (2000) as demonstrating that "biliteracy varies along several continua—personally, interpersonally, culturally, and geographically—in terms of the characteristics and development of individuals, contexts of language use, relations of status and power, and facets of communication media" (Cumming, 2001b, pp. 9–10). Literacy is thus currently viewed by many researchers as more than simply a cognitive process resulting in an individual skill, what Brian

Street has called "autonomous literacy" (1984). Street's argument was that by itself literacy could not autonomously confer benefits to individuals or societies outside particular valuings of particular kinds of literacy. For example, multiple literacies in different languages are valued differentially depending on the status of the languages in question and their speakers, as are multiliteracies, that is, literacy in different modalities, such as computer literacy, visual literacy (New London Group, 1996), or comic book literacy (Norton & Vanderheyden, 2004). In this sense literacy is not only multi or multiple and not merely social or culturally embedded but also ideological, since, if literacies are valued differently, then literacy inevitably indexes power differentials; that is, the literacies of the less powerful elements of society may not even be valued as literacy at all (e.g. comic book literacy or literacy in a nondominant language or one not highly socially esteemed). The question Street raises is how to implement New Literacy Studies' understandings of literacy in educational contexts (Street, 2005), a question especially significant for L2 writing scholars.

Perhaps as a sign of the maturing of a discipline, and of a growing interest in personal narratives at least in part stimulated by feminist research methods and their influence on L1 writing research, an increasing amount of the metadisciplinary discourse has recently begun to document L2 professionals' reflections on teaching and learning L2 writing. These writers have examined and written about the nature of their own experiences either of becoming L2 writing professionals (Blanton & Kroll, 2002; Casanave & Vandrick, 2003) or of going from being L2 English learners to accomplished professionals and teachers of writing to both other non-native English speakers (NNESs) and native English speakers (NESs) (Belcher & Connor, 2001; Braine, 1999b). These kinds of reflections on L2 writing have both created and been created by a broadened perspective on the discipline (Silva & Leki, 2004), one that has been termed and explored as the opening of a postprocess era in L2 writing. See Brauer (2000) as well as articles by Atkinson (2003a, on the idea of postprocess, 2003b on culture and writing), K. Hyland (2003a on genre), Kubota (2003 on issues of gender, class, and race), Matsuda (2003c on disciplinary history), Casanave (2003 on sociopolitical issues), and Leki (2003a on interdisciplinary issues) in the special issue of the *Journal of Second Language Writing*, guest edited by Atkinson (vol. 12, no. 1, 2003).

Reflecting the maturation of the discipline, this book is organized to explore three main topic areas: contexts for writing; curriculum, instruction, and assessment; and basic research on L2 writing. We feel this approach broadly accounts for the research on L2 writers interacting with contexts, with instruction, and with texts over the 25-year span considered here, although we recognize that the body of literature examined in this volume might also have been divided in other ways.

I: Contexts for L2 Writing

This section on contexts for writing reflects recent understandings of literacy as ideological. The section explores the broad situational issues shaping the development of L2 writing and impacting on the experiences of L2 writers. Drawing on information about the writers themselves and their experiences from case studies, surveys, questionnaires, and interviews, the research reviewed traces some of the settings of L2 writing at the whole-person level, the struggles and motivations of writers, the contextual and situational obstacles they face, and the strategies they have used to overcome them. Generally, studies were excluded from this section if the L2 writers or the settings they worked in were essentially anonymous and were included when the research personalized the writers and writing contexts. This section incorporates work on child L2 writers; L2 writers in secondary schools; undergraduate L2 writers; L2 writers in graduate school; L2 writers in community, resettlement, and adult education settings; L2 writers in the workplace; L2 writers in academic, scholarly, or professional contexts; and identity issues that arise for L2 writers as well as political, sociopolitical, and ideological issues embedded in L2 writing.

II: Curriculum, Instruction, and Assessment

This section highlights and synthesizes the educational issues appearing across the various contexts investigated in research on L2 writing. The first chapter in this section (chapter 9) addresses curricular and instructional issues. These focus on the conceptual foundations of L2 writing curricula, including theoretical orientations and teachers' pedagogical knowledge. A second focus has been on the varied purposes and policy contexts of L2 writing curricula and means of organizing them: for example, through benchmark standards, the integration or separation of writing from other curriculum components, aspects of writing taught, and studies of instructional interactions. The second chapter in this section (chapter 10) reviews research on the assessment of L2 writing. Studies of formative assessment have considered pedagogical issues such as describing teachers' practices for responding to L2 students' writing and analyses of their effects, different media and modes of responding, and peer- and self-assessment. Studies of proficiency assessment have focused on issues related to institutional policies and the design and validity of formal tests of L2 writing, including analyses of the L2 discourse written for tests and of raters' processes for evaluating L2 writing.

III: Basic Research on Writers, Their Composing Processes, and Their Texts

This section constitutes a synthesis of the findings of reports of empirical research on second language writing published between 1980 and 2005. The focus is on basic research: that is, inquiry into the phenomenon of L2 writing, as opposed to a focus on L2 writing instruction or assessment—which are addressed in section II. The section includes four chapters: The first, chapter 11, focuses on L2 writer variables (for example, L2 writing ability, L2 proficiency, and L2 writing development); the second, chapter 12, looks at L2 composing processes (for example, planning, formulating, and revising); the third, chapter 13, examines discoursal issues in the L2 writers' texts (for example, cohesion, organizational patterns, and textual modes and aims); and the fourth, chapter 14, addresses grammatical issues in L2 writers' texts (for example, parts of speech or form classes, sentence elements, and sentence processes). Additionally, each chapter includes a discussion of the breadth and depth of the research reported on in that chapter. The section also includes an appendix: two tables, one alphabetical by author, the other chronological, listing all of the studies analyzed, which provide author names, publication dates, sample sizes, subjects' first language(s), and subjects' second language(s). The section is meant to be used primarily as a reference work, pointing to studies and findings relevant to a particular area or subarea of interest—as a sort of prose database.

The need to place some kind of boundary around the research to be synthesized here has unfortunately meant making choices about what to exclude. For example, although we recognize the importance of reading to writing, we decided not to include the literature that made that connection unless it substantially focused on writing rather than reading. Furthermore, covering L2 writing in English alone meant covering a great deal of ground; attempting to include studies of writing in all languages internationally would have created problems in accessing material (and have exceeded our own language resources). In generally limiting ourselves to L2 English writing in North America, furthermore, we have not systematically reviewed the extensive literature on the Australian Sydney School and its teaching of power genres (see Belcher, 2004); the growing literature on foreign language writing, including English (see Reichelt, 2001; see also the online database CLEAR at Michigan State University); the work of L2 English writing researchers associated with Lancaster University/BALEAP (see Lea & Street, 1998); or the relatively newly formed European Association of Teachers of Academic Writing (EATAW). Consequently, any conclusions we may draw here cannot be assumed to apply outside the North American or L2 English context. We encourage others to take on the task of synthesizing writing done in languages other than English or in locales other than English-dominant regions of North America. We have, however, occasionally cited work from outside North America or outside our designated time frame when an issue under discussion required it.

Section I

Contexts for L2 Writing

Since the early 1980s the L2 writing profession has increasingly acknowledged that it is counterproductive to analyze English learners' writing or language development without embedding the inquiry in the human, material, institutional, and political contexts where they occur. This section on Contexts for L2 Writing is predicated on views of language use and education as the enactments of particular discourses (Gee, 1996, 2005). Taking an ecological view of activities, human agency, and contexts as enmeshed and woven together, the approach in this section has been to describe the contexts in which L2 writers write by constructing a loosely thematic narrative based on the study of the individuals and groups who have been the focus of L2 writing research in the last 25 years.

Some of the categories selected for inclusion in this section presented themselves as obvious to such an endeavor, for example, the chapter covering research on L2 undergraduates in North American universities. In other cases, categories that incorporated a body of literature were included even when that body was relatively small, for example, the chapter on workplace writing; though a relatively small category in L2, nevertheless the context of writing in the workplace presents an intriguing and important intersection of concerns for L2 writing professionals. Finally, in some cases, such as L2 writing in secondary schools, research on writing itself could not be properly discussed without consideration of the institutional, social, cultural, and affective contexts in which the writing was embedded.

Any discussion of L2 writers requires an acknowledgement that it is difficult to come to a decision about how to refer to them, or indeed, whom to include in the discussion. Terms referring to these writers such as English as a Second Language (ESL), English as an Additional Language (EAL), bilingual, multilingual, and others are each inappropriate in some ways for the many varieties of writers that might be included here. However, since some term is required, we have for the most part settled upon L2 writers as one of the more neutral.

Chapters 2, 3, 4, and 5 group writers working in educational contexts, prekindergarten through graduate school in English-medium institutions in North America. The students in each of these levels of education might be grouped differently, for example by legal status as visa students versus more permanent residents, and these different categorizations would unquestionably have led to a different kind of synthesis of the literature. The decision was made to group these writers instead by the educational context in which they worked and lived and consequently by the literacy demands encountered there. We nevertheless recognize that these demands are inevitably perceived, experienced, and responded to differently depending in part on the students' length of residence in the target community, intended length of residence, language proficiency, educational background, and a host of other factors so disparate as to make the resulting discussion too diffuse to be useful to understand the phenomenon of L2 writing. In categorizing research by writing context we are also making a claim about the importance and impact of context on all individuals and hoping at the same time to avoid the knotty issue of dividing people themselves into categories.

The next section (chapters 6, 7, and 8) examines the literature on L2 English writing outside classrooms, in the community, the workplace, and the professional settings of scholarly publications in English. The role of writing in these contexts varies widely, and the accomplishment of writing tasks is less individual and often more widely distributed among the members of the social or professional group. Finally, permeating all these previous contexts are the broader sociopolitical dimensions of L2 writing in English. The literature on these dimensions encompasses some of the social identities of these writers and examines the political and ideological climate surrounding L2 writing in English and the influence of that climate on pedagogical practices and disciplinary and societal attitudes.

Chapter 1

Young Writers

Research on the writing of young beginning L2 writers over the last 25 years has been characterized by its consistent portrayal of these writers as capable, usually able to do more with writing than might be imagined. Unlike descriptions of the wrenching disruptions and loneliness of many teen L2 writers, the story of younger L2 writers has generally been hopeful, more often reporting success and increasing power, self-confidence, and flexibility in writing. (See, however, darker pictures of how schooling is experienced by young L2 learners in Toohey, 1998, 2000, and Hawkins, 2005, and the influence of school programs on beginning writers in Edelsky, 1996.)

Researchers of the 1980s were well aware of the differences between early L1 writing and early L2 writing among children. First, unlike L1 writers, L2 writers may have little oral language to draw upon in developing literacy, and thus are not and cannot be moving from oral to written forms in their writing development, an analysis often offered in discussing L1 beginning writers. The second significant potential difference is that L2 beginning readers and writers may already be literate to some degree in L1 and can therefore potentially rely partially on that literacy both to create texts and to advance their developing L2 literacy (Edelsky, 1986).

Nevertheless, because many of the efforts of researchers in the 1980s were specifically focused on improving instruction, including in bilingual education programs, their initial apparent mission was to show

1 that beginning L2 writers were much like beginning L1 writers and that

2 in supportive, meaning-oriented writing contexts, beginning L2 writers brought with them and were able to draw upon a variety of resources and strategies to successfully create expressive texts that communicated meaning (Ammon, 1985; Blanton, 1998, 2002; Edelsky, 1986, 1989; Genishi, Stires, & Yung-Chan, 2001; Han & Ernst-Slavit, 1999; Hudelson, 1989a; Peyton, 1990; Urzua, 1986, 1987).

Like beginning L1 writers, L2 writers were also observed to use invented spellings (Edelsky, 1986; Hudelson, 1989a); to use marks (such as drawings) other than letters to supplement texts (Blanton, 1998; Han & Ernst-Slavit, 1999; Hudelson, 1989a; Huss, 1995); to show awareness that print conveys meanings (Hudelson, 1984); to respond positively to opportunities to write (Hudelson, 1984, 1989a, 1989b); to use writing for a variety of purposes, including non-narrative writing (Early, 1990), and to shift stances for different audiences (Edelsky, 1986; Hudelson, 1984, 1986; Urzua, 1987); to demonstrate the ability to look at text as text and critically evaluate it (Samway, 1993); and to exhibit a general sense of what writing looks like, including across different script systems, for example, knowing that Arabic is written right to left rather than left to right (Huss, 1995) or that Chinese characters have a particular boxy look (Buckwalter & Lo, 2002). Much of this research worked against prevailing dogma and served to debunk such myths as the following notions:

- L2 writers must learn to speak before learning to read or write. Rather, young learners may feel more comfortable writing and be more willing to write than speak (Hudelson, 1984, 1986; Saville-Troike, 1984); furthermore, their writing differs from their speech even in early stages (Edelsky, 1986).
- L2 writers must learn to read before they can write. Instead learners use existing knowledge as best they can to accomplish their goals (Han & Ernst-Slavit, 1999; Hudelson, 1984, 1986).
- Children must learn correct spellings from the beginning or they may develop bad spelling habits that will be difficult to break later (Edelsky, 1986; Hudelson, 1984).
- Grammar instruction aids literacy development. In fact it appears to have little effect (Elley, 1994; Saville-Troike, 1984).
- Reliance on L1 serves only to confuse children and so should be discouraged. Rather, L1 has been shown to be an important resource (Carlisle, 1989; Dávila de Silva, 2004; Hudelson, 1989a; Long, 1998; Moll, Saez, & Dworkin, 2001; Saville-Troike, 1984).
- Because writing is a solitary affair and an individual cognitive achievement, children should each work to develop their writing abilities and texts individually. Instead, children have been shown to work best with the timely help of peers and teachers (Blanton, 1998, 2002; Clark, 1995; Dávila de Silva, 2004; Early, 1990; Goodman, 1984; Hudelson, 1986; Urzua, 1987).

Research in the 1980s and early 1990s also supported a drive away from copying texts in lieu of creating them, filling in blanks instead of writing more extended language, and encouraging (or forcing) children to function in only the target language instead of making use of L1 borrowing or code-switching strategies (Early, 1990; Edelsky, 1986; Elley, 1994;

Francis, 2000). It also generally supported Whole Language approaches (Edelsky, 1996; Freeman & Freeman, 1989; Hudelson, 1989a, 1989b; Kitagawa, 1989; Westerbrook & Bergquist-Moody, 1996), the notion that writing helps develop other language and social skills (Hudelson, 1984; Urzua, 1987), and the potential importance of teachers' roles (Francis, 2000; Goodman, 1984).

Although case studies were not infrequent, because the thrust of this research was to argue a position, or at least minimally to describe contexts that promoted literacy acquisition in this population, the emphasis was somewhat synchronic, looking at groups of young writers often within bilingual programs (Ammon, 1985; Edelsky, 1982, 1986; Geva & Wade-Woolley, 1998). Nevertheless, a consistent finding in these studies was the wide variation shown between individual young writers and individual pieces of writing by the same child (Hudelson, 1986; Saville-Troike, 1984). Perrotta (1994) offered a useful summary of the positions that researchers were taking for granted by the beginning of the 1990s. At the end of the 1990s a report sponsored by a series of government, health, and education agencies (addressing reading rather than writing, however) reviewed the research to date on schooling and literacy generally for L2 students (August & Hakuta, 1997).

In this body of literature, as in others focused on writing, the 1990s saw a "social turn" (Trimbur, 1994), on one hand, and on the other a more diachronic focus with greater emphasis on the complicated paths that writing skill development took with individual children and on the way writing skills interacted with identity, positioning, and variations in familial or cultural orientations (Edelsky, 1996; Goodman, 1984; Hudelson, 1986; Hunter, 1997; Maguire & Graves, 2001; Solsken, Willett, & Wilson-Keenan, 2000; Volk & de Acosta, 2003). Recurring themes through 2005 centered around the importance to writing of talk, including talking to one's self; this meant not learning to talk *before* writing, as had been promoted in the 1970s, but using oral interaction to scaffold text construction and model texts (Gutierrez, 1994; Han & Ernst-Slavit, 1999; Patthey-Chavez & Clare, 1996) and to build influential social relations with peers and teachers (Blanton, 2002; Day, 2002; Gutierrez, 1994; Hawkins, 2005; Hunter, 1997; Huss, 1995; Long, 1998; Maguire, 1997; Nassaji & Cumming, 2000). McCarthey, Garcia, Lopez-Velasquez, Lin, & Guo (2004) found that the lack of opportunity to talk (between students and teachers and among teachers) about expectations for writing tasks and topics led some young English learners to transfer L1 schooling understandings about writing to their English learning context in ways that were not particularly helpful, for example, believing that care in handwriting and forming letters was highly valued.

Writing was also seen as a means of allowing children to explore and make connections between home or native culture and school or target culture (Edelsky, 1996; Han & Ernst-Slavit, 1999; Long, 1998; Maguire,

1997; Maguire & Graves, 2001; Masny & Ghahremani-Ghajar, 1999; Patthey-Chavez & Clare, 1996). In addition, examining children's journal writing became less an exercise in discovering the nature of L2 beginning writers' texts, as it had been in earlier research, and more a means of monitoring these writers' social, educational, and cultural adjustment experiences (Gutierrez, 1994; Kreeft, Shuy, Staton, Reed, & Morroy, 1984; Maguire & Graves, 2001; Nassaji & Cumming, 2000; Peyton, 1993). In contrast to the previous several years of research, with those assessments came also a recognition of the frustration experienced by these children as they lost self-confidence in their literate abilities and developed a sense of their own incompetence (Platt & Troudi, 1997), causing in some cases a loss of interest in extended reading and writing for school (Han & Ernst-Slavit, 1999; Long, 1998), though not necessarily in self-initiated writing (Long, 1998). (Similar findings occur for high school students and community writers; see for example Fu, 1995, and Guerra, 1998.)

As sociocultural theories came to predominate over more developmental and cognitive orientations, the roles and attitudes of teachers in particular were considered critical in delimiting or opening literacy possibilities for the children (Gutierrez, 1994; Masny & Ghahremani-Ghajar, 1999; Platt & Troudi, 1997). See also Toohey (1998, 2000) and Toohey and Day (1999); although not focused on literacy development specifically, this research richly contextualizes sample environments in which child literacy develops in schools. In recognition of the importance of teachers, L2 child writing researchers began also to urge that both teachers and administrators learn more about the cultural and family backgrounds of L2 students in their classes (Masny & Ghahremani-Ghajar, 1999; McCarthey, 2002; McCarthey et al., 2004) and exercise particular critical vigilance so as not to be led by dominant school-based discourses to undervalue the hybridity of young writers' texts as they weave social and personal agendas and varying background cultures into their writing (Solsken, Willett, & Wilson-Keenan, 2000). Trends in the early 2000s have converged around the examination of how writing develops in biliterate children and how being bilingual affects literacy development in both languages, in other words, the examination not of the similarities between monolingual and bilingual beginning writers but of their differences, with the differences viewed as advantages rather than as deficits (Buckwalter & Lo, 2002; Durgunoglu, 1998; Durgunoglu, Mir, & Arino-Martin, 2002; Francis, 2000; Reynolds, 2002). See especially Perez (2004a) for a useful discussion of L1/L2 literacy development in children from a variety of L1 backgrounds.

An important line of research traces the influence that opportunities and encouragements to write a variety of texts in mainstream (Au, 1993; Gutierrez, 1992; Moll, Saez, & Dworkin, 2001; Reyes, 1992) and heritage language schools and at home exert on nascent L2 literacy, on the continued development of L1 literacy, and on children's attitudes toward writing in L1 and L2 (McCarthey & Garcia, 2005; McCarthey et al., 2004; McCarthey, Guo, & Cummins 2005; Xu, 1999) with successes reported particularly in school contexts that encouraged writing in both (or more) languages (Manyak, 2001; Moll, Saez, & Dworkin, 2001). Biliterate children demonstrated a range of literacy competencies inside (McCarthey et al., 2004) and outside school contexts and the ability to strategically engage them (Jimenez, 2000; Solsken, Willett, & Wilson-Keenan, 2000). Furthermore, McCarthey's (2002) series of case studies demonstrated how L2 students appropriated, resisted, and transformed school literacy contexts to suit their own culturally and historically developed sense of how to use writing to further preferred school identities. Also noted was the importance of parents' attitudes toward their children's development of biliteracy as well as the parents' own educational and socioeconomic backgrounds (Hawkins, 2005; G. Li, 2002; McCarthey & Garcia, 2005; McCarthey et al., 2004; McCarthey, Guo, & Cummins 2005; Xu, 1999). Other factors examined in relation to the effort to develop L2 literacy included the degree of respect demonstrated by school systems for the children's language and cultural heritage (August & Hakuta, 1997; Reyes, 1992; Solsken, Willett, & Wilson-Keenan, 2000; Townsend & Fu, 1998) and the immigrant community's success in maintaining strong intracultural ties (Divoky, 1988). Despite the evidence arguing for L1 literacy development and maintenance, researchers have documented evidence that recent obsessive testing programs, particularly in Texas (McCarthey, 2002), have forced teachers' and administrators' focus away from maintenance and encouragement of L1 writing among young bilingual writers with debilitating effects (McCarthey & Garcia, 2005; McCarthey, Guo, & Cummins, 2005; Xu, 1999).

Summary

In all, far from viewing L2 literacy development among young learners as a simple matter of teaching and practicing L2 reading and writing in classrooms, over the 25-year period examined researchers have become increasingly aware of the complex and often unpredictable constellations of individual histories, understandings, and resources and other kinds of contextual factors, including social standing among peers, that give young English learners access to the literacy practices and desirable subject positions that promote development of school language and literacy (Hawkins, 2005). Finally, Harklau (2002) and Elley (1994) have made explicit a previously implicit argument that second language acquisition research, historically focused primarily on spoken language, can benefit from more in-depth study of L2 writing and literacy development, particularly among young writers in elementary and secondary schools, where literacy is an essential modality for communicating subject matter (Harklau, 2002). In this sense the study of young L2 writers potentially contributes not only to an understanding of literacy development but also to the field of second language acquisition by capturing on paper the dynamic shifts of young learners' language evolution.

Chapter 2

Writing in Secondary School

Not much of the published literature on junior and senior high school for L2 learners through the 1980s focused specifically on L2 writing. Rather, researchers were concerned primarily to suggest pedagogical possibilities (Freeman & Freeman, 1989) and explore issues related to bilingual education and teaching ESL through the content areas (Cantoni-Harvey, 1987; Chamot & O'Malley, 1987; Crandall, 1987; Rigg & Allen, 1989; Scarcella, 1990). Research from the early 1990s forward, however, has included a more direct focus on L2 writing development. Much of this research on L2 writing and writers in secondary schools has been qualitative in orientation, primarily involving observational and case studies of students and/or high schools, but also including questionnaire and interview research, some quantitative analyses of outcome data, and, especially abroad, investigations of pedagogical innovations. But in fact this adolescent population has generally suffered from a lack of attention to its writing needs in L2 (Harklau, 2000, 2001; Reynolds, 2001; Wald, 1987). Moreover, unlike the pervading optimistic tone of research on child or community L2 writers, the research literature on high school L2 students and their writing experiences paints a consistently pessimistic portrait of the overall predicament of high school L2 learners and writers. The qualitative focus of much of this research gives insight into the personal sadness, loneliness, stress, embarrassment at being placed into classes with younger domestic students, homesickness, and social isolation of many of these students. Most of the research has focused on students of Spanish-speaking, Asian, or Southeast Asian background; this distribution of interest probably more or less fairly represents the visible secondary school L2 student population in North America.

It is not possible to talk about writing research on L2 secondary students without first clarifying some of the complications inherent in that setting. Of all the contexts in which L2 writing occurs, high school is probably the most fraught and the most complex. Its complexity stems from several factors. In North America, high school is mandatory up to a certain age (though not free in Canada to students older than 19 [Watt, Roessingh,

& Bosetti, 1996] or available at all to students over a certain age in some U.S. school districts [Muchinsky & Tangren, 1999]). This means that all immigrant teens, regardless of their previous literacy and educational background, are required to attend. They cannot simply choose not to attend, as both tertiary and adult or community learners can. And, unlike younger learners, the basic reality of high school English language learners is their stark variability along several dimensions. Although learners placed into the same level of high school may initially share a similar level of oral language proficiency (and sometimes not), the same high school ESL classroom may well hold students who have never been to school before at all, students with fourth grade L1 educations and little L1 literacy (Welaratna, 1992), some whose previous teachers themselves had little education (Garcia, 1999), students who already have high school degrees from their home countries (Fu, 1995; Muchinsky & Tangren, 1999), some whose education came from refugee camps, and others from elite private schools (Harklau, 1994a). Welaratna (1992), for example, described the case of a Khmer student who came to the US at age 17 after only 5 years of formal education in Cambodia, whose English at that time was limited to greetings, and who was placed into the sophomore year of high school.

To understand how literacy development constitutes a central means of educational communication in secondary school it is necessary to look at the broader picture of L2 students' experiences there. If an 8-year-old English language learner begins school in the US having never been to school before, certainly the child has adjustments to make and quite a bit of catching up to do. But if a 17-year-old has never been to school, the catching up required is dramatic and in fact is unlikely to take place in the time left for attending high school. Well known, often-cited research by Collier (Collier, 1987, 1989; Collier & Thomas, 1989) and Cummins (1986, 2001) estimates that getting up to grade level for academic subjects in an English-medium elementary school may take a youngster 5 to 7 years, an astonishingly long time, and this is for children who experienced normal access to education in L1 before entering English-medium schools. Collier (1995) noted that even high school students with excellent previous L1 educational backgrounds studying in an affluent U.S. school district who made steady progress each year had not reached the 50th percentile on standardized tests in such subjects as reading and science after 6 years of all English schooling, such is the slow pace of language and academic development for teens in an L2. Progress is variable (Early, 1989, 1992), but some evidence for certain L2 groups points to little development of writing skills between eighth grade and freshman year in college (Hartman & Tarone, 1999; Tarone et al., 1993; Valdes & Sanders, 1998).

Language difficulties may coexist with sophisticated cognitive skills, and academic development grows with language proficiency (Harklau, Losey, & Siegal, 1999; Valdes, 2001). But the difficulties of studying in an L2 are reflected in research comparing the academic achievement of international students studying at North American colleges and universities who completed high school in their own language with that of L2 students who have graduated from North American high schools. Contrary to perhaps the common sense view, research fairly consistently shows the international students doing better. This pattern holds more generally; the more time students spent studying in their native language high schools, the better they did in L2 academic settings (Muchinsky & Tangren, 1999). Part of this advantage comes from simply knowing better how to do school, knowing what the school script is. Part is building academic knowledge and understandings that can then compensate for lack of language proficiency in a way in which language proficiency cannot compensate for lack of academic knowledge and understandings. Muchinsky and Tangren (1999) noted the example of an immigrant student who needed the concept of *narrator* explained, whereas an international student is more likely merely to need the word translated in order to grasp its meaning. Overall, the best predictor of academic success in college for these students is number of years spent in high school in L1 before immigration (Bosher & Rowenkamp, 1992; Cummins, 2001).

As these learners are attempting to learn a foreign language and working on learning content through the foreign language that they are still in the process of learning, they are also at the same time, and arguably toughest of all, coming of age. High school years are a period of life when many learners are likely to be at the peak of their sensitivity to issues of identity (Harklau, 2007; Kanno & Applebaum, 1995) and peer relations (Heller, 2001; Ibrahim, 1999; S. McKay & Wong, 1996), no longer looking primarily to parents for social and psychological support, as children might, and not yet formed enough to have a clear sense of themselves and their identities or to have developed reliable means of maneuvering in the social world, as older learners might. Yet peer relations with domestic students are a pervasive and persistent problem for L2 learners in North America (Duff, 2001; Fu, 1995; Kanno & Applebaum, 1995; Lay, Carro, Tien, Niemann, & Leong, 1999; S. J. Lee, 2001; Leki, 1999; S. McKay & Wong, 1996; L. Olsen, 1997), with language and cultural differences sometimes working against them (Heller, 2001).[1] The high school experience for these students has been described as "a social and academic minefield" (S. J. Lee, 2001, p. 516). Research from the 1980s suggested that, by the high school years, students, at least in the US, self-segregate

---

1   Relations with domestic peers are an issue at all levels of schooling but the research literature suggests that these are particularly acute for secondary schoolers.

along racial, ethnic, or cultural lines and may refuse to cooperate across those borders (Kagan, 1986). L2 high school learners report that they are, perhaps predictably, ignored, laughed at, shown impatience, isolated, rejected, pressured to abandon home values, styles, and preferences (to stop acting, say, Chinese), and pressured to refuse target culture values, styles, and preferences (to stop trying to act, say, North American) (L. Olsen, 1997). They may sense both the need to interact with domestic students and a fear of them and the culture of high school, sometimes including fears of drugs, sex, and/or violence. In some cases second generation and newly arrived immigrant students have fundamental differences that cause conflicts within a single language or cultural group (S. J. Lee, 2001). Teachers as well may show impatience and prejudice against English learners (Lay et al., 1999; L. Olsen, 1997). For some L2 students a confusing or limited and limiting set of identity categories may be all that is made available to them in high school, with some successfully resisting the dominant culture of the mainstream to find identity links in counter- or minority cultural expressions (Heller, 2001; Ibrahim, 1999) and others giving up, as reflected in the continued "abysmally high" dropout rate of English language learners (Hawkins, 2005, p. 59). Furthermore, these immigrant students may have family obligations unusual for adolescents (e.g. serving their parents as translator for interactions with authorities) (Johns, 1991b; Lay et al., 1999; S. J. Lee, 1997; Losey, 1997; Orellana, Reynolds, Dorner, & Meza, 2003; Rodby, 1999; Valdes, 1996).

But the issue here is not merely social; it is educational as well. One of the persistent questions in L2 K–12 (kindergarten through twelfth grade) education is when to "mainstream" the students, that is, take them out of an ESL curriculum and integrate them into regular classes with domestic students. Arguments for continuing ESL support for as long as possible include the observations that L2 learners are more comfortable and at ease in these classes and so are more willing to speak up (Duff, 2001; Harklau, 2001; Valdes, 2001), some even finding them a haven, a "safe space" (S. J. Lee, 2001, p. 515) in an otherwise intimidating institution; that unlike many mainstream teachers, ESL teachers are trained and interested in dealing with these students (Youngs & Youngs, 2001); and that this continued support recognizes that academic and language development is a long-term process (Duff, 2001; Harklau, 1994a; Hartman & Tarone, 1999; Valdes, 2001).

But ESL classes, particularly in high school, have many problems of their own, prompting reference to "ESL Lifers" (L. Olsen, 1997) and the "ESL ghetto" (Valdes, 2001), an isolating, sometimes chaotic, stigmatized, self-perpetuating space that keeps students in a holding pattern till graduation and focuses them on minutiae of grammatical form (Derwing, DeCorby, Ichikawa, & Jamieson, 1999; Duff, 2001; Fu, 1995; Garcia, 1999; Harklau, 1994a, 1994b, 1999a; Hartman & Tarone, 1999; Lay et al., 1999; Leki, 1999; Valdes, 1999, 2001). The notion of the high school

ESL class as a ghetto arises from research that documents students spending many hours a day in ESL classes and not mixing with non-ESL high school students except in activity-based classes such as physical education, cooking, or music, which make few language demands. Although the situation in North America varies dramatically by school district, it is sometimes the case that students who enter ESL classes under these ghettoizing conditions simply never leave. Even rooms designated for ESL classes are reported to be the leftovers, old, small spaces deemed not good enough for other classes (Schmidt, 2000). All of these negative features can, under good conditions (Harklau, 1994a; Walqui, 2000), be corrected with better ESL instruction and responsible administration, except one: isolation. The protective shelter of ESL classes necessarily isolates L2 learners from their domestic peers and, at a time in life when peer interaction is crucial, the pressure to behave in socially appropriate ways (behavior that is learned through those interactions) may be at its most intense, and peer intolerance of deviation from social norms may be greatest.

In terms of language development, the high school ESL class has a dual focus. On one hand, it must provide instruction and practice in the kind of language that will promote expansion of academic skills (referred to as Cognitive Academic Language Proficiency, or CALP; Cummins, 1986). On the other hand, the ESL class should also equip students with the kind of everyday language that would allow their eventual integration into high school social life (often referred to as Basic Interpersonal Communication Skills, or BICS; Cummins, 1986). Development of BICS allows English language learners to interact with their peers in ways that will promote not only a sense of belonging socially but also the language development and cultural knowledge necessary for academic success (see below).

But the role played by oral skills in the development of academic writing is complex in this setting. Some L2 learners feel they require oral interaction with domestic peers to fuel writing proficiency by helping them gather vocabulary, develop fluency, and become familiar with the host country culture and current affairs (Duff, 2001; Kanno & Applebaum, 1995; Valdes, 2001). For these students, language forms may be absorbed and then first emerge primarily during oral interaction. They may feel more comfortable writing if they feel they have enough oral language to allow them to do so (Kanno & Applebaum, 1995; Valdes, 2001). Those with an extensive education in their L1 may find that much of their L1 literacy skill and academic knowledge transfers readily to L2 (Wald, 1987) so that they need little or no help with academic work but expect that secondary school will allow their integration into high school social life and provide them with opportunities to develop L2 oral skills by facilitating interaction with domestic classmates (Adger & Peyton, 1999).

Ironically, however, since the effort to develop BICS often takes place in the ESL class, it separates English language learners out from their monolingual English peers, the very conversation partners that BICS is aimed at. The issue then becomes when exactly in their school day the L2 students will have the opportunity to use these oral skills. Some evidence suggests that in fact in mainstream classes, outside the ESL ghetto, L2 learners may engage only rarely in oral interactions with domestic students, who may be uninterested in L2 learners (Heller, 2001; Kanno & Applebaum, 1995; Leki, 1999). Harklau's L2 students produced no more than one or two utterances a day, usually brief how-are-you exchanges with a teacher (Harklau, 1994a; Lay et al., 1999). Thus, moving into the mainstream gets these students out of the ESL ghetto but may exacerbate the problem of oral noninteraction (Miller, 2000), particularly for students reluctant to speak in settings that mix bilingual and monolingual students (Kanno & Applebaum, 1995; Valdes, 2001). Furthermore, L2 students may experience peer pressure from compatriots to speak their L1s and not English (Duff, 2001).

On the other hand, other English learners have little patience with a focus on BICS or oral interactional skills in ESL classes because this kind of fluency building may (however appropriately) entail game playing or story writing, which some L2 students may regard as inappropriate as high school activities. These adolescents may then become bored and disruptive or may simply tune out (Valdes & Sanders, 1998), criticizing their ESL classes for not only isolating them from domestic peers but also in effect infantilizing them through activities designed to allow them to learn how to interact with those peers when they would prefer to be developing academic language and skills (Derwing et al., 1999; Fu, 1995; Garcia, 1999; Kanno & Applebaum, 1995; Leki, 1999; L. Olsen, 1997). For students who are reluctant to speak, it is writing rather than oral interaction that serves to solidify an incipient, tentative grasp of language features and allows writers to try out and build on an academic vocabulary base that they can then use in mainstream or content courses (Wald, 1987; Weissberg, 2000).

Whatever the focus of ESL classes, mainstream high school classes also present problems for L2 students, and here the distinction between BICS and CALP blurs somewhat for L2 writing studies. High schoolers are expected to begin to move away from strictly personal interests and experiences (discussable with BICS) toward the broader social world, a move which in high school requires greater knowledge of popular culture, media culture, and news events, knowledge domains that are not strictly academic and yet may be essential to success in high school and become increasingly prominent as writing subject matter in secondary school (Duff, 2001). In addition, in an effort to keep domestic high school students interested, mainstream high school teachers may specifically work at providing experiential relevance by joking, being sarcastic, using asides, and making references to pop culture and current events (Duff, 2001; Harklau, 1994a). English learners at this age then are called upon to develop both the ability to manipulate academic topics and at the same time a familiarity with the taken-for-granted cultural background of high school peers in order to follow discussions in mainstream classes. As isolating and sometimes stigmatizing as the ESL class may be, L2 students may feel equally isolated in mainstream classes, when they cannot follow the speedy, idiom-laden language and when teachers are too busy with high maintenance (Duff, 2001; Harklau, 1994a) domestic students to accommodate their needs.

The nature of writing instruction in high school ESL classes is reported as ranging from careful, supportive, meaning-focused approaches in which language errors are considered a normal part of the language learning process (Frodesen & Starna, 1999; Harklau, 1994a, 2001) to, unfortunately, more frequently reported ESL writing classes largely focused on grammar and mechanics, using such techniques as controlled composition or copying individual sentences (Fu, 1995; Garcia, 1999; Hartman & Tarone, 1999; Lay et al., 1999; Trueba, 1987; Valdes, 1999, 2001, 2004). Sadly, this approach to L2 writing instruction has been documented into the late 1990s and beyond (Valdes, 1999, 2001, 2004). It should be noted, however, that ESL classes can rarely afford to focus on writing alone (Valdes, 1999) and that professional preparation for high school ESL teachers rarely includes specific instruction in teaching composition generally or L2 writing in particular (Diaz, Moll, & Mehan, 1986; Schmidt, 2000; Valdes, 2001). Furthermore, in a telling statement on the relative status of the field, some of those asked to teach high school ESL classes have no ESL training whatsoever, let alone training in teaching L2 writing (Harklau, 1994a; Valdes, 2001). Given this state of affairs, the continued existence of the old-fashioned, detail-focused approach to writing instruction, highlighting neatness and grammatical accuracy, distressing as it is, comes as no surprise. Its consequences can, however, be devastating for students, particularly for those whose literacy educations in L1 stopped early and who in effect need to learn not neatness, grammaticality, or even composition but literacy, that is, to learn literate behaviors and take on literate practices (Blanton, 2005). Although learning grammaticality and even neatness may have some use, the implication of this research is that a real understanding of what literacy is must take precedence.

On the other hand, in a long-term ethnographic investigation, Harklau (1999a) documented writing instruction in a particular ESL high school class that clearly worked toward the promotion of academic, composition, and language skills, more so than the mainstream classes Harklau detailed in this study. Ironically, perhaps, or perhaps inevitably, some students even in this successful ESL class felt they were not as well served as they might have wished because they failed to recognize (or perhaps appreciate) the teacher's fluency-building agenda (in addition to building academic competence) and as a result felt that activities meant to promote

BICS were too easy, boring, a waste of their time. Furthermore, in another study Harklau (2003) documented writing classes in which the teacher, delighted with the apparent commitment of the L2 writers, encouraged the immigrant students to constantly replay the immigrant experience in their writing, constructing them as the "perpetual foreigner" or "exemplars of ethnolinguistic identities" (p. 90) rather than as individuals.

In some contexts where the ESL class is intended as only a transitional class, once exited from the ESL ghetto, L2 students may find themselves tracked into low track English classes, often with a non-college-prep orientation. The problems for L2 students there are the same as they are for L1 students: The courses typically make fewer cognitive demands, require little extended prose, expose students to only a few genres, focusing on ones that are supposedly the most practical but are least academic, and so make it even more difficult for the students to develop the kinds of fluency with academic genres and registers that might be required in college, thus condemning them to stations in life in which a college education does not figure. It is no news that, the longer the student is in low track courses, the less likely he/she is to ever build the academic skills and knowledge that would allow escape (Harklau, 1994b; Losey, 1997). If L2 students then continue to have problems in writing, it becomes unclear whether the source of the difficulty is in language development or in lack of writing experience (Frodesen & Starna, 1999; Valdes, 1999).

If these L2 high school students do continue to higher education, they may find themselves at another disadvantage compared with their international peers. In North American writing classes they are unlikely to develop the familiarity with and understanding of formal features of grammar that usually can be and often are assumed in college L2 writing instruction for international students (D. Ferris, 1999b; Harklau, 1994a), leaving the graduates of the North American high schools, at any rate, once again running to catch up.

Interestingly, although writing is variously important to and plays different roles for different English learners (S. McKay & Wong, 1996; Peyton, 1993), the outcome of all these different types of high school ESL or mainstream classes may actually be depressingly similar for all L2 students who subsequently enroll in college. The research literature examines several cases of students who, after spending years in high school ESL classes, find themselves in ESL classes again in college, much to their frustration (Frodesen & Starna, 1999; Harklau, 2000; Holmes & Moulton, 1995; Lay et al., 1999). Such a finding reiterates the protracted nature of L2 writing development but also suggests that this development cannot be the domain of the writing or ESL teacher alone. Yet it appears that mainstream content area high school teachers have mixed reactions to ESL students in their classes (Hartman & Tarone, 1999; Youngs & Youngs, 2001). On one hand, some teachers praise L2 learners' diligence and respect for school (Harklau, 2000). In those classrooms and schools where L2 learners are quiet and hard working and domestic students more unruly (Duff, 2001), the L2 students can be constructed by their high school teachers as exemplary, "an inspiration" for domestic high school students, and held up to their classmates as models to emulate (Harklau, 2000).

But on the other hand research also portrays high school teachers, with their hands undeniably full already, as feeling that it is the job of the ESL teacher to make sure that students are ready for their science class or their history class, and that it is not their job to make sure that the course content in their science or history class is in a real sense available to L2 learners. Despite attempts to help mainstream English teachers and content area teachers provide appropriate instruction for English learners (Lucas, Henze, & Donato, 1990; Roessingh, 1999; Short, 1997; Trueba, 1987; Valdes, 1999), teachers may not know what to do, simply not be willing to do anything at all, or believe that if L2 students have been mainstreamed this must mean they can handle the mainstream classes without further intervention on their part (Clair, 1995; Duff, 2001; Hartman & Tarone, 1999; Schmidt, 2000; Valdes, 1999; Wolfe-Quintero & Segade, 1999). Some believe that ESL students should be kept out of their classes altogether, with ESL teachers assigned to deal with them; still others believe that ESL classes should not exist at all because they pamper or coddle L2 learners (Harklau, 2001; Schmidt, 2000).

Furthermore, like their students, ESL high school teachers themselves may work in isolation from their colleagues (Harklau, 2001; Schmidt, 2000). There is perhaps some element of xenophobia and even racism in the behaviors and reactions of some of the mainstream teachers (Vollmer, 2000). But more generally there is an amazing failure of awareness on the part of, particularly monolingual, mainstream teachers and, more to the point, of administrators, of what is involved in learning a language and of how they might make their classes more accessible to English language learners. The highly politicized nature of bilingual education and ESL, at least in the US, also means that the rules under which English learners attempt to study may change with the political whims of local leaders and populations (L. Olsen, 1997).

It is perhaps because of the complexity in this high school context that so many different approaches have been suggested, and tried, to teach L2 English in high school: separate ESL classes, bilingual classes, dual literacy classes, sheltered instruction, content-based courses (Garcia, 1999; Valdes, 1999). The fairly depressing picture that most of the literature presents of the plight of L2 high school students is only partly offset by reports of successful programs (Derwing et al., 1999; Faltis & Wolfe, 1999; Harklau, 1994a; Leki, 2001a; Valdes, 2001; Walqui, 2000) and courses such as the junior high school science class proposed in Moje,

Collazo, Carillo, and Marx (2000), in which students' home and community discourse would be integrated with that of science and academics.[2] More frequently researchers focusing on secondary students lament the piecemeal approach of school systems in accommodating L2 students, with mainstream teachers believing that the language and writing development of L2 learners is not their concern but that of the ESL teacher and with administrations feeling they have done their job by hiring one ESL teacher and tucking these students away into that class, sometimes for nearly the entire day (Harklau, 1994a; Hartman & Tarone, 1999). However that may be, dropout rates remain high among L2 students regardless of their language abilities and educational backgrounds (Derwing et al., 1999; Watt & Roessingh, 1994, 2001).

Rare instances in the research literature of L2 teens successfully negotiating satisfying identity construction, peer interaction, and writing seem to take place outside the school context, indexing a wide variety of forms of literacy that students engage in on their own, for example poems, letter writing (Guerra, 1996, 1998; Johns, 1991b; Orellana et al., 2003), or electronic communications (Lam, 2000), non-academic genres bordering on oral forms that carry little cultural capital in some academic settings but that nevertheless might in fact be a road in toward the development of more academic writing genres. But, because these types of literacies are extracurricular and as such imbued with little academic status, these students may still be considered non-writers (Hornberger & Skilton-Sylvester, 2000).

Summary

If research on the writing of this group of English learners is relatively sparse, it is perhaps because writing researchers have been overwhelmed by the more immediate and serious problems observed in the contexts in which that writing might take place. The importance of writing and writing instruction is dwarfed by the more dramatic, threatening, and far-reaching issues these learners face and the seriousness of the other language, identity, and agency issues their cases present. These students vary widely among themselves and enter into widely varying secondary schooling situations. Fu (1995), for example, described the adolescent members of the same family all enrolled in the same school but with far-reaching differences among them in background education, predispositions, and

2 See, however, Villalva (2006). Perhaps, having documented many of the pressing problems associated with L2 high school literacy development, in the future researchers will be free to explore in more detail the characteristics of positive writing environments. It is notable that in this study of successful bilingual student writing the two focal students relied significantly on social networks to move their projects forward.

interest in literacy and equally far-reaching responses from the different teachers they encountered in that single school. Overall, the pervading gloom of the research published between 1980 and 2005 on L2 students in secondary school suggests that, except for relatively rare cases noted above, in many instances L2 students and the schools they entered were not ready for each other. Although it would seem that the clear but unmet onus is on the schools to accommodate the L2 students, whose attendance is required, the schools have often been historically underfunded and sometimes ill-staffed, with perhaps the result that high numbers of L2 students vote with their feet and drop out.

Chapter 3

Undergraduate Writing

The bulk of research on L2 writing has explored the undergraduate context in North America and worldwide. Most curricular decisions and innovations, most examination of texts, most exploration of writing strategies and difficulties have been directed at this population, who often studied and worked in the same institutions as the researchers themselves. As the nature of this population has shifted over the years, so has the focus of research attention in terms of language and cultural background, gender, residence status (visa-holding international students versus immigrant or second generation or "Generation 1.5"), and academic status (beginning with undergraduates and more recently moving toward graduate students). The undergraduate students researched in North American universities came from a variety of writing backgrounds: some from non-English-medium settings, often abroad; others from U.S. high schools where they may or may not have had special ESL classes, where they may or may not have done much writing either in ESL classes or in other content area classes, where they may or may not have begun to (or wanted to) acculturate to U.S. teenage life and make English speaking friends; still others from intensive English programs, usually preuniversity institutions in an English-dominant country, that typically included academic writing instruction (Atkinson & Ramanathan, 1995). Questions about appropriate academic support for these students' L2 advanced literacy development included whether they could best be served by developmental or basic writing courses (Matsuda, 2003a) and whether they should take the first-year writing course required in most U.S. settings with English-dominant students or in separate classes for L2 students (Silva, 1994). While a great deal of research has been published about these undergraduates, documenting their preferences and performance in the L2 writing classrooms and beyond, in recent years the students' broader, more contextualized experiences in L2 writing classes have undergone scrutiny and increasingly the students themselves been heard from systematically through interview research (Leki, 2001b).

Early research on these students was focused on pedagogical issues, texts, and composing processes; state-of-the-art publications in 1987 and 1993 reflected those primary interests (Connor, 1987; Silva, 1993; Zamel, 1987). However, a strong additional strand of L2 writing research directed outside the L2 writing classroom around this time was in the area of needs analysis, in particular, studies of the kinds of writing required in undergraduate general education and disciplinary courses. Quantitatively oriented research methodologies such as surveys predominated in the early years, investigating both writing task requirements across the curriculum and nonwriting faculty response to L2 student writing, primarily error gravity studies (that is, research into how serious a given error is considered to be).

Researchers gathered information about the types of writing required in undergraduate courses in the context of a developing interest among L2 writing practitioners in the mid-1980s in moving away from writing instruction as form-focused and in importing process writing pedagogies from L1 writing instruction (Zamel, 1976). The predominantly expressivist orientation of these early imports initiated a flurry of disputes (Hamp-Lyons, 1986; Horowitz, 1986a; Liebman-Kleine, 1986; Spack, 1988) about where L2 writing instruction should concentrate: Would L2 writing proficiency develop best if writers could first experience what it was to be a writer by finding (often personal) meaning through writing (Zamel, 1982); or, given the pressure on undergraduates to perform their writing immediately in response to curricular demands, should L2 writing instruction help writers prepare to meet those demands more directly (Horowitz, 1986a, 1986b; Johns, 1995)? In either case, those demands then needed to be further assessed and categorized (Braine, 1989, 1995; Bridgeman & Carlson, 1984; Carson, Chase, & Gibson, 1993; Carson, Chase, Gibson, & Hargrove, 1992; Hale et al., 1996; Horowitz, 1986b; Johns, 1981; Kroll, 1979; Spack, 1988). Students were also questioned about their own sense of their academic literacy needs and the degree to which L2 studies courses were providing for them (Christison & Krahnke, 1986; Ostler, 1980; Smoke, 1988). Bridgeman and Carlson's (1984) study was particularly revealing in its analysis of the differences between the writing qualities valued by English departments (greater focus on organizational and stylistic issues) and those valued by other academic departments (greater focus on content). In some cases the findings of these needs analyses led to curricular alterations such as content-based instruction, sheltered study, and linked courses, for which an entire body of literature exists. (See for example Benesch, 1988, and Brinton, Snow, & Wesche, 1989, for initial discussions.)

Early studies of the kinds of writing required in undergraduate courses across the curriculum were primarily descriptive, but these have more recently expanded both toward very detailed corpus linguistic analyses of academic discourse (Biber, Conrad, Reppen, Byrd, & Helt, 2002) and toward more ecological approaches that take into account specific course contexts (Allison & Wu, 2002; Jackson, 2002) and specific students' interactions with and responses to those writing demands (Currie, 1993; Fishman & McCarthy, 2001; Frodesen & Starna, 1999; Leki, 1995a; Leki & Carson, 1994, 1997; Storch & Tapper, 1997; Zamel, 1990, 1995). See also discussion of case studies below.

In addition to writing tasks, L2 students also faced a variety of faculty responses to their writing (Janopoulos, 1992; Johns, 1991a; Rosenthal, 2000; Santos, 1988; Vann, Lorenz, & Meyer, 1991; Vann, Meyer, & Lorenz, 1984; Zhu, 2004) and sometimes to their very presence in courses across the curriculum (Zamel, 1995). Although responses to L2 writing were shown to vary across the curriculum in relation to such factors as respondents' age, gender, and content area, for the most part this research described faculty across the curriculum as generally able and willing to overlook L2 errors in favor of content, with certain types of errors (ones, for example, that caused the most disruption of meaning or were the most "foreign," such as subject deletion) causing more distraction and irritation than others. (Anecdotal accounts of more cranky responses to L2 student writing abound; published accounts of such reactions are relatively rare, however, perhaps owing to faculty reluctance to be officially or publicly unwelcoming. See, however, Johns, 1991a, and Zamel, 1995.)

Another aspect of the undergraduate context examined included issues surrounding the gatekeeping functions of writing exams, both entrance and exit exams: the question of whether different standards did or should apply to L2 writers (Janopoulos, 1995); the anxiety and pain these exams caused for L2 students (Mlynarczyk, 1998; Sternglass, 1997); the additional, and unfair, hardships L2 writers experienced on timed, one-shot writing exams (Braine, 1996; Haswell, 1998; Ruetten, 1994). (See chapter 10 on assessment for a fuller treatment of writing exams.) Of particular interest was Johns' (1991b) study of Luc, a Vietnamese immigrant student who repeatedly failed his university's English writing exam while managing to do successful work, including writing, in his biology major and to handle the literacy demands occasioned by his family's business. Despite some evidence that Luc's case may not have been typical (Byrd & Nelson, 1995), this study served as local and immediate research evidence for a bid to broaden L2 studies' perspectives on the meaning of literacy and of success in L2 writing. This broadening was also taking place at the theoretical level through Street's (1984) argument that literacy was not an autonomous cognitive skill but should be thought of rather as embedded social activity that could take a variety of forms of literacy practices and necessarily reflected power differentials. The writing exam that Johns' Luc repeatedly failed, reflecting traditional views of literacy, was grounded in the notion of autonomous literacy; yet the institutional undervaluing or dismissal of Luc's L2 literacy practices and the continued imposition of a culturally inappropriate writing exam demonstrated concretely the appropriateness of Street's alternative term "ideological literacies," which was gaining currency at this time.

As the central players in their own academic experiences, L2 writers' opinions, perceptions, goals, attitudes, and preferences have increasingly been explored, initially by more quantitative means and later in more richly individualized portraits. Studies have provided insight into learners'

- feelings, attitudes, and perceptions in relation to L2 writing and L2 writing courses, such as feelings about writing in English (Frodesen & Starna, 1999; Riley, 1996; Zamel, 1982, 1990), writing apprehension (Betancourt & Phinney, 1988; Gungle & Taylor, 1989), sense of growth in their L2 writing skills and strategies (Sasaki, 2004; Shi & Beckett, 2002), sense of personal growth in addition to developing writing skills as a result of L2 writing courses (Katznelson, Perpignan, & Rubin, 2001; Pally, Katznelson, Perpignan, & Rubin, 2002), feelings of success in L2 writing courses (Basturkmen & Lewis, 2002), views of their own background in writing (H. Kobayashi & Rinnert, 2002), perceptions of U.S. education (Chamberlin, 1997), perceptions of multiculturalism (McQuillan, 1994), perceptions of disconnect between L2 writing instruction and L2 undergraduate writing needs across the curriculum (Leki, 1995b; Leki & Carson, 1994, 1997), and, most recently, reactions to increased use of computer-assisted technologies in L2 writing classrooms (Belcher, 1999; Bloch & Brutt-Griffler, 2001; Yoon & Hirvela, 2004);
- personal goals for learning to write in English (Cumming, Busch, & Zhou 2002) and, in the specific situation of bilingual Canada, for choosing to develop disciplinary literacy in English at an Anglophone institution in French-speaking Quebec while yet valuing and hoping to maintain full biliteracy (Gentil, 2005);
- preferences for specific pedagogical approaches and techniques in L2 writing classrooms, such as journal writing (Holmes & Moulton, 1995), new approaches to writing instruction (Pennington, Brock, & Yue, 1996), preferences for ESL versus mainstream writing classes (Braine, 1996), preferences for and responses to feedback (Cumming & Riazi, 2000; Enginarlar, 1993; D. Ferris, 1995; Hedgcock & Lefkowitz, 1994, 1996; G. Jacobs, Curtis, Braine, & Huang, 1998; Leki, 1991a; Radecki & Swales, 1988; Saito, 1994; S. Zhang, 1995); and
- experiences in L2 writing classes and in writing tasks across the curriculum: for example, developing writing strategies for writing

tasks (Leki, 1995a), experiences in writing group work and peer responding (Carson & Nelson, 1994, 1995; de Guerrero & Villamil, 1994; Leki, 2001c; McGroarty & Zhu, 1997; Nelson & Carson, 1998; Nelson & Murphy, 1992; Tang & Tithecott, 1999; W. Zhu, 2001, Zhu being one of the very few that show L2 undergraduates in socioacademic relationships with domestic students), and experiences as L2 undergraduates (Leki, 1999, 2001c, 2003b, 2007).

Interestingly, despite heavy use of writing centers by L2 writers, until recently the bulk of publications related to L2 writers in writing centers were suggestions addressed to writing center tutors and intended to improve writing center tutors' ability to address L2 students' needs and expectations in recognition of the fact that these may conflict with standard principles of writing center interactions (Blalock, 1997; Harris & Silva, 1993; Thonus, 2003; Williams, 2002; see also many contributions in publications devoted to writing centers, such as *Writing Center Newsletter* and *Writing Center Journal*). The gist of many of these publications was to note that the needs of L2 students in the writing center often did not match writing center ideology. Writing center pedagogy promoted nondirective tutoring practices, discouraging a focus on sentence-level language features in a piece of writing and employing Socratic-style questioning to prompt writers to come to their own decisions about their writing based on their shared cultural sense of what sounded right, worked, or constituted a convincing argument. These kinds of choices proved difficult for L2 students to make, creating frustration for both tutors and students seeking more directive support.

Less research focused on L2 writers' experiences in or attitudes toward writing centers, individual tutoring, or writing conferences with their teachers (Conrad & Goldstein, 1999; L. Goldstein & Conrad, 1990; Harris, 1997; Powers & Nelson, 1995; Thonus, 2002; Young & Miller, 2004). But 2004 saw the publication of a book-length collection of articles (Bruce & Rafoth, 2004, directed primarily at educating an audience of writing center directors and tutors) and a special issue of the *Journal of Second Language Writing* reporting research on interactions within the writing center (Thonus, 2004; Weigle & Nelson, 2004; Williams & Severino, 2004) and, importantly, adding to the scanty literature on L2 writers' post-writing-center revisions (Conrad & Goldstein, 1999; L. Goldstein & Conrad, 1990; Williams, 2004).

Increasing numbers of case studies of undergraduate L2 writers have complexified understandings of how a variety of factors interact to produce a particular portrait of L2 literacy development. In these we see the focal students

- interacting with aspects of L2 writing courses and their cultures (Harklau, 1999b; Leki, 1999; Losey, 1997; Rodby, 1999) and assignments (Losey, 1997; Tucker, 1995), including journals (Lucas, 1992; Mlynarczyk, 1998), teacher feedback (F. Hyland, 1998, 2000, 2003), and technology (Bloch & Brutt-Griffler, 2001; Yoon & Hirvela, 2004); many of these interactions were less than fully successful for a variety of reasons, such as conflicting expectations of students and teachers, or teachers' lack of awareness of students' adopted language learning strategies;

- dealing with requirements of writing university exams (Johns, 1991b; Mlynarczyk, 1998; Sternglass, 1997);
- responding to specific undergraduate course demands for L2 literacy (Currie, 1998; Fishman & McCarthy, 2001; Leki, 2003b, 2007; Spack, 1997a; Sternglass, 1997);
- developing L2 literacy and academic competence (Bernstein, 2004; Currie, 1993; Gentil, 2005; Johns, 1992; Kutz, Groden, & Zamel, 1993; Leki, 2007; Smoke, 1994; Spack, 1997a; Sternglass, 1997), often in the face of institutionally created obstacles to learning and language development, such as heavy emphasis on testing, and sometimes as a result of sociopolitically conditioned lack of access to privileged literacy modes (Leibowitz, 2005);
- finding ways to cope with literacy demands through compensatory strategies (Adamson, 1990, 1993; Leki, 1995a, 1999, 2003b; Rodby, 1999); and
- finding their identities socially constructed for them by teachers and institutions as first and foremost ESL students (Harklau, 2000).

The most extensive of these case studies foreground the combined effects of the student's past and present cultural, educational, family, and personal context (see for example Leki, 2007). Other studies more pointedly focused on the intersection of educational and cultural backgrounds in L2 writing, including interrupted educations (Bosher & Rowenkamp, 1998), age of immigration (Tarone et al., 1993), cross-cultural responses to writing instruction (Newman, Trenchs-Parera, & Pujol, 2003), reading–writing relationships in L1 and L2 (Belcher & Hirvela, 2001; Carson, Carrell, Silberstein, Kroll, & Kuehn, 1990; Carson et al., 1992), L1 literacy backgrounds (Dong, 1998), the struggles and gradual development of writing expertise in a small group of undergraduates (Sternglass, 1997), and the (not always successful) effects of transferring successful L1 learning strategies to L2 writing contexts (Leki, 1995a; Spack, 1997a; see also Bell, 1995, for a description of the difficulties of an adult English-speaking learner of Chinese writing). F. Hyland provided a detailed series of studies on a small group of L2 students' responses to feedback (F. Hyland, 1998, 2000, 2003). In addition, and in accord with critical applied linguistics analyses of the colonizing spread of English worldwide, case studies of L2 writers also revealed a variety of agentive stances in relation to the acquisition of academic writing in English in South Africa

(Angelil-Carter, 1997; Thesen, 1997) and India (Canagarajah, 2002a), as well as varying degrees of willingness to invest in English literacy and language (Norton, 2000; Russell & Yoo, 2001). For international students in BANA countries (Britain, Australia, North America), resistance to the hegemony of English academic writing has been discussed primarily in relation to graduate students (see below).

Both within the writing class and in other courses across the curriculum, the issue of plagiarism has excited special interest in the case of L2 writers because of their potential lack of familiarity with the culture-bound concept of plagiarism (Deckert, 1993), a sometimes presumed culturally based special deference to printed text and received knowledge (Ballard & Clanchy, 1991; Fox, 1994; Matalene, 1985), but also a more limited range of linguistic possibilities open to them as language learners to avoid using already printed text (Currie, 1998; F. Hyland, 2001; Pecorari, 2003).[1] The discourse on L2 writers' use of plagiarism went from seeing it as (a) a problem to be solved through instruction through (b) an activity to be understood within historical (Pennycook, 1996a) and cross-linguistic (Ballard & Clanchy, 1991) contexts to (c) a strategy used to compensate for lack of L2 language proficiency (Currie, 1998; Pecorari, 2003). Others have attempted to understand views on plagiarism that exist for languages other than English and in cultural settings outside the West (J. Bloch, 2001; LoCastro & Masuko, 2002; Sapp, 2002), to determine adequacy of description of and consistency of warnings against plagiarism in informational materials and official definitions from English-medium universities (Pecorari, 2001; Sutherland-Smith, 2004; Yamada, 2003), and to propose consciousness-raising pedagogies for L2 writers, including graduate students (Barks & Watts, 2001). In light of the issues raised by the intersection of L2 writers and English academic writing practices, L2 writing researchers have also worked to problematize received understandings and assumptions about plagiarism in the West (Angelil-Carter, 2000; Pennycook, 1994a, 1996a; Scollon, 1995), questioning, among other things, precisely what the relationship is between plagiarism and learning in academic settings in a global context of English dominance (Sapp, 2002), describing inconsistent views among teachers and administrators, as well as students, on what constitutes plagiarism (Pennycook, 1994a; Sutherland-Smith, 2004), and distinguishing between intertextual borrowing that did and did not intend to defraud (Pecorari, 2003; Chandrasoma, Thomson, & Pennycook, 2004).

To understand the literacy backgrounds of L2 writing students in the aggregate and the broad contexts surrounding literacy development

---

1 The issue of plagiarism is discussed in this chapter primarily because the literature on the subject has tended to focus on undergraduates, for example, in writing classes. But similar issues arise for graduate student and L2 professional or academic writers.

worldwide, researchers examined literacy practices and preferences in other languages, nations, and cultures and the ways those practices were taken up through education: in Sri Lanka (Canagarajah, 1993a, 1993c, 1996, 2002a, 2002b), in India (Ramanathan, 2003), in China (Carson, 1992; Erbaugh, 1990; X.-M. Li, 1996; Parry & Su, 1998; You, 2004a, 2004b), in Europe generally (Johns, 2003a), in Germany (Reichelt, 2003), in Hong Kong (Pennington, Brock, & Yue, 1996), in Japan (Carson, 1992; H. Kobayashi & Rinnert, 2002), in Ukraine (Tarnopolsky, 2000), in Poland (Reichelt, 2005; Zydek-Bednarczuk, 1997), in Kenya (Muchiri, Mulamba, Myers, & Ndoloi, 1995), and, in collections of studies, in several other contexts internationally (Brock & Walters, 1993; Dong, 1998, 1999; Dubin & Kuhlman, 1992; Duszak, 1997b; Foster & Russell, 2002; Kaplan, 1995; Purves, 1986, 1988; Street, 1993, 2001; see also chapters in Perez, 2004b). Experiences of non-native-English-speaking L2 writing and literacy teachers added insight into how cultural backgrounds shaped the shapers of English L2 literacy as well (Belcher & Connor, 2001).

Specifically in relation to issues in rhetoric, initial efforts to contextualize L2 writers' literacy development revolved around the notion of contrastive rhetoric, the study of how rhetorical strategies and practices differ from one culture to the next. Contrastive rhetoric was one of the few elements of L2 literacy that penetrated L1 writing research with any success, as a cross-cultural, and so palatable if often facile, explanation of L2 writer differences. But contrastive rhetoric came under increasing fire in L2 studies for its serious methodological problems (Y. Kachru, 1995; Leki, 1991b). Mohan and Lo (1985) charged contrastive rhetoric explanations with confounding cultural with developmental and educational issues. Contrastive rhetoric was also criticized for its tendency to essentialize and reify cultures, rhetorics, and writers, freeze them in time, and implicitly create hierarchies (Kubota, 1997, 1999; Kubota & Lehner, 2004; Spack, 1997b; Susser, 1998), and most recently for its failure to adequately develop a theory of culture in which to ground contrastive studies (Atkinson, 2004). Furthermore, a study of Chinese English-language professionals reported some of these writers describing English writing in the same terms contrastive rhetoric studies had used to describe Chinese writing, and vice versa (Shi, 2003). Response to the backlash against contrastive rhetoric insisted on the importance of cultural shaping in attempting to understand L2 students' experience (Carson, 1998; Liebman, 1988; Nelson, 1998), developed more fully contextualized and historically and institutionally grounded explorations of cultural differences in literacy practices and preferences, particularly among L2 authors writing professionally (Canagarajah, 2002c; Connor, 1996, 2002, 2004, 2005; X.-M. Li, 1996; Panetta, 2001; Ramanathan, 2003; Shi, 2003; Thatcher, 2000; Wu & Rubin, 2000), and led to closer examination of and challenges to values implicitly and explicitly promoted in English academic writing and to proposals for a new contrastive rhetoric (Connor, 2002) and a critical contrastive rhetoric (Kubota & Lehner, 2004). These discussions included critiques, from a cross-cultural or relativist perspective, of the emphasis in English academic writing and writing textbooks (Ramanathan, 2002) on individualism (Ramanathan & Atkinson, 1999), on voice (Helms-Park & Stapleton, 2003; Ramanathan & Kaplan, 1996), and on "critical thinking" (Atkinson, 1997) as imposition of English-language cultural norms on L2 writers. See Casanave (2004) for a discussion of the controversies surrounding contrastive rhetoric.

In response, researchers have examined the practice of developing and displaying individual voice in writing not as culture-bound but as a widespread, even universal, impulse varyingly instantiated (Lam, 2000; Matsuda, 2001, 2002). By the same token the display of critical thinking was analyzed as crucially dependent not on background culture but on the amount of content knowledge a writer brought to a given subject (Leki, 2004; Stapleton, 2002). Of special poignancy in this regard were graduate students, some of whom were established professionals in their fields with multiple publications in their L1s, who chafed under the requirement to produce an alien voice in English (Fox, 1994; Hirvela & Belcher, 2001; Ivanic & Camps, 2001).

Summary

The bulk of the literature on L2 writing in English in North America has covered undergraduates and over the last 25 years has examined a wide variety of features of that writing and its context. The purpose of much of this research has been to feed back into tertiary-level writing classrooms, and so it has aimed directly or indirectly at improving writing instruction there. Since nearly all undergraduate students are required to take writing classes, sometimes in separate sections especially designated for L2 writers, sometimes in course sections together with domestic undergraduates, the proliferation of studies devoted to undergraduate L2 writing may reflect the sense of urgency that L2 writing professionals felt to make these courses as beneficial to L2 undergraduate students as possible and to prepare them for the writing they were assumed to encounter in courses across the undergraduate curriculum in English-medium settings. The wide variety of dimensions inherent in the undergraduate experience was reflected in the wide variety of subjects that have intrigued writing researchers and prompted them to attempt to find answers to the question of how best to provide writing instruction for L2 students. The trajectory of the answers these researchers have proposed over the years is discussed in section II.

Chapter 4

Graduate Student Writing

As numbers of L2 graduate students in North American institutions have increased over the last 25 years, research attention has shifted from L2 undergraduates toward the L2 graduate student population. As noted in the section on identity below, graduate students may experience particular threats to their identities as they make the transition to the unfamiliar ways of writing demanded by their disciplines in English-dominant educational environments. Often much is at stake for these students, who may leave jobs and family behind to pursue degrees abroad, be required to make significant financial investments in their education or have them made on their behalves by their employers or governments, experience threats to their disciplinary expertise (for example, being regarded as or assumed to be less expert than they really are), and be required, in addition to studying, to work as teaching or research assistants in contexts they have never themselves experienced before.

Much of the initial research on L2 English graduate student writing focused on what these writers needed to do to enter and thrive in the discourse communities of their disciplines. As L2 writing research broadened away from the analysis of target texts as ultimate goals for graduate student writers, other issues came to the fore: how disciplines may be inimical to graduate students from certain backgrounds and may function to exclude the students' experiences; what the effect was of social relations with faculty and others involved in a graduate program; how other (oral) genres, such as seminar presentations, impacted L2 writers.

During the 1980s and early 1990s most of the research focusing on graduate students acknowledged that disciplinary communities constituted communities of practice into which these students sought entrance; this research attempted to establish writing requirements (conceived of as more or less static) within these disciplines, usually in terms of genre, disciplinary language, and discourse conventions for papers written for graduate courses, for articles written for publication often in collaboration with advisors, and for theses and dissertations (Canseco & Byrd, 1989; Casanave & Hubbard, 1992; Cooley & Lewkowicz, 1997; Gosden, 1996;

Huckin & Olsen, 1984; Jenkins, Jordan, & Weiland, 1993; McKenna, 1987; Samraj, 1994). Other research examined texts produced by L2 graduate students in response to genre requirements (S. Jacobs, 1982; James, 1984; Swales, 1990b) or explored ways of teaching genres (Swales & Lindemann, 2002; Swales & Luebs, 2002).

An early and particularly eye-opening and influential self-report was that of Fan Shen (1989), who described his difficulties taking on English rhetorical style in writing as a graduate student in English literature. The impact of Shen's much-cited essay was eventually reflected in research methods that moved away from documentary evidence alone and from pedagogical issues toward case study, interview, and observational research with L2 graduate students. The focus shifted toward the kinds of resources students accessed in meeting disciplinary requirements (Riazi, 1997), including reliance on L1 educational and disciplinary experience (Connor & Kramer, 1995; Connor & Mayberry, 1996), and the types and degrees of difficulty these graduate students faced in writing (Angelova & Riazantseva, 1999; Belcher, 1989; Casanave, 2002; Casanave & Hubbard, 1992; Cooley & Lewkowicz, 1997; Dong, 1996; Leki, 2006; Raymond & Parks, 2002; Riazi, 1997) and in required oral presentations (Weissberg, 1993) as neither entire insiders nor entire outsiders to the disciplinary community or the L2 culture (Shaw, 1991). Master's students in particular found themselves poised between being novices and budding experts, still seeing themselves essentially as students and thus anchored primarily to courses and grades rather than seeing themselves as beginning to participate in a community's literate activities (Casanave, 2002). But even PhD students needed to learn the types of literacy practices typical of their disciplines; Belcher's students, for example, were unconvinced that criticism of others' work took place in publications in their disciplines (Belcher, 1995). The students' difficulties included not knowing how to position themselves in their writing in relation to the received knowledge of the discipline (Belcher, 1995; Cadman, 1997) and not knowing where to turn for help (Belcher, 1989; Dong, 1998).

Furthermore, unlike most domestic graduate students, for L2 students an enormous disparity might exist between their disciplinary knowledge and sophistication and their ability to write in English (Hirvela & Belcher, 2001; Ivanic & Camps, 2001; Schneider & Fujishima, 1995), a difference of which they reported being acutely aware (Silva, 1992). Although many, perhaps most, graduate students eventually experienced success (Gentil, 2005; Silva et al., 2003), research on L2 graduate students reported their struggles in finding themselves called upon to write discipline-specific texts, including theses and dissertations, with the curricular aid of only elementary and general-focus L2 writing courses, courses whose practices did not always support and at times even conflicted with disciplinary practices

(Hansen, 2000; Schneider & Fujishima, 1995). In addition, unlike the case in most undergraduate courses, in graduate courses, course and writing task objectives often remained implicit (Carson, 2001; Casanave, 2002; Raymond & Parks, 2002; Yang & Shi, 2003). As Tardy (2005b) noted, the whole idea of disciplinary writing as rhetorical, as a form of implicit argument, is likely to remain occluded for these students. Furthermore, in some cases students faced the anomalous situation of completing course work in their disciplines having done relatively little writing, receiving little feedback on their writing, and yet then being expected to plunge directly into writing theses and dissertations (Leki, 2006).

Whereas early studies assumed that, in order to become members of disciplinary communities, the students would need to do whatever they could to conform to disciplinary standards, later work investigated the degree to which these students experienced frustration with the expectations and assumptions of the target community (Fox, 1994) or resisted conforming to them, sometimes successfully (Belcher, 1994, 1997; Canagarajah, 1999, 2001a; X.-M. Li, 1999), sometimes less so (Casanave, 1992). Belcher's work (1994, 1997) demonstrated, for example, that the students she studied were more successful and more satisfied with their experience in graduate school when their faculty advisors did not assume that the students would simply align themselves to disciplinary standards; instead, the students who thrived had advisors who assumed that the students would alter the disciplines they were entering and would bring to the disciplines their unique perspectives as bicultural operators. Furthermore, some students specifically worked to maintain their ability to function professionally in multiple languages, a desire that sometimes required considerable effort (Gentil, 2005; see also chapter 7 on scholarly writers).

Research in the later 1990s and 2000s provided detailed examinations of how graduate students made choices in view of local factors at play in graduate student writing.[1] The factors include the interactions of students with each other (including with linguistic compatriots; Gentil, 2005) and with faculty, and the interactions of students' current understandings of various course and disciplinary requirements with students' past experiences. Past experience with disciplinary activities appeared to significantly aid particularly master's students in their L2 studies (Casanave, 2002;

---

1 Studies of graduate students in non-English-dominant countries who are required to write theses or dissertations in English are also beginning to appear. See for example Y. Li (2005), which documents, among other strategies, one graduate student's heavy reliance on previously published materials from which to borrow rhetorical and linguistic moves and, to meet the school's PhD graduation requirement, his eventual publication of three papers in journals included in the *Science Citation Index*.

Connor & Kramer, 1995; Yang & Shi, 2003); the students who most comfortably took up master's work in TESL (Teaching English as a Second Language) studies in Casanave's (2002) study at the Monterey Institute were those who had previously taught English themselves.

L2 graduate students were often acutely conscious of themselves and their placement and budding roles within their chosen disciplines (Hirvela & Belcher, 2001; Ivanic & Camps, 2001), experienced disconcerting contacts with campus life (Braine, 2002), had sometimes suffered a considerable loss in status from social, professional, and familial positions they had occupied at home (Fox, 1994; Hirvela & Belcher, 2001), and were sensitive to the fact that, in hoping to succeed, they were also competing against domestic students, whose understanding of the context of study may have been far greater (Beer, 2000). In addition, even class participation patterns, which varied, served to position the L2 students differently depending on such local conditions as the student, the class, and the professor's reaction to them (Morita, 2004), although some graduate students actively and strategically manipulated their dialogic interactions with others to best suit their purposes, including the furthering of their writing goals (Braxley, 2005). Other students voiced resentment at the lack of intercultural and cross-language sophistication of some of their professors (Myles & Cheng, 2003).

For the students studied by Casanave (1995) and Prior (1991, 1998), the broader disciplinary community itself had less formative potency than these other local, immediate, and historical or personal factors in the students' experiences. In general the role of social factors was increasingly recognized (Beer, 2000; Braine, 2002; Ferenz, 2005; X.-M. Li, 1999; Myles & Cheng, 2003; Prior, 1995; Riazi, 1997; Stein, 1998), even among research supervisors, who reported evaluating graduate research proposals in terms of the person who wrote it rather than based strictly on genre features (Cadman, 2002). Understanding shifted away from the notion of one-way disciplinary enculturation of L2 graduate students toward the perception, particularly at the PhD level, of joint construction of disciplinarity through oral and textual interactions among and between newcomers and more proficient others such that both texts produced and lives lived were tweaked in the direction of realignment with the new community, which itself was reconceived as local rather than as an abstract, the discourse community of the profession. In other words, graduate students were not merely seen to be enculturated by faculty or others into disciplinary communities but were seen as shaping those communities as well, particularly at the local level. The downside of this emphasis on the local community, however, was that it required L2 students, already less socially plugged in, to negotiate vagaries of individual campuses and departments with care and subtlety (Casanave, 2002; Prior,

1998), sometimes experiencing catastrophic difficulties when they established little social contact (Schneider & Fujishima, 1995).[2]

The role of faculty, most especially thesis and dissertation advisors, in the initiation and socialization of L2 English graduate students became increasingly evident (Belcher, 1989, 1994; Cho, 2004; Tardy, 2005b), particularly because these students drew on fewer other social resources, such as peers or members of their degree committees (Dong, 1998), and generally worked in greater isolation than their domestic classmates, despite the fact that the majority of L2 graduate students studied in science and technology fields and thus often worked in labs together with other graduate students. According to survey research by Dong (1998), as science and technology students, some of these L2 graduate students were not only writing in English for the first time but writing for the first time at all at any length. Counterintuitively, and to the students' disadvantage, their advisors required fewer revisions from them than they did from domestic students and were less likely to direct these students toward dissertations that consisted of article compilations with the director as co-author. Thus, in addition to the L2 students' greater lack of experience with writing and greater social (and so academic) isolation, they were further disadvantaged by getting fewer opportunities to work through drafts of papers and to collaborate with their advisors on publications, thereby in turn giving them less opportunity to establish a professional presence and a list of publications on their resumes. The L2 students sought and got less help than domestic students although their advisors did not perceive this difference and although the students generally craved more, not less, intervention in their work (Dong, 1998; Leki, 2006). They were, however, assertive to varying degrees about the processes of initiation and socialization they underwent, chafing at both insufficient and excessive guidance, oversight, and intervention by faculty, finding it difficult to achieve a balance between support and constraint. On the other hand, some L2 doctoral candidates who collaborated with peers and mentors in education and social science disciplines experienced success in attempting initial forays into professional research and publication activities and, significantly, were able to rely on their own local knowledge, derived from their experiences crossing language and cultural boundaries, to contribute to and expand center-based knowledge with their own perspectives (Cho, 2004). What was characterized as "low-demand" participation with

---

2 Early research on levels of general satisfaction among L2 students with their graduate experiences focused on their isolation from host country members and on the adaptations that L2 students needed to make to fit in better and, as a result, to have a better experience. By the mid-1980s and 1990s, however, researchers questioned instead the "inadequacies of the higher education community that fails to provide a policy, program, or concern about the problems that face international students" (Perrucci & Hu, 1995, p. 496).

mentors in joint projects (Prior, 1998) at times advantaged L2 students by providing gradual initiation into difficult activities and at other times disadvantaged them by limiting their opportunities for full participation (Cho, 2004). Another key to the development of rhetorical knowledge appeared to be the exigency of the writing task, with graduate students required to make abrupt leaps in expertise as the result of intense investment in certain high-stakes writing projects (Tardy, 2005b).

Choice of dissertation topics among L2 students was affected by language and local knowledge considerations as well as by recommendations of advisors. Investigations of constraints experienced by L2 graduate students suggested a preference for quantitatively oriented rather than qualitatively oriented dissertation research because of its lesser reliance on language and greater generic transparency (Chang & Swales, 1999; Cho, 2004; J. Flowerdew, 1999a). However, despite active discouragement, desire to pursue intellectually appealing topics as well as philosophical commitment to the more fuzzy genres and perspectives of qualitative research drove the choices and sustained the energy of some L2 graduate students to engage in qualitative research as well (Belcher & Hirvela, 2005).

Looking toward the positions L2 students would eventually take up after graduate school and drawing on the research on the difficulties of professional writing in English by NNES users, Tardy (2004) reported on L2 graduate students' mixed feelings about the role English would eventually play in their professional lives, both as a medium of international scientific communication and as the cause of potential obstacles to their full participation in professional activities (research, publication, conferences) and of resultant loss of scientific information written in languages other than English.

Summary

Perhaps the most salient feature of the L2 graduate student experience exposed in the research literature in the last 25 years was the disparity between the students' high level of disciplinary expertise and their lower degree of familiarity with language, writing, and sometimes cultural issues, and the difficulty of getting focused help with overcoming these obstacles. By the same token, one of the previously most occluded features of the L2 graduate student experience was the need to negotiate social roles within graduate departments and with graduate advisors, as it became clearer that success in L2 graduate writing was often tied to success in managing departmental social relations, including in the production of joint publications. Finally, the initial heavy focus on L2 undergraduates has shifted since the 1990s to greater emphasis on graduate students. Part of this shift has been fueled by, and has in turn fueled, increasing interest in disciplinary genres and genre research.

Chapter 5

L2 Adult Newcomer, Resettlement, and Community Literacy

After the end of the U.S. war in Vietnam and into the early 1980s, hundreds of thousands of Southeast Asian refugees immigrated to North America and flooded resettlement camps in places such as the Philippines (Auerbach & Burgess, 1985) in the "largest refugee resettlement program in U.S. history" (Tollefson, 1989, p. x). Most of the publications related to L2 Adult Basic Education in the early 1980s consisted of either quantitative studies of large populations or curriculum-related materials focused on teaching "survival English" in response to this influx and in an effort to quickly get L2 learners ready for lives in English. By the mid-1980s the English language programs developed in the US and in refugee resettlement programs began to draw serious criticism for their adoption of then current communicative, competency-based language teaching methodologies. These survival English curriculums purported to teach the amount and type of practical English actually needed and used in daily tasks to allow refugees and other immigrants to learn enough basic English to get a job. Analyses of these programs (particularly by Auerbach & Burgess, 1985, and Tollefson, 1986, 1989), heavily influenced by Freirian critiques of these types of materials as reflective of banking models of education (Freire, 1970), argued persuasively that they trained and led refugees and immigrants to expect to remain at the lowest socioeconomic levels, regardless of their previous education and experience. Auerbach and Burgess (1985, p. 484) cited an excerpt from materials at the time intended to wryly capture the essence of the employment conflict for many newcomers:

> 14. A. What did you do in Laos?
>   B. I taught college for 15 years. I was Deputy Minister of Education for ten years and then . . .
>   A. I see. Can you cook Chinese food?
>   (The Experiment in International Living, 1983, p. 177, cited in Auerbach & Burgess, 1985)

Because of their employment and survivalist orientation, these refugee and immigrant programs had no reason to include much writing besides filling out forms, and perhaps as a result, little research into these programs was dedicated strictly to writing. (Tollefson's 1989 account of the curriculum in the camps and later in-country programs, for example, barely mentions writing, and then only in relation to testing, in chapter 6. T. Goldstein's 1996 account of workplace language teaching and use likewise does not mention writing.) Furthermore, modes of language perception, production, and interaction were blended so that writing was used to help teach language generally and as a springboard for oral skills, rather than considered a skill to develop for some intrinsic value of its own. Although writing was helpful to language learning in a variety of ways, it seemed indisputable that for most of the learners, though not all (see Derwing & Ho, 1991), L2 writing was in fact the least important language skill to develop.

Although the flurry of response to L2 adult language learning and literacy needs has diminished, according to 2000 statistics English learners still made up half of the students attending Adult Basic Education (ABE) classes in the US in 1998, with the research literature over the last 25 years focusing mainly on Southeast Asians (especially Vietnamese, Cambodian, Hmong, Khmer, and Laotian) and Spanish speakers. Although native English speakers and English learners in adult literacy classes shared certain experiences (e.g. stigmatization for lack of English literacy) and goals (e.g. empowerment and perhaps independence in relation to the demands of life in literate societies), there was much that differentiated them as well, beginning with their legal status. Developing adult L2 literacy in the US was tightly bound up with a number of issues surrounding immigration. Laws passed in 1917 required literacy (though not necessarily in English) for immigration; although these laws were subsequently overturned, literacy in English is still a requirement for citizenship in the US and, in some cases, for permanent resident status (S. McKay & Weinstein-Shr, 1993; Moriarty, 1998). Thus, L2 literacy learners were under a certain amount of legal pressure to become literate. [1] (For an analysis of the situation in Canada, see Burnaby, 1992, and Burnaby & Cumming, 1992.)

English learners were also sometimes outsiders in the community, unfamiliar with local customs, including on the job, and some had such limited "economic and educational options" that they often had little choice but to live in "highly segregated racial and ethnic communities out of which they rarely venture" (Guerra, 1998, p. 5). Rarely venturing out of their L1-speaking community meant rarely interacting with English speakers; the desire for such interaction was one motivation for attending

---

1 These requirements for literacy may be honored more in theory than in practice but the requirement to *read*, *write*, and speak ordinary English is nevertheless in place.

ESL or ABE classes for many of these people (Cumming & Gill, 1991; Malicky & Derwing, 1993; S. McKay, 1993; S. McKay & Weinstein-Shr, 1993). An image of helpless, clueless immigrants, however, was contradicted by the research evidence of many of these groups' clear vision of their own needs and resourcefulness in meeting them (Auerbach, 1989; Duffy, 2004; Guerra, 1998; Klassen & Burnaby, 1993; S. McKay, 1993; S. McKay & Weinstein-Shr, 1993; Norton, 2000). Nevertheless, the L2 literacy acquisition experiences of refugees, immigrants, newcomers, or other adult community English learners were complex.

In several respects the literacy acquisition processes of this population were different from those of other ABE learners, who were fluent English speakers, and they added to the complications of becoming literate in a second language. First, English learners had no oral English to draw on to support literacy growth; they were learning to read and/or write in English without already knowing English. Some adult English learners may have had little or no access to education in their L1 and might not be literate in their own languages or spoke languages that had no written form, making these adults relatively unfamiliar with print generally, as well as with schooling practices. The degree of difference between the learners' L1 and English also impacted the learner's task, for example, whether the L1 was alphabetic or not.

On the other hand, other English learners had multiple literacies in a variety of languages and scripts (Saxena, 1994), a great deal of education, and a high degree of sophisticated literacy skills, only not in English. As a result, their education and literacy carried with it "little social value" (Norton, 2000) and did not bring them social benefit or access to material resources. If the wider culture tended to view illiterate English-speaking adults as cognitively impaired (Fingeret, 1984, cited in S. McKay, 1993), the cognitive abilities of those who were literate in their L1 but not in English were sometimes not recognized or valued until they could display them in English.

A mix of learners representing these initial states in a single ESL or adult literacy class was not uncommon, particularly during periods, such as the one just after the end of the U.S. war in Vietnam, of intense resettlement (Collignon, 1993). What all these L2 learners had in common, however, was likely to be a lack of familiarity with local social and cultural habits and assumptions. In some cases, then, for example with rural Hmong or Cambodian refugees, language courses included cultural information, especially about expectations on the job or about getting a job, with information and admonitions that seemed to differ relatively little from those of early twentieth-century Americanization classes, in which immigrants learned "the American way" to brush their teeth or wash their dishes. More modern versions of this kind of approach informed students that they must always arrive on time to work and discouraged them from enrolling in school while they were collecting public assistance (Auerbach & Burgess, 1985; Tollefson, 1986).

The literature focusing on this population during the early 1980s, a period of resettlement, consisted of either pedagogical materials or criticisms of those materials, in both pre-arrival and in-country literacy courses, and of the resettlement programs (Auerbach & Burgess, 1985; Tollefson, 1986). Although by the later 1980s and throughout the 1990s there was still little research focused specifically on the actual L2 writing of this population, most of the research attention had turned away from institutional issues and toward investigations of smaller groups, in recognition of the fact "that literacy is *not* essentially the same phenomenon wherever it is found" (Klassen, 1991, p. 40). These studies documented:

- the ways that these learners and their families and communities used literacy, and resisted using literacy (Reder, 1987), including writing, in both L1 and L2: L1 literacy often served to construct and maintain family and community bonds; L2 English served a more bureaucratic function (Klassen & Burnaby, 1993; S. McKay, 1993; Reder, 1987; although see Weinstein-Shr, 1993, for an opposite analysis);
- the social meaning of literacy in different cultures (Besnier, 1993; Hartley, 1994; Klassen, 1991, 1992; Kulick & Stroud, 1993; Reder, 1987; Rockhill, 1987; Street, 1993);
- how these adults coped in English dominant countries in everyday situations despite limited English literacy by relying, for example, on combinations of memorization (of locations), painstaking copying of written information onto forms, and relying on sympathetic service personnel (Cumming & Gill, 1991; Gillespie, 2000; Guerra, 1998; Klassen, 1991; S. McKay, 1993; Norton, 1998; Weinstein-Shr, 1993);
- these learners' goals for attending literacy classes (Klassen & Burnaby, 1993; Malicky & Derwing, 1993; Manton, 1998; Norton, 2000);
- patterns of participation in literacy classes, including obstacles and support structures (Cumming & Gill, 1992; Hayes, 1989; Klassen, 1992).

These reports, mostly observational and case studies, emphasized the strategic pooling of family and community resources that allowed immigrants or refugees to manage the literacy requirements of their daily work lives, dealings with bureaucracies and schools, commercial transactions, and even intercommunity disputes satisfactorily (Duffy, 2004; Guerra, 1998; Hartley, 1994; Klassen & Burnaby, 1993; S. McKay, 1993; S. McKay & Weinstein-Shr, 1993; Norton, 2000; Weinstein-Shr, 1993). In fact high dropout rates from literacy classes supported evidence that most of the experiences of literacy failure took place in the ESL/literacy classes themselves, not in the real world (Klassen, 1991), leading to ongoing criticisms of pedagogies and programs (Currie & Cray, 2004) but even more so of the refusal or inability of government and other agencies to adequately fund literacy development efforts, even in Canada and Australia, where official government policy has been more welcoming to immigrants than it has in the US (Fergusson, 1998; Klassen & Burnaby, 1993; S. McKay & Weinstein-Shr, 1993). Despite the high dropout rate in adult education courses, English learners were reported to be eager to take the English courses offered; it was often the opportunities to enroll that were inadequate, with potential learners being turned away because of overdemand (Guerra, 1996).

Several researchers also noted the overrepresentation of women in these classes (Cumming & Gill, 1991; Guerra, 1998; Malicky & Derwing, 1993; Norton, 1998), the literacy roles open to women within families as managers of household writing (Klassen, 1991; Rockhill, 1987) or closed to them (Hartley, 1994), and the special interest writing held for some of these women, particularly writing diaries (Norton, 1998) and letters in efforts to maintain community ties (Guerra, 1998; Klassen & Burnaby, 1993), leading Guerra to refer to the "feminization of literacy" (1998, p. 103).

Differential success depending on age of community learners in literacy classes sometimes led to generational conflicts (Guerra, 1996) and loss of status for older community members who were either slower to learn English or literacy or did not learn at all (Delgado-Gaitan, 1987; Klassen, 1991). Unless special care was taken to support them in maintaining their traditional positions of importance, they could become irrelevant and were then displaced as community leaders (Malicky & Derwing, 1993). In other cases, social disharmony was caused when those who did learn to write were then on call for the rest of the community, sometimes against their will and even for fraudulent purposes (Weinstein-Shr, 1993). On the other hand, in communities with community exchange networks, literacy could become another useful item to barter (Hartley, 1994).

For a variety of reasons, many L2 learners in adult literacy or community ESL classes were reported to show relatively little interest in learning to write in English. For some, literacy in English was irrelevant or viewed as simply unattainable; what was significant and within the realm of possibility was acquisition of literacy in their native language (Klassen, 1991). These learners wanted to be able to write letters to family, for example, in Spanish; after all, they had no one to write letters to in English. Furthermore, they felt that lack of Spanish literacy was getting in the way of learning oral English. Thus, they were interested in becoming literate, but not in English (Klassen & Burnaby, 1993). For these learners, the main usefulness of the ESL classes was for putting them in touch with other Spanish speakers, often women, who could then increase their mutual support networks. For others, no particular goal was perceived as achieved through writing in English (Cumming & Gill, 1991); since writing appeared to have little functional value, these learners were uninterested in learning to write. In some communities, as Kulick and Stroud (1993) noted about Papua New Guinea, "there is no notion that everyone should learn to write" (p. 33); adult learners coming from such communities also saw limited use for writing (Guerra, 1998). Furthermore, learners' own views on what learning to write might mean may not correspond to those of their instructors (Rigg, 1985). Finally, in some contexts being able to *speak* English was far more important than being literate at all, even in a home language, as was the case, for example, in the complex situation of apartheid South Africa, according to Kerfoot (1993). Thus, the benefits of knowing how to read and/or write a non-prestige language were outweighed by the importance of familiarity, even without literacy, with the prestige language.

Part of the reason for this lack of interest in learning to write in these literacy classes was that, as noted above, these learners managed to accomplish a variety of literacy tasks without L2 literacy (Delgado-Gaitan, 1987; Gillespie, 2000; Klassen, 1991). Furthermore, the various uses of literacy were divided between L1 and L2 within the community such that what one language could not provide could be provided by the other (S. McKay, 1993; Weinstein-Shr, 1993), one offering an opening out to the community, the other the possibility of maintaining the intimacy of family links. Thus, literacy was described as practiced within communities not as an individual "autonomous" literacy (Street, 1993), but as social literacy, spread out among community members, with all the literacy talent needed present in one or another member in one or another language (Gillespie, 2000; Reder, 1987). Where literacy was viewed as a community experience and resource, a single writer or reader in the family or community might serve as scribe in jointly written letters, which were exchanged between families, not individuals (Hartley, 1994). Thus, individuals were reported to have felt no particular need to become literate when the community could fulfill their literacy needs. These kinds of perspectives made it clearer that, although a given learner might not have been reading or writing individually, L2 language users took on different roles in a variety of literate practices (Vasquez, 1992).

In 1991 Cumming and Gill noted that little research had yet focused on writing specifically in this population. By 2000, Gillespie could still assert: "To date we know relatively little about how the development of writing ability in adult literacy learners compares with that of young children or of basic writers at the college level" (p. 91). Nevertheless, the late 1990s and early 2000s saw an increased appearance of work related to writing. An early issue addressed from a curricular point of view was the question of interaction between L1 and L2 literacy, leading to an unresolved debate about whether, for those with little or no L1 literacy, the best approach would be to teach literacy in L1 first, thus allowing the learners to rely on the support of oral L1 language fluency to support initial literacy in L1, or to teach literacy directly in English along with developing oral English. Several researchers supported the position that any amount of L1 literacy gave the learner an advantage in approaching L2 literacy (Malicky & Derwing, 1993; Robson, 1981; Weinstein, 1984). However, as S. McKay (1993) argued, other research did not show L1 writing abilities as useful support for developing L2 literacy, at least not with extended prose, until a certain level of L2 proficiency was achieved (Cumming, 1989); L1–L2 interactions are complicated, with L1/L2 differentially and mutually affecting both L1 and L2 reading and writing (Carson et al., 1992). But the studies cited by S. McKay pertain to academic writing, and it appears to be the general consensus that even the smallest amount of L1 literacy is helpful in the development of L2 literacy, beginning for example with the understanding that print carries meaning.

As noted above, some learners themselves expressed interest in learning L1 literacy before or along with L2 literacy (Klassen & Burnaby, 1993; Malicky & Derwing, 1993). Being able to do so in a course required the assistance of a teacher literate in the students' L1. Because that was not always feasible, some suggested using bilingual or bicultural teacher aides from the community (Auerbach, 1993), who would provide the additional advantage of fulfilling learners' expectations about what a teacher did or was (Hardman, 1999).

In an effort to determine where adult learners needed to concentrate efforts in learning to write more than short phrases, research by Cumming and Gill (Cumming, 1991; Cumming & Gill, 1991) homed in on three areas: vocabulary; self-monitoring, for example, being able to remember knowledge they had and use it in creating texts; and bridging the disconnect between their experiences and writing, for example, by using writing to document their experiences. The designation of this last category of need arose in response to observations that the learners these researchers followed had difficulty filling out sections of job applications that included categories asking about health histories or hobbies. The writers had trouble determining what kind of information was being asked for, what to include from their own lives. This research stands out in its attempt to understand and delineate metacognitive substrates of L2 adult literacy needs.

More typically, research on how learners learn to write at this level noted that learners needed all kinds of language and print skills, including speaking (Collignon, 1993) and deciphering maps (Collignon's focal student had never seen a map of her own country, Laos), and that, when given the opportunity, adult L2 literacy students were willing and able to actively recruit text production assistance from the variety of sources and people at hand, including peers in literacy classes (Hardman, 1999). Their texts were often primarily a springboard or support for oral development and as such for the most part revision was not a part of the kind of writing done in adult literacy classes (McGroarty & Scott, 1993).

Autobiographies and diaries have also been used to study L2 literacy learners' experiences (Guerra, 1996, 1998; Norton, 1998, 2000). Analyzing how the relatively educated Canadian immigrant women in her study used the journals they wrote in English, Norton (1998) noted that they used them to critique aspects of their educational experience, to document their own progress in L2, and to note discrepancies between what they were told about Canada and what they experienced. Norton pointed out, however, that these diaries were different from those typically used in writing classes because they had an explicit purpose, to inform the researcher's research, which thus gave the writers more compelling reason to write than most L2 journals or diaries might. In a further analysis, Norton noted that the writers used the diaries to inform both her and their classmates (since they read portions out loud), to construct their L2 identities, and to reflect on that construction. Gender issues arose in these studies as well.

Two research reports in 2004 captured an interesting counterpoint in L2 adult/community literacy studies and reiterate, on one hand, the resiliency and resourcefulness of communities in their engagement with L2 literacy and, on the other hand, the disappointing features of ESL adult literacy classes, which resulted in ineffectiveness and high rates of learner dropout. Duffy (2004) analyzed an exchange of letters to the editor from a Midwest U.S. newspaper between 1985 and 1995 initiated by anti-immigrant members of the Anglo community who wrote to complain bitterly about the Hmong refugees living there. Duffy demonstrated how members of the Hmong community were able to contest their positioning as welfare cheats, criminals, and dog eaters by redeploying the very tropes and other rhetorical tools used in the anti-immigrant letters, at the same time creating forms of civic writing that had not theretofore been attested within the Hmong community. Members of the Hmong community were thus being socialized by their adversaries into particular literacy practices that empowered them against those very adversaries and toward a more positive construction of their own identities.

The counterpoint to this example of effective and creative refugee community literacy within the context of civic life was the approach to literacy development in newcomer classes described by Currie and Cray (2004). Although the adult students in these classes had a clear understanding of the broad and varied uses of writing in their real lives, their L2 literacy classes were disappointingly disconnected from writing as social engagement or from the kinds of writing the learners did or needed in their public lives; the classes focused instead on low-level writing practice, spelling, copying, and grammatical accuracy. Having been socialized into a particular view of what literacy is, neither the students nor their teachers took exception to the literacy practices in these classes, thereby re-inscribing this limited view of literacy into their belief systems. It was this kind of vision of what participation in L2 literacy and community means that underlay the Chinese cook anecdote with which this chapter began.

Summary

Literacy issues for immigrant or resettlement clients fall into two categories: (a) the nature of the demands for literacy within the daily lives of these L2 users and the individual and community responses to these demands and (b) the content and focus of adult L2 literacy classes. The research indicates generally that these L2 users and their communities have been quite resourceful in fulfilling their literacy needs, often by distributing literacy skills through the community rather than concentrating them in each autonomous individual. Although these learners have looked to L2 literacy classes to further their aims, the classes have been less successful than they might have been, sometimes because the focus of the classes themselves was inappropriate, sometimes because the learners' goals, made explicit or not, did not converge with the goals of the literacy class, and sometimes because the life circumstances of the potential students caused them to find attendance at these classes simply too difficult to negotiate when balanced against the real or expected return. In the meantime the study of the processes of adult acquisition of L2 literacy remains somewhat underdeveloped.

Chapter 6

Workplace Writing in L2

Workplace writing refers to writing required or associated with the daily workplace environment and typically produced for in-house consumption by co-workers at the same work site, such as a factory, or within the same business. Workplace writing is thus to be differentiated from, for example, scholarly writing (discussed in chapter 7), which is associated with a profession rather than a worksite and is directed to other professionals within the same discipline but typically operating in physically dispersed work settings, such as universities or scientific laboratories internationally. L2 studies have a long history of attending to writing in the workplace, including writing for science and technology, industry, business, and the medical fields; other research has considered oral L2 interactions, including on the factory floor (T. Goldstein, 1996; Harper, Peirce, & Burnaby, 1996; Peirce, Harper, & Burnaby 1993). For the most part, the research in this area has focused on needs analysis (Cameron, 1998; Duff, Wong, & Early, 2000; Huckin & Olsen, 1984; Katz, 2000; Lepetit & Cichocki, 2002), that is, identifying what kinds of writing are required at particular job sites; cross-linguistic text analysis (Connor, 1988; Dennett, 1988; Jenkins & Hinds, 1987; Maier, 1992; Selinker, Todd-Trimble, & Trimble, 1978; Sims & Guice, 1992), that is, how L1 versus L2 writers respond to the writing demands at these sites or how the demands differ from each other across language and cultural groups; and materials development or other pedagogical issues (Hutchinson & Waters, 1987; Myers, 1988; L. Olsen & Huckin, 1983; Platt, 1993; Selinker, Tarone, & Hanzeli, 1981), that is, the kinds of instructional programs that might best be generated from the research findings to be used in writing courses, often ones sponsored by the company or worksite itself. Less attention has focused on the L2 writers producing the workplace documents or on their writing contexts (Parks & Maguire, 1999). The findings of those few that have focused on writers and contexts (Belcher, 1991; Parks, 2000, 2001; Parks & Maguire, 1999) are provocative in their repeated findings that writing in these settings is heavily embedded in the social dimensions of the workplace.

Belcher's (1991) early study of L2 writers in a technical corporate setting notes their anxiety about writing, their awareness that lack of English writing skills would likely get in the way of their professional advancement, and their sense that they needed a writing class focused on grammar, lexis, and rhetoric. Comparing documents and behaviors of successful writers at the company with those of her students, however, Belcher drew a different picture. Because of their writing anxiety and their fear that miscommunication would cause them to be seen as less competent than they were, her students avoided writing, hoping to protect themselves from drawing the negative attention of supervisors. But this also meant that they lost opportunities both to self-promote and create social bonds with their co-workers through their writing and to improve their writing through practice and feedback. She noted that, in contrast, successful writers in the company used informal writing, such as volunteering to take on onerous note-taking chores at staff meetings, to build bonds of solidarity with co-workers. The L2 writers already had restricted social interactions with their native English-speaking co-workers, leading in part to lack of opportunity to develop the language for social regulation that would allow them to use writing to portray themselves to their advantage as knowledgeable, friendly, and hardworking. Such lack of opportunity for interaction with NESs has been noted in other workplace studies (Duff, Wong, & Early, 2000). In effect, what her students needed to improve their writing was not grammar and rhetoric instruction but situated literate activity, social interaction centered on text.

Although Belcher's students had the option of avoiding writing at their worksite, and did, the Francophone nurses in the extended series of studies by Parks (2000, 2001) and Parks and McGuire (1999) were required to read and create daily nursing notes and nursing care plans and did so in a context of extensive formal and informal mentoring and collaborative interaction with co-workers and supervisors and of readily available model documents. Parks' research reported the intensely social nature of these L2 writers' initiations into the local literacy culture of this hospital setting.

L2 writers like those in Belcher's study may have been reluctant to write in workplace settings, particularly if writing was not required, but other L2 writers appeared to succeed at writing in the kinds of activity systems (Dias, Freedman, Medway, & Paré, 1999) where writing was functional and a part of everyone's job, where they experienced repeated exposure to examples of exactly the type of writing they were to produce themselves, where they could get mentoring on the spot rather than writing in isolation, and where the document was not an end in itself but merely a tool, a means leading to a commonly sought goal, such as patient care. In such settings because the writing itself was not as important as the goal that the writing furthered, L2 and other types of errors in the document were ignored when the writing could be otherwise easily and accurately deciphered.

From studies of workplace writing, it is clear that all new employees, L1 or L2 English, experience a learning curve as they appropriate new disciplinary and institutional genres; the difference between the two groups in this regard is primarily a matter of degree. To be sure, language is an issue for L2 writers. But in studies of both workplace and academic writers (Parry, 1991; Pearson, 1983), L2 writers and readers have been shown to struggle not with technical or discipline-specific vocabulary so much as with what has been called subtechnical vocabulary that NES writers could probably take for granted. Pearson (1983, p. 387) gave the following as examples of subtechnical workplace vocabulary: "parameter, discrete, comprise, hypothesis, preliminary, corroborate, projected, issue." Furthermore, whereas L2 writers may have little trouble processing the kinds of heavy noun phrases standard in technical fields, such as "radiation dose computation model, cycle counter diagnostic program, or emissions control monitor" (p. 388), producing these phrases with the modifying nouns in the anticipated order presented a difficulty that language study by itself was unlikely to successfully overcome.

Nevertheless, what may most distinguish L2 writers from the L1 writers discussed in the extensive L1 literature on workplace writing probably centered less around directly linguistic issues and more on social issues. Working closely with workplace mentors and collaborators impacted L1 and L2 writers differentially in that L2 writers did not have the same range of linguistic resources to draw upon as L1 writers and so were able to profit from those contacts less than were their L1 counterparts. They may have had less ready access to workplace social interactions that would instigate the kind of spontaneous collaboration that promoted both linguistic development and genre enculturation. Furthermore, even L2 workers who might have been inclined to seek out social relationships on the job in order to help themselves further their linguistic and literacy skills may also have preferred or felt under social pressure to remain within their home language groups. Studies such as T. Goldstein (1996) and Rockhill (1991) documented how the importance of maintaining social solidarity with compatriots on the job directed learners away both from English and from interactions with English speakers. Interactions between the L2 workers and English speakers could be unfavorably viewed by the L2 work community as attempts to curry favor with the dominant group and thus gain advantage over co-workers. For these L2 workers, the many benefits, including material, that accrued from remaining within the home community and language clearly outweighed the often illusory benefits promised in the discourse on immigrant assimilation.

Summary

A substantial body of research on workplace literacy in L1 English exists alongside L2 research on needs analysis, text analysis, and recommended pedagogical interventions at worksites. Perhaps because writing at the worksite is often avoidable, there is a scarcity of research in North America on the role writing plays for L2 workers and the development of writing skills among them. The most significant findings of this line of research to date are related less to the literacy or textual demands of this writing and more to the social and interpersonal components surrounding workplace writing, a finding also noted in the L1 literature.

Chapter 7

Scholarly Writing in L2

English has increasingly become the language for science and technology publishing, squeezing out other national languages even in their home countries (Pennycook, 1994b; Phillipson, 1992; Phillipson & Skutnabb-Kangas, 2000; Swales, 1997) and forcing researchers with little or no interest in English itself to learn to write in English or to take on collaborators that do. Many discussions of L2 writers publishing in English begin with reference to this dominance of English in international publications (Canagarajah, 1996, 2002b; Gosden, 1992; Parkhurst, 1990; St. John, 1987; Swales, 1997), referring to the "English monoculture in the scholarly community" (Duszak, 1997b, p. 3) and to English as the *Tyrannosaurus rex* of languages (Swales, 1997). As J. Flowerdew (1999a) points out, international databases such as the *Science Citation Index* and the *Social Sciences Citation Index* primarily list English-language journals, libraries subscribe to journals in such databases, scholars consult journals in libraries, articles published in these journals get more citations and attention and so attract more scholars to try to publish in them, and as a result of this whole inexorable process (St. John, 1987), "the ascendancy of English is self-perpetuating" (Gibbs, 1995, in *Scientific American* cited in J. Flowerdew, 1999a, p. 243). In some non-English-dominant countries hiring, promotion, tenure, and even conferral of PhD degrees requires publishing in international journals, which in many instances means in English (Braine, 2005; Casanave, 1998; Curry & Lillis, 2004; J. Flowerdew, 2000; Gosden, 1992, 1996). Curry and Lillis (2004) reported, for example, that in Slovakia, where academic professional activities are rated on a point system for purposes of raises and promotions, a publication in an English-medium journal merits twice the number of points as one in a Slovak-medium journal. In other cases scholars publish in English in order to add their voices and home country's perspectives to the international conversation in their professions (Casanave, 2002), noting, as one scholar put it, that publishing in English is necessary because "you never get cited when you write in [the scholar's L1]" (Curry & Lillis, 2004, p. 679).

Research into professional L2 writing in English over the last 25 years has focused on the following:

- Cross-linguistic, cross-cultural, and cross-disciplinary text analysis (Duszak, 1997b), in part to discover what rhetorical features contribute to the success of a research article or other kinds of discourse (see especially the extensive coverage in Candlin's 2002 collection).
- Surveys and interviews with novice (J. Flowerdew, 2000; Gosden, 1996) and successful L2 authors of scholarly publications about their processes and strategies for creating L2 text as well as the problems they have encountered in attempting to produce and publish them (Canagarajah, 1996, 2002b; Curry & Lillis, 2004; J. Flowerdew, 1999a, 1999b; Gosden, 1995; Kaplan, 1993, 2001; Matsumoto, 1995; Medgyes & Kaplan, 1992; Parkhurst, 1990; Phillipson & Skutnabb-Kangas, 2000; St. John, 1987). Some of these problems included length of time and effort required to produce a publishable manuscript, a sense of being somewhat limited to a simple style and a quantitative research paradigm, and the difficulty of making claims with the proper amount of force and revealing or concealing the author's commitment to those claims. In J. Flowerdew's (1999b) survey 29 percent of respondents cited prejudice of editors against non-native English writers as a cause for difficulties in getting published.
- Surveys and interviews of editors of international publications on the reception accorded submissions from L2 writers (J. Flowerdew, 2001; Gosden, 1992; Shi, 2003) and on the potential difficulties of prospective L2 authors in interpreting and responding to reviewers' commentary (Gosden, 2003). The editors Gosden (1992) surveyed worried most about "clear and logical presentation of results" from L2 authors and noted that superior science could override problems with communication but that ordinary or "mediocre" science could not (p. 132).
- Case studies of bilingual authors (Casanave, 1998; J. Flowerdew, 2000; Shi, 2003).
- The variety of communities that these scholars envision as their audience and the cross-national and cross-disciplinary variability of demands and rewards for publications in English (Canagarajah, 2002b; Curry & Lillis, 2004).
- First-person accounts by L2 scholarly authors writing in English (Belcher & Connor, 2001; Braine, 1999b; see particularly Connor, 1999 and X.-M. Li, 1999 for linguistically and biculturally sensitive accounts of writing professionally in L2).

In addition to the challenges that confront any scholarly author, L2 writers, especially those in developing or Outer Circle countries (B. Kachru, 1992), face an array of obstacles from lack of material support (libraries, typewriters or computers, email, even paper) (Canagarajah, 1996) to need to control linguistic and rhetorical features of English (J. Flowerdew, 2000; Gosden, 1996; Sionis, 1995; St. John, 1987) to a sense of being outside, away from the center of the disciplinary conversation (J. Flowerdew, 2000). The possibility arises as well that a certain prejudice exists among journal editors and reviewers either against L2 writers generally or against potential contributors from certain parts of the world (J. Flowerdew, 1999a; Gosden, 1992). But the situation of these scholars is even more subtly complicated.

Graduate training and disciplinary reading in English creates a special bilingualism such that some writers have become so accustomed to engaging their discipline in English that they are, in effect, unable to think or write about disciplinary issues in their L1s; their disciplinary language is English (Casanave, 1998; J. Flowerdew, 2000; Shi, 2003). This lack of L1 disciplinary fluency may account for linguistically naive evaluations of English as inherently better suited than other languages for science writing (Shi, 2003), although it is also possible that some vernacular languages worldwide may not have undergone the kind of language status or corpus planning that results in the development and promotion of an academic or scientific register. Nevertheless, since "all languages can in principle be used for all purposes" (Phillipson & Skutnabb-Kangas, 2000, p. 32), the conditions that would allow such development are less linguistic than economic, political, and social (Ahmad, 1997; J. Flowerdew, 1999b; St. John, 1987) and less likely to come about when English is already fulfilling the role of scholarly language.

Yet, despite their L2 English fluency, as some scholars noted with embarrassment or irritation (J. Flowerdew, 2000; Curry & Lillis, 2004; Parkhurst, 1990), their manuscripts may be criticized by reviewers and editors with such comments as "Obviously, . . . not . . . written by a native speaker. There are many problems with language usage," as reported in J. Flowerdew (2000, p. 135). Furthermore, except for L2 writers who were also linguists, applied linguists, or otherwise involved in language education (Belcher & Connor, 2001; Braine, 1999b), other authors of L2 English publications were reported to have no interest whatsoever in language learning (Sionis, 1995; St. John, 1987) and wished only to get their research published, doing whatever that required in an English-dominated publishing world. Despite the assertion of editors that language issues did not cause a report of superior research to be rejected, most scientific research in fact is "ordinary" rather than revolutionary science (Kuhn, 1962) and, as the best journals receive a glut of submissions and look for a reason to reject manuscripts, language does play a role in the decision to publish (J. Flowerdew, 2001; Gosden, 1992, 1995). For the scholarly writers, being forced to write in an L2 caused them to waste a considerable amount of time and effort in an enterprise unrelated to their area of interest, generating texts in English, translating from L1, compiling lists of useful rhetorical expressions (Gosden, 1992; Matsumoto, 1995; Parkhurst, 1990; St. John, 1987), writing in hybridized combinations of L1 and L2 (Gosden, 1996), and working with language editors (Burrough-Boenisch, 2003; Lillis & Curry, 2006).

An entire industry of English-language editors exists worldwide to edit, rewrite, or help such authors revise their manuscripts; these practices in themselves create a number of problems (Burrough-Boenisch, 2003). Such services are expensive, it is often not the easily correctable surface language features that require alteration (see J. Flowerdew, 2000, for an example), these language editors may not be familiar with the writer's disciplinary discourse, and the resulting text may be, as one L2 physicist noted, "delicately different from the original . . . well organized in English, but, bad in Physics" (Gosden, 1996, p. 125). When the language editor is familiar with disciplinary discourse and can be of greatest assistance, the ethical issue apparently arises of whose text it is that is being published (Quian, 1995); in other words, the language editor's collaboration may be so extensive as to merit citation as co-author of the article. Furthermore, seeing English as a lingua franca rather than as "owned" by those in English-dominant countries, some L2 authors have expressed a desire to not become homogenized into sounding like a NES and would prefer to keep their distinctive written "accents" (Duszak, 1997a; Matsumoto, 1995; St. John, 1987; Yakhontova, 2002).

Subtle issues of national loyalty and professional advancement may be at play as well in the use of English for professional publication. Despite the pull on one side to publish in English, some scholars experienced a counterpull to do more to participate in and contribute to the development of their home academic communities (Sri Lanka, Canagarajah, 2002b; Thailand, Nagavajara, 1995, cited in Duszak, 1997a, p. 35) or to publish in L1 in order to establish and encourage the networking relationships with local scholars necessary for professional advancement (Hong Kong, Braine, 2005; Japan, Casanave, 1998). As Casanave (1998) pointed out, bilingual, bicultural academics of this type may feel it essential to write in both languages, although they experienced the two publishing worlds as fulfilling different professional roles and making different professional demands. Shi's (2003) study of professionals educated in English-dominant Western countries reported not only ways in which these scholars perceived themselves as more well-rounded than their monolingual counterparts but also the ways they themselves subsequently furthered the expansion of English in China, some requiring, for example, that their students use English conventions even when they wrote in Chinese, thus making academic writing a "site of penetration" (p. 384) of English into China. Shi warned that TESL (Teaching English as a Second Language) preparation programs need to become more critically conscious of their self-replicating potential on the international graduate students who return to academic positions at home. Some Chinese scholars publishing in Chinese in China in fact have already adopted English-language style conventions, viewing themselves as pioneers at the forefront of a coming general shift to English style (Shi, 2002).

The increasing dominance of English in science and technology research reports has had a variety of other consequences not only for the individual scholar but for the rest of the world as well. The requirement to publish in English may result in L2 scholars engaging in message reduction (Sionis, 1995), allowing ideological reformulation by reviewers and editors (J. Flowerdew, 2000), or choosing not to publish at all, in each case potentially causing information of vital scientific interest to be distorted or to go unreported (Baldauf, 1986; Baldauf & Jernudd, 1983; Canagarajah, 2002b; J. Flowerdew, 1999a; Tardy, 2004). Furthermore, as Phillipson and Skutnabb-Kangas (2000) reported, publication of scientific research exclusively or primarily in English may result in scholars being unable to communicate their scholarly findings appropriately in their L1 to their L1 audiences and in focusing on issues of importance to the international community at the expense of locally significant issues.

Summary

The study of L2 scholarly writing in English in the last 25 years entailed the exploration of the global spread of English, uncovering certain negative consequences, for example, the displacement of other languages as likely means of scholarly communication and the distortion of scientific knowledge and skewing of meta-analyses (Gregoire, Derderian, & LeLorier, 1995) through the failure to include material published in languages other than English (Tardy, 2004). This work then becomes "lost science" (Gibbs, 1995). Reported reactions of L2 scholars have ranged from acceptance of the unavoidable (Phillipson & Skutnabb-Kangas, 2000) to irritation, frustration, and a sense of being discriminated against or disadvantaged. The dominance of English in scholarly writing has also resulted in the emergence of expensive professional English-language editing services. Perhaps ironically, as L2 graduate students return home after advanced studies in English-medium settings abroad, their experience and familiarity both with English language and with the world of English publishing work to enhance the validity of an increasingly English-only world of scholarly publication.

Chapter 8

Ideological, Political, and Identity Issues in L2 Writing

Ideology and Politics

The political and ideological discussions that emerged surrounding L2 writing research from 1980 to 2005 centered essentially on the hegemony of English (and its current academic writing preferences) and on the role of a critical perspective in L2 writing instruction. During the 1980s L2 writing's political and ideological agenda focused on advocacy for L2 English learners, often in face of institutional and educational policies detrimental to L2 learners (Benesch, 1988; Edelsky, 1996; Smoke, 1998) and often, responding to immediate inequities, with a practical more than theoretical orientation. During this time as well, applied linguists showed signs of interest in exploring the nefarious aspects of the spread of English language worldwide (Fairclough, 1989, 1995; Phillipson, 1992; Skutnabb-Kangas, 2000; Swales, 1997). But pointed disciplinary discussion of the ideological aspects of teaching L2 English writing was sparked by two publications in the early 1990s. The first was an article by Terry Santos (1992) in the inaugural issue of the *Journal of Second Language Writing*. Santos made the argument that the L2 writing field had not become as overtly ideological as its L1 English counterpart for two primary reasons. First, unlike L1 English, the roots of L2 English in North America were not in the humanities, with literature, but in the social sciences, with linguistics and applied linguistics. This historical disciplinary allegiance resulted in a bias in favor of empirical rather than hermeneutical research and a more practical, less theoretical collective turn of mind, all tending to nudge the field away from more ideological considerations. The second influence on L2 writing was the conservatizing effect of its international clientele and focus. Sensitivity to the practices and values of other cultures made English for Academic Purposes (EAP) teachers reluctant to take on classroom roles that might seem to impose U.S. or Western practices and values, including a focus on ideological and political questions. Furthermore, burning ideological issues in the US, for instance, may simply be irrelevant to many internationals. In addition, in some cases for those teaching abroad, discussion of ideological issues may have carried social sanctions or even security risks that were not worth taking, either for the teachers or for their students. About the same time Suresh Canagarajah published a short article (1993b) calling for promotion of local knowledge in face of the hegemony of L2 academic writing in English.

These two articles then marked the beginning of a period of increased published debate about the appropriate political role of EAP, which to a great degree, particularly at the more advanced level, meant L2 writing instruction. On one hand was a pragmatic argument, partially based in genre teaching traditions, that when international undergraduate and graduate students study in BANA countries they have a short period of time in which they must quickly improve their writing skills in order to be able to succeed in these English-medium systems; the core goal of EAP classes was for students to develop the tools they needed to succeed academically (Allison, 1996; Johns, 1995; Ramanathan, 2002; Santos, 2001). They did not have time for debates on, for example, the U.S. social issue of the day; a class billed as a writing class should teach writing (Silva, 1997). The argument on the other side noted that teaching English was unavoidably ideological (Benesch, 1993; S. McKay, 1993; Severino, 1993) and failing to overtly frame it as such was taking a political position affirming the status quo, a status quo that worked against students' educational, and so material, interests and was characterized by social injustices more broadly (Benesch, 1993, 1995, 1996). Discussion in the 1990s and 2000s explored issues in critical pedagogy (Benesch, 2001; Canagarajah, 2002a; Hammond & Macken-Horarik, 1999; Pennycook, 1997, 1999), critical EAP (Allison, 1996; Benesch, 1993, 1996, 1999, 2001; Harwood & Hadley, 2004), student rights analysis, which aimed to go beyond needs analysis by exploring the power dimension inherent in students' academic lives and the possibility of helping students negotiate that power (Benesch, 1999), critical literacy (Pennycook, 1996b, 2001), and the negotiation of competing discourses inherent in the integration of multilingual literacies (Belcher & Connor, 2001; Canagarajah, 2001a, 2001b, 2002c). The politics of L2 writing instruction at the institutional level in North America also emerged as an area of concern (Currie, 2001; Matsuda, Ortmeier-Hooper, & You, 2006).

Two other strands of interest in ideological issues are worth noting here. The first, with a postcolonial perspective, came from abroad in the form of discussions of the impact of Western notions of professional participation (i.e. academic and professional writing) on scholars, researchers, and writers from non-metropole countries or those where English was not the dominant language. The problem was that, in the interests of wider international circulation, increasing numbers of professional journals halted publication in indigenous/native languages and began to accept submissions only in English. This meant, for example, that a Taiwanese journal of medicine required Taiwanese authors writing for Taiwanese colleagues to submit their articles in English. At the same time institutions worldwide increased their pressure on scholars to publish and to move away from their previous participation in local, sometimes mainly oral, professional exchanges toward publication in international, not local, journals (increasingly in English), with hiring and promotion decisions resting on such publication (Braine, 2005; Canagarajah, 2002b; Casanave, 1998; J. Flowerdew, 1999a; Gosden, 1996). Given the trauma that North American academics experience in preparing for tenure and promotion, these new administrative decisions to require publication in international journals created increased anxiety for individuals writing in L2 and further undermined the position of local publications and languages. As Belcher and Hirvela have phrased it in relation to L2 graduate students, these academics writing in L2 English were "being forced to play the Ginger Rogers role to their L1 peers' Fred Astaire, doing everything that Fred does but in high heels and backwards" (Belcher & Hirvela, 2005, p. 201). Requirements to operate in English, with the resultant unequal distribution of material goods, were shown to percolate throughout postcolonial settings. Ramanathan (2003) documented the repercussions for students in India of a vernacular high school education; those educated not through the medium of English but rather in the local language ultimately experienced differential access to social benefits, in particular to higher education, benefits which were made available to those whose educations took place in English-medium institutions.

A second strand of ideological inquiry was the exploration of ethnicity, class, and to a lesser degree gender. Most discussions of ethnicity and class focused on immigrant issues, often on K–12 or in community settings with adults (see those chapters of this section). Although many of these discussions focused on lower-income writers, Vandrick (1995) pointed out the anomalous situation of wealthy international undergraduates in writing classes in the US finding themselves for the first time on an equal footing with classmates who might have been their servants at home and exposed to ideas of social justice that made of them the perpetrators of injustices. Vandrick also focused attention on gay and lesbian issues (Vandrick, 1997) and on gender issues, as have others (Belcher, 1997, 2001; Boyd, 1992; D. Johnson, 1992; Kubota, 2003; Vandrick, 1994).

Finally, a number of issues with significant political content and implications (for example, the question of essentializing ethnicity and culture) are taken up in other chapters, including the central challenge of World Englishes with its piercing question of who owns English (Nero, 2000), discussed below.

Identity

Much of the work on voice in writing and on multiliteracies, which became increasingly prominent during the 1990s and early 2000s, implicitly dealt with issues of identity such as how L2 English literacy intersected with old identities and engendered new, hybridized identities.[1] Researchers in this area were often critical of institutions that were unable or unwilling to recognize this hybridization and respond to it, or uninterested in doing so (Ferdman, 1990; Jimenez, 2000; Kells, 2002), including responding to learners' fear of losing their L1 literacies, identities, and voices (Crisco, 2004; Jimenez, 2000), as though the identities played out through an L1 were mere annoying obstacles to educational and life improvements that would bloom in L2. Among multiliterate school learners of English writing, some researchers found that ability to write in languages other than mainstream English might be entirely dismissed by the school, and the writer labeled nonwriter or at the least required to study English writing as though mainstream English alone defined literacy (Anderson & Irvine, 1993; Buijs, 1993; Fox, 1994; Fu, 1995; Guerra, 1998; Hornberger & Skilton-Sylvester, 2000; Martin-Jones & Bhatt, 1998; Nero, 2000). Both English-dominant students and English learners in writing classrooms participated in maintaining language myths with implications for identity assignment (Kells, 2002). Literacy that carried lesser cultural capital, such as that in an L1 (Guerra, 1998), in a nonprestige dialect of English (Martin-Jones & Bhatt, 1998; Nero, 2000), or in nonacademic uses, was discounted (Johns, 1991b). Particularly for stabilized dialects of English or World Englishes these kinds of findings led to questions such as: Who owns English? How long is a learner still an ESL student or a language learner? When does a learner become a native speaker or writer of English? What is a native speaker or writer of English (Chiang & Schmida, 1999; Norton, 1997; Valdes, 2000)? Questions also arose about the usefulness of such terms as native speaker or mother tongue (Rampton, 1995).

At the individual level as well, writers questioned and negotiated the sometimes problematic, sometimes exhilarating relationships among their literate identities: the one they intuited and the one projected or threatened by English writing (Angelil-Carter, 1997; Belcher & Hirvela, 2001; Braine, 1999a; Cadman, 1997; Canagarajah, 1993c, 2002b, 2004; Casanave, 1998; Chiang & Schmida, 1999; Cho, 2004; Cmejrkova & Danes, 1997; Harklau, 1999b, 2000; Hirvela & Belcher, 2001; Ivanic & Camps, 2001; Kramsch & Lam, 1999; X.-M. Li, 1999; Norton, 2000; Peirce, 1997; Shen, 1989; Shi, 2003; Silva et al., 2003; Stein, 1998;

---

1 Issues related to identity and language generally (i.e. not writing in particular) are richly and subtly explored in quite a large literature. For examples focusing mainly on English L2, see Pavlenko and Blackledge (2004) and the 1997 special issue of the *TESOL Quarterly* on identity.

Thesen, 1997) or by their L1 writing after many years with English (Connor, 1999) as they struggled to inhabit desired identities or resisted unwanted transformations. Many of these L2 English writers were graduate students or professionals with a well established sense of their L1 selves in the world. Starfield's (2002) research analyzed the text features that prevented an undergraduate L2 writer from projecting an authoritative discursive identity and resulted in his being constructed as a plagiarizer. But other L2 writers were able to make use of their multiliteracies to explore aspects of the transition between literacies or to document thoughts about, for example, immigration experiences (Kramsch & Lam, 1999; Lvovich, 2003; Norton, 2000).

Claims have been made in the literature for the liberating effect on fixed identity categories of electronically mediated exchanges. The reduction in physical indexes of identity available to the reader may allow the writer to in effect take on different, perhaps more powerful identities, and perhaps allow the historically disadvantaged a better chance at equal participation (Casanave, McCornick, & Hiraki, 1993, as reported in Casanave, 2004; Lam, 2000). Belcher (1999) discussed a graduate class's electronic communications that opened up some of her students to voice, allowing them to take on the persona of knowledgeable and helpful informant to their classmates; other students, however, four out of five of them women, refused to participate. Matsuda discussed (his own) identity hiding and its consequences (2003b) as well as the negotiation and establishment of "vertical" hierarchical relationships among a group of Japanese electronic media users, though along alternative rather than the traditional lines of age or gender (Matsuda, 2002). J. Bloch (2002) analyzed the range of rhetorical strategies L2 graduate students were able to use in internet exchanges to regulate their interactions with their teacher. But most of the studies on electronic writing and L2 relate to pedagogical issues, including peer interactions (e.g. Braine, 2001), rather than identity issues.

Identity issues have become increasingly evident in research on children developing L2 literacy. Although not specifically on writing, work by Hawkins (2005) and Toohey (2000) demonstrated how the identities that the children were allowed in their classrooms created successes or failures for them. Within specific communities of practice, some, and not other, identity positions were made available to the children, identity categories to which they might be summoned and that they might then try to resist, positing their own identities. But the L2 children's proposed identities could only be understood and/or accepted if they already existed as possibilities within those communities. Elaborating on how this dance played out specifically in writing, McCarthey's (2002) research documented children enacting their identities through their interactions with writing in school, some children accepting the writing tasks, which they saw as fitting in with their preferred views of themselves, and others not seeing or accepting them in this way. Other researchers investigated contexts in which younger English learners were able to establish satisfying new visions of themselves through writing (Day, 2002; Maguire & Graves, 2001; Willett, 1995), including through internet writing, which allowed the writer to use English not to project an English self but to link to a Chinese diaspora (Lam, 2000), for example, and to other internationals.

Finally, L2 writing research has not gone very far in exploring the intersection of L2 writing and gender, class, race, or sexual orientation as identity issues. In a special 2004 issue of the *TESOL Quarterly* on gender, for example, L2 writing was not featured. Nevertheless, second language studies have increasingly focused on questions of how gender is imposed on, for instance, immigrant women or other L2 speakers and how gender is discursively constructed. See for example Pavlenko (2001a, 2001b, 2001c). Although issues related to class, gender, race, and sexual orientation have been addressed to some degree in relation to ESL classes (Belcher, 1997; Vandrick, 1994, 1995, 1997), only a little of this research has directly reflected composition issues (Benesch, 1998; D. Johnson, 1992; Kubota, 2003).

Summary

Because it crosses linguistic and cultural boundaries, L2 writing research has always shown some level of awareness of ideological issues, but these issues came to the forefront in the early 1990s and remained significant into the 2000s. Areas of exploration centered on equity for L2 writers and on the ethics surrounding the export of English (especially academic) writing worldwide. One aspect of investigations of equity issues related to identity both created and suppressed by writing in a second language and often manifested in studies of voice in writing. As a result of considerations of these kinds of questions, a great deal of research in the mid-2000s on contexts for L2 writing included overt recognition of their ideological dimensions.

Section II

Instruction and Assessment

Most activities involving L2 writing are done for educational purposes. Accordingly, pedagogical purposes have, to varying degrees, shaped the nature of much research on L2 writing. The goals motivating this inquiry have, if only implicitly, been to improve educational practices and learning opportunities, increase the knowledge available to teachers or program administrators, or resolve key problem issues in educational policies. The present section of this book synthesizes publications about research that has addressed topics conventional to the field of education, recognizing that pedagogical interests also underlie many of the studies of social contexts addressed in section I and of basic issues in L2 writing described in section III of this book.

Chapter 9 focuses on studies of curriculum and of instruction. Sequenced from a macro- to a micro-perspective, the chapter first considers the conceptual foundations of L2 writing curricula and the professional knowledge of L2 writing instructors. Second, we recount how the purposes of L2 writing curricula are shaped by some of the social contexts of L2 writing already surveyed in section I. The third part of chapter 9 considers three ways in which the published research has portrayed the organization of L2 writing curricula: (a) through benchmark standards; (b) as options for relating L2 writing to other aspects of language ability, study, or student populations, focused on particular aspects of writing and with greater or lesser specificity of purposes; and (c) through descriptions of the actual teaching of L2 writing, classroom discourse in these contexts, or experiments on specific instructional approaches.

Chapter 10 reviews studies of the assessment of L2 writing. The first half of the chapter addresses formative assessment, acknowledging its integral relations to issues of pedagogy featured in chapter 9. We summarize the extensive research on teachers' responding to L2 writing in respect to the aspects of L2 writing attended to and the media, modes, and timing of responses. Related studies of peer- and self-assessment are then reviewed. The second half of chapter 10 focuses on formal assessments of L2 writing proficiency, observing that formal tests of writing and other language abilities tend to serve institutional purposes of selection, certification, or credentialing. This portion of the chapter demonstrates how research has focused on task design, validation, and rating processes in tests of L2 writing ability.

Given that pedagogical concerns motivate much research on L2 writing, it is striking that relatively few research studies have directly addressed issues of L2 writing curriculum and instruction. There may be three reasons for this orientation. One reason is that publications about curriculum in second language education have tended to treat matters holistically—combining writing together with topics like reading, listening, speaking, grammar, vocabulary, and culture (e.g. R. K. Johnson, 1989; Markee, 1997; Nunan, 1988; Stern, Allen, & Harley, 1992). Moreover, the organization of most L2 curriculum policies in schools, intensive language programs, settlement programs, and higher education also tends to combine, rather than differentiate, these related dimensions of language learning and teaching. Analyses of L2 curricula tend to be conceived at the level of an overall program rather than of a particular course (such as L2 writing), even for curricula designed to fulfill specific, rather than general, purposes (e.g. Hutchison & Waters, 1987; Widdowson, 1983). A further issue behind the relative neglect of curriculum issues is that courses in L2 writing, and indeed many L2 programs, are seldom designated as official subjects in school curricula or as credit-bearing or core courses of study in higher education. ESL curricula tend to perform a marginal, service function for academic programs in North American educational institutions (Santos, 1992; Silva, Leki, & Carson, 1997). Even foreign language studies occupy a negligible role in most curricula, as evidenced in Goodlad's (1984, p. 216) estimate of their accounting for only 2 to 4 percent of staffing resources in schools in the US.

A second, related point is that analyses of L2 curricula have tended to adopt Tyler's (1949) conventional rationale for and sequence of curriculum design: Determine educational purposes, select or devise relevant learning experiences, organize them, and then evaluate students' achievements of them. L2 writing courses have seldom adopted newer, more radical, or broad-based theories about curriculum. For instance, the aims of most L2 writing courses are much narrower than the broad goals for schooling that appear in Joseph, Bravmann, Windschitle, Mikel, and Green's (2000) goals of "curriculum as culture": training for work and survival, connecting to the canon, developing self and spirit, constructing understanding, deliberating democracy, and confronting the dominant order. In turn, as demonstrated in section I of the present book, only recently, and in selective instances, have L2 writing programs or researchers taken up the radical, ideological conceptualizations of curriculum that often feature in English literacy education or the agenda proposed for multiliteracies (e.g. Bascia, Cumming, Datnow, Leithwood, & Livingstone, 2005; Cope &

Kalantzis, 2000; Lo Bianco, 2000). Likewise, studies of L2 writing have scarcely distinguished between curriculum positions that emphasize the transmission (e.g. associated with Skinner, 1954, or the philosophy of John Locke), transaction (e.g. associated with Dewey, 1916), or transformation (e.g. associated with Freire, 1970) of knowledge and abilities— an analytic distinction conventional in curriculum studies (e.g. Miller & Seller, 1985). Nonetheless, aspects of these ideas may be applied widely and tacitly in educational practices. For example, a transmission position in L2 writing would emphasize the presentation and students' practice of rhetorical or grammatical forms; a transaction position would involve students composing texts and then receiving feedback from peers and their teacher to improve their drafts; and a transformation position would aim to emancipate the social positions of disadvantaged student populations through their literacy development. From this perspective (and other perspectives detailed in chapter 9), principles for organizing L2 writing curricula appear highly eclectic and variable.

A third reason for the relative neglect of curriculum and instructional issues in studies of L2 writing is that they have been overshadowed by research on the qualities and characteristics of L2 students' texts and composing (as documented in section III of this book) or of the social contexts of L2 writing (as documented in section I of this book). Pedagogical purposes underlie these other research foci: Instructors need to understand better the qualities and dimensions of L2 students' writing as well as social contexts related to writing outside of or within classrooms. Nonetheless, it remains the case that research on L2 curriculum and instruction has tended to dwell primarily on oral communications in classrooms (e.g. Chaudron, 1988), thereby neglecting the integral role of writing. Elley (1994) has charged that this focus on oral aspects of second and foreign languages carries over from audiolingual methods of language teaching and has greatly constrained the literacy of schoolchildren in many parts of the world, particularly where English or other international languages are the medium of instruction.

At the same time, trends since the 1980s for increased accountability in education have prompted expansions and developments in research on L2 writing assessment (Brindley, 1998b; Cumming, 1997). In response to calls for increased accountability and improved professional standards, most major tests of English language abilities have been refined or redesigned in recent decades (Cumming, 2007; Spolsky, 1995; Weir & Milanovic, 2003). Accompanying advances have appeared in the methods, technologies, and conceptualizations of language testing (Alderson & Banerjee, 2002; Bachman, 2000; Cumming, 2004). Validation research, in particular, has burgeoned following a professional consensus on the centrality of construct validation and the need for multiple forms of evidence to demonstrate that the measurements, processes, uses, and consequences of language assessments all correspond to the intended construct being assessed and not other, unintended phenomena (Bachman, 2000; Chapelle, 1999; Kunnan, 1998). The scope of research on language assessment has likewise broadened to consider systematically issues such as fairness (Kunnan, 2000; Shohamy, 2001), usefulness (Bachman & Palmer, 1996), and the value of classroom formative assessment (*for* learning, rather than just *of* learning: Darling-Hammond, Ancess, & Falk, 1995; Rea-Dickins, 2001).

Chapter 9

Curriculum and Instruction

The preceding chapters in this book have described the diverse contexts in which L2 writing is taught and learned. Integral to, and cutting across, these varied contexts are common pedagogical principles for education in L2 writing. These pedagogical purposes are guided at a macro-level by curriculum and program policies. At a micro-level, they are enacted by instructional practices and activities in courses or informal contexts for learning. Curricula and policies for L2 writing may be formulated explicitly or enacted implicitly—or combinations of both—and organized at a program, institutional, state, or national level. Teaching L2 writing fundamentally involves individual instructors' choices, ongoing decisions, and actions to organize activities relevant to the learning purposes of a group of participating students as well as their curriculum, institutional, and societal contexts.

Research in recent decades has demonstrated that curricula for L2 writing involve several interacting dimensions. One dimension involves the conceptual foundations that inform ideas about writing, language, learning, teaching, and social contexts. Key to these conceptual foundations is the knowledge that L2 writing instructors possess to guide their teaching as well as to develop themselves professionally. A second dimension of L2 writing curriculum involves the purposes and population of students that an educational program serves. A third dimension involves the organization and sequencing of activities and resources for teaching and learning. Any or all of these dimensions may be specified formally and explicitly as policies, or just acted upon tacitly, by the teachers, students, and other stakeholders (such as administrators, families, employers, or instructors or professors in related programs) who have an interest in an educational program.

Conceptual Foundations of L2 Writing Curricula

Most L2 writing curricula have a pragmatic orientation: to help L2 students develop their textual, cognitive, and discoursal abilities (Santos,

1992; Silva & Brice, 2004). To this end, curricula for L2 writing typically involve the organization of learning activities for students to develop abilities to produce (a) meaningful, accurate written texts (b) by composing effectively and (c) engaging in the discourse appropriate to specific social contexts and purposes. As the authors of previous reviews of L2 writing research have observed, these three aspects of learning are informed by different conceptual foundations, each of which has progressively ascended to prominence in research over the past two decades (Cumming, 1998, 2001b; Grabe & Kaplan, 1996; K. Hyland, 2003a; Matsuda, 2003d; Raimes, 1991, 1998; Silva, 1990).

Linguistic and rhetorical theories provide tools and terms to describe the texts and language forms that L2 students produce or might need to learn. Concepts and theories from psychology provide tools and terms to describe the ways L2 students think or act while composing written texts, suggesting how these might be improved. Sociocultural, political, pragmatic, or critical theories provide tools and terms that describe the qualities of interaction and the cultural values that shape L2 students' writing within specific social contexts, seeking explanations for, or reasons to challenge, their actions or societal conditions. Analyses of social contexts have predominated in recent years, though research on all three aspects of L2 writing has persisted because these three perspectives are complementary as well as integral to L2 writing curricula.

Studies about L2 written texts, learning, and intergroup relations have tended to serve one of two roles—foundational or descriptive—with regard to L2 writing curricula. The foundational role has provided concepts that inform certain aspects of L2 writing curricula. The descriptive role has documented or evaluated L2 writing curricula as they have appeared, for example by describing "best" pedagogical practices or exemplary programs or by surveying, comparing, or assessing their characteristics. Theorists such as Luke (2005) have argued that curriculum policies, particularly for literacy education, should draw on and synthesize diverse sources of theoretical ideas and empirical evidence. But L2 writing curricula have seldom enjoyed the resources or administrative structures to realize such aims on a large scale. L2 writing curricula do tend to be informed by diverse conceptual foundations, but more in an ad hoc, eclectic manner, born out of pragmatic necessity, local influences, and affiliations with related fields such as English mother-tongue composition, applied linguistics, and minority education (Grabe & Kaplan, 1996; Matsuda, 1998, 2003d).

Indeed, one would be hard pressed to identify foundational concepts that have aspired to provide a single, guiding basis on which to organize L2 writing curricula comprehensively. As Grabe (2001) put it, there is no single grand theory of L2 writing, nor could there probably ever be one, because of the competing and conflicting demands, contexts, and interests the theory would have to satisfy. Other authors have likewise observed that little research and few models of L2 writing have tried to relate curriculum content directly with L2 students' writing achievements (Cumming & Riazi, 2000; Ellis, 2003; Mohan & Lo, 1985; Valdes, Haro, & Echevarriarza, 1992).

Rather, the tendency has been to devise L2 writing curricula through eclectic combinations of relevant information and established pedagogical practices. For example, the abundant research that has accumulated about contrastive rhetoric (synthesized in Leki, 1991b; Connor, 1996) or about L2 composing processes (synthesized in section III of the present book) may inform certain curricular decisions about teaching, assessment, or the sequencing of activities for specific learner groups. But that information relates only to a minor aspect of any L2 writing curriculum or teacher's thinking. It does not provide overarching principles for curriculum organization. Expectations vanished several decades ago that any single theory might guide L2 writing curricula, as had been previously expressed in, for example, Lado's (1964) principles of contrastive analysis, Hughey, Wormuth, Hartfield, and Jacobs' (1983) enthusiastic advocacy of ideas about L2 composing processes, or Krashen's (1984) efforts to amalgamate previous research on writing within his psycholinguistic theory of comprehensible input.

Theoretical Orientations

Theoretical orientations do underpin certain L2 writing curricula, nonetheless. A notable instance (and striking exception to the trend suggested above) has been the adoption of theories of genre as a conceptual framework for ESL writing curricula. Previous reviews by Johns (1997, 2003b), K. Hyland (2004b), Hyon (1996), Paltridge (1997, 2001), and Tardy (2006) have documented the extent of research and L2 writing curricula founded on genre theory. Three different "schools" have prevailed, each with differing histories and theoretical underpinnings but a common emphasis on identifying and teaching the semiotic, linguistic, and social organization of written and spoken discourse as distinctive genres or text types. In Australia particularly, theories of systemic–functional linguistics (e.g. Christie, 1999; Halliday & Hasan, 1985; Martin, 1992) have directly informed most curricula and research on L2 writing (Feez, 1998; Hammond, 1987; Paltridge, 2001). Related frameworks and analyses emphasizing ESL learners' acquisition of the semiotics of discourse in education have appeared in North America and elsewhere (e.g. Early, 2001; K. Hyland, 2004b; Mohan, 1986; Mohan & Slater, 2005; Schleppegrell & Colombi, 2002). But most conceptualizations of genres in North American L2 writing instruction have arisen from two differing sources: either analyses of texts in professional, technical, or academic communications (Bhatia, 1993; Biber et al., 2002; L. Flowerdew, 2000; Jacoby, Leech, & Holten, 1995; Swales 1990a; Swales & Feak, 1994) or analyses of the socialization, discourse, and ideologies associated with membership in specialized discourse communities (Berkenkotter & Huckin, 1995; Dias & Paré, 2000; Freedman & Medway; 1994; Parks, 2001; Spack, 1997a).

The educational applications of genre theory have perhaps reached a zenith in the pedagogy of multiliteracies proposed by the New London Group, emphasizing multimodal discourse communications, social futures, and equality of educational opportunity (Cope & Kalantzis, 2000; Luke, 2005; Street, 1993). But applications of genre theory to L2 writing have long been accompanied by distinctive curricular and pedagogical approaches. Swales (1990a, pp. 68–82) influentially proposed "tasks" as a fundamental unit for organizing and negotiating pedagogical activities. Australian educators have adopted a common cycle of teaching and learning that passes through phases of context building, modeling and deconstructing a text, jointly constructing a text, independently constructing a text, and finally linking to related texts (Burns & Hood, 1995; Feez, 1998; Hammond, 1987). Mohan (1986) and colleagues developed and have applied a set of core "knowledge structures" to guide the analysis, organization, and construction of curricula and pedagogical activities.

Other instances of foundational theories guiding the organization of L2 writing curricula systematically and comprehensively have appeared sporadically, locally, or as notable innovations. These include adoptions of Hornberger's (2003) continua of biliteracy (e.g., Bloch & Alexander, 2003), Vygotskian sociocultural theory (Moll, 1989; Moll & Diaz, 1987; Parks, 2001; Prior, 1998; Wald, 1987), critical and postmodern theories (Canagarajah, 1999, 2002b; Gentil, 2005; Ramanathan, 2004), or Freirian emancipatory principles (Auerbach, 1992; Benesch, 1998, 2001; Quintero, 2002). At a more applied level of educational principles, various L2 writing curricula have adopted principles of content-based instruction (Adamson, 1993; Early, 1989, 1990; Mohan, 1986; Roessingh, 1999; Sheppard, 1994; Shih, 1986; Short, 1999; Snow & Brinton, 1997) or of whole-language teaching (Edelsky, 1996; Freeman & Freeman, 1992; Urzua, 1987; Westerbrook & Bergquist-Moody, 1996).

From the viewpoint of analyzing aspects of L2 writing curricula in action, three theoretical concepts have been prominent. One involves sociocultural theory as a rationale or explanation for the roles of instruction in learning L2 writing. For instance, the verbal interactions of instructors and students focused jointly on their L2 writing enact optimal circumstances to observe learning in the Vygotskian zone of proximal development. Sociocultural theories have featured as explanatory frameworks in analyses of tutoring L2 writing (Aljaafreh & Lantolf, 1994; Cumming & So, 1996; Gutierrez, 1994; Harris & Silva, 1993; Williams

& Severino, 2004), teacher–student conferences (Blanton, 2002; Conrad & Goldstein, 1999; L. Goldstein & Conrad, 1990; Patthey-Chavez & Clare, 1996; Patthey-Chavez & Ferris, 1997), dialogue journals (Moulton & Holmes, 1994; Nassaji & Cumming, 2000; Peyton & Staton, 1993), or students' reflective analyses on portfolios or other collections of their writing (Cumming, Bush, & Zhou, 2002; Donato & McCormick, 1994; Hamp-Lyons & Condon, 2000). Similarly, sociocultural theories justify the organization of L2 curricula around tasks that involve students talking, collaborating, and writing together on projects, demonstrating how such interactions extend students' linguistic resources and establish purposeful activity systems for learning (de Guerrero & Villamil, 2000; DeVillar & Jiang, 2001; Liu & Hansen, 2002; McGroarty & Zhu, 1997; Parks, Huot, Hamers, & Lemonnier, 2005; Shi, 1998; Swain & Lapkin, 1995, 1998; Villamil & de Guerrero, 1996).

Relatedly, theories of language socialization have helped to conceptualize the conditions for learners' progressive adoptions of L2 writing abilities or socioeducational constraints in their doing so. Various ethnographic, ethnomethodological, and case studies have demonstrated how L2 learners come to adopt particular, multiple identities as students and writers through the discourse and power relations they experience in schools and colleges, interacting with peers, teachers, and families and through the genres of popular, local, or academic culture (Currie, 1993; Duff, 2001, 2002; Early, 1992; Edelsky, 1986; Harklau, 1994a, 2000, 2001; Hunter, 1997; Ivanic & Camps, 2001; Leki, 1995a; Losey, 1997; Martin-Jones & Jones, 2000; S. McKay & Wong, 1996; Prior, 1998; Ramanathan, 2003, 2004; Riazi, 1997; Spack, 1997a; Toohey, 2000; Vandrick, 1997; Willett, 1995). Other analyses, as well as innovative L2 literacy curricula, have tried to bridge discontinuities between language and literacy practices in formal education and among culturally diverse families (Auerbach, 1989; Cumming & Gill, 1991; Cummins, 2001; King & Hornberger, 2005; Moll, 1989; Valdes, 1996; Wilson-Keena, Willett, & Solsken, 2001).

A third, recent conceptual orientation concerns new multimedia technologies and expanded notions of literacy as multiliteracies (Cope & Kalantzis, 2000; Lo Bianco, 2000; Street, 1993). Computer technologies facilitate the means by which L2 writing is produced, for example, enabling revisions through word processing and spelling and grammar checkers. They also expand definitions of multimedia forms of literate design, of the resources available through internet sites and communications with various communities of respondents internationally, of hybrid and multimodal forms of textual and visual discourse, and of students' potentials and capacities for learning (Bloch, 2004; Cummins & Sayers, 1995; Hirvela, 2005; K. Hyland, 2002, 2003b; Kern, 2000; Kern & Warschauer, 2000; Lam, 2000; Pennington, 1993, 1996; Warschauer, 1999).

L2 Writing Teachers' Knowledge

The conceptual foundations of L2 writing curricula are also embedded within, and enacted through, the knowledge that teachers have and use in their pedagogical practices. Researchers have started to document the knowledge that teachers have about L2 writing, identifying key differences in their individual orientations to teaching and writing within programs as well as across them internationally, related to their personal, professional, and cultural experiences, beliefs, and intentions (Cumming, 2003; X.-M. Li, 1996; Shi & Cumming, 1995). Such information specifically about L2 writing is integral to guide teacher education (Bell, 1997; Blanton & Kroll, 2002; Winer, 1992). It is also integral to facilitate the accommodation of innovations in L2 writing curricula (Burns & Hood, 1995; Clachar, 2000; Cumming, 1993; Pennington, Brock, & Yue, 1996; Pennington et al., 1997). Moreover, understanding teachers' knowledge helps to appreciate or plan the long-term professional development of educators, particularly in cross-cultural contexts or across curricular programs in higher education (Belcher & Connor, 2001; Bell, 1997, 2002; Braine, 1999b; Casanave & Schecter, 1997; Crandall, 1993; Fishman & McCarthy, 2001; Leki, 1992; Spack, 1997a; Zamel, 1995).

Curriculum Purposes and Contexts

Curricula for L2 writing are also circumscribed by the purposes for which people are learning. These purposes reflect the status in a society of the language being learned, the functions and value of literacy in that language, as well as the characteristics, intentions, and status of the learners and of the institutions in which they study. The diversity of contexts for learning L2 writing, exemplified in initial chapters in section I of this book, tend to conform to a few categories of curriculum purposes. It is worth briefly recapping and consolidating these here because, from a curriculum perspective, the rationale for teaching L2 writing tends to relate to the institutional contexts and social purposes for which L2 writing is learned.

The vast majority of research on teaching L2 writing has involved learning English for *academic purposes*. In English-dominant countries, courses in L2 writing are organized for young adults whose strongest language is not English in order to ensure their academic success, either in schools or in preparation for higher education, to pass entrance exams for colleges or universities, or as a requirement upon entry to such institutions (Cheng, Myles, & Curtis, 2004; Leki, 2001a; Powers & Nelson, 1995; Rosenfeld, Leung, & Oltman, 2001; Williams, 1995). Likewise, in situations of immigrant settlement, L2 writing instruction features prominently in the education of children or adolescents whose home language differs from that of the dominant language in society (Adger & Peyton, 1999; Carrasquillo & Rodriguez, 1996; Edelsky, 1986; Faltis &

Wolfe, 1999; Gibbons, 1993; Harklau, Losey, & Siegal, 1999; Hudelson, 1989b; Maguire, 1997; Walqui, 2000). Settlement programs for recent adult immigrants also teach L2 writing, though often for the purposes of *cultural adaptation* to the host society or for *specific purposes*, such as training for employment (Burnaby & Cumming, 1992; Cumming, 2003; Feez, 1998; McGroarty, 1992; So-Mui & Mead, 2000; Spener, 1994; Svendsen & Krebs, 1984; Thatcher, 2000).

These contexts contrast with the many circumstances internationally in which L2 writing is taught as a *foreign language* (i.e. not widely used in the local community). Such curricula may have the purposes of preparation for future travel, work, or academic studies, particularly in internationally prevalent languages, such as English, French, German, Italian, Japanese, Mandarin, and Spanish, about which a distinctive body of research on L2 writing is starting to emerge (Reichelt, 1999; Silva & Brice, 2004). A limited number of studies have begun to document how curricula and policies related to L2 writing are organized within particular countries— such as Poland (Reichelt, 2005), Ukraine (Tarnopolsky, 2000), Japan (H. Kobayashi & Rinnert, 2002; Kubota, 1999), or China (You, 2004b)—or comparatively across countries (Brock & Walters, 1993; Cumming, 2003; Dickson & Cumming, 1996; Purves, 1988). L2 writing also features in curricula that have the purposes of *language maintenance*, for example of aboriginal, ancestral, religious, or community languages in minority situations, either for children or adults (Edelsky, 1986; Hornberger, 2003; Martin-Jones & Jones, 2000).

Organization of L2 Writing Curricula

How are L2 writing curricula organized? Three perspectives on this question emerge from the published literature. One is that sets of benchmark standards have, over the past two decades, been established as curriculum frameworks for most large-scale educational programs that involve L2 writing (as well as other aspects of language ability). A second perspective is that a range of options appear in curricula in regards to such issues as the relationship of writing to other language abilities or topics of study, the curricular focus on particular aspects of writing as well as the degree of specificity or generality about them, and the inclusion or segregation of L2 writers with or from other student populations. A third perspective emerges from observational studies of classroom L2 writing instruction as well as training studies involving specific aspects of L2 writing.

Language Standards

Increasingly in recent years, educational systems and professional associations have developed sets of benchmark standards, competencies, or attainment targets that define intended levels of achievement for students at particular points within the educational systems and also prescribe content for teaching or assessment. Innumerable curriculum standards have appeared at a state or national level. Notable international or national examples are the Common European Framework of Reference (Council of Europe, 2001), TESOL's Standards (TESOL, 2001), ACTFL's Proficiency Guidelines (ACTFL, 1986), the Canadian Language Benchmarks (Centre for Canadian Language Benchmarks, 2000), and the Australian Certificates in Spoken and Written English (New South Wales Adult Migrant English Service, 1995). These frameworks describe language abilities broadly and comprehensively (i.e. to include writing, reading, speaking, and listening). But key aspects of the research and development of assessment, professional development, and teaching tools accompanying the frameworks have focused on L2 writing in, for example, Australia (Brindley, 1998b, 2000; P. McKay, 2000) and Europe (Alderson, 2005b; Little, 2005; North, 2000). Indeed, the explicit, describable nature of writing performance has foregrounded writing as a symbolically important aspect of L2 student ability in these frameworks as well as other curriculum and assessment contexts. The appearance of language standards follows general trends for increased accountability in education, even though professional consensus has tended to be the means for developing these language standards rather than much empirical or theoretical inquiry (Brindley, 1998b; Cumming, 2001a; P. McKay, 2000, 2007; TESOL, 2001).

Standards are also set implicitly for L2 writing in many curricula through high-stakes proficiency tests that determine certification for completion of secondary education or screen applicants for admission into programs of higher education or for certification in professions or trades. Tests such as the IELTS (International English Language Testing System), MELAB (Michigan English Language Assessment Battery), or TOEFL (Test of English as a Foreign Language) exert a powerful influence by gatekeeping internationally to higher education in English-medium universities. These and other such tests require demonstrations of L2 writing proficiency that in turn influence curricula around the world for students preparing for these tests. Research related to these tests is discussed in the next chapter of this book.

Options for Curriculum Organization

Cumming (2003) identified three sets of options that distinguish the organization of curricula for L2 writing internationally. The first curriculum option concerns whether L2 writing is taught as a separate subject or is integrated with other aspects of language, content, or subject-matter study. For example, courses in ESL composition exist at most universities in North America but, at the same time, many curricula value the integration of instruction in reading and writing as complementary aspects of L2 literacy (for reasons substantiated by much research on reading–writing relations, e.g. Belcher & Hirvela, 2001; Carson & Leki, 1993; Grabe, 2003; Hirvela, 2001, 2004; Johns, 1993, 1997; Zamel, 1992). Likewise, writing features prominently in most L2 curricula that follow principles of content-based instruction, though in conjunction with other media of communication and the study of subject-matter knowledge (Mohan, 1986; Sheppard, 1994; Shih, 1986; Snow & Brinton, 1997).

The second curriculum option concerns whether L2 writing is taught (a) for specific purposes related to one job function or type of communication situation (e.g. business letters or reports in a particular format or for a specific discipline, field, or job) or (b) to develop general capacities and full L2 literacy. Many L2 writing courses for adults are designed to serve specific purposes or fields (e.g. Jacoby, Leech, & Holten, 1995). The content of specific-purpose writing courses is often based on extensive analyses of the writing required in target situations (e.g. Biber et al., 2002; Braine, 1989, 1995; Bridgeman & Carlson, 1983, 1984; Canseco & Byrd, 1989; Carson, 2001; Casanave & Hubbard, 1992; Connor & Kramer, 1995; Hale et al., 1996; Huckin & Olsen, 1984; Horowitz, 1986b; Jenkins et al., 1993; Leki & Carson, 1994; Raymond & Parks, 2002; Zhu, 2004). In contrast, theorists such as Widdowson (1983) and Leki and Carson (1997) have argued compellingly that language education should help students develop broad, creative capacities for writing to address future situations that could not be predicted in advance by curriculum planning. Extensions of this view appear in courses that foster critical analyses in L2 writing (Atkinson, 1997; Belcher, 1995; Benesch, 1996, 1998; Hammond & Macken-Horarik, 1999) or students' assumption of individual responsibility to define and monitor personal goals for writing improvement (A. Brown, 2005; Cresswell, 2000; Cumming, 1986, 2006; Frodesen, 1995; Hoffman, 1998).

The third curriculum option concerns the focus of instructional activities. Curricula inevitably focus on certain conceptualizations of L2 writing. These foci may vary from each other but also overlap in practice. Such foci represent relatively distinct theoretical positions about L2 writing as well as conventional repertoires of pedagogical practices in respect to, for example, composing processes (Susser, 1994; Urzua, 1987; Zamel, 1982), genre theory (Feez, 1998; Hyon, 1996; Johns, 1997, 2003b), grammar teaching (Byrd & Reid, 1998; Frodesen & Holten, 2003; Llewelyn, 1995; Shih, 2001), or content-based language instruction (Mohan, 1986; Sheppard, 1994; Shih, 1986; Snow & Brinton, 1997). As observed above, these conceptualizations may represent complementary aspects of L2 writing rather than competing pedagogical methods that produce wholly different outcomes. Indeed, as Cumming and Riazi (2000) concluded, evaluating the outcomes of L2 writing curricula is highly contingent on contextual factors, particularly in situations of cultural diversity. So such curricula might best be considered as a set of variable achievements that arise from the interaction of diverse types of instruction and opportunities for learning experienced by students of varying characteristics and backgrounds with differing intentions for L2 writing.

Other alternatives for the organization of L2 curricula arise from the nature of learner populations and their social contexts. One fundamental issue is whether curricula should separate L2 learners from their mother-tongue counterparts. Although comparative research on this point is limited, several studies highlight the differences in cultural environments for learning, and their sometimes stigmatizing consequences, that appear when curricula segregate ESL students from their mainstream peers in separate classes in universities (Atkinson & Ramanathan, 1995; Braine, 1996; Zamel, 1995) or in schools (Carrasquillo & Rodriguez, 1996; Harklau, 1994a, 1994b; Sheppard, 1994). A radically different basis for curriculum organization appears in innovative literacy programs for minority populations, which have foregrounded the cultural values of minority communities as the basis of relevance and purposes for writing in their home language and that of the dominant society (Auerbach, 1992; Cumming & Gill, 1991; Maguire, 1997; Moll, 1989; Moll & Diaz, 1987; Walsh, 1994; Wilson-Keena et al., 2001). A third issue concerns curricula in postcolonial countries, where teachers and learners alike may resist developing L2 writing because of macrostructural issues in society related to perceptions about the ex-colonial language and values associated with it, for example in settings such as Sri Lanka (Canagarajah, 1993c, 2002b) or Hong Kong (Pennington, Brock, & Yue, 1996).

Instructional Interactions

There have been surprisingly few research-based descriptions of L2 writing classroom instruction. The scarcity of such inquiry contrasts markedly with the many analyses of classroom discourse that feature in research on the teaching of oral aspects of L2 learning (e.g. Chaudron, 1988). Nonetheless, as is discussed in the next section of this book, considerable research has focused on one aspect of pedagogical practice: teachers' evaluative responses to L2 students' writing. The few naturalistic studies that have documented interactions in L2 writing classrooms have pointed toward the value of instructors combining regular routines for writing practice with explicit instruction on text forms and composing processes and individualized responses to written drafts (Cumming, 1992; Riazi, Lessard-Clouston & Cumming, 1996; Shi, 1998; Weissberg, 1994; Yeh, 1998). Similar conclusions appear from the few training studies that have evaluated, under experimental-type conditions, certain explicit approaches to L2 writing instruction in, for example, rhetorical structures (Connor & Farmer, 1990; Yeh, 1998) or specific points of grammar

(Frantzen, 1995; Harley, 1989; Ransdell, Lavelle, & Levy, 2002; Shih, 2001). The eclectic, diverse principles and practices that constitute L2 writing instruction likewise appear in various reflective testimonials that have documented experiences teaching L2 writing courses (e.g. D. Ferris, 2001; Franco, 1996; Shih, 2001; Wald, 1987) or organizing programs for L2 literacy (e.g. Hamilton, Barton, & Ivanic, 1994; Hood & Knightley, 1991; Morgan, 1998; Perez, 2004b; Westerbrook & Bergquist-Moody, 1996).

Summary

The curriculum and instructional praxis has been a perplexingly over-looked and underrepresented aspect of research on L2 writing. Certain theories have influenced the conceptualizations of L2 writing curricula, notably versions of genre theory, rhetoric, sociocultural theory, language socialization, and new literacies. But their applications have been isolated, perhaps constrained by the diversity of contexts and interests that such curricula must serve, as documented in section I of this book. Practices of L2 writing curriculum organization and instruction appear to be pragmatic and eclectic rather than comprehensively principled. Research has produced few substantive guidelines for designing and implementing L2 literacy instruction, but modest efforts have been made to suggest principles for designing and teaching courses of L2 writing (e.g. Benesch, 2001; Ferris & Hedgcock, 2005; Grabe & Kaplan, 1996; K. Hyland, 2003b; Reid, 1993, 2001). Future research needs to continue to investigate the pedagogical practices of teaching L2 writing and the development of teachers' knowledge in this domain as well to propose, analyze, and evaluate new and current curriculum standards and other policies.

Chapter 10

Assessment

There are two major purposes for assessing writing in second languages, related to different educational functions. Related to teaching and learning, formative assessments involve locally focused, continuous feedback on students' writing. Formative assessments have the purpose of helping to improve the writing of individual students, to inform instruction, and to evaluate achievements or completion of courses or programs. Research on formative assessments tends to appeal to values of educational relevance, utility, ongoing interpersonal relations, and individual writing development. In contrast, formal tests or examinations of proficiency in writing (and of course other modes of communication, such as reading, speaking, and listening) are related to program and institutional policies. They inform decisions about admissions or placement into programs or graduation from them, certification of individual abilities, or evaluations of program effectiveness. Research on formal tests tends to appeal to values of construct validity, reliability, and fairness for diverse populations and situations.

Formative Assessment

Formative assessments of students' writing are integral to L2 pedagogy. Instructors routinely evaluate students' writing in order to know what to teach students individually (for diagnostic purposes) or collectively (to inform their curriculum or lesson planning). Teachers also want to know how well students might have done in their writing or assignments, and they are obliged to evaluate and report on students' progress and achievements. Students, in turn, expect feedback from their instructors in order to know how well they have succeeded in their writing or task requirements and what they should try to learn or improve in their writing. Formative assessments combine (a) instructional functions, through teachers' feedback and responses to students' writing, with (b) functions of constructing literate communities within classrooms, through peer-assessment and collaboration, as well as (c) assessment functions, through teachers' evaluations or self-evaluations of written drafts or texts.

These pedagogical functions vary on several dimensions. Sources of variation include the conceptualizations of L2 writing of individual teachers as well as particular curricula (Cumming, 2001a, 2001c; D. Ferris, 2003), learners' levels of L2 proficiency (Grabe & Kaplan, 1996) or ages (Hudelson, 1989b), as well as the extent to which curriculum policies prescribe uniform approaches to assessment or whether instructors have individual discretion or share group responsibilities for student assessment (Brindley, 2000; Darling-Hammond et al., 1995; Lynch & Davidson, 1994; TESOL, 2001).

A key theme historically in this research has been the realization that formative assessment is embedded heavily in local curriculum contexts, and so cannot be isolated from teachers' and students' particular purposes, situations, prior experiences, or intentions. This realization contradicts the idea that there may be universally preferable methods of responding to L2 students' writing. That illusory idea was evident in early inquiry into this topic, based on simple survey or impressionistic methods (e.g. Cumming, 1985; Zamel, 1985) and ideological prescriptions, reflecting more the authors' beliefs than much empirical evidence, about what might be "proper" approaches to responding to students' writing (D. Ferris, 2003; Leki, 1990). X.-M. Li's (1996) comparative, sociohistorical analysis of highly regarded writing instructors in China and the US revealed as much variation, and differing values in their guiding rationales for assessing students' writing, among instructors within the two countries as exist across them. Nonetheless, D. Ferris' (2003), L. Goldstein's (2005), and K. Hyland and F. Hyland's (2006) recent book-length reviews of this research do highlight a range of established pedagogical principles and findings from inquiry about responding to students' L2 writing. Research into these matters has focused on questions of what, how, and who: What aspects of writing should formative assessments address? How might this be done? To what effect? By, with, or for whom?

Teachers' Responses to Students' Writing

Conventionally, teachers are assumed to have a professional responsibility for assessing students' writing. To enable them to do so, they are assumed to have proficiency in the L2, knowledge about writing and the local curriculum, and a repertoire of relevant techniques for responding to their students' writing. Following this assumption, most research on teachers' responses to students' L2 writing has taken either a descriptive or evaluative approach. Descriptive approaches have asked: What responding practices do certain teachers use? What aspects of writing do they attend to? What occurs in this process? What preferences for feedback on their L2 writing do students have? Evaluative approaches have asked: What aspects of writing should teachers focus on? What are the results of their doing so? Both approaches have obtained data from macro-level as well as micro-level perspectives, including surveys of teachers and students, reflective interviews, observations of classroom interactions, analyses of feedback on written drafts, analyses of teacher–student discourse, and quasi-experiments on relevant variables, conditions, or treatments. The focus on responding to students' written compositions has overshadowed other functions of L2 writing teachers' assessment practices, such as assigning grades or marks for courses or evaluating students' long-term L2 writing achievement. Nonetheless, a key message arising from this research is that, for L2 teachers to realize the pedagogical value of formative assessment, they often need to separate their (a) assessor roles of evaluating students' texts critically from (b) their instructional roles of responding meaningfully to the ideas and content that students are attempting to convey in their written drafts.

Aspects of L2 Writing

L2 writing instructors tend to respond to a relatively broad range of their students' written texts, including their ideas, rhetorical organization, grammar, word choices, spelling, and punctuation (Cohen & Cavalcanti, 1990; Conrad & Goldstein, 1999; D. Ferris, 1995, 1997; Ferris, Pezone, Tade, & Tinti, 1997; Hedgcock & Lefkowitz, 1994; Reid, 1994; Saito, 1994). Emphases on any one of these aspects of L2 writing may arise from differences in curriculum contexts, variable pedagogical goals, or teachers' beliefs or emerging relationships with their students (Conrad & Goldstein, 1999; Cumming, 2001c; F. Hyland & K. Hyland, 2001; X.-M. Li, 1996; Porte, 1997).

Errors are an inevitable, defining characteristic of writing with limited proficiency in a second language. How, or whether, to respond to errors is a point of much pedagogical controversy. Debate has centered on Truscott's (1996) argument that correcting errors in L2 students' writing is not beneficial, and even counterproductive, to students' writing development. D. Ferris (1999a, 2002, 2003) and L. Goldstein (2001, 2005) have responded by synthesizing diverse evidence to demonstrate the value of judicious, purposeful error correction as well as principles to guide such pedagogy. The concept of "error" in writing is difficult to define precisely, identify reliably, and relate directly to writing or language development because research has demonstrated that more fluent writers produce more and different types of errors (Grant & Ginther, 2000; Haswell, 1988; Jarvis, Grant, Bikowski, & Ferris, 2003; Polio, 1997; Rifken & Roberts, 1995). Likewise, the perceived severity of errors varies by aspects of language or texts as well as the situations or interests of the people assessing them (Janopoulos, 1992; T. Kobayashi, 1992; Santos, 1988; Vann et al., 1991).

For these and other reasons, evaluative research has found it difficult to establish that teachers' error corrections actually improve L2 students' writing (Chastain, 1990; Fazio, 2001; Kepner, 1991; Leki, 1990; Polio, Fleck, & Leder, 1998; Robb, Ross, & Shortreed, 1986). Many L2 students do, nonetheless, appear able to interpret teachers' error corrections and other types of feedback to improve their writing, though in variable ways and to varying extents (Ashwell, 2000; Cardelle & Corno, 1981; Chandler, 2003; Cohen, 1987; Cohen & Cavalcanti, 1990; Connor & Asenavage, 1994; Conrad & Goldstein, 1999; Fathman & Whally, 1990; D. Ferris, 1997; Ferris & Roberts, 2001; F. Hyland, 1998; F. Hyland & K. Hyland, 2001; Lalande, 1982; Patthey-Chavez & Ferris, 1997; Qi & Lapkin, 2001; Semke, 1984; Storch & Tapper, 2002; Warden, 2000; Yates & Kenkel, 2002). In surveys and analyses of their interactions, L2 students have distinctly expressed their desires for teachers to correct errors in their writing, particularly at the final draft stage of composing (Cohen, 1987; Cumming & So, 1996; D. Ferris, 1995; Ferris & Roberts, 2001; Hedgcock & Lefkowitz, 1996; Nelson & Carson, 1998; Radecki & Swales, 1988; Saito, 1994; S. Zhang, 1995). An intriguing pedagogical issue, highlighted in Aljaafreh and Lantolf (1994), Hoffman (1998), and Makino (1993) is whether teachers gradually encourage students, over time, to assume greater responsibility and self-control for handling errors in their L2 writing.

Media, Modes, and Timing of Responses

Teachers respond to L2 writing in various media and modes and at different stages of drafting written texts. Written comments on students' written texts appear to prevail as the most common, conventional pedagogical practice, though often supplemented by oral conferences or tutoring with individual students. As demonstrated in the studies cited in the paragraphs above, teachers' responses may refer directly (i.e. explicitly) or indirectly (e.g. by underlining, codes, or verbal hedges) to aspects of students' texts. Responses may involve various types of speech acts (e.g. praise, criticisms, questions, requests, directions, corrections or editing, advice, providing information, or general impressions). Responses may be conveyed verbally, orally, through print or computer media, on audio tapes, with symbols or graphic markers, in margins, over or above particular phrases, or on separate sheets or forms. Responses may be given on initial, second, or final drafts, on portfolios of collections of written texts or drafts, as well as in dialogue journals that model language forms while engaging students in continuing, written "conversations" (Peyton & Staton, 1993). The learning potential in these interactions resides in teachers providing diverse forms of "scaffolding" to support L2 students' writing, awareness, self-control, and ultimately learning (Aljaafreh & Lantolf, 1994; Conrad & Goldstein, 1999; Gibbons, 1993; Nassaji & Cumming, 2000; Patthey-Chavez & Clare, 1996; Qi & Lapkin, 2001; Williams, 2004). The power and control that teachers exert over students in these contexts, however, can also create a forum for biases or prejudices to play out (Losey, 1997; Patthey-Chavez & Ferris, 1997).

Peer and Self-Assessment

Formative assessment in peer writing groups can build local communities of writers while producing particular styles of spoken discourse in groups that may influence L2 learning or text revisions (Carson & Nelson, 1996; Cheng & Warren, 2005; de Guerrero & Villamil, 1994; Franken & Haslett, 2002; Hedgcock & Lefkowitz, 1992; Kong & Pearson, 2003; Liu & Hansen, 2002; Lockhart & Ng, 1995; McGroarty & Zhu, 1997; Mendonca & Johnson, 1994; Nelson & Carson, 1998; Paulus, 1999; Storch, 2002, 2005; Swain & Lapkin, 1995; Tsui & Ng, 2000; Zhu, 2001). Studies have established the value of coaching or training L2 students how to do peer response (Berg, 1999; Rothschild & Klingenberg, 1990; Stanley, 1992). But such studies have also revealed issues of cultural or individual differences or experiences that can hamper the dynamics of L2 student groups (Franken & Haslett, 2002; G. Jacobs, 1987; Mangelsdorf, 1992; Mangelsdorf & Schlumberger, 1992; Nelson & Murphy, 1993; Samway, 1993). Computer environments are increasingly providing supportive, engaging media for L2 peer collaboration—inside, outside, and across classrooms—as well as tools and resources for individual writing development, such as spelling and style checkers, dictionaries, and self-evaluation feedback (Cummins & Sayers, 1995; Hirvela, 2005; New, 1999; Pennington, 1993, 1996; Sullivan & Lindgren, 2002; Warden, 2000; Warschauer, 1999).

Various approaches to self-assessment of L2 writing have also developed in the contexts of classroom or self-directed study or of diagnostic or proficiency tests that include writing components (Alderson, 2005a; Alderson & Huhta, 2005; Bachman & Palmer, 1989; A. Brown, 2005; Ekbatani & Pierson, 2000; Little, 2005; Porto, 2001). Self-assessments also appear in writing instruction that invites students to formulate their own goals for L2 writing improvement then monitor their own progress (Cumming, 1986; Cumming, Busch, & Zhou, 2002; Hoffman, 1998) or that may emerge implicitly through reflection and self-analysis in the contexts of writing portfolios (Donato & McCormick, 1994; Hirvela & Sweetland, 2005; Koelsch & Trumbull, 1996; Little, 2005; Song & August, 2002).

Proficiency Assessment

Most of the systematic research and development about formal L2 writing assessment has focused on tests for students internationally seeking admission to university or college programs in English-dominant countries, such as the United States, the United Kingdom, Canada, Australia, and New Zealand. Within many countries, L2 writing assessments are also conducted at a national or state level through tests that certify completion of secondary education, determine admission to programs of higher education, or (in Europe, Australia, New Zealand, and Canada) evaluate the L2 proficiency of applicants for immigration decisions, placement in settlement programs, or employment or professional certification. In all these contexts, L2 writing is usually considered to be one integral component ability among many (including reading, speaking, and listening) that comprehensively constitute proficiency in the second language.

Research on L2 writing for these assessment purposes has reflected three different perspectives on the fundamental issue of determining and validating what L2 writing ability is. This focus follows recent theories of language testing that have asserted the centrality of construct validity— knowing that a test assesses what it claims to assess (Alderson & Banerjee, 2002; Bachman, 2000; Kunnan, 1998). Evidence for construct validation needs to be gathered from various, complementary perspectives. For L2 writing assessments, one perspective concerns designing, sampling, and measuring L2 writing in ways that are feasible, reliable, fair, and educationally relevant. A second perspective has involved evaluating the characteristics of L2 writing that testees produce in order to refine or validate the measurements or guide adaptation of new task types or media. A third perspective has involved describing and analyzing raters' processes of scoring L2 writing assessments.

Design of Formal L2 Writing Assessments

Over the past century, a convention has emerged of testing L2 writing abilities through tasks that involve examinees writing one, two, or several timed compositions on fixed topics in conventional genres, such as brief arguments, expositions, narratives, recounts, or summaries. Trained and experienced raters then impressionistically evaluate the resulting compositions in reference to rating scales that describe and demarcate the qualities of the writing. These scales may take the form of general, overall, holistic descriptions of the qualities of writing (i.e. on a single scale with four to nine score points) or they may involve multiple traits on separate scales that describe, at each score point, categorical features of language use, content, and rhetorical organization or other such task-specific traits (Cumming, 1997; Hamp-Lyons, 1991; Kroll, 1998; Spolsky, 1995;

Weigle, 2002). The rationale for this approach to L2 writing assessment was articulated influentially in Carroll's (1975) skills model of language proficiency, which considered writing to be one of four integral skills (in addition to reading, listening, and speaking) that should be evaluated directly through examinees' production of written compositions (rather than indirectly through tests of knowledge about grammar, vocabulary, or style). Carroll's arguments for performance assessments of writing built on conventions of assessments already established both for L2 (Lado, 1961; Spolsky, 1995) as well as L1 composition tests (e.g. Diederich, 1974). Considerable wisdom and practical advice have now accumulated about the design of such L2 writing tasks (Kroll & Reid, 1994) as well as the types of tasks and evaluation criteria appropriate to different levels of L2 writing proficiency (Grabe & Kaplan, 1996; Weigle, 2002).

Two tests have dominated the markets, and correspondingly the research activities, related to English proficiency assessment internationally. In North America, the Test of English as a Foreign Language (TOEFL) is developed and administered by Educational Testing Service (ETS). In the United Kingdom, Europe, Australia, and New Zealand, the International English Language Testing System (IELTS) is developed and administered by the University of Cambridge Local Examinations Syndicate (UCLES). Stoynoff and Chapelle (2005) have recently reviewed research on these and other specific ESL/EFL tests, including those that feature writing.

Test designers have utilized, and typically combined, three approaches to determine the tasks and criteria for formal L2 writing assessments: needs analysis, theory-based conceptualizations, and analyses of writing among examinee populations. Needs analyses have surveyed professors, students, and course syllabi to ascertain the types of writing tasks and levels of performance required in the target environment, such as university programs (Bridgeman & Carlson, 1983; Canseco & Byrd, 1989; Carson, 2001; Epp, Stawychny, Bonham, & Cumming, 2002; Ginther & Grant, 1996; Hale et al., 1996; Horowitz, 1986b; Kroll, 1979; Nunan, 1988; Rosenfeld, Leung, & Oltman, 2001; Waters, 1996). An extension of this approach has been to collect and analyze corpora of the actual written discourse in target contexts to serve as a basis for the design of writing tests as well as curricula (Bhatia, 1993; Biber et al., 2002; Bosher & Smalkoski, 2002; L. Flowerdew, 2003; K. Hyland, 2004b; K. Hyland & Milton, 1997; K. Hyland & Tse, 2005; Swales, 1990a, 1990b).

This latter group of studies of written genres exemplifies, as well, how theoretical conceptualizations have guided the design of certain L2 writing assessments. A notable instance is the theory of systemic–functional linguistics (deriving from, for example, Halliday & Matthiessen, 2004; Martin, 1992) that has informed the design and content of the Adult Migrant Education Program's (AMEP) Certificates in Spoken and Written English and various other language tests for migrant populations in Australia (Brindley, 1998a, 1998b, 2000; Brindley & Wigglesworth, 1997; Feez, 1998). Concepts of communicative competence—such as those proposed by Bachman (1990) or Harley, Allen, Cummins, and Swain (1990)—have also informed the general characteristics of many L2 proficiency tests, but with limited empirical evidence about specific constructs such as L2 writing (Bialystok, 1998; Chapelle, 1999; Sasaki & Hirose, 1996).

More commonly, the design of L2 writing tests has tended to draw eclectically on a variety of relevant research findings and theories (e.g. Clapham & Alderson, 1996; Connor, 1990; Cumming, Kantor, Powers, Santos, & Taylor, 2000; H. Jacobs, Zinkgraf, Wormuth, Hartfiel, & Hughey, 1981; Stansfield & Ross, 1988). Indeed, the prevalent approach to developing formal writing assessments has been through bottom-up, empirically grounded analyses of samples of writing from relevant student populations to devise and verify rating scales and evaluation criteria (Hamp-Lyons & Henning, 1991; Hawkey & Barker, 2004; H. Jacobs et al., 1981; Stansfield & Ross, 1988; Tyndall & Kenyon, 1996). Some of these analyses have followed from, or even led to, conceptual frameworks and curriculum standards, such as the rating scales and diagnostic assessments for L2 writing developed in relation to the Common European Framework of Reference for Languages (Alderson & Huhta, 2005; North, 2000), Stewart, Rehorick, and Perry's (2001) adoption of the Canadian Language Benchmarks for writing assessments, or the adoption of the Certificates in Spoken and Written English as the basis to evaluate progress in the competency-based curriculum for adult ESL education in Australia (Brindley, 1998b, 2000; Feez, 1998).

Four issues and types of analyses are central to the implementation of large-scale, formal L2 writing assessments. One is establishing the reliability of scoring writing tasks (Brindley, 2001; Stansfield & Ross, 1988). A second is the value of training raters to establish and maintain such consistency in scoring (Shohamy, Gordon, & Kraemer, 1992; Weigle, 1994, 1998). Most recently, sophisticated analyses have been able to account for interactions between scoring methods, raters, and writing tasks (Kondo-Brown, 2002; Lumley, 2005; Schoonen, 2005; Weigle, Boldt, & Valsecchi, 2003). A further concern is distinctions between different types of writing tasks and prompts and the qualities of writing that they produce for assessment purposes (Cumming et al., 2005; Schneider & Connor, 1990; Spaan, 1993; Zwick & Thayer, 1995). On this last point, a recent debate concerns relations between reading and writing abilities for assessment purposes. Should writing and reading be assessed separately to avoid dependencies across task types and language skills, as in recent revisions to the IELTS (Charge & Taylor, 1997; Clapham & Alderson, 1996; Wallace, 1997)? Or should writing and reading be assessed together, and even in conjunction with source information in aural media, in tasks that evoke the "content responsible" (Johns, 1993; Leki & Carson, 1997) demands of academic writing in relation to source readings, and the multimodality of multiliteracies, as in recent revisions to the TOEFL (Cumming et al., 2000; Hamp-Lyons & Kroll, 1997; see also Way, Joiner, & Seaman, 2000; Weigle, 2004)?

A related, major point of controversy is the negative backwash that writing tasks in high-stakes admissions tests such as the TOEFL or IELTS may have on teaching and learning. If such tests define the construct of L2 writing too narrowly or simply, they may elicit pedagogical practices, or even coaching, that simply involve test preparation rather than legitimate writing development (Alderson & Hamp-Lyons, 1996; Bailey, 1999; Crusan, 2002; Cumming, Grant, Mulcahy-Ernt, & Powers, 2004; Greenberg, 1986; Hamp-Lyons & Kroll, 1997; Raimes, 1990). This debate raises the larger issue of the usefulness of formal assessments of L2 writing to inform and support educational, learning, and societal purposes (Burrows, 2001; Cumming, 1994, 2001a; Green, 2005; Hamp-Lyons & Kroll, 1997; Kunnan, 1998; Lynch & Davidson, 1994). Some, but little, research has probed into other complicated, ethical issues related to formal L2 writing assessments such as writing or test anxiety (E. Hall, 1991; Johns, 1991b), the computer skills required to perform in writing in computer media (H. Lee, 2004; Taylor, Kirsch, Jamieson, & Eignor, 1999), or the accommodations appropriate for ESL students on large-scale tests administered in schools (Abedi, Hofstetter, & Lord, 2004).

Discourse Analyses as Validity Evidence

A long-standing approach to provide validity evidence for L2 writing assessments involves analyses of the discourse characteristics of the written compositions that L2 learners at different levels of proficiency produce on a test. This approach dates back to Kaplan's (1966) impressions of culturally different rhetorical patterns while reviewing a sample of ESL compositions from a test at his university and to Perkins' (1980) quest for objective indicators, based on text analyses, to validate impressionistic methods of scoring L2 writing. Most recently, this approach has led to various programs for automated scoring of compositions, based on models of lexical or syntactic features derived from large corpora of composition samples. But applications of automated scoring to L2 writing are hampered seriously by the idiosyncratic or erratic spelling, lexical choices, and error types associated with the writing of language learners, despite the reliability of computer analyses in comparison with the impressionistic scoring of writing by human raters (Foltz, Kintsch, & Landauer, 1998; Powers, Burstein, Chodrow, Fowles, & Kukich, 2002; Shermis & Burstein, 2003). A further constraint is the conclusion demonstrated by Jarvis et al. (2003) that L2 compositions tend to display clusters of variable text features rather than strictly linear dimensions of development that could be modeled easily by computer programs.

Nonetheless, a considerable amount of research has attempted to trace, mostly through cross-sectional research designs, progressive differences in a range of morphological, syntactic, lexical, rhetorical, and pragmatic aspects of L2 written compositions at different score points on L2 tests representing levels of L2 proficiency (Archibald, 1994; Bardovi-Harlig & Bofman, 1989; Cumming et al., 2005; Cumming & Mellow, 1996; de Haan & van Esch, 2005; Engber, 1995; D. Ferris, 1994a; Frase, Faletti, Ginther, & Grant, 1999; Grant & Ginther, 2000; Intaraprawat & Steffensen, 1995; Ishikawa, 1995; Jarvis, 2002; Jarvis, Grant, Bikowski & Ferris, 2003; Kern & Schultz, 1992; Larsen-Freeman, 1978; Larsen-Freeman & Strom, 1977; Laufer, 1991; Laufer & Nation, 1995; Ruetten, 1994; Sweedler-Brown, 1993; Tedick & Mathison, 1995; Turner & Upshur, 2002). As Brindley (1998a) and Cumming (2001a) have observed, a rating scale on a test of language ability presumes, if only implicitly, a hypothetical progression in language development, and so warrants empirical substantiation from analyses of learners' texts. In turn, meta-analyses and replication studies have begun to synthesize and rigorously evaluate the robustness and usefulness of indicators of accuracy, complexity, and fluency commonly used in L2 writing research and tests (Ortega, 2003; Polio, 1997, 2003; Wolfe-Quintero, Inagaki, & Kim, 1998).

Rating Processes

A second approach to establishing the validity of formal L2 writing assessments concerns the criteria and decision making that raters use to score written texts. For impressionistic, holistic, or analytic scoring of writing, raters' evaluations play as important a role as the text features of examinees' writing do. Indeed, impressionistic scoring can be defined as the interaction between rater's interpretive evaluations and the discourse features of examinees' texts. This fundamental issue was initially suggested for L2 writing by Homburg (1984) then pointedly articulated in Connor-Linton's (1995b) call to "look behind the curtain" of L2 writing assessments to understand the significance of raters' decision making and thinking processes. Analyses of these processes have shown that, in evaluating L2 compositions, issues arise that are distinct from assessments of L1 writing, related to raters' consideration of language features, cultural orientations, their own knowledge and experiences, rhetorical structures, and the institutional purposes of the assessment (Cumming, Kantor, & Powers, 2002; Lumley, 2005).

Numerous case studies have recently used introspective methods (such as think-aloud or stimulated recall protocols) to describe the criteria, thinking processes, and decisions that raters use to evaluate L2 writing in specific tests and tasks (Connor & Carrell, 1993; Cumming, 1990a; Cumming, Kantor, & Powers, 2001, 2002; Hamp-Lyons & Mathias, 1994; Janopoulos, 1992; Lumley, 2002, 2005; Milanovic, Saville, & Shen, 1996; Sakyi, 2001; D. Smith, 2000; Vaughn, 1991). These studies have all shown raters' thinking to involve highly interactive, but also contingent and tentative, processes of interpreting texts and forming evaluation judgments, focused on a complex range of language, content, rhetorical, institutional, and task-specific concerns. Cumming, Kantor, and Powers. (2002) concluded, for example, that experienced raters typically use 27 different thinking behaviors during a few minutes' evaluation of a single L2 composition. Lumley (2005, p. 310) has proposed that the process of rating L2 writing usually follows three stages: "A first reading, during which scores are not typically discussed, although this appears to be the stage at which raters make up their minds about the quality of the text; a scoring stage, during which the scores are given and justified, in relation to the scoring categories; and a third stage, when the scores are implicitly or explicitly confirmed or revised."

Many studies have demonstrated that the criteria applied to evaluate L2 writing involve not only the descriptive criteria prescribed by rating scales but also raters' personal, cultural, or professional knowledge and orientations. Some studies have contrasted the performance of experienced and inexperienced raters of writing, pointing out that inexperienced raters, such as student teachers, tend to have and act on only partial representations of L2 writing, compared to the full set of criteria and complex decision making that experienced raters apply (Cumming, 1990a; Schoonen, Vergeer, & Eiting, 1997; Shohamy et al., 1992). Other studies have analyzed the criteria applied by different groups of raters, revealing differences related to their professional roles (such as ESL vs. English L1 instructors, J. D. Brown, 1991; Mendelsohn & Cumming, 1987; Song & Caruso, 1996), pedagogical experiences or purposes (Erdosy, 2001; Land & Whitley, 1989), or cultural backgrounds (Connor-Linton, 1995a; H. Kobayashi & Rinnert, 1996; Rinnert & Kobayashi, 2001; Shi, 2001). These findings point to the centrality of cultural values and personal interpretations for assessing L2 writing. Correspondingly, in the contexts of formal assessments, these findings highlight the need for explicit procedures for rater training, moderation, and calibration to ensure fairness and consistency (Weigle, 1994, 1998).

Summary

Assessment policies, practices, and methods have been studied extensively in respect to L2 writing in recent decades, prompted by concerns for accountability, fairness, and validity in education generally. Knowledge about L2 writing assessment has advanced on many dimensions, producing useful information about the variability and impact of teachers' responses to students' writing, the value of peer- and self-assessment for writing development, principles for designing formal writing tests, the types and qualities of evidence required to ensure validity of writing tests, and the diverse influences on and complex processes of evaluating L2 writing. As Hamp-Lyons (2007) has observed, these developments have bifurcated into two distinct cultures: one concerned with teaching and learning, related to formative functions of assessment in classrooms and other pedagogical settings, and the other culture concerned with exams, related to the design and analysis of formal tests and institutional policies. The distinctions between these purposes of assessing L2 writing, and the "cultures" developed around them, suggest that they may continue, in the future, to develop in differing, antithetical directions, despite the prospect (and often reality) that, in educational practices, information arising from research in either area can mutually inform the other.

Basic Research on Second Language Writing

Studies

Section III focuses on basic research on L2 writers, their composing processes, and their written texts. As in the two foregoing sections of this book, the selection of studies has been limited to those in published form—books, book chapters, and journal articles. Not included are conference proceedings, ERIC documents, and unpublished theses and dissertations. Studies in which writing is the medium but not the focus are also excluded, as are studies in assessment, which are addressed in section II. We have included here analyses of research done outside North America where the studies were just too important to leave out or where looking at only North American studies would have seriously distorted the findings of basic research on L2 writing.

Caveats

The studies examined here are generally sound, but they all have limitations—as does any body of research. We have not evaluated these limitations; judgments about the quality of individual studies are left to the reader. Our representation of the findings of these studies are a function of our reading of the studies, interests, biases, and limits of knowledge and expressive abilities—as would be the case with any endeavor such as this. Consequently, we do not claim that what follows is objective or disinterested; it does constitute, however, a serious attempt to provide an account that is honest, fair, useful, and accessible. Again it is up to the reader to judge whether this attempt has been successful or not. Furthermore, statements about the results of the studies should be seen as tentative and interpretive rather than definitive; the reader is urged to read each statement as though it were preceded by the following phrase: On the basis of the authors' reading and analysis of these studies, it is believed that . . . .

Using This Section

This section can be used in at least two ways. It can be read in its entirety to give a general overview of this body of research. Or it can be used as a reference work—pointing to studies and findings relevant to a particular area of interest—a sort of prose database that can be used as a springboard for reading or doing research in a specific area. To facilitate this latter use, we have done three things. First, we have attempted to make the presentation of findings in all parts of this section (chapters, categories, subcategories) self-contained. Second, we have made the structure of the chapters uniform and transparent. Thus, each chapter begins with a brief introduction and a chapter outline, and the organizational principle for the presentation of findings in subsections, categories, and subcategories is from most to fewest findings. Each chapter concludes with a tally of the categories with the most findings (to assess depth) and the categories with the most subcategories (to assess breadth). We have also cited examples of sustained research programs in the general area addressed in the chapter. Third, two tables have been included at the end of the section that provide information on each study's author name(s), publication date, sample size, and subjects' first and second language(s).[1] The tables include the same information, but one is organized alphabetically by (first) author's last name; the other by date of publication. This information is intended to provide some (authorial and historical) context for and easy reference to each of the studies cited in this section.

---

1 We have chosen to use "subjects" instead of "participants" here and elsewhere in this section because we judged "participants" to be too broad. We intend "subjects" to refer only to the people whose characteristics, processes, and texts were examined, rather than including other participants in the research such as researchers, scorers, or coders.

Writer Characteristics

Introduction

The focus of this chapter is second language writers, specifically second language writer variables. These variables have been divided into five basic categories: second language variables, first language variables, transfer, psychological and sociological variables, and demographic variables. The organizing principle for the ordering of these categories is most to least findings. The order of the presentation of these categories and their subcategories is indicated in the chapter outline below.

Chapter 11 Outline

L2 variables
    L2 writing ability
        Writer characteristics
        Composing processes
        Written text
    L2 proficiency
        Writer characteristics
        Composing processes
        Written text
    L2 writing development
        Writer characteristics
        Composing processes
        Written text
    L2 reading
    L2 writing confidence
    L2 writing grammatical ability
    L2 writer perceptions
L1 variables
    L1 writing ability
        Positive relationship

> Negative/inverse relationship
> No/weak relationship
> L2 proficiency level
> L2 education
> L2 vocabulary
> L2 speaking ability
> Time in L2 context
> L1 reading
> L1 education
> Confidence in L1 and L2 writing

Transfer
Psychological and social variables
> Motivation
> Apprehension
> Emotion
> Learning style
> Identity
> Metaknowledge
> Extroversion/introversion
> Field dependence/independence
> Collectivism/individualism
> Political background
> Assertiveness

Demographics
> Grade level
> SL vs. FL
> Educational level
> L2 instruction starting age
> Graduate vs. undergraduate
> Time in L2 context
> Age
> Grade of entry
> L2 writing experience
> L1 education
> L1 background

Findings

L2 Variables

L2 Writing Ability

WRITER CHARACTERISTICS

In the research, students with high levels of L2 writing ability, i.e. more skilled L2 writers (as opposed to less skilled L2 writers) tended to be older and female. They spent more time in English-speaking countries (Hirose & Sasaki, 1994), were exposed to writing at home and with peers, and had received rhetorical instruction in both first and second languages (Skibniewski & Skibniewska, 1986). They exhibited confidence in their second language writing ability (Hirose & Sasaki, 1994; Sasaki & Hirose, 1996), a sense of purpose, an awareness of audience (Skibniewski & Skibniewska, 1986), and a commitment to the writing task (Victori, 1999).

More skilled L2 writers had a thorough understanding of what should be included in each component of an essay. They saw composing as flexible, with no restricting assumptions, and saw the nature and requirements of a writing task and their own writing problems as broad and complex (Victori, 1999). They did not see formal writing as very difficult (Hirose & Sasaki, 1994).

More skilled L2 writers regularly practiced free L2 composition beyond the paragraph and wrote summaries of materials read in their first language in high school (Sasaki & Hirose, 1996). They voluntarily did more second language writing (Hirose & Sasaki, 1994) and were involved in more self-initiated writing than were less skilled L2 writers. They were less apprehensive about writing (Skibniewski & Skibniewska, 1986), and less concerned with surface features (Hirose & Sasaki, 1994). They felt little difficulty in writing for academic purposes (Sasaki & Hirose, 1996), and less often assumed that the reader knew what was going on in the writer's mind (R. Wong, 1993).

COMPOSING PROCESSES

More skilled L2 writers employed a hierarchical composing process (Skibniewski, 1988) and more often had a preconceived plan (Skibniewski & Skibniewska, 1986; Victori, 1999). They did more planning overall (Hirose & Sasaki, 1994; Raimes, 1987; Skibniewski, 1988), more global planning (Sasaki, 2000), and more planning of organization (Hirose & Sasaki, 1994; Sasaki, 2000). They did more global goal setting (Skibniewski, 1988) and rehearsing (Raimes, 1987). They thought on a larger, more global scale than did their less skilled counterparts (Sasaki, 2000).

More skilled L2 writers did more revising overall (Raimes, 1987; Skibniewski, 1988; Hirose & Sasaki, 1994) and more global and extensive revision (Skibniewski, 1988; Skibniewski & Skibniewska, 1986). They focused on high-level revision (Skibniewski & Skibniewska, 1986) and revising at the discourse level and did more rescanning (Raimes, 1987), rereading (Hirose & Sasaki, 1994; Uzawa, 1996), rewriting (Skibniewski & Skibniewska, 1986), and editing than less skilled L1 writers did. They interacted more with text as it emerged on paper (Raimes, 1987).

More skilled L2 writers were more concerned with and attentive to organization overall (Hirose & Sasaki, 1994; Sasaki & Hirose, 1996;

Victori, 1999), both before and while writing (Sasaki & Hirose, 1996), and concentrated more on organizational and structural changes (Skibniewski & Skibniewska, 1986) than their less skilled counterparts did. They paid more attention to choosing their words and assessing them (Hirose & Sasaki, 1994; Victori, 1999) and left blanks when they could not think of a word and pursued their point (R. Wong, 1993). More skilled writers also paid more attention to grammar (Hirose & Sasaki, 1994) and accuracy (Sasaki & Hirose, 1996) and more often stopped to translate and refine expression in the second language (Sasaki, 2000). They paid more attention to spelling (Hirose & Sasaki, 1994).

More skilled L2 writers were more fluent (Hirose & Sasaki, 1994; Sasaki, 2000) in their first and second languages (Sasaki & Hirose, 1996) and more focused on production (Hirose & Sasaki, 1994) at the global text level than were less skilled L2 writers (Victori, 1999). They spent more time on task (Raimes, 1987) and more often wrote directly in English (Hirose & Sasaki, 1994). They did less pausing to stop and think while writing (Hirose & Sasaki, 1994; Sasaki, 2000) and translated less often (contradiction noted) (Hirose & Sasaki, 1994).

More skilled L2 writers attended more to content (Hirose & Sasaki, 1994), referring more to audience, especially in terms of modifying content and presenting stronger or weaker opinions; their main objective was convincing the reader of their opinion (Victori, 1999). They used more rhetorical strategies (Sasaki, 2000).

WRITTEN TEXT

More skilled L2 writers wrote longer texts (Grant & Ginther, 2000; Intaraprawat & Steffensen, 1995; Sasaki, 2000) that exhibited more complex development (Sasaki, 2000). They used more metadiscourse (and used it more correctly), and their texts exhibited more and a wider range of metadiscourse types (Intaraprawat & Steffensen, 1995). They used more sequential topics and fewer parallel topics (Schneider & Connor, 1990) and more schematic links than did less skilled L2 writers (R. Wong, 1993).

With regard to parts of speech, more skilled writers used more adjectives, adverbs, articles, nouns, verbs, personal pronouns, prepositions (Grant & Ginther, 2000), and conjunctions (Kiany & Nejad, 2001). In terms of functional categories, they used more amplifiers (e.g. *definitely*), conjuncts (e.g. *however*), demonstratives (e.g. *this*), downtoners (e.g. *barely*), emphatics (e.g. *really*) (Grant & Ginther, 2000), illocutionary markers (e.g. *we claim that*), and more correctly used code glosses (e.g. *in other words*), commentaries (expressions that address the reader, e.g. *dear friends*), emphatics (e.g. *undoubtedly*), hedges (e.g. *probably*), and narrators (expressions that inform readers of the source of information, e.g. *according to*) than their less skilled counterparts (Intaraprawat & Steffensen, 1995).

More skilled L2 writers used more grammatical features, including more modals, nominalizations, past tense, present tense, subordination (especially complementation and adverbials rather than relative clauses), third person pronouns (Grant & Ginther, 2000), and passives (Grant & Ginther, 2000; Kameen, 1980, 1983), and fewer second person pronouns (Grant & Ginther, 2000) than less skilled L2 writers did. They had longer clauses, more words per T-unit (Kameen, 1980, 1983), and more T-units per essay (Intaraprawat & Steffensen, 1995; Schneider & Connor, 1990).

More skilled writers used more words, lexical features, lexical specificity (in terms of type–token ratio, i.e. number of different words/number of words), and longer words (Grant & Ginther, 2000), and exhibited more lexical individuality/originality (Linnarud, 1986).

L2 Proficiency

WRITER CHARACTERISTICS

A higher level of L2 proficiency was related to higher L2 writing ability (Aliakbari, 2002; Kiany & Nejad, 2001), greater fluency (Hirose & Sasaki, 1994), higher L1 writing ability (Aliakbari, 2002), lower L1 writing ability (contradiction noted) (Carson & Kuehn, 1992), and less use of L1 (Wang & Wen, 2002). The higher the level of L2 proficiency, the less significantly it predicted L2 writing ability (Ma & Wen, 1999). A lower level of L2 proficiency was related to better L1 writing skills (contradiction noted) (Carson & Kuehn, 1992), more difficulty in L2 writing (Zainuddin & Moore, 2003), and less transfer between L1 and L2 (Wu & Rubin, 2000).

L2 proficiency was distinguished from academic level (Carrell & Connor, 1991), influenced the correlation of L1 and L2 composing (Kamimura, 1996), did not predict developmental stage in L2 writing (Bosher, 1998), and appeared to explain part of the difference in strategies and fluency (Sasaki, 2000). Written L2 proficiency lagged behind spoken fluency (Blanton, 2005). A certain level of L2 proficiency was a required but not sufficient condition for L2 writing (Aliakbari, 2002). L2 proficiency was not independent of L1 writing ability (Sasaki & Hirose, 1996), and was not mutually interdependent with literacy skill (Yasuda, 2004).

COMPOSING PROCESSES

A higher level of L2 proficiency was related to having writing strategies similar to those of L1 writers (Zamel, 1982), ability to apply writing strategies as efficiently to L2 composing as to L1 composing (Kamimura, 1996), and greater interaction among composing processes (Roca, Marin, & Murphy, 2001). More L2 proficiency was positively related to better plans in L1 and L2 (Akyel, 1994), less use of the L1 for generating text (Wang & Wen, 2002), and all aspects of revision, except at the essay level (H. Kobayashi & Rinnert, 2001).

A lower level of L2 proficiency was related to a less effective process (Jones & Tetroe, 1987), not employing a wider range of compensatory strategies (V. Smith, 1994), and less planning (Jones & Tetroe, 1987). It did not impede the ability to restructure, irrespective of purpose (Roca, Murphy, & Manchón, 1999), and was related to greater composing difficulties when writing in L2 in the third person (Kamimura & Oi, 2001).

L2 proficiency made a distinct (from writing expertise) contribution to processes (Cumming, 1989) and appeared to explain part of the differences in strategies (Sasaki, 2000). L2 proficiency operated independently of goal setting (V. Smith, 1994); was related to how often L1 was used during L2 writing; was related to task difficulty; did not uniformly affect the frequency and duration of language switching (Woodall, 2002); was significantly related to revision; was most strongly related to revision at the intersentential level, but not to that at the essay level; might have been independent of or separable from essay-level knowledge and concerns that underlie revision (H. Kobayashi & Rinnert, 2001); and affected revising strategies less than did past experience (Yasuda, 2004). An L2 proficiency threshold level may have been a necessary condition for fully deploying L2 writing ability (Roca et al., 1999).

WRITTEN TEXT

A higher level of L2 proficiency was associated with, in L2 writing, higher ratings on content, organization, and language use; higher scores on persuasive and descriptive texts (Cumming, 1989), higher holistic scores (Carrell & Connor, 1991; Kamimura & Oi, 2001), better L1 and L2 compositions (Akyel, 1994), and more developed stories (Kamimura & Oi, 2001). It was also related to higher L1 composition scores (Sasaki & Hirose, 1996) and lower L1 reading and writing scores (contradiction noted; Carson et al., 1990). It accounted for a large portion of variance in text quality (Cumming, 1989).

A lower level of L2 proficiency was related to lower L2 writing scores (Flahive & Bailey, 1993; H. Kobayashi & Rinnert, 1992; Kubota, 1998), greater use of first person pronouns and hedges (Wu & Rubin, 2000), less use of conjunctions (Kiany & Nejad, 2001), and less effective use of information from background readings and referencing of source, author, and text information. It was also related to reliance on copying as a primary method of text integration (Campbell, 1990).

L2 proficiency made a distinct (from writing expertise) contribution to written texts (Cumming, 1989); with competence in text production, it was a discrete aspect of L2 writing (V. Smith, 1994), and, with L1 writing ability, influenced the quality of writing. It significantly explained L2 composition scores (Sasaki & Hirose, 1996), contributed to the quality of writing (Hirose & Sasaki, 1994), and was the most significant variable in predicting L2 writing scores (Kiany & Nejad, 2001).

With composition score, L2 proficiency explained most of the variance in L2 composition total variance, but uniquely explained only a small fraction of that variance (Hirose & Sasaki, 1994). It had more impact on quality of writing than did L1 writing quality. With L1 writing ability, L2 proficiency predicted only a small amount of variance, suggesting that other factors may be involved (contradiction noted) (Aliakbari, 2002). L2 proficiency had little correspondence to judgment of writing ability for placement (Raimes, 1987), showed no significant interaction with writing expertise, and did not visibly affect composing processes (Cumming, 1989).

L2 Writing Development

WRITER CHARACTERISTICS

Age was negatively related to development of L2 writing (Carson & Kuehn, 1992) and was a decisive factor in the greater use of syntactic patterns (e.g. coordination, subordination). The age of 12 may have been a "turning point" in the foreign language (FL) acquisition process; at that age there was a "sudden spurt" in grammatical development (Torras & Celaya, 2001).

Development in writing was different for FL and second language (SL) students. SLs continued to improve; FLs declined in L2 writing ability. However, both SLs and FLs had a net gain over time in terms of development of writing ability. FLs and SLs tended to see development in "product-oriented" variables, but SLs saw more gains in "process-oriented" variables. L2 writing instruction in FL settings could have had an impact, but additional intensive L2 writing training was needed to continue development (Sasaki, 2004).

Literacy development in one language had a positive effect on development in the other by presenting concepts that carried between the two. Access to meaning through one language meant that development in that language would surpass development in the other. The learner's strong or weak identification with a culture and language further enhanced the development of literacy. Children had no tendency to confuse literacy development in languages that are orthographically different, even at young ages, prior to formal instruction. Access to writing materials and books simultaneously did not have negative effects on the development of the easier language. The availability of language support and materials enhanced the development of literacy (Buckwalter & Lo, 2002).

Other factors that affected L2 writing development include previous educational experience (Mohan & Lo, 1985); length of time in the US (development of L2 writing proficiency did not correlate with it); aptitude development; L2 academic environment; loss of L1 writing ability (Carson & Kuehn, 1992); attitudes toward L2 writing; time; practice and study; active (vs. passive) learning; cognitive and social growth (Sasaki, 2004); an early (vs. late) start in L2 learning (Torras & Celaya, 2001); recognizing different discourse needs and associated styles (Reynolds, 2002); multiple opportunities to write in many genres (McCarthey et al., 2005); access to and participation in disciplinary and vernacular discourses in L1 (Gentil, 2005; Tardy, 2005a); a rhetorical view of texts (focusing on not just what content to transmit to readers, but how to transmit it persuasively); and mentoring and collaboration, identity, and situational and task exigency (Tardy, 2005b).

COMPOSING PROCESSES

More prewriting time on planning reflected development for both FL and SL groups (Sasaki, 2004). Less extensive use of translation (from L1 to L2) as a conscious strategy reflected development (Elliot, 1986). Higher L2 proficiency level, more writing experience (Skibniewski, 1988), increasing automaticity, more concern with the needs of the reader, and greater ability to select from alternative wordings reflected development in revision. Less frequent but longer pauses also reflected development (Elliot, 1986).

WRITTEN TEXT

L2 writing development was measured by a number of textual variables: rhetorical organization (development of this ability came late: McCarthey et al., 2005; Mohan & Lo, 1985); features of written English (gradually acquired/developed); repertoire of cohesive links; consistency in the use of the past tense and learning how the past tense is formed; genre development (learning gradually to differentiate genres: Elliot, 1986); organization of content with more semantic ties (P. Johnson, 1992); T-unit development; number of clauses per T-unit; coordination of independent clauses; sentences beginning with coordinating conjunctions (from oral to written style); use of content words (Casanave, 1994); quantity of writing (Sasaki, 2004); appropriate use of language conventions such as capitalization and punctuation; subject–verb agreement; tense; focus on topic; idea elaboration; metaphorical language; and word choice (McCarthey et al., 2005).

With regard to accuracy, complexity, and fluency, development did not take place at the same rate or uniformly. Fluency developed faster and achieved higher levels than complexity or accuracy. Complexity seemed to develop least. Extensive use of memorized sequences or patterns aided fluency and accuracy. Fluency was favored over accuracy in the production of longer, more varied sentences (Torras & Celaya, 2001). Difference in L2 writing fluency appeared to be explained in part by L2 proficiency or a lack of it (Sasaki, 2000).

L2 Reading

L2 reading ability (measured by written recalls) was significantly related to L2 writing (as measured by scores on holistic scales: Carrell & Connor, 1991). L2 reading comprehension scores were significantly, but modestly, correlated with holistic writing scores (Flahive & Bailey, 1993). The correlation of L2 reading and writing abilities was different for L2 writers with different language backgrounds (Carson et al., 1990).

L2 reading-habit variables were not significantly related to L2 writing performance (Hedgcock & Atkinson, 1993). L2 pleasure reading was not significantly related to writing ability (Flahive & Bailey, 1993), but L2 pleasure reading correlated with L2 writing proficiency (contradiction noted: Janopoulous, 1986). The amount of free voluntary L2 reading was positively related to L2 writing performance and engaging in free writing in the L2, and negatively related to L2 writing apprehension and writer's block (S.-Y. Lee, 2005).

L2 Writing Confidence

More confidence in L2 writing was exhibited by more skilled writers (Sasaki & Hirose, 1996). More confidence in L2 writing might have resulted from students' initial competence in L1 writing and could result in less confidence in L1 writing. Less confidence in L2 writing was gained when writing was perceived as school-only—especially when parents did not engage in it frequently. Less confidence may have resulted from teachers' high expectations and teacher feedback emphasizing criticisms and accuracy. Confidence in writing improved when it was linked meaningfully to contexts, goals, and audiences (McCarthey & Garcia, 2005).

L2 Writing Grammatical Ability

L2 writing ability (measured by holistic writing scores) strongly correlated with L2 grammatical ability (in the form of CELT scores and number of error-free T-units). Reading and writing ability were statistically related to L2 grammatical ability. L2 grammatical ability might have been part of a unified language proficiency factor underlying it, reading comprehension, and writing ability (Flahive & Bailey, 1993).

L2 Writer Perceptions

The most commonly cited differences in L2 writer perceptions related to writing, planning, vocabulary, sentences, and phrases; on the whole, fewer differences were noted in rhetoric. L2 writers perceived that their limited vocabularies meant they were unable to express themselves accurately and precisely. Grammar and vocabulary were the L2 writers' main concerns (Silva, 1992).

LI Variables

LI Writing Ability

POSITIVE RELATIONSHIP

There was evidence to suggest that L2 writing ability could be predicted by L1 writing ability (Ma & Wen, 1999). L2 writing ability was transferred from L1 discourse competence (Carson & Kuehn, 1992). L2 writing ability significantly correlated with L1 writing ability, at least in some L2 writers (Carson et al., 1990). Poor L2 writing skills reflected poor L1 writing skills (Doushaq, 1986). L2 writers were handicapped by low L1 writing ability (Carson & Kuehn, 1992). Fewer L2 writing resources were a result of lower L1 writing ability (Zainuddin & Moore, 2003). Writers' L2 writing ability could be significantly predicted by L1 writing ability at different L2 proficiency levels (Ma & Wen, 1999). L2 and L1 writing exhibited a moderate positive correlation for students who had L2 education and had been in an L2 context more than 6 months (Carson & Kuehn, 1992). L2 writing was indirectly affected by L1 writing ability, which directly affected L2 oral expression ability, L2 vocabulary comprehension, and L2 discourse comprehension ability (Ma & Wen, 1999).

NEGATIVE/INVERSE RELATIONSHIP

Proficiency gain in L2 writing may have developed with concomitant L1 writing ability loss (Carson & Kuehn, 1992; McCarthey et al., 2005). Students functioning at the highest L2 writing level exhibited lower L1 writing ability (Carson & Kuehn, 1992). High L2 writing ability was related to low L1 writing ability with high L2 proficiency (Aliakbari, 2002). High L2 writers who were low L1 writers were younger and had less L1 education, but had L2 educational experiences. Low L2 writers who were high L1 writers were older and had a lower L2 educational level, despite a comparatively long time in the L2 context. L2 writing ability and L1 writing ability exhibited a small negative correlation for students with no formal L2 education who had been in the L2 context using their L2 in academic writing less than 6 months (Carson & Kuehn, 1992).

NO/WEAK RELATIONSHIP.

L2 writing ability was not significantly correlated with L1 writing proficiency (Carson & Kuehn, 1992). L2 writing ability had no meaningful relationship with L1 writing (Aliakbari, 2002). L2 writing ability was not simply correlated with L1 writing ability (Carson & Kuehn, 1992). L2 writing ability and L1 writing ability were two separate tasks; that is, writing in L2 was a language-specific phenomenon, not a writing problem. L2 writing ability may not necessarily have been helped by or have been transferred from L1 writing. L2 writing ability was impacted less by L1 writing ability than by L2 proficiency. L2 writing performance could be predicted by L1 writing and L2 proficiency; however, the low correlation suggested that other factors may have been involved (Aliakbari, 2002).

L2 Proficiency Level

Students functioning at the lowest L2 level exhibited better L1 writing skills. Students functioning at the highest L2 level exhibited lower L1 writing skills (Carson & Kuehn, 1992). High L2 proficiency with low L1 writing ability was related to high L2 writing ability (Aliakbari, 2002). As L2 proficiency increased, L1 writing scores tended to decrease (Carson et al., 1990). L2 proficiency had more impact on L2 writing ability than did L1 writing ability. L2 proficiency and L1 writing could predict L2 writing performance; however, the weak correlation suggested that other factors might have been involved (Aliakbari, 2002).

L2 Education

Slightly more L1 and L2 educational experience was related to lower L1 and L2 writing scores for students who had low L1 and L2 scores. With students who had had L2 education and had been in an L2 context more than 6 months, L1 and L2 writing exhibited a moderate positive correlation. High L1 writers who were low L2 writers were older and had a lower L2 educational level, despite their comparatively long time in an L2 context; low L1 writers who were high L2 writers were younger and had less L1 education, but had L2 educational experiences (Carson & Kuehn, 1992).

L2 Vocabulary

The effects of L2 productive vocabulary on L2 writing ability were greater than those of L1 writing ability and L2 speaking ability. L2 productive vocabulary, together with L1 writing ability and L2 speaking ability, exerted direct effects on L2 writing ability. Through its effects on L2 vocabulary comprehension, L2 oral expression ability, and L2 discourse comprehension, L1 writing ability affected L2 writing ability (Ma & Wen, 1999).

L2 Speaking Ability

L2 speaking ability, along with L1 writing ability and L2 productive vocabulary, explained most of the variance in L2 writing ability. The effects of L2 speaking ability and L1 writing ability were lesser than the effects of L2 productive vocabulary (Ma & Wen, 1999). When English functioned mainly as an oral language for L2 writers, their written English proficiency lagged behind their spoken fluency, and their writing and speaking skills were not meaningfully related (Blanton, 2005).

Time in L2 Context

For writers who had been in an L2 context for more than 6 months and had L2 education, L1 and L2 writing exhibited a moderate positive correlation. Despite their comparatively long time in an L2 context, high L1 writers who were low L2 writers were older and had a lower L2 educational level (Carson & Kuehn, 1992).

L1 Reading

L1 reading ability was significantly correlated with L2 reading ability, L1 writing ability, and L2 writing ability (Carson et al., 1990). Neither L1 (Flahive & Bailey, 1993; Hedgcock & Atkinson, 1993; Janopoulos, 1986) nor L2 pleasure reading (Flahive & Bailey, 1993; Hedgcock & Atkinson, 1993) had a significant relationship with L2 writing ability. L1 reading tended to decrease as L2 proficiency increased (Carson et al., 1990).

L1 Education

Slightly more L1 and L2 educational experience was related to lower L1 and L2 writing scores. Younger writers who had less L1 education but had L2 educational experiences were low L1 writers and high L2 writers (Carson & Kuehn, 1992).

Confidence in L1 & L2 Writing

L1 writing ability was related to more confidence in L2 writing, but with some loss of L1 confidence (McCarthey & Garcia, 2005). For multilingual writers who lacked confidence in their L2 skills and might have been hesitant to challenge generic norms in the verbal mode, visuals might have offered an alternative means of expressing one's individuality (Tardy, 2005b).

Transfer

A number of factors were seen as causes of or influences on L1–L2 transfer in L2 writing: culture (Indrasuta, 1988; Zainuddin & Moore, 2003);

L1 background; educational experience (Carson et al., 1990); previous knowledge; metalinguistic awareness (Khalil, 1999); L2 proficiency level; nationality (due to cultural conventions or school training: Wu & Rubin, 2000); and linguistic, conceptual, and organizational differences between L1 and L2 (Ghrib-Maamaouri, 2001). Other factors were seen as not contributing to transfer: individuality, collectivism, and psychological differences (Wu & Rubin, 2000).

There is research to suggest that differences in L1 and L2 texts could be caused by things other than L1 negative transfer (interference). These included a lack of instruction on organization (Mohan & Lo, 1985), better organizational skills in L2 than in L1, good L2 skills, conscious or unconscious use of dissimilar structures based on a perception about culturally preferred rhetorical patterns or preference for a certain pattern, poor organization, low L2 proficiency, lack of composing experience in L2, cultural conventions, and a lack of ability to organize a coherent text in the L1 (Kubota, 1998).

A number of studies described the transfer of rhetorical qualities. These included rhetorical redundancy (e.g. lexical repetition used for emphasis: Bartelt, 1982, 1983), L1 rhetorical patterns (Achiba & Kuromiya, 1983; H. Kobayashi, 1984; Norment, 1986), text relating and text restating in general statements (H. Kobayashi, 1984), general statements (Leung, 1984), text structure (Choi, 1986, 1988), introduction of additional claims (Choi, 1986), narrative discourse features, appropriateness of language, conventional rhetorical style (Indrasuta, 1988), concern with "saving face" for readers (Zainuddin & Moore, 2003), rhetorical strategies (i.e. parallelism & subordination) (Khalil, 1999), and audience awareness in persuasive tasks (Zainuddin & Moore, 2003). Other studies suggested areas of no or little transfer. These included rhetorical structure, discourse-level phenomena (Stalker & Stalker, 1989), and L1-specific patterns (Kubota, 1998).

A number of studies described the transfer of linguistic features and processes. These included L1 linguistic patterns (Achiba & Kuromiya, 1983), writing errors (Cronnel, 1985), orthography (resulting in L2 spelling errors), L1 rules (Janopoulous, 1986), appropriateness of language (Indrasuta, 1988), grammar errors (inappropriate verb forms, articles, noun forms, and prepositions), hypercorrection, overgeneralization of grammar rules, mechanical problems (minor role), use of coordinators (Hinkel, 2001), and spelling errors (Ghrib-Maamaouri, 2001).

A number of studies described transfer of skills and processes. These included L1 writing skill, the quality, though not the quantity, of planning (Jones & Tetroe, 1987), discourse competence, lack of language aptitude, and composing competence (Hirose & Sasaki, 1994).

Psychological and Social Variables

Motivation

Motivation was greater for L2 writers born and schooled in the US, with regard to trying harder and participating in school-related discussion with teachers. Motivation for L2 writers born and schooled outside the US was associated with the advantage of initial education in the L1 rather than with purely linguistic considerations (Ferris & Politzer, 1981).

Among L2 writers, some exhibited intrinsic motivation, and others appeared to be extrinsically motivated. L2 writers exhibited three types of intrinsic motivation:

1 intrinsic knowledge motivation: pleasure in satisfying intellectual curiosity and expanding one's knowledge;
2 intrinsic accomplishment orientation: pleasure in the process of meeting a challenge and surpassing oneself;
3 intrinsic stimulation: enjoyment of the aesthetics of the experience, or the appeal of something rather more elusive.

Intrinsically motivated L2 writers showed signs of identified regulation (valuing an activity as an important goal for the self). L2 writers with extrinsic motivation were less uniform and less stable in their characteristics than intrinsically motivated L2 writers. Both intrinsically and extrinsically motivated L2 writers exhibited numerous self-efficacy characteristics: mastery experience (sense of self-efficacy coming from experience in surmounting obstacles, not from easy success), social modeling (observing others like oneself succeed at various tasks), social persuasion (which relies more on expert coaches), and stress management (Belcher & Hirvela, 2005).

Apprehension

More writing apprehension was felt by less skilled L2 writers than by more skilled writers and graduate students (Betancourt & Phinney, 1988; Skibniewski & Skibniewska, 1986). Apprehension's sources were different for different groups and for different levels of writing experience. More apprehension occurred in L1 rather than in L2. Apprehension decreased as bilingual writing experience increased (Betancourt & Phinney, 1988). Higher writing apprehension correlated with lower quality of writing (Skibniewski & Skibniewska, 1986). Writing apprehension and writer's block were interrelated; however, neither L2 writer's block nor writing apprehension was associated with writing performance (S.-Y. Lee, 2005).

Free reading was found to significantly and negatively predict writing apprehension and writer's block; that is, more free reading was related to less apprehension about writing. Free voluntary reading helped reduce writer's block in a second or foreign language and was found to be a predictor of writing performance. It was not the case that, the more free writing one did, the less writing apprehension and writer's block one would experience. It was also not the case that L2 writers who had more faith in reading and writing instruction would score higher in writing performance and show less blocking and apprehension (S. -Y. Lee, 2005).

Emotion

In one study, L2 writers were asked to write in response to two topics: one believed to elicit an emotional paper; the other a non-emotional paper. In the emotional paper, students spent more time on lexicomorphosyntactic issues while writing because they may have felt compelled to faithfully represent their intended meaning. When planning the emotional paper, students spent less time on global-level considerations because they were more concerned with the semantic value of specific lexical units and associated linguistic structures, thus reducing memory space available for more global discourse planning. When revising the emotional paper, students spent more time on pragmatic- and textual-level processing because they were more concerned about whether the *whole* text delivered their intended ideas. In the non-emotional paper, revisions were mostly microstructural changes which did not alter the gist of the text. The emotional topic did not prompt students to attend to global issues to the same extent that they did on the non-emotional topic (Clachar, 1999).

Learning Style

With regard to personality type, as measured by the Myer–Briggs Type Indicator (MBTI), L2 writers were not like traditional college age L1 writers. The L2 writers were very homogeneous: 8 of the 16 personality types were not represented at all, and over half of L2 writers were Introversion/Sensing/Thinking/Judging (ISTJ) or Extroversion/Sensing/Thinking/Judging (ESTJ). L2 writers who scored higher on the Thinking scale had higher holistic ratings, wrote more, and wrote with greater syntactic complexity. The opposite was true for those with higher scores on the Feeling scale. L2 writers who scored higher on the Intuition scale wrote with more lexical diversity; L2 writers who scored higher on the Sensing scale exhibited less. L2 writers who scored higher on the Judging scale had greater syntactic complexity than those who scored higher on the Perceiving scale (Carrell & Monroe, 1993).

Identity

L2 writers presented academic-oriented and non-academic-oriented identities; correspondingly, their goals were seen as academic (achieving an academic career, either as a lecturer or as a researcher), professional (non-academic environment), and personal (individualistic). Within an

EFL environment, the L2 writers' identities and goals appeared to impact the nature of their networks, which in turn influenced each student's L2 advanced academic literacy acquisition. Academic-oriented social networks were reported to reinforce the social and cultural features of advanced academic literacy, whereas the non-academic-oriented social networks were reported to emphasize general literacy practices (Ferenz, 2005).

Metaknowledge

In one study, metaknowledge of L2 expository prose (e.g. of topic sentences) did not significantly contribute to explaining L2 composition total scores (Hirose & Sasaki, 1994). But in another, metaknowledge test scores had positive significant correlations with L2 composition total score. And metaknowledge test scores, L2 proficiency level, and L2 composition total score each significantly explained the English composition total score. Metaknowledge of L2 expository writing influenced the quality of L2 writing (Sasaki & Hirose, 1996).

Extroversion/Introversion

Extrovert L2 writers were more ambitious, wrote and researched independently, and took professors' feedback seriously. Introverts tended to be satisfied with B grades, preferred group work, and were indifferent to feedback (Angelova & Riazantseva, 1999).

Field Dependence/Independence

Field-independent L2 writers were more ambitious, wrote and researched independently, and took professors' feedback seriously (Angelova & Riazantseva, 1999); field-dependent L2 writers tended to be satisfied with B grades, preferred group work, and were indifferent to feedback (Angelova & Riazantseva, 1999).

Collectivism/Individualism

Whereas collectivist features (e.g. indirectness) were more often observed in the L2 writers' texts than in those of the L1 writers, collectivism exerted no significant effect on usage of any of the textual features examined (e.g. collective virtue passages, humaneness passages, thesis statements, anecdotes, proverbs, hedges, first person pronouns; Wu & Rubin, 2000).

Political Background

L2 writers' political background (influenced by previous experience with potential reprisals in home countries) caused a general reluctance to criticize openly or to take sides in writing (Angelova & Riazantseva, 1999).

Assertiveness

Assertiveness (a lack of hedge words) was not significantly related to differences in directness, first person singular pronouns, or proverbs/canonical expressions (Wu & Rubin, 2000).

Demographics

Grade Level

In two studies of L2 writers in forms three, five and seven (grades nine, eleven, and thirteen), grade level was related to increased syntactic complexity (Yau & Belanger, 1984, 1985). Higher grade level was associated with increases in overall essay length, T-unit length, clause length, number of clauses per T-unit, number of nominals, and number of adverbials per 100 T-units. Higher grade level was not associated with an increase in number of coordinations per 100 T-units (Yau & Belanger, 1985).

In a study of L2 writers in grades three and six, roughly one-fourth of the errors made by third graders were considered to be influenced by L1 usage; roughly one-third of the errors made by sixth graders were considered to have possible L1 influences (Cronnel, 1985).

In a study of fourth and sixth grade L2 writers, grade level correlated significantly and positively with rhetorical effectiveness, overall quality, syntactic maturity, and productivity. Grade level did not correlate significantly with error frequency. Sixth graders generally wrote longer, better, and more complex papers than fourth graders (Carlisle, 1989).

In a study of Deaf and Hearing fourth and sixth grade L2 writers, grade level was not associated with Hearing students' use of significantly more conjunctions than Deaf students. Between grades four and eight, Hearing students increased the use of some categories of cohesion while they decreased in others but did not use a greater variety of ties. By eighth grade, the Deaf students' weak use of cohesive devices evident in fourth graders appeared to have improved considerably (Maxwell & Falick, 1992).

In a study of fifth through eighth grade L2 and L1 writers, regularity markers (*and, then, when, in*), which express a relation between events but do not impose any notion of agency, and are typical of oral speech, were more frequent than power markers (*because, so, therefore, thus, by, through, with, thus*), which do recognize agency and have been associated with written informational genres, for both L1 and L2 writers across both topics and all grade levels. There was no evidence of transition away from regularity markers toward power markers for either L1 or L2 writers. There was evidence, however, that the two groups responded to the topic variable in different ways: L2 writers showed little differentiation between two topics, but L1 language arts students used a more oral pattern on one topic and a more written pattern on another (Reynolds, 2002).

SL vs. FL

In a longitudinal study, both FL and SL writers improved their L2 writing in the long term; increased quantity and speed of L2 writing; increased their use of strategies until their junior year, and then dropped; paid more attention to rhetorical refining (consideration of audience needs); and thought about audience-effective writing after, but not while, writing (Sasaki, 2004).

FL writers used fewer strategies and cited limited opportunities to write long English texts as the reason for their lack of improvement on composition scores. FL writers who continued to rely on translation cited a need for better expressions and limited vocabulary; had explained their decrease in prewriting planning by limited opportunities to practice English writing; and were not concerned with producing better content (Sasaki, 2004).

SL writers used more strategies; decreased their use of translation; slipped back into local planning strategies (owing to tight deadlines in L2-context schools preventing planning of every possible detail); did less translation on account of their overseas experiences and intensive study; showed a decrease in prewriting planning because they had become experienced and comfortable in writing; and were concerned with producing better content (Sasaki, 2004).

Educational Level

Educational level seemed not to be a valid indicator of L2 reading and writing differences (Carrell & Connor, 1991), and educational level did not correlate with development of L2 writing proficiency. For writers with no formal L2 education who had been in the L2 context using academic L2 less than 6 months, there was a small negative correlation between L1 and L2 writing; however, for students who had L2 education and had been in the L2 context more than 6 months, there was a moderate positive correlation between L1 and L2 writing. Comparing students with high L1 and L2 writing scores with students who had low L1 and L2 scores, the low L1 and L2 writers had slightly more L1 and L2 educational experience. High L1 writers who were low L2 writers were older and had a lower L2 educational level, despite their comparatively long time in the L2 context. Low L1 writers who were high L2 writers were younger and had less L1 education, but had L2 educational experiences (Carson & Kuehn, 1992).

L2 Instruction Starting Age

Early starter (ES) and late starter (LS) groups of L2 writers showed development in fluency, accuracy, and complexity, but this development did not take place at the same rate or uniformly. For both ES and LS L2 writers, fluency developed faster and achieved higher levels than complexity or accuracy. There was significant improvement in lexical complexity for both groups, and in both groups age was a decisive factor in the greater use of syntactic patterns (e.g. coordination, subordination; Torras & Celaya, 2001).

In the ES group, development was more pronounced in accuracy than in fluency, but complexity was the area that seemed to develop least, and the ES group made extensive use of memorized sequences or patterns in their writing, aiding fluency and accuracy scores. The LS group developed more rapidly than the ES group in terms of complexity; produced longer, more varied sentences, thus favoring fluency over accuracy; and did better than the ES group in rate and level of attainment (Torras & Celaya, 2001).

Graduate vs. Undergraduate

Graduate L2 writers, who were more accurate than undergraduate L2 writers, edited all the time as a habit, so that editing became recursive, occurring throughout the writing process; undergraduate L2 writers, who were less accurate, often did not edit their papers at all or were overwhelmed by the amount of editing that had to be done on a final draft. Graduate L2 writers continually worked to develop their linguistic competence in English and showed an awareness of what they considered their biggest grammar problems; undergraduate writers were often unaware of the types of errors they were producing. Graduate L2 writers were more aware of grammatical patterns at the discourse level, not just at the sentence level; undergraduate L2 writers edited far more locally than did the graduate L2 writers (Shih, 1998).

Time in L2 Context

The length of time in the L2 context correlated with the level of L2 education achieved; did not correlate with the development of L2 writing proficiency; (for students with no formal L2 education who had been in academic English less than 6 months) was related to a small negative correlation between L1 and L2 writing; and (for students who had had L2 education and had been in the US more than 6 months) was related to a moderate positive correlation between L1 and L2 writing. And, despite their comparatively long time in the L2 context, high L1 writers who were low L2 writers were older and had lower L2 educational levels (Carson & Kuehn, 1992).

Age

Age was related to increases in syntactic complexity (Yau & Belanger, 1984); positively correlated with length of time in the US; negatively related to development of L2 writing; and was unrelated to the development of academic writing skills in L1. Older writers with lower L2 educational levels were high L1 writers and low L2 writers, despite their comparatively long time in the US. Younger writers with less L1 education but more L2 educational experience were low L1 writers and high L2 writers (Carson & Kuehn, 1992).

Grade of Entry

Grade of entry into the school system, number of years in the L2 context, and age of arrival in the L2 context had the lowest correlation with organization (out of accuracy, fluency, organization, and coherence). Grade of entry was not a better predictor of writing performance than age on arrival. Early entry may have provided a significant advantage in L2 writing (Tarone et al., 1993).

L2 Writing Experience

L2 writing experience was related to better writing ability and stronger language skills, higher writing scores (Kubota, 1998), and increased revising ability (H. Kobayashi & Rinnert, 2001; Takagaki, 2003); a lack of L2 English writing experience was related to low writing scores and/or English proficiency and to a focus on sentence-level translation rather than to a focus on expressive or rhetorical differences (Kubota, 1998).

L1 Education

Neither amount of L1 writing in high school nor previous formal instruction in L1 or L2 class differentiated more and less skilled L2 writers. More skilled L2 writers regularly practiced L2 free composition beyond the paragraph level and writing summaries of paragraphs on materials read and regularly wrote more than one paragraph in a L2 (Hirose & Sasaki, 1994).

L1 Background

L1 background was related to the amount and pattern of transfer in L2 writing. Of two groups of L2 writers with different first language backgrounds, both showed significant relationships between L1 reading and L2 writing. However, only one group showed significant correlations between L1 writing and L2 writing and a strong correlation between L2 reading and writing abilities (Carson et al., 1990).

Discussion

There were clear differences in terms of the number of findings among the five major categories of writer characteristics. L2 variables had the most (51%) (with L2 writing ability, L2 proficiency, and L2 writing development the three largest subcategories), followed by demographic variables (15%), transfer (12%), psychological and sociological variables (11%), and L1 variables (11%). It is assumed that more findings in a particular area may reflect greater depth in the research in that area.

There were also clear differences in terms of number of subcategories per major category of writer characteristics. Demographic and psychological and sociological variables had the most categories (26% each), followed by L1 variables (21%), L2 variables (17%), and transfer (10%). It is assumed that more subcategories of a particular category may reflect greater breadth in the research in that category.

Only a small fraction of the individual findings reported here were supported by more than one study. Only fifteen findings (4% of all findings) were supported by evidence from two studies, and only seven (2%) were supported by evidence from three studies. All the other individual findings here were supported by only one study.

The foregoing suggests the inquiry into L2 writer characteristics has had few sustained programs of research. There are, however, some notable exceptions, for example Carson and her colleagues (e.g. Carson & Kuehn, 1992; Carson et al., 1992) and Sasaki and Hirose (e.g. Hirose, 2003; Hirose & Sasaki, 1994; Sasaki, 2000, 2004; Sasaki & Hirose, 1996).

Composing Processes

Introduction

The focus of this chapter is second language composing process variables. These variables include revision, planning, general composing processes, formulation, translation, restructuring, dictionary use, audience and purpose, editing, linearization/verbalization, monitor use, first language use, text generation, backtracking, fluency/pausing, thinking, topics and prompts, problem solving, idea generation, processing, rereading, metacognitive strategies, goal setting, organizing, and drawing. The organizing principle for the ordering of these categories is most to least findings. The order of presentation of these categories and their subcategories is indicated in the chapter outline below.

Chapter 12 Outline

Revision
    Writer
        Writer perception
        Instruction
        L2 proficiency
        More skilled vs. less skilled
        Audience
        Development
        Writing experience
    Process
        Strategy
        Levels of processing
        Errors
        Cognition
        When in the process
        First and second revisions
        More revision
        Concern/purpose of revision

Text
    Types/levels of changes
    Lexical issues
    Drafts
    Cognition
Planning
    L2 proficiency
    Planning in L1/L2
    Global/local
    Skill level
    Language
    Goals
General composing processes
    L1 vs. L2
    Writing patterns
    Strategies
    Difficulty
    L2 proficiency
Formulation
Translation
    Translation task vs. writing task
    ESL/EFL
    More/less skilled
    General
Restructuring
Dictionary use
Audience and purpose
Editing
Linearization/verbalization
Monitor use
L1 use
Text generation
Backtracking
Fluency/pausing
Thinking
Topics/prompts
Problem solving
Idea generation
Processing
Rereading
Metacognitive strategies
Goal setting
Organizing
Drawing

Findings

Revision

Writer

WRITER PERCEPTION

L2 writers perceived the revision process as an activity that affected surface aspects of their texts (Porte, 1997): checking for errors (Lai, 1986) and proofreading (Porte, 1997). They felt that they should revise until the final draft had no mistakes in form (Parkhurst, 1990). They also perceived that evaluation by teachers inhibited the kind of revisions made (Porte, 1997). Their perceptions about their revising activities were very different from their concerns about their writing as a whole (Yasuda, 2004), and their revising intentions were similar across languages (Takagaki, 2003).

L2 writers' saw vocabulary as the main tool of revision and felt that revision was important because it was conducive to the improvement of the final grade awarded to their texts—that their teachers would rank range of vocabulary higher than the content (Porte, 1997).

INSTRUCTION

Few L2 writers recalled any explicit instruction in revision; this professed lack of instruction in revision techniques left many to their own devices concerning how to revise (Porte, 1997). Explicit instruction played an active role in students' essay-level revisions and use of correction strategies (H. Kobayashi & Rinnert, 2001). Past writing instruction seemed to correlate with the quality of writing (Skibniewski & Skibniewska, 1986), and past writing experience was a stronger basis for their revising strategies than proficiency level (Yasuda, 2004). Instructional context seemed to have a positive effect on the participant's approach to revision and use of revision strategies. Teacher focus on form was seen to affect attitude toward revision and use of revision strategies; it might have made L2 writers feel incompetent about their own writing. Written feedback corresponded to more revision and high-level revisions when working on one's own (Sze, 2002).

L2 PROFICIENCY

L2 proficiency was significantly and positively related to all aspects of revision performance except for those at the essay level. L2 proficiency was most strongly related to revision at the intersentential level. Thus, L2 proficiency may be somewhat independent of or separate from essay-level knowledge and concerns that underlie revision skill at this level (H. Kobayashi & Rinnert, 2001). In addition, past writing experience was a stronger basis for revising strategies than proficiency level (Yasuda, 2004).

L2 proficiency did not correspond with the placement of L2 writers in writing courses (Raimes, 1987), and, regardless of proficiency level, L2 writers all used different strategies for "getting into" their topic (Zamel, 1983).

MORE SKILLED VS. LESS SKILLED

More skilled L2 writers rewrote (Skibniewsi & Skibniewska, 1986) and revised (Raimes, 1987) more, revised more extensively (Skibniewsi & Skibniewska, 1986), and did more global revising than did less skilled L2 writers (Skibniewski, 1988). More skilled L2 writers concentrated more on higher-level organizational and structural changes (Skibniewsi & Skibniewska, 1986); less skilled L2 writers made fewer revisions (Skibniewski, 1988) and were more apprehensive about L2 writing than were more skilled L2 writers (Skibniewsi & Skibniewska, 1986).

AUDIENCE

L2 writers' gearing of the message to the intended audience was not done with sufficient thoroughness or effectiveness (Arndt, 1987). Audience addressed in a teacher–learner dialogue context resulted in a slightly higher rate of overall revision; audience addressed in a teacher-as-examiner context resulted in twice as many revisions (Butler-Nalin, 1984).

DEVELOPMENT

Development of L2 revision ability was reflected in more automaticity, more concern with the needs of the reader, more ability to select from alternative wordings (Elliot, 1986), and a greater capacity for critical self-evaluation (Arndt, 1987).

WRITING EXPERIENCE

There was a positive and significant relationship between L2 writing experience and revision performance (H. Kobayashi & Rinnert, 2001).

Process

STRATEGY

In a study of the revision strategies of a reluctant high school L2 writer, this writer did not perceive a need to revise, did no revision at all unless required to do so, did not employ available resources to revise, paid little attention to feedback on grammar because of lack of capability of dealing with error, and did not focus on specific comments on grammar, organization, and content given in the margin. However, feedback from the student's teacher/researcher affected not only the total number of revisions but also the types of revisions made (Sze, 2002). Another study reported the use of different revising strategies at different points in the composing process (some delayed until they finished writing; others revised as they wrote) (A. Wong, 2005).

LEVELS OF PROCESSING

In a study in which students wrote in response to two different topics—one emotional; the other nonemotional—it was reported that pragmatic-level processing rose during revision on the emotional paper, but that lexicomorphosyntactic-level processing rose during revision of the non-emotional paper. Pragmatic and textual level processing got more time during revision in the emotional paper because of a concern for whether the whole text delivered the writer's intended ideas. Microstructural changes, which did not alter the gist of the text, characterized the revisions of the nonemotional text (Clachar, 1999). In another study it was claimed that text production management placed a far greater burden on revision in L2 than in L1 (C. Hall, 1990).

ERRORS

L2 writers were able to detect and correct a good portion of their errors, and they could better detect errors than problems of reader interpretability. Error detection worked better for some errors than for others, and most error correction was done at the word or clause level; text-level problems were often overlooked. And self-correcting of errors facilitated by teacher input improved error detection (Chandrasegaran, 1986).

COGNITION

L2 writers concentrated on cognitively easier operations when making revisions. Cognitively easier operations (addition, deletion, substitution) were the main foci of these writers. L2 writers shifted to cognitively harder operations when given more time and chances to revise (Lai, 1986).

WHEN IN THE PROCESS

Revising was done throughout the writing process (Zamel, 1983). Content was revised early in the process, as opposed to during proofreading, done later (Zamel, 1982). Over half of revisions were made during drafting (C. Hall, 1990). Between-essay changes were more frequent than ongoing ones and included more text reconstructions (Lai, 1986).

FIRST AND SECOND REVISIONS

In L2 first revisions, both lower- and higher-level intentions were used whereas in L2 second revisions there was a greater focus on lower-level revisions. This pattern was also observed in L1 first and second revisions (Takagaki, 2003).

MORE REVISION

One study reported that revisions increased when writing in L2 (Skibniewski & Skibniewska, 1986), and a second claimed that L2 writers had more revising episodes (C. Hall, 1990), but a third reported that revision was more frequent in L1 than in L2 (Takagaki, 2003).

CONCERN/PURPOSE OF REVISION

Finding precise expressions (St. John, 1987) and making more sense (Urzua, 1987) were the purposes of revision and major concerns during revision (St. John, 1987).

Text

TYPES/LEVELS OF CHANGES

Surface changes (formal and meaning-preserving changes) accounted for most L2 revision (Lai, 1986; Sze, 2002); text-based changes accounted for little revision (Lai, 1986). Lexical substitutions were the most common revisions for both L1 and L2. Changes affecting information were the most numerous revisions for both L1 and L2; mechanical and cosmetic changes were the next most numerous (C. Hall, 1990). Lower-level revisions were made by less successful L2 writers (Butler-Nalin, 1984).

Intersentential or paragraph-level revisions were similar in quantity for undergraduates with and without writing instruction. Undergraduate L2 writers with writing instruction outperformed undergraduate L2 writers without writing instruction in terms of essay-level revision. Graduate L2 writers outperformed undergraduate L2 writers without instruction at all three levels (intersentential, paragraph, and essay) of revision, but outperformed undergraduate L2 writers with instruction only at the intersentential level (H. Kobayashi & Rinnert, 2001).

LEXICAL ISSUES

Lexical issues were a major factor in revision for L2 writers. They were seen as an annoyance (Zamel, 1983) and a source of frustration (Kelly, 1986). The word was the predominant syntactic unit students concentrated on (Lai, 1986), and the lexical level was where L2 writers tended to revise (Butler-Nalin, 1984). Word order or choice (St. John, 1987) and word- and phrase-level changes accounted for most revision. Lexical substitutions were the most common revisions at the highest level, for both L1 and L2 writers (C. Hall, 1990).

DRAFTS

There is a developmental tendency of movement for L2 writers from lower- to higher-level revision through successive drafts (Butler-Nalin, 1984). L2 drafts had more revision than L1 drafts (C. Hall, 1990), and successful L2 writers wrote more drafts per assignment than did unsuccessful L2 writers (Butler-Nalin, 1984).

COGNITION

L2 writers focused on cognitively easier operations when making revisions; cognitively more difficult operations occurred when L2 writers were given more time and chances to revise (Lai, 1986).

Planning

L2 Proficiency

L2 writers with higher L2 proficiency using L2 for planning had significantly higher mean scores for plan and composition quality and wrote better plans than did lower-proficiency L2 writers when planning in L1 and in L2 (Akyel, 1994). Lower L2 proficiency reduced the quantity, though not the quality, of planning and affected planning behavior (Jones & Tetroe, 1987). For lower L2 proficiency writers, using L2 for planning had a significant effect on plan detail and quality (Akyel, 1994). Contrary to the claim in Jones & Tetroe (1987), L2 proficiency level affected the quality of plans, regardless of the language used for the plans. Both higher and lower L2 proficiency writers felt that planning in L2 was more helpful than planning in L1 (Akyel, 1994).

Planning in L1/L2

L1 and L2 planning patterns were seen as very similar (Armengol-Castells, 2001; Hirose & Sasaki, 1994), with quality, though not the quantity, of plans transferring from L1 to L2. The level of abstraction of the planning process was similar in L1 and L2 (Jones & Tetroe, 1987). Neither L1 nor L2 planning involved making elaborate initial plans (Kelly, 1986). And it was claimed that rhetorical planning may be a manifestation of linguistic intelligence transcending L1/L2 differences (Sasaki, 2000). L2 planning required more mental capacity than did planning in a first language. Regardless of the similarity of level of abstraction of planning, writers performed less well in their L2 than in their L1 (Jones & Tetroe, 1987).

Global/Local

With regard to local and global planning, expert L2 writers were able to partially adjust their global plans as a result of elaborate but flexible goal setting (Sasaki, 2000), but most planning was local, addressing how the writers would proceed and what they would include in their compositions (Armengol-Castells, 2001). When responding to an emotional topic, writers spent less time on global-level considerations because they were more concerned with the semantic value of specific lexical units and associated linguistic structures, thus reducing memory space available for more global discourse planning (Clachar, 1999).

Skill Level

As opposed to less skilled L2 writers, more skilled L2 writers did more planning overall (Hirose & Sasaki, 1994; Lay, 1983; Raimes, 1987; Skibniewski, 1988; Victori, 1999), had preconceived plans when writing (Skibniewski & Skibniewska, 1986), and did more planning of organization (Hirose & Sasaki, 1994; Sasaki, 2000; Sasaki & Hirose, 1996). More skilled L2 writers did more global planning (Sasaki 2000; Skibniewski, 1988) and were more able to adjust their global plans while writing (Sasaki, 2000). They did more (Skibniewski, 1988), more elaborate, and more flexible goal setting and had the ability to assess the characteristics of a task for successfully achieving their goals (Sasaki, 2000).

Language

In match condition (when the language of writing was the same in which the content was learned), writers' plans were longer, more detailed, and of superior quality (Friedlander, 1990). Another study (not considering match condition) reported that the language of the plan did not make a significant difference in the resulting compositions (Akyel, 1994).

Goals

L2 writers planned in more complex ways when given goals to work with (Jones & Tetroe, 1987).

General Composing Processes

LI vs. L2

ESL writers who were ready to compose, i.e. had reached a threshold level of L2 proficiency, had writing strategies similar to those of L1 writers (Albrechtsen, 1997; Zamel, 1982). A number of studies foregrounded similarities between L1 and L2 composing processes: L1 and L2 writers used similar strategies when writing, rereading, jumping around in text, reevaluating organization, asking questions, and changing vocabulary (Lay, 1983); L2 writing studies reflected the findings of Flower and Hayes' work with L1 writers (Kelly, 1986); writers who were skilled in L1 writing were also skilled in L2 writing (Skibniewski & Skibniewska, 1986); composing strategies were common to both L1 and L2 writers (Raimes, 1987); writers exhibited similar writing methods in their L1 and L2 writing—and this may have been true for L2 writers operating well below the university level (Albrechtsen, 1997); and L1 and L2 literacy in children developed along the same cognitive and social lines (Urzua, 1987).

A number of studies point out similarities and differences between L1 and L2 composing strategies. L2 composing behavior was similar to that of L1 writers in some respects, but language was still a factor that limited performance; advanced L2 writers' needs appeared to be the same needs as those of L1 writers, but there were extra needs: difficulty with language, more at the rhetorical and stylistic level than in sentence grammar (Kelly, 1986). L2 writers used similar composing processes in L1 and L2, but their efficiency in reaching goals differed (Moragne e Silva, 1989).

Writing Patterns

L2 writers exhibited a systematic approach to writing (Victori, 1999). Writing was a means of discovery as well as expression (Zamel, 1983), and the ability to write well depended more on the writers' mastery of rhetorical skills than in which language they composed (Skibniewski & Skibniewska, 1986). Whereas two studies reported that the composing process, the construction of textual meaning, was not linear (Zamel, 1982, 1983), another claimed that (at least scientific) L2 writing was primarily linear (St. John, 1987).

In another study, L2 writers' general writing patterns fell into two categories: a sectional pattern (isolating and allocating attention to specific writing elements for focus and development, similar to knowledge transformers), and a linear pattern (involving uncensored transfer of ideas to paper without consideration of relevance or fit, similar to knowledge tellers; Ferenz, 2005).

Strategies

A broad range of strategies was used in L2 composing, and L2 writers had a common repertoire of composing strategies, including metacognitive, cognitive, and affective strategies; however, they differed in individual strategies, that is, they had different levels of comfort with each strategy (A. Wong, 2005).

Difficulty

One study found that the composing process was difficult for L2 writers (Lay, 1982); L2 writers in another study did not see L2 composing in and of itself to be problematic (Zamel, 1983).

L2 proficiency

L2 proficiency did not appear to visibly affect L2 composing strategies (Raimes, 1987; Cumming, 1989).

Formulation

Data suggest some sequential structure within a fairly autonomous formulating (writing/transcribing, as opposed to planning or revising) process. Tentative formulation in L1 and L2 problem solving was clearly an L2-specific process. The most typical sequence for tentative formulation in L2 was evaluation–acceptance–writing with coarticulation–repair (Zimmerman, 2000).

Simplified tentative formulations had a much higher frequency in L2 writing than in L1 writing. Tentative formulations in L1 preceded those in L2 and were much more frequent than text revisions in L1 as well as in L2 text production. There were more repeated tentative formulations in L2 writing. Tentative formulations were distinct from reflections (Zimmerman, 2000).

The act of repair in writing was placed outside formulating. The mechanical act of writing came between most formulating processes and repair. The reformulating part of repair had the same structure as text formulation. Although it was possible to influence repair by proposing various partitioning strategies, this seemed to be impossible or much more difficult with tentative formulations, owing to their more spontaneous and associative character (Zimmerman, 2000).

Formulation was concentrated more in the central stages of composition as opposed to the beginning and end, regardless of language (first or second) being used. Around 60% of composition time devoted to formulation might have been the minimum, at least for time-compressed tasks. The predominance of formulation over planning and revising across languages confirms the nonoptional nature of this process. Once a threshold of proficiency was reached, writers were more likely to share time between formulation and other processes (Roca et al., 2001).

Percentage of time devoted to formulation was similar across languages. High school students formulated for longer periods of time than university students or recent university graduates, who spent relatively equal amounts of time on formulation. The high school group spent less time on formulation as the task wore on. This group's diminished use of formulation over the task indicates a gradual depletion of ideas (Roca et al., 2001).

In L1 tasks, writers used five times more fluent (unproblematic) formulation procedures than problem-solving ones. In L2 tasks, the ratio dropped to 2:1. The lower ratio of fluent formulation vs. problem-solving formulation in the L2 indicated the difficulty of generating text in an L2. These ratios held across proficiency levels (Roca et al., 2001).

Less skilled L2 writers exhibited a lack of control, using a "what next strategy," whereas more skilled L2 writers generally knew what they wanted to do and how to do it, shifting between a well-formed plan and local, specific decisions (Cumming, 1989).

Translation

Translation Task vs. Writing Task

In a translation task, most L2 writers did not operate at a sentence-by-sentence level, and instances of restructuring beyond the sentence level were frequent. L2 writers were freed from the cognitive activities of generating and organizing ideas and were able to concentrate on linguistic activities. L2 writers generally regarded both translation and L2 writing tasks as helpful for learning and improving L2 writing (Uzawa, 1994).

In L2 writing tasks, metacognitive-level attention—particularly to content—was relatively high, but was very low in a translation task. Linguistic-level attention was very high in translation and very low in writing tasks (Uzawa, 1996). With regard to L2 high-level goals, scores on L1 and L2 writing tasks were similar, but translation scores were significantly better. English expressions in translation were more vivid than in L2 essays. Participants found the translation exercise to be more helpful than essay writing because they were forced to use words and expressions slightly beyond their current levels (Uzawa, 1996).

ESL/EFL

Comparing ESL and EFL writers, ESL writers did less translation because of their overseas experiences and intensive study, and those ESL writers who slipped back into local planning strategies attributed this to their time abroad—tight deadlines in U.S. schools preventing planning of every possible detail. EFL writers who continued to rely on translation cited limited vocabulary and a need for better expressions (Sasaki, 2004).

More/Less Skilled

Less skilled L2 writers often stopped to translate their generated ideas into English; more skilled L2 writers often stopped to refine English expression. L2 proficiency or lack of it appeared to explain part of the difference in strategies and in fluency—less skilled writers still had to stop often to translate and were forced to think on smaller, local scales (Sasaki, 2000).

General

There was evidence that some students would write an entire paper in L1 and then translate this directly into the L2 (Gosden, 1996; Zamel, 1982), using a phrase-by-phrase translation strategy (Gosden, 1996). Translating directly from L1 disrupted thought processes because some low-level skills were not fully automatic in the L2 (Moragne e Silva, 1989). In one study, L2 writers translated L2 into L1 in the process of sentence construction (McCarthey et al. 2005).

Restructuring

Restructuring was a complex phenomenon that served different purposes in the complex and multilevel nature of L2 composing. Ideational restructuring (change in meaning) was used by L2 writers for message abandonment, message elaboration, and message reconceptualization. Textual restructuring (change beyond the clausal level) was used for manipulation of coherence/cohesion, stylistic concerns, obeying register requirements, and textual structuring of information. Linguistic restructuring (compensating for lack of L2 linguistic resources or the instability of interlanguage knowledge) was used on lexical problems, morphosyntactic problems, and markedness (marking connections between clauses). Linguistic processing in L2 writing inhibited the formulation of syntactic alternatives at both the ideational and textual levels and constrained the number of upper-level restructuring episodes, but not their quality or variety. Concern with producing alternative syntactic structures remained more or less constant when either proficiency decreased or when writers composed in L2 (Roca et al., 1999).

L2 writers were capable of restructuring their discourse while simultaneously constructing and retaining a global representation of the text. The ability to restructure, irrespective of purpose, was not impeded by a lack of L2 ability. However, there was evidence of a possible threshold level of L2 competence as a necessary condition for writing ability to be fully deployed in L2 (Roca et al., 1999).

Writers with greater L2 proficiency (advanced) were more (but not significantly more) concerned with the production of syntactic alternatives. These writers devoted more than twice as much time as intermediates to elaboration of ideas, theme–rheme orderings, and structuring of information. Writers with less L2 proficiency (intermediates) exhibited only small, nonsignificant differences between the amount of restructuring time in L1 and L2 compositions. These writers devoted seven times as much time as the advanced group to restructuring discourse for compensatory purposes. Whereas the intermediate group's restructuring time remained balanced for both upgrading of meaning and compensating for lack of linguistic resources, the imbalance of purposes on the part of the advanced group was quite conspicuous, global concerns being far more dominant (Roca et al., 1999).

Dictionary Use

More successful or more advanced language learners did not necessarily use dictionaries more effectively than less successful or less advanced language learners did (Christianson, 1997). Frequent use of dictionaries in L2 writing resulted in more time on written planning and the writing process in general and increased the number of stops during the writing process (Skibniewski & Skibniewska, 1986). However, the use of a dictionary did not have any major effect on the quality of the composing process (H. Kobayashi & Rinnert, 1992). Furthermore, one dictionary-use strategy did not suffice for all users in all situations. That is, for some students, their strategies were successful; for others, the same strategies were not (Christianson, 1997).

In one study, it was reported that, although the use of bilingual dictionaries could lead to errors of certain types (generally, inappropriate lexical choice from a selection provided in the dictionary, but also including incorrect forms of those choices), it was not shown that the use of a bilingual dictionary led to errors where no errors would otherwise occur (H. Kobayashi & Rinnert, 1992).

In another study, it was reported that dictionary use did not provoke errors and that it had not been shown that skillful dictionary use could help writers avoid a certain percentage of errors or suggest which type of errors could have been avoided. Only a tiny fraction of words were looked up in a dictionary (1.6% of the total corpus); 42% of those words were used incorrectly. However, students who read the example sentences and related them to the writing task at hand made fewer mistakes. Overall, accurate production relied more on the sophistication of the user than on that of the dictionary (Christianson, 1997).

Audience and Purpose

L2 writers showed varying degrees of awareness of audience (Kelly, 1986). Differences in audience awareness were related to the writers' ability to construct an image of their audience's potential traits (Zainuddin & Moore, 2003). Skilled writers had better audience awareness than unskilled writers (Skibniewski & Skibniewska, 1986) and made more reference to audience, in terms of modifying their content and presenting stronger or weaker opinions (Victori, 1999). Less skilled bilingual writers exhibited a lack of attention to audience, which could be linked to previous L1 training and experience—mainly for classes and exams. Exposure to different types of writing for varieties of audiences was more influential than similar educational or cultural background with regard to level of writing skill (Zainuddin & Moore, 2003).

L2 writing showed diverse mental representations of audience and rhetorical purpose. Perception of audience determined purpose of text. These variables had an impact on the composing strategies used (e.g. taking fewer risks when writing for the teacher; taking more risks when writing for self). When the audience was the teacher, the rhetorical purpose was to relate the writer's experience to the teacher; strategies had a narrow range and were less frequent and less recursive. The main goal was to get it right the first time. When the audience was the teacher as coach, the rhetorical purpose was to try out ideas for feedback; strategies involved a large number of revisions. When the audience was other students, the rhetorical purpose was to enable the writers to learn more; strategies involving planning and rhetorical goals were important. When the audience was the self, the rhetorical purpose was reflection; there was a broad range of composing strategies and more recursion (A. Wong, 2005).

Editing

One study reported that more skilled writers were less concerned with surface features of their texts at the outset, leaving them to the end of the composing process; they seemed to have developed many strategies that allowed them to pursue their communicative goals without being sidetracked by formal issues (Zamel, 1983).

However, other studies claimed that more skilled L2 writers were consistently involved in more editing than were the less skilled (Raimes, 1987) and edited all the time as a habit, so that editing became recursive, occurring throughout the writing process. They were able to edit more carefully from the start of the writing process, not waiting until the final draft to concentrate on editing (Shih, 1998). Less skilled L2 writers were distracted by local problems from the very beginning, were bogged down in error avoidance (Zamel, 1983), and edited far more locally (Shih, 1998).

Improvements were made when L2 writers began to see editing as a different kind of reading process from normal reading, using a different focus for each reading cycle. Editing also improved when writers approached the editing task more slowly, taking apart longer sentences or reviewing texts for specific usages they had practiced in the past (Shih, 1998). Also, L2 writers edited far less than they revised and edited at different points in the writing process (A. Wong, 2005).

Linearization/Verbalization

Different operations might be triggered that vary according to the knowledge and executive control procedures of the L2 writer. These operations could be divided into two main sets: backward operations, basically repetition (serving as a retention mechanism) and rereading (as a generative power), and forward operations, which comprised a number of problem-solving behaviors (Roca, 1996).

Verbalization of the text written down provided information about whether the linearization process occurred smoothly and fluently or was interrupted by problems and/or backward movements. Verbalizations above and beyond the written text were the aspects of writing the L2 writer was supposed to be attending to while facing the problem; these included language use, discourse organization, gist, intention, and procedures for writing (Roca, 1996).

Writing problems were approached in several different ways: problem identification, no search or compensatory action needed; problem identification, search or compensatory action needed but not accomplished; problem identification, search or compensatory action needed and accomplished. Heuristics, such as generating and assessing alternatives, translating, assessing in relation to a rule or reasoning about linguistic choices, and setting or resetting a goal, were also used (Roca, 1996).

L2 writers, when facing the task of putting ideas in linear form, had different possibilities: producing a stretch of text more or less automatically or getting into trouble (Roca, 1996).

Monitor Use

Heavy use of the monitor taxed the short-term memory of the user, effectively limiting production to small chunks, and overuse of monitoring did not lead to improved writing (Jones, 1985).

Overuse involved pausing more frequently and for much longer periods of time, writing fewer words between pauses, monitoring writing during pauses, making far fewer changes to the text once it was written down, writing in much shorter chunks—suggesting that the main composing unit was no more than a phrase—taking more time, and making writing less satisfying (Jones, 1985).

Underuse involved pausing less frequently and for shorter periods of time, writing more words between pauses, searching for an appropriate lexical item during pauses, making more changes to the text once it was written down, not developing a flow, writing in much longer chunks—suggesting that the main composing unit was more than a phrase—not monitoring during the formulation of the text but checking the text only after it began to appear on the page, taking less time, and making writing less satisfying (Jones, 1985).

Both overuse and underuse resulted in a similar number of errors (Jones, 1985).

LI Use

L1 use/dependency in L2 writing declined with the development of the writers' L2 proficiency, L2 writing experience, and L2 writing skill level. The L2 writing process was a bilingual event. The L1 was used overwhelmingly in the L2 composing processes and was more likely to occur in process-controlling, idea-generating, and idea-organizing activities than in text-generating activities. The amount of L1 use was not related to the difficulty level of the composing activity (Wang & Wen, 2002).

Language-switching in thinking processes underlying L2 composing might be caused by factors related to high-level knowledge demands; those factors included an implicit need to encode a nonlinguistic thought in the L1 to initiate a thinking episode, a need to facilitate the development of a thought, a need to verify lexical choices, and a need to avoid overloading the working memory. Conceptual knowledge was shared across L1 and L2 and might be tied to a shared rather than a separate store in a bilingual's memory. Language-switching facilitated rather than inhibited L2 composing processes (Qi, 1998).

L1 use was greater in more demanding writing tasks (Qi, 1998) and in narrative writing (as opposed to argumentative writing), though this might have been because of differences in writing prompts (Wang & Wen, 2002).

Text Generation

More skilled writers focused on global text-level production; less skilled writers focused on vocabulary and grammatical issues (Victori, 1999). The mean number of words produced was just about the same for more and less skilled writers (Raimes, 1987).

Differences in fluency are associated with length of burst (language-generating segments terminated by pauses or revisions) and with measures of revision performance. Increased linguistic experience was associated with an increase in fluency, an increase in burst length, a decrease in the frequency of revision, and an increase in the number of words that are accepted and written down (Chenoweth & Hayes, 2001).

The act of writing generated ideas, both in the sense of creating ideas and in the sense of creating the language to express those ideas (Kelly, 1986). Text-generating strategies were consistent across languages. Writers relied on internal resources for generating content. Writing, rehearsing, reading, repeating, and, sometimes, pausing alternated while dealing with text transcription. As for text-generating strategies, reading and repeating while rehearsing helped writers construct their meaning and shape their texts. They relied on written text for text generating, rather than on orally verbalized ideas (Armengol-Castells, 2001) and asked and then answered their own questions for the purposes of generating text (A. Wong, 2005).

Backtracking

Language used to backtrack (taking stock of ideas and constraints in the text produced so far) did not seem to be dependent on degree of writing expertise. Below a threshold level of L1 use in the composing process, writers tended to backtrack using the L1; above a threshold level, there must have been another variable at work that explains L2 writers' backtracking behavior. The independent variable needed to explain the differences in individual backtracking behavior was dominant language in the composing process (Manchón, Roca, & Murphy, 2000).

Backtracking through the L1 and backtracking through the L2 are distinct operations. L2 backtracking involved rereading the prompt, rereading notes, and rereading already written text; L1 backtracking involved direct translation, translation with omissions, and paraphrasing. Direct translation was the type of L1 backtracking used most frequently. Writers showed distinct behavior in terms of how often they reread their texts (Manchón et al., 2000).

Writers used backtracking in the L2 more in narrative tasks than in the argumentative essays. Writers maintained their percentage of use of L2 backtracking and their choice of backtracking in L1 or L2 across tasks (Manchón et al., 2000).

Fluency/Pausing

More skilled L2 writers wrote longer texts with more complex development at greater speed than did less skilled L2 writers, and L2 proficiency or lack of it explained part of the difference in fluency (Sasaki, 2000). Quantity and speed of writing increased slowly over time (Sasaki, 2004).

Increased experience with the L2 was associated with increased fluency in writing that language, and increased linguistic experience was associated with an increase in burst length, a decrease in the frequency of revision, and an increase in the number of words that were accepted and written down (Chenoweth & Hayes, 2001).

There was an increase in the number of pauses when writing in L2 (Skibniewski & Skibniewska, 1986). More skilled L2 writers composed sentences without much pausing (Hirose & Sasaki, 1994), and their most productive pauses tended to be longer ones (Bosher, 1998). Writers paused at intervals during the composing process, and some stopped for lengthy periods and were silent (Kelly, 1986). Frequent use of dictionaries when writing in L2 was related to a greater number of stops during the writing process (Skibniewski & Skibniewska, 1986).

Thinking

Writing expertise was significantly related to episodes of combined ideational and linguistic thinking. Thirty percent of all the writers' time was devoted to thinking about gist (meanings and ideas) and language concurrently; proficient writers devoted 60% of their time to combined linguistic and gist-related thinking (Cumming, 1990b).

The most conspicuous activity was the search for the right phrase, followed by comparisons of cross-linguistic equivalents, then reasoning about their linguistic choices. There were five common features in the decision-making episodes of the writers: their thinking was often meta-linguistic and ideational at the same time, it was categorically focused (attention was constrained by syntactic or other information), the behavior was very productive, it was negotiatory, and it led to a consolidation of knowledge (Cumming, 1990b).

Thinking in a language was a real phenomenon, not a figure of speech. Students said they thought in the L2. The reasons were that they had learned the material in English and that they needed English to discuss the topic with others (Shaw, 1991).

Topics/Prompts

L2 (child) writers were most able to develop a distinctive voice in writing when they were allowed to choose the topic (Urzua, 1987). Writers liked topic-related classroom discussions to help them generate ideas before writing, and mentioned strategies for idea generation when the topic was unfamiliar, e.g. having an internal conversation about the topic (Zamel, 1982). Certain topics generated more L1/L2 switching (Lay, 1983). An emotional topic did not prompt writers to attend to global issues to the same extent that they did on a nonemotional topic. Thus there was risk involved in applying fixed definitions of competency to the entire range of writing strategies with respect to topics of emotion (Clachar, 1999).

There was more referring back to the prompt in the L1 than in the L2, which may reflect a stronger long-term memory in the L1 (Moragne e Silva, 1989). Many differences between the protocols were likely due to the difference between the writing prompts (Albrechtsen, 1997).

Problem Solving

L2 writers with high levels of literate expertise generally used higher-order thinking to resolve problems, whereas those with lower levels of expertise tended to focus more at the verbatim levels, rarely trying to construct an overall situational representation of the passages. Educated adults tended to use equivalent problem-solving strategies while performing challenging reading and writing tasks in their L1 and L2. The frequency and qualities of these strategies related closely to the literate expertise the individual had developed (Cumming, Rebuffot, & Ledwell, 1989). There was a vast difference in the proportions of problem-solving behaviors for basic, average, and professional L2 writers (Cumming, 1989).

The use of problem-solving strategies was highly consistent across L1 and L2 performances and between reading and writing in both languages (Cumming et al., 1989). Rhetorical problems were identified and solved in both languages (Moragne e Silva, 1989).

Idea Generation

Skilled writers typically did global rereadings, which acted as a springboard for generating ideas (Victori, 1999). Less skilled writers mostly generated ideas in the L1 first and translated them into the L2 (Hirose & Sasaki, 1994).

The act of writing generated ideas, both in the sense of creating ideas and in the sense of creating the language to express those ideas (Skibniewski & Skibniewska, 1986). L1 writing generated ideas (which later turned into text) in response to problems established throughout the process. L2 writing involved a lot of oral generating (mostly for content clarification), but little of the material generated made it into text (Moragne e Silva, 1989). Topic-related classroom discussion helped students generate ideas before writing. For unfamiliar topics, the strategy of internal conversation about the topic aided idea generation (Zamel, 1982). Reading aloud also facilitated the generation of ideas (Albrechtsen, 1997).

Processing

There were greater occurrences of lower-level processing for an emotional topic than for a nonemotional one. For the emotional topic, lexico-morphosyntactic-level processing accounted for 56% of all procedures, whereas textual-level processing accounted for 33%, and pragmatic-level processing 11%. For the nonemotional topic, lexicomorphosyntactic-level processing accounted for only 42%, whereas textual-level processing accounted for 39% and pragmatic-level processing 19% (Clachar, 1999).

During revision, pragmatic-level processing rose from 11% to 27% on the emotional papers; for the nonemotional topic, lexicomorphosyntactic-level processing rose from 42% to 69%. During revision of the emotional paper, students spent more time on pragmatic- and textual-level processing because they were more concerned about whether the whole text delivered their intended ideas; revisions of the nonemotional text were mostly microstructural changes which did not alter the gist of the text (Clachar, 1999).

Rereading

More skilled writers reconsidered units of text, from a sentence or two to whole paragraphs, that transcended sentence boundaries (Zamel, 1983); rereading was a key part of the skilled writers' processes (Raimes, 1987; Skibniewski, 1988). Less skilled writers typically did global rereadings, which served as a springboard for generating ideas or as a form of proofreading (Victori, 1999).

Writers reread their already written work in order to determine how well it was integrated with later ideation and how well or clearly it represented their intentions. Rereading was especially helpful for writers who became stuck—an essential part of the process of making and evaluating the expression of meaning (especially with regard to the assessment of clarity and reader accessibility) and an important part of error correction (Zamel, 1983).

Metacognitive Strategies

More and less skilled writers used basically the same metacognitive strategies; the difference was that less skilled writers assessed task demands differently, and therefore used different approaches to tackle the writing task. More skilled writers were distinguished by their use of schematic links; the less skilled writers assumed that the reader knew what was going on in their minds. More skilled writers' were less concerned with surface features than were the less skilled writers in the L2. More skilled writers left blanks when they could not think of a word, and pursued their point; less skilled writers did not (R. Wong, 1993).

Goal Setting

Goal setting seemed to be a skill that operated independently of proficiency (V. Smith, 1994). More skilled writers partially adjusted their global plans, based on elaborate but flexible goal setting; this behavior appeared to be a manifestation of writing expertise that cannot be acquired over a short period of time (Sasaki, 2000).

Four main categories of L2 writing goals were identified: content, organization, style-oriented, and rhetorical (A. Wong, 2005). During L2 writing, it was difficult to go from high-level goals to transcription because some low-level skills were not fully automatic in the L2 (Moragne e Silva, 1989).

Organizing

Overall organization at the discourse level was one of the most conspicuous attributes of more skilled L2 writing (Hirose & Sasaki, 1994). More skilled L2 writers had an overall concern for organizing ideas; less skilled L2 writers started with a variety of ideas, which they believed they would reorder while writing or rewriting the final draft—this did not happen (Victori, 1999).

Drawing

For L2 child writers, drawing was a means of expression and rehearsal for writing. Their drawings were more complex and complete than their writing. These writers were eager to share drawings and made up narratives to accompany them, but they could not easily be persuaded to write about their drawing (Hudelson, 1989a).

Discussion

Of the 25 categories in this chapter, the six largest categories (revising, planning, general composing processes, formulating, translating, and restructuring) together accounted for more than half of the findings reported. Revising alone accounted for roughly a quarter of the findings. The percentage of findings supporting these categories were for revising 25%, planning 8%, formulating 7%, general composing processes 6%, translating 5%, and restructuring 4%. The categories with the highest number of subcategories were revising (19), planning (6), general composing processes (5), and translating (4). All of this suggests that a handful of issues in L2 composing have been looked at in both breadth and depth.

Additionally, a very small fraction of individual findings reported here were supported by more than one study. There were seven individual findings (2% of total findings) supported by two sources, one finding supported by three sources (0.3%), and one supported by five (0.3%).

The foregoing would suggest that in the inquiry into L2 composing there are few sustained programs of research. There are, however, some notable exceptions: for example, Cumming and his colleagues (e.g. Cumming, 1989, 1990b; Cumming et al., 1989); Sasaki and Hirose (e.g. Hirose & Sasaki, 1994; Sasaki, 2000, 2004; Sasaki & Hirose, 1996); and Manchón, Roca, and Murphy (e.g., Manchón et al., 2000; Roca, 1996; Roca et al., 1999; Roca et al., 2001).

Written Text

Textual Issues

Introduction

The focus of this chapter is textual issues in second language written text. The textual features examined include cohesion, organizational/rhetorical patterns, modes/aims, metadiscourse/metatext, statements, coherence, paragraphs, themes and rhemes, proposals, gender, productivity, ideas, repetition, expressions of disciplinarity/individuality, letters of recommendation, content, obliqueness, text quality, topics, moral statements, style, politeness, background information, rhetorical redundancy, attention-getting devices, thesis statement, integration, details, audience, paraphrase, position, main idea, orientations, appeals, and parallelism. The organizing principle for the ordering of these categories is most to least findings. The order of presentation of these categories and their subcategories is indicated in the chapter outline below.

Chapter 13 Outline

Cohesion
    General
        L1/L2
        More/less effective compositions
        Distance
        Cohesion and Coherence
    Lexical
        Relative frequency
        L1/L2
        Error
        More/less effective compositions
    Conjunction
        L1/L2
        Error
        Relative frequency

Reference
Elliptical
Substitution
Organizational/rhetorical patterns
General
Japanese
Korean
Chinese
Arabic
Spanish
Modes/aims
Narration
Chinese
Thai
Arabic
French
Vietnamese
Argumentation
Exposition
Description
Persuasion
Metadiscourse/metatext
Statements
Coherence
Paragraphs
Similarities
Differences
Themes and rhemes
Proposals
Gender
Productivity
Ideas
Repetition
Expressions of disciplinarity/individuality
Letters of recommendation
Content
Obliqueness
Text quality
Topics
Moral statements
Style
Politeness
Background information
Rhetorical redundancy

Attention-getting devices
Thesis statement
Integration
Details
Audience
Paraphrase
Position
Main idea
Orientations
Appeals
Parallelism

Findings

Cohesion

General

L1/L2

In the analysis of cohesion (the network of lexical, grammatical, and other relations that link various parts of a text) there were more similarities than differences between L1 and L2 texts (Indrasuta, 1988). There was no significant difference between L1 and L2 writers in terms of the frequency/percentage of different cohesive ties (Hu, Brown, & Brown, 1982), or density of cohesion (cohesive tie per T-unit ratio). General cohesion density was not as good a discriminator of L1/L2 writing as was a lack of variety in lexical cohesion (Connor, 1984).

Texts written by L2 writers seemed less frequently linked conceptually than those of L1 writers and often were uninterpretable to judges, in spite of the use of cohesive ties. For L1 writers, the ties did their job of tying; for the L2 writers, they often did not. Over time, L1 writers increased the use of some categories of cohesion while they decreased the use of others but did not use a greater variety of ties. However, L2 writers' weak use of cohesive devices, which was evident early, improved considerably (Maxwell & Falick, 1992).

Compositions written in L2 exemplify a developmental stage in the use of language and the organization of content, from argumentative or descriptive compositions with more semantic ties (reiteration and collocation) in L1, to expository writing with more syntactic ties (reference and conjunction) in L2 (P. Johnson, 1992).

MORE/LESS EFFECTIVE COMPOSITIONS

One study reports that more effective compositions (in L1 or L2) were not more cohesive than less effective compositions, in the number of cohesive items either per sentence or per composition (P. Johnson, 1992), but another claimed that composition scores were highly correlated with the total number of cohesive devices used (Liu & Braine, 2005). The type of cohesive item varied in comparisons of more effective compositions written in L1. More effective compositions in L1 (Malay) had more semantic ties through reiteration of words than did less effective compositions; in contrast, more effective L1 (English) compositions had more syntactic, conjunction, and reference ties. More effective L2 compositions had more syntactic ties than less effective L2 compositions (P. Johnson, 1992). There was no statistically significant difference between more and less effective L2 essays in terms of frequency of use of cohesive ties (M. Zhang, 2000).

DISTANCE

The majority of L2 ties were either immediate (relating to an item in a nearby sentence) or remote (relating to an item in a sentence further away), whereas mediated ties (relating to an item in a distant sentence, but mediated by elements in intervening sentences) were rarely used. There was not much difference among L2 groups of differing writing ability in terms of distances characterizing cohesive ties. There was no statistically significant relationship between essay scores and distances that characterized the ties (M. Zhang, 2000).

COHESION AND COHERENCE

It has been claimed that to be cohesive, an L2 essay needs to be coherent (Connor, 1984); that cohesive ties are the result of textual coherence and not the creators of it (Maxwell & Falick, 1992); and that the relationship/correlation between cohesion and coherence is very weak (Khalil, 1989).

Lexical

RELATIVE FREQUENCY

In L2 texts, lexical cohesive features were the most common (Liu & Braine, 2005; M. Zhang, 2000); they were much more common than grammatical ties (P. Johnson, 1992; Khalil, 1989) and were followed by conjunction and reference cohesion (P. Johnson, 1992; Liu & Braine, 2005; M. Zhang, 2000). Of the five categories of lexical ties used by L2 writers, repetition/reiteration was used most (Khalil, 1989; Liu & Braine, 2005; M. Zhang, 2000), followed by collocation and synonym (Liu & Braine, 2005; M. Zhang, 2000), followed by general word and superordinate ties (M. Zhang, 2000). Reiteration and collocation made up approximately 75% of total cohesive ties, with syntactic ties (reference and conjunction) comprising the remaining 25% (P. Johnson, 1992).

However, it was reported in another study that collocation made up a small percentage of lexical cohesion (Khalil, 1989).

Among reference devices, pronouns had the highest percentage of use (*they*, *it*, *them*, *these*, *we*, and *I* were most common; *this* and *these* were much more common than *that* and *those*), followed by definite articles and comparatives (Liu & Braine, 2005).

L1/L2

Lexical cohesion was the only cohesive feature that distinguished L1 and L2 writers; variety in lexical cohesion was a better discriminator of L1/L2 writing than general cohesion density. L2 essays lacked a variety of lexical cohesion devices that held L1 essays together (Connor, 1984). L2 writers used lexical cohesion much more than L1 writers did but, unlike the L1 writers, the L2 writers relied very heavily on same-item repetition. The L1 writers found new ways to express semantic repetition and tie their writing together; the L2 writers tended to repeat words and phrases (Maxwell & Falick, 1992).

ERROR

L2 writers underused lexical cohesion (repetition of items, collocations, synonyms) (Johns, 1984). Their lexical cohesion involved problems with personal pronouns and collocation (Johns, 1984; Liu & Braine, 2005) and a restricted choice of lexical items (Liu & Braine, 2005). L2 writers were generally weak in lexical cohesion and had some difficulty in using correct words. Their essays showed a limited lexical repertoire (M. Zhang, 2000). However, it was also reported that L2 writers overused lexical cohesive ties, especially reiteration (Khalil, 1989).

MORE/LESS EFFECTIVE COMPOSITIONS

L2 composition scores were highly correlated with the number of lexical devices (Liu & Braine, 2005). However, it was also reported that there was little difference in the means of cohesive ties among L2 groups at three composition score levels; lexical ties appeared slightly more frequently in the highest scoring group (M. Zhang, 2000).

Conjunction

L1/L2

L2 writers used far more internal conjunctive cohesion than L1 writers. In terms of additives, L1 writers tended to use *also*, *and*, and *too*, whereas L2 writers tended to use *moreover* and *furthermore* to a greater extent (these words were not used by the L1 writers at all) and showed a tendency to rely on *actually* and *on the other hand* (Field & Oi, 1992). L2 writers

(Arabic) used significantly more coordinate conjunctions than L2 writers from three other language backgrounds (Chinese, Spanish, English) (Reid, 1992).

ERROR

L2 writers overused additive and temporal conjunctive ties. The most frequently recurring conjunctive error was the misuse of adversative conjuncts (Johns, 1984; M. Zhang, 2000), often used where a temporal or a causal tie would have been more appropriate, and often out of proximity to the phrase or sentence that they were meant to create contrast with (Johns, 1984). Many of these problems were attributed to L1 transfer (M. Zhang, 2000).

RELATIVE FREQUENCY

Conjunctive ties (along with reference ties) were about 25% of cohesive ties (P. Johnson, 1992). Conjunctive ties in L2 texts were less common than lexical ties and more common than reference ties (M. Zhang, 2000). Among conjunctions, additive devices were the most common, followed by temporal, causal, adversative, and continuative (Liu & Braine, 2005; M. Zhang, 2000).

Reference

L2 essays had a high percentage of reference cohesion (Khalil, 1989). Reference cohesion (along with conjunction), however, comprised only 25% of cohesive ties (P. Johnson, 1992). Reference cohesion was the third most frequent type of cohesion used, following lexical and conjunctive cohesion. More highly rated texts used slightly more reference ties. Less highly rated essays' references were more ambiguous than those in better essays. Mediated ties were also associated with reference ties (M. Zhang, 2000).

Among reference ties (comparative, demonstrative, and pronominal), comparatives were the least used. References were sometimes used without an explicit referent or with no agreement with previous text, especially in less effective essays (M. Zhang, 2000). Problems with reference devices included shifted use of pronouns, omission or misuse of the definite article (Liu & Braine, 2005; M. Zhang, 2000), and underuse of comparatives (Liu & Braine, 2005).

Elliptical

L1 writers used elliptical ties; L2 writers did not (Hu et al., 1982). L2 essays had no ellipsis (Khalil, 1989).

Substitution

L2 essays had a low percentage of substitution (Khalil, 1989).

Organizational/Rhetorical Patterns

General

L2 writers with greater writing experience and greater L2 proficiency received substantially higher ratings on organization (Cumming, 1989). Organization scores had the lowest correlation with three demographic variables: the number of years in the US, age of arrival in the US, and grade of entry into the school system. L1 writers' organization was rated significantly higher than that of L2 writers. Advanced-level international students' performance on organization was similar to that of immigrant writers (Tarone et al., 1993). Writers with organizational difficulties in L1 writing also have discourse problems in their L2 writing (Leung, 1984). When L2 writers made more switches to their L1 and used more L1 as they wrote, the essays were of better quality in terms of organization (Lay, 1982, 1983). Most writing was organized by association, meaning that one idea essentially triggered the next, with the most common basis being time (Edelsky, 1986).

Japanese

Japanese rhetorical patterns involved both linear and circular approaches. In L2 compositions, there were more linear patterns (34%) than circular patterns (27%). In L1 there were more circular patterns (46%) than linear patterns (29%). The same person could use both linear and circular approaches, depending on the audience. In a number of cases, when English and Japanese essays were written by the same student, the rhetorical pattern of the English and Japanese compositions was the same. The L2 (English) essays of the Japanese students were influenced by their Japanese language and rhetorical patterns. The inductive approach of the English essays, the didactic remark at the end of the English essays, and usage such as *as you know, think, because,* and *although* in the English essays were categorized as problems of interference from Japanese (Achiba & Kuromiya, 1983).

Four groups of writers—AEA (American students writing in English in the USA), JJJ (Japanese students writing in Japanese in Japan), JEA (Japanese students writing in English in the USA), and JEJ (Japanese students writing in English in Japan)—differed from each other in their use of rhetorical patterns and general statement types. In terms of rhetorical patterns, AEA students frequently chose the general to specific pattern; JJJ students frequently chose the specific to general pattern. The two Japanese groups writing in English showed different tendencies: the JEA students fell between the two culturally different groups writing in their first language (JJJ and AEA), whereas the JEJ students (English majors in Japan) reflected very closely the preferences of the JJJ group. The findings suggested the existence of cultural preferences for certain rhetorical patterns and types of general statements and a tendency for Japanese ESL learners to use L1 patterns and general statement types when writing in English (H. Kobayashi, 1984).

In terms of organizational pattern, a significant difference between Japanese (L2) and English (L1) writers was observed in Reservation (where a writer shows understanding of an opposing opinion) but not in Thesis Statement, Conclusions, and Hesitation (where a writer withholds judgment—does not take a for or against decision). More than half of the Japanese and American students incorporated a thesis statement and conclusions into their writing (thus using a general–specific pattern). Far more instances of reservation were observed in the Japanese group than in the American group (Kamimura & Oi, 1998).

Similarities and differences were found in the writing of L2 (Japanese) students. The similarities: No negative transfer of L1-specific patterns (those patterns used almost exclusively in Japanese) was observed. Negative transfer was *mainly* poor organization. There were many instances of positive transfer. The differences: Dissimilar rhetorical patterns generally resulted in the same effect as similar patterns, but sometimes resulted in above-average L2 scores and below-average L1 organization scores due to one or a combination of the following: better organization in English than in Japanese, good English language skills, and conscious or unconscious use of dissimilar structures based on a perception about culturally preferred rhetorical patterns or preference for a certain pattern—for example, believing that only English could have a deductive structure. The poor organizational quality often identified in L2 writing may not be so much the result of using cultural conventions as it is a manifestation of the lack of ability to organize a coherent text in L1. Lower L2 scores seemed to be related to students' low English proficiency and/or lack of composing experience in English (Kubota, 1998).

In one study, organization of L1 and L2 texts in terms of location of main idea, rhetorical pattern, and summary statement was identical for 40% of the participants and similar for 33.3%. Deductive organizational patterns appeared in both L1 and L2 compositions, but there was no significant correlation between organizational scores in either language on that basis. Overall L1 and L2 text quality were significantly dependent on factors beyond organization. Students favored a deductive organizational pattern for argumentative writing, regardless of language. Rhetorically successful Japanese writing did not categorically follow a deductive pattern (Hirose, 2003).

L2 essays received higher scores than L1 essays in expository and persuasive modes. In the expository group, 45% were dissimilar between L1 and L2; in the persuasive group, 54%. The similar group in each mode showed a larger decrease in scores from L1 to L2. The interaction effect between use of (dis)similar rhetorical structures and organization scores in each mode was marginal (Kubota, 1998).

Korean

There was a preferred structure for the English essays: claim + justification + conclusion; but Korean essays showed no such structural preference. In the L1 writing of the Korean speakers, each essay had a different organizational pattern (Choi, 1986, 1988). L1 Korean essays often introduced an additional claim somewhere in the essay; however, the same components (claim, justification, and conclusion) were the main components for each language. The Korean pattern was more circular than linear (Choi, 1986). In essays authored by Koreans in English, some showed the preferred structure of the English writers whereas others were organized in different patterns partially similar to the Korean essays (Choi, 1988).

Chinese

Different organizational patterns and structures were reported between Chinese and English subjects, but not for Chinese subjects across mode or language. L2 (Chinese) narratives made frequent use of initial, additive, and explanatory sentences, showing a centrifugal intersentential development pattern. In terms of logic categories (sentence types, e.g. initial, additive, adversative), there were shared patterns of usage of sentences by Chinese subjects writing in Chinese in the narrative and expository modes. For Chinese subjects, rhetorical patterns were similar regardless of mode or language; the number of sentences differed across modes, but not significantly (Norment, 1986).

Arabic

Even though Arabic speakers used *and* more often than non-Arabic speakers, this did not have a major effect on the global organization of their texts. Most of the students used coordination as a low-level or local rhetorical strategy rather than a global strategy for paragraph development. When L2 learners organized their writing in ways that did not conform to the norms of English discourse, it might not have been the result of transfer. Other factors such as the subjects' unfamiliarity with acceptable writing techniques, even in their L1, or interlanguage development factors common to all L2 learners might have been a more plausible explanation (Fakhri, 1994).

Spanish

Emotion affected the quality of the L2 written product in terms of both the quantity and types of errors made in organization. Errors peculiar to the essays on emotional topics included the introduction of irrelevancies, lack of transitions, unfocused paragraphs, and unclear progression of ideas (Clachar, 1999).

Modes/Aims

Narration

CHINESE

For Hong Kong students, the expository mode of writing made more demands on the writers' syntactic resources than the narrative mode of writing did (Yau & Belanger, 1984).

L1 (Chinese) narratives averaged 519 sentences each, with frequent use of initial, additive, and explanatory sentences, showing a centrifugal intersentential development pattern. L2 (English) narratives averaged 478 sentences each, with explanatory and initial type sentences the most frequent. In terms of logic categories, there are shared patterns of usage of sentences by Chinese subjects writing in Chinese in the narrative and expository modes (Norment, 1986).

Two groups (English- and Chinese-speaking writers writing in English) displayed a similar global structure with respect to the main constituents of a narrative: orientation, initiating and complicating events, a high point, and a coda. There were remarkable differences between groups with regard to the distribution of the moral. In the L1 writers' texts the moral was not only in the coda, but also in other narrative constituents, but for the L2 writers the moral was only in the coda. Similarities and differences in narrative structure and rhetoric between the two distinct language and cultural groups were seen as closely connected with the literacy and cultural conventions of the English and Chinese languages (M. Lee, 2003).

THAI

In the narratives written in English by native English speakers and in English and Thai by native Thai speakers, the analysis of narrative components and discourse analysis indicated more differences than similarities. The factors that influenced the differences seemed to be cultural rather than linguistic. For American students, it was claimed that narratives were for entertaining and informing, so they used more actions to make the story interesting. For Thai students, it was claimed that narratives were for instruction and should have explicit moral themes and teach moral values, so they used more descriptions of mental states. When the Thai students wrote in the L2, they brought with them the appropriateness of language use and conventional rhetorical style from their L1. Since the Thai L1 group was more different from the American group than from the Thai L2 group, it was concluded that Thais were following the Thai conventional model of narrative, whereas the American group followed the Western model (Indrasuta, 1988).

FRENCH

For the L1 (French) and L2 (English) texts written by native French speakers, scores for narratives and expositions were more strongly related to one another when analytic rather than holistic scoring was done. Even though there was a strong relationship among analytic scores for the four types of writing (French narrative, French exposition, English narrative, and English exposition), each type was nonetheless in some way distinct from the others (e.g. a student's analytic score on an English narrative was not necessarily an accurate predictor of the same student's analytic score on a French narrative; Canale, Frenette, & Belanger, 1988).

ARABIC

With regard to the English narratives of native speakers of English and native speakers of Arabic, the most significant results were related to patterns for storytelling. The English (L1) and Arabic groups (L2) wrote directly, with clear forward movement and little reflection. The Arabic students, even though they had been exposed to English literary forms for most of their school lives, still gave more information about scene, which appeared to be a feature of the Arabic literary style (Söter, 1988).

VIETNAMESE

With regard to the English narratives of native speakers of English and native speakers of Vietnamese, the most significant results were related to patterns for storytelling. The English (L1) group wrote more directly, with clear forward movement and little reflection. The Vietnamese (L2) group showed a greater allocation of time for the telling of the story and emotional and mental processes of the characters, as well as setting the context for the story (relationship between storyteller and listener; Söter, 1988).

Argumentation

L1 writers' ability to produce longer essays than their L2 writer peers may have put them at an advantage when constructing argumentative compositions, as a short essay may simply not be able to address all of the components of effective persuasion, while their use of counterarguments and low subtopic-to-sentence ratio showed that they anticipated audience reactions and kept their topic in focus (Ferris, 1994b).

Differences in argumentation in L1 and L2 were reported. Regarding decisiveness of argument, L2 writers did writing as self-expression and included thinking processes; their writing included phrases such as *I'm not sure, I don't really know,* and *difficult for me.* L1 writers thought first, reached a conclusion, then wrote and supported the answer (even if the final answer included qualifications and reservations); their writing included phrases such as *I believe, I do approve,* and *one-hundred percent [in favor]*. With regard to consistency of argument, the L2 writers sometimes included a progression from "I disapprove of euthanasia privately" to "but, I approve the part of euthanasia". In terms of development of arguments, the L2 students writing was often unsupported; L1 students' writing contained more explanation (Oi, 1999).

In terms of argumentation the writers' L1 and L2 texts exhibited more similarities than differences. Organization in terms of location of main idea, rhetorical pattern, and summary statement were identical for 40% of participants, and similar for 33.3%. All students placed their main opinion initially in L2, and 73.3% did so in L1. Students favored a deductive organizational pattern for argumentative writing, regardless of language (Hirose, 2003).

Exposition

For L2 writers, all syntactic factors showed more complexity in the expository mode than in the narrative mode. The expository mode of writing made more demands on the writers' syntactic resources than did the narrative mode of writing (Yau & Belanger, 1984). L1 expository texts were longer than L2 expository texts. In terms of logic categories, there were shared patterns of usage of sentences by L2 subjects writing in L1 in the narrative and expository modes (Norment, 1986).

L2 composition writers exemplified a developmental stage in the use of language and the organization of content, from argumentative or descriptive compositions with more semantic ties in L1 to expository writing with more syntactic ties in L2 (P. Johnson, 1992).

L1 essays received higher scores than L2 essays in the expository mode. Of these expository texts, 45% exhibited dissimilarities between L1 and L2 (Kubota, 1998).

Description

More skilled writers in L1 and L2 used more specific and fewer general descriptions in their L2 writing (Lanauze & Snow, 1989). For L2 writers, descriptive texts were easier than persuasive texts (Carrell & Connor, 1991). Compositions written in L2 exemplify a developmental stage in the use of language and the organization of content, from argumentative or descriptive compositions with more semantic ties in L1 to expository writing with more syntactic ties in L2 (P. Johnson, 1992).

Persuasion

Reading both descriptive and persuasive L2 texts was significantly related to writing persuasive L2 texts. Descriptive texts were easier than persuasive texts, but the evidence was primarily for reading, not for writing (Carrell & Connor, 1991).

Metadiscourse/Metatext

More metadiscourse (details that allow writers to address their audiences, explicitly mark the structure of text, and increase the clarity of writing) was used incorrectly more often in lower- than in higher-quality L2 essays; problems occurred most in the use of connectives (expressions encoding information about text organization and how different parts of the text are related), the most frequently used category, and least in low-frequency categories: code glosses (expressions helping readers to grasp intended meaning), illocutionary markers (expressions that state what act the writer is performing), and hedges (expressions that allow writers to convey their reservations about their statements). Although more metadiscourse was used incorrectly in poor L2 essays, code gloss errors were among the least frequent errors. Good L2 essays showed more than twice as many code glosses as did poor L2 essays, almost twice the proportion of correctly used narrators (expressions informing readers of information sources or authorities being cited), and three times as many commentaries (expressions addressing the reader, eliciting a reader response, or anticipating reader response; Intaraprawat & Steffensen, 1995).

Higher-quality L2 essays evidenced a greater range of words/expressions in employing particular categories of metadiscourse. Despite the differences in the number of metadiscourse markers used in higher- and lower-quality L2 essays, both showed similar distribution patterns, using certain markers more or less than others. Similar overall metadiscourse distribution patterns may have been related to some not requiring a particularly high level of insight into reader needs (Intaraprawat & Steffensen, 1995).

With regard to frequency of higher-level metatext in L2 PhD theses, in terms of scope, there were more linear text references at lower levels than at higher levels; in terms of distance, there were more linear text references at the lower levels than at the chapter level. With regard to proportion of higher-level metatext, the texts had an average of 4% of the text devoted to metatext, that is, at chapter level or thesis scope or chapter distance. Thus, it was argued that metatext at higher levels plays a greater role in the cohesion and coherence of the text as a whole. With regard to distribution of higher-level metatext, the use of previews and reviews in intermediate chapters was much less consistent than in the first and last chapters. Chapter-end reviews were usually longer than a chapter preview. In some cases metatext was not used at all. It was reported that a key differentiating aspect of dissertation writing would probably be a much greater use of metadiscourse. Also, writers were generally more consistent in their use of metatext at thesis level than at chapter level (Bunton, 1999).

In metadiscourse in graduate L2 writing, writers used slightly more interactive (helping to guide the reader through the text) than interactional (involving the reader in the argument) forms, and hedges (the withholding of a writer's full commitment to a proposition) and transitions (expressions of semantic relations between main clauses) were the most frequent devices overall. Writers in social science disciplines employed more metadiscourse. Computer science tended to differ from this general picture of impersonality in scientific discourse, displaying relatively high frequencies of both self-mentions (explicit references to the author) and engagement markers (explicit reference to or the building of a relationship with a reader). The broad disciplinary hard and soft groupings were relatively more balanced overall in their use of interactive metadiscourse. Biology dissertations showed a very high use of evidentials (references to information from other texts) due to the greatest density of citations in the field (K. Hyland, 2004a).

Regarding metatextual deixis (pointers such as *above, below, this story*), it did not occur at all in the texts of those with low L2 writing ability; there was one inappropriate case in the texts of those with mid-level L2 writing ability; the few cases of appropriate metatextual deixis were all in the texts of those with high L2 writing ability. It was concluded that metatextual deixis may be an indicator of multilevel global discourse strategies used by skilled writers (Evensen, 1990).

Statements

In terms of general statements, Japanese students writing in English in Japan and Japanese students writing in Japanese in Japan tended to use Text Relating (revealing personal values, beliefs, feelings, and experience in relation to the content of a composition), whereas Japanese students writing in English in the US and American students writing in the US used Text Restating (summarizing or generalizing the content of a composition) more frequently. It was claimed that this suggests the existence of cultural preferences for certain types of general statements and a tendency for Japanese ESL learners to use L1 general statement types when writing in English (H. Kobayashi, 1984).

Lower English proficiency L2 writers used twice as many simple statements as did higher English proficiency writers (Bermudez & Prater, 1994).

L2 writers' organization, in terms of location of summary statement, was very similar in L1 and L2 writing. In both L1 and L2, some writers led into the initial placement of their main opinion with neutral statements. Those who did not do so in L1 attributed it to spontaneous writing, instead of a more consciously guided approach. Seventy-three percent of L1 writing had summary statements; L2, 60%. Those who did not have a summary statement reflected on the need for summary statements only in their L1 work—possibly a cultural inclination toward "bottom-heavy" writing. Summary statements were clear, contradicting prior claims about

Japanese writing. Lack of a summary statement did not necessarily mean a lack of intent to write one (Hirose, 2003).

There was a significant difference in use of direct statements (showing interpersonal involvement between characters and readers) in L1 and L2 writers' texts; density of direct statements for L1 writers was 2.5 times greater than in L2 writers' texts. Density and approaches of moral statements for L1 and L2 writers were different (M. Lee, 2003).

Coherence

It was reported that writers with coherence problems in L1 also had coherence problems in their L2 writing (Leung, 1984); that L1 writers' coherence was significantly higher than L2 writers' (Tarone et al., 1993); that less skilled writers were not able to adhere to global and local coherence at the same time and were not able to create the multilevel, hierarchical coherence typically found in the work of more skilled writers (Evensen, 1990); and that advanced-level international student writers' level of coherence was similar to that of immigrant L2 writers (Tarone et al., 1993).

It was also reported that coherence accounts for major differences in text quality (Maxwell & Falick, 1992). Four types of coherence breaks were reported: misleading lexical items, lack of adequate justifying supports, insufficient linking of the inductive statement to the preceding discussion, and lack of crucial information or explanation. The total number of coherence breaks was greater for L2 writers than for L1 writers; and there were similar numbers and similar types of coherence breaks in both the L2 and L1 texts of L2 writers (Choi, 1986).

Reasons for incoherence included poor elaboration and/or development of detail in L2 writing (Khalil, 1989), a lack of signal words and the use of pronouns such as *it* when the reference was not clear (Khuwaileh & Al Shoumali, 2000), lower levels of metatext (Bunton, 1999), the introduction of irrelevancies, lack of transitions, unfocused paragraphs, and unclear progression of ideas (Clachar, 1999).

The relationship between coherence and cohesion was very weak (Khalil, 1989). Coherence pattern—or the organization of idea units—rather than cohesion characterizes text quality (P. Johnson, 1992). Cohesive ties are the result of coherence and not the creators of it (Maxell & Falick, 1992).

Paragraphs

Similarities

L2 writers produced introductory paragraphs with the preferred L1 rhetorical structure taught for the introductory paragraph in an argumentative academic essay (Stalker & Stalker, 1989). L2 writers showed a lower, but not significantly lower, mean involvement of bonds at paragraph boundaries than did L1 writers (Reynolds, 1995). Even though L1 (Arabic) writers used *and* more often than L1 (English) writers did, its use did not have a major effect on the global organization of their texts; most used coordination as a low-level or local rhetorical strategy rather than a global strategy for paragraph development. L2 (Arabic) writers never used *and* at the beginning of a paragraph. According to the researcher, *and* in this position is common in Arabic writing. It was claimed that the Arabic writers knew this use was unacceptable in English and monitored their writing during the task (Fakhri, 1994).

Differences

Most L2 writers exhibited a serious lack of knowledge about how to organize articles or essays at the paragraph level. Sequencing, development, subject unity (presentation of a general main idea and relating other ideas to that idea), and coherence were paragraph-level problems or weaknesses for L2 writers (Doushaq, 1986). L2 writers exhibited misleading paragraph division, two types of which were identified: where there was a need to break a long paragraph into shorter ones and where there was a need to combine several short paragraphs into one. The unjustified change of paragraphs accounts for most instances of misleading paragraph division (Wikborg, 1990). Exceptions to the patterns of normal paragraph development were mostly produced by the L2 writers (Mauranen, 1996). One of the problems of L2 writers was unfocused paragraphs, when writing essays on emotional topics (Clachar, 1999).

Themes and Rhemes

L2 writers tended to have rhemes (elements that are new or focal—the core of the sentence) repeat the essential meaning of the preceding rhemes instead of developing new meanings; this was mainly owing to the manipulation of L2 syntactic structures for realizing theme (elements that are given or known—what the sentence is about). L2 writers had problems in using themes in the L2 that they did not have in their mother tongue. Though the principles of thematic progression in a good text were found to be highly similar at a relatively abstract functional level in both L1 and L2, the actual realizations of these principles in text did not run smoothly in the L2 texts (Mauranen, 1996).

Participant themes (e.g. people) are used more by lower-proficiency than higher-proficiency L2 writers. Nominal nonparticipant themes (e.g. things) are used more by advanced than by lower-proficiency L2 writers. Marked themes (e.g. *it* and *there* predicates) are used more by advanced than by lower-proficiency L2 writers (Hawes & Thomas, 1997).

L2 writers used more marked themes than did L1 writers. L1 writers used unmarked themes (themes that come first in the sentence); the marked themes (themes that are not in sentence initial position) they used were typically infinitive phrases. As a result of L1 influence L2 writers used marked themes more (Hu et al., 1982). L2 writers used explicit themes whereas L1 writers used implicit themes (Indrasuta, 1988). L1 writers were more able than L2 writers to establish a theme clearly and unambiguously (Scarcella, 1984).

Proposals

There were fewer or no overt sections in unsuccessful L2 proposals, with one exception. The number of overt sections was not a direct indicator of the degree of functional organization, but suggested an element of audience awareness. Reference sections were present in all proposals. Two successful proposals were substantially longer than the other six proposals. Successful L2 proposals contained, on average, 1.5–3.0 sections, compared with 0–1, on average, in the unsuccessful proposals. Significant differences in frequency were found in seven lexical items: Four occurred more often in successful proposals than in unsuccessful proposals (*research, analysis, theory,* and *knowledge*), and three occurred more often in unsuccessful proposals than in successful proposals (*important, me,* and *question*). Successful L2 proposal writers contextualized their own expertise effectively within a larger research community. Organizationally, this was realized through selective adaptation of section headings, sequence, and contents as suggested in departmental guidelines. Lexically, these L2 writers referred to *the research* more frequently. Unsuccessful L2 proposal writers failed to convince their reviewers, they covered too many issues and research traditions too superficially or covered too few, their textual organization was generally less elaborate, and there were also fewer lexical references to their proposed research (Allison, 2005).

Gender

L2 women writers used fewer compliment intensifiers (e.g. *very* interesting) than did L1 women writers, and they exhibited less variation according to gender of audience than did the L1 writers. L2 women writers used less personal referencing than did their L1 counterparts, and they did not use the L1 pattern of using substantially more personal references in compliments addressed to women. Almost all of the writers used an opening compliment, but a much higher percentage of L1 women writers used a closing compliment to a female than to a male addressee, whereas a higher percentage of L2 women writers used a closing compliment to a male addressee than to a female. Although L2 women writers used some aspects of the L1 women writers' female–female complimenting style, they did not vary their language use according to gender of addressee to the degree or in the same ways that the L1 women writers did (D. Johnson, 1992). L2 essays written by females show a clearer attempt to express the writer's point of view and a greater degree of elaboration than did those of males; this is attributed to different socialization experiences (Bermudez & Prater, 1994).

Productivity

In general, L2 writers produced shorter texts than did L1 writers. L2 compositions had fewer words than L1 compositions (Benson, Deming, Denzer, & Valeri-Gold, 1992; Bouton, 1995; Ferris, 1994b; Moragne e Silva, 1989; Reynolds, 1995). However, in one study, L2 writers' business letters were longer than those of L1 writers; greater length was due primarily to unnecessary professional information about the L2 writers' backgrounds (Sims & Guice, 1992).

Regarding variables associated with L2 text length, grade level correlated significantly and positively with productivity. Bilingual program students outscored submersion program students on productivity (Carlisle, 1989). Writers in match condition—writing in the language in which the topic was experienced—produced longer texts (Friedlander, 1990). Low-proficiency L2 writers' texts were shorter than those with higher proficiency levels (Kamimura & Oi, 2001). More skilled/experienced L2 writers wrote longer texts than did less skilled/experienced L2 novice writers (Sasaki, 2000).

In L2 writing, as language switching increased, text length decreased (Woodall, 2002). And L2 writers unable to produce longer essays may have been at a disadvantage when constructing argumentative compositions, as a short essay may simply not have been able to address all of the components of effective persuasion (Ferris, 1994a).

Ideas

When L2 writers made more switches to their L1 as they wrote, their essays were of better quality in terms of ideas (Lay, 1982). Errors in compositions whose topics are emotionally evocative included an unclear progression of ideas (Clachar, 1999). A lack of difference in the quantity of cohesion between the compositions of more and less skilled L2 writers suggests that coherence pattern or the organization of idea units, rather than cohesion, must characterize quality (P. Johnson, 1992).

Both high and low L2 proficiency groups had more idea units in a first person than in a third person task and fewer external idea units (describing scenes and outward behavior) on the third person task. Higher L2 proficiency level students writing in first person had slightly more internal idea units (describing the character's internal thoughts and feelings) than when writing in third person; lower proficiency level students had many more. Higher L2 proficiency level students writing in third person first had many more internal idea units in first person writing; lower L2 proficiency level students had more idea units in third person writing (Kamimura & Oi, 2001).

Repetition

With regard to frequency of different types of repetition, only the use of simple paraphrase showed a significant difference, with L1 writers using almost twice as much as L2 writers. In terms of ratio of repetition to paraphrase, L2 writers showed a higher ratio than L1 writers, which indicated that the L2 writers showed a greater preference for repetition over paraphrase than did the L1 writers (Reynolds, 1995).

Qualitatively, there was little difference between the L1 and L2 groups with regard to the degree of repetition used. However, the qualitative comparison of representative essays showed that the two groups were not indistinguishable. Based on quantitative measures, no significant differences were found between the L2 and L1 groups in terms of the degree at which repetition makes a text more cohesive. Qualitative analyses showed that repetition varied among the L2 and L1 writers (Reynolds, 1995). Repetition in L1 was significantly higher than in L2 (Khalil, 1999).

Expressions of Disciplinarity/Individuality

L2 writers adopted the traditional introduction–method–results–discussion organization. They made frequent use of discipline-specific terminology. L2 writers used visuals particularly common to scientific discourse (for example, tables, graphs, and schematic diagrams). Their use of color in their PowerPoint presentations fell within expected conventions of their disciplinary fields. For multilingual writers, who often lacked confidence in their language skills and may have been hesitant to challenge generic norms in the verbal mode, visuals offered an alternative means of expressing one's individuality (Tardy, 2005b).

Color, background design, and use of images were some of the elements that L2 writers manipulated according to their own tastes, purposes, and sense of self. Through their presentation slides, the L2 writers portrayed themselves as members of their disciplinary communities through organizational structures, lexical choices, visual images, and slide color. They were aware of the expectations for the genre that their readers/viewers held, and they worked within this range of variation (Tardy, 2005b).

Letters of Recommendation

L1 writers wrote longer letters than the L2 writers. Similar numbers of L1 and L2 writers used separate paragraph introductions, included their introduction in a larger paragraph, and included no introduction. L2 writers used more direct recommendations than L1 writers. L1 writers used more indirect recommendations than L2 writers. With regard to the frequency of content features in the opening sentences of introductions, recommendation appeared more often in L2 than in L1 texts; relationship appeared more often in L1 than in L2 texts; and traits/achievements appeared in similar numbers of L1 and L2 texts. With regard to the frequency of content features (recommendation, relationship, and traits/achievements—further categorized as academic, personal, and workplace) in the introduction, recommendation appeared more often in L2 than in L1 texts. Relationship, academic traits/achievements, personal traits/achievements, and workplace traits/achievements appeared more frequently in L1 than in L2 texts (Bouton, 1995).

Content

In terms of content, four qualities with regard to parents (love, understanding, communication, and spending time) appeared in the papers of both L1 and L2 groups; however, the number of times each was used differed for the two groups. L1 basic writers wrote more about love and understanding from parents, whereas L2 writers described parents more as teachers and providers (Benson et al., 1992).

In business letters, L2 writers' letters included more unnecessary professional information, unnecessary personal information, and inappropriate requests; L2 writers' business letters differed from L1 writers' letters in the use of accepted salutations, complimentary closings, tone, and information (Sims & Guice, 1992).

In letters of recommendation, content features in the opening sentences of introductions included more recommendation in L2 than in L1 letters. In terms of the frequency of content features in the introduction, the L1 texts included more recommendation, relationship, academic traits/achievements, personal traits/achievements, and workplace traits/achievements than did the L2 texts (Bouton, 1995).

Obliqueness

Obliqueness in less skilled L2 student writing stemmed from limitations in ability to define the rhetorical problem inherent in the question, which then led to the writer setting goals that confined focal attention to recount of topic content and sentence production. The analysis of theme and rheme showed how information structuring at sentence level (choice of items for theme and rheme positions) could affect a reader's perception of obliqueness or directness of answer. Cognitively, an oblique answer was generated by a writing process driven by content-based and sentence-level goals rather than by a global rhetorical goal, or it arose from limitations in the mental processes of task interpretation and rhetorical goal setting. Inappropriate choice of information for theme position in sentences contributed to the gap between an oblique answer and the question (Chandrasegaran, 2000).

Text Quality

A number of writer variables were positively associated with L2 text quality. These included grade level (Carlisle, 1989), literate expertise (Cumming, 1989), L2 proficiency (Cumming, 1989; Kamimura & Oi, 2001), match condition (writing in L2 on a topic learned about in L2; Friedlander, 1990), and gender (Bermudez & Prater, 1994). A number of text variables were positively related to L2 writing quality. These included word length; words per clause (Ferris, 1994a); T-unit length (Intaraprawat & Steffensen, 1995); number of T-units (Intaraprawat & Steffensen, 1995; Schneider & Connor, 1990); essay length (Intaraprawat & Steffensen, 1995); coherence pattern or the organization of idea units, rather than cohesion (P. Johnson, 1992); counterarguments; closings; parallel progressions (when the topical subject is semantically identical to the topical subject of the previous sentence; Ferris, 1994a); percentage of interpersonal features; use of all metadiscourse types; range of words/expressions in employing particular categories of metadiscourse (Intaraprawat & Steffensen, 1995); a shift from third person to first person for high L2 proficiency writers (Kamimura & Oi, 2001); and factors beyond organization (Hirose, 2003).

Topics

Three groups of essays (from low, mid, and high scoring L2 writers) did not differ in proportion of extended parallel topics (where T-unit topics are semantically identical). The three groups of essays differed in proportion of parallel topics and proportion of sequential topics (topics derived from the content of the comment in the previous T-unit). There were significant differences between essays rated low and high and between those rated mid and high. The low and mid rated essays contained a greater proportion of parallel topics than did the high; the highs had a greater proportion of sequential topics than did the low and mid scoring writers. The highest rated essays contained more sequential topics and fewer parallel topics, proportionally, than either the low or middle rated essays (Schneider & Connor, 1990).

Moral Statements

Frequency and approaches of moral statements for L1 and L2 writers were different; half of the L1 writers included a moral to the story whereas 83% of the L2 writers did. Also, the L1 writers approached the moral implicitly whereas the L2 writers approached it explicitly. Frequency of presenting the moral from an additional character in L2 texts was three times higher than that of L2 writers; L2 writers usually presented the moral from a senior individual (parent or teacher). In terms of distribution of the moral, there was a remarkable difference between groups: the moral of L1 writers was not only in the coda, but also in other narrative constituents; for L2 writers, the moral only appeared in the coda (M. Lee, 2003).

Style

It was reported both that L2 writers bring with them the conventional rhetorical style from their L1 (Indrasuta, 1988) and that, at the discourse level, no unconscious transfer of L2 rhetorical structures/styles was evident (Stalker & Stalker, 1989). L2 writers used more impersonal, conversational styles (Reynolds, 2005). L2 writers' texts (letters) gave the impression of being too casual, too desperate, too personal, or too detached, whereas the L1 writers' letters all appeared to be more professional (Maier, 1992). L1 writers showed a clearer, more distinctive personal sense of style (Huie & Yahya, 2003). Writers generally developed styles consistent with the local norms of the schools: focusing on one topic, organization, elaboration on an idea, metaphorical language, and word choice (McCarthey et al., 2005).

Politeness

There were striking differences in politeness strategies used by L1 and L2 writers. In business letters apologizing for a missed appointment, L1 writers used more negative politeness strategies to preserve the addressee's face: They mitigated their apologies more; expressed thanks more often; and were more pessimistic and less direct. The language they used stressed the severity and extreme nature of the circumstances. L2 writers used more potentially risky positive politeness strategies and were more informal and direct in using these strategies than were the L1 writers (Maier, 1992). In letters of recommendation, L2 writers used more exaggerated politeness than L1 writers and used more inappropriate salutations and closings (Sims & Guice, 1992).

Background Information

L2 writers with less L2 proficiency, L2 writers with more L2 proficiency, and L1 writers all used more background information in the introduction than in any other part of the text, with both L2 groups using more than the L1. Little acknowledgement of source was given, with the L2 groups acknowledging the source more often than the L1 group. The L1 writers were better able to incorporate background information without a change in voice – the L2 writers' paraphrases, near copies, quotations, and exact copies produced momentary elaborative discourse within the context of their otherwise simpler language (Campbell, 1990).

Rhetorical Redundancy

Rhetorical redundancy, which was used for emphasis, clarification, conventions of courtesy, and persuasion (Bartelt, 1982, 1983), was a major discourse feature evident in L2 written texts; this feature seemed to be the result of language transfer of a similar device that existed in the L1. Redundancy for particular purposes in L1 can be assumed to represent an interaction between language transfer of redundancy and L2 discourse constraints (Bartelt, 1982). This rhetorical redundancy resulted in unnatural written L2 discourse. The degree of rhetorical redundancy varied according to the context (Bartelt, 1983).

Attention-getting Devices

L1 writers engaged their readers' attention in their first sentences and used the following attention-getting devices: cataphoric reference, interrogatives, direct assertions, structural repetition, short abrupt elements, sentence-initial adverb + verb sequences, and historical context. Although all of the L1 essays contained one or more of these attention-getting devices, only 58% of L2 essays contained such devices. Moreover, L2 essays lacked the range of attention-getting devices employed by the L1 writers. The L2 writers primarily used historical context and direct assertions (Scarcella, 1984).

Thesis Statement

L2 writers had clearer theses in their introductions than did L1 writers (Stalker & Stalker, 1989). There was no significant difference between L1 and L2 writers with regard to the presence of a thesis statement; more than half of the L2 and L1 writers incorporated a thesis statement, that is, used a general to specific pattern (Kamimura & Oi, 1998). L1 students placed their thesis statements earlier in essays (Wu & Rubin, 2000).

Integration

L2 writers showed some overintegration and overexplication of encoding relationships. There appear to be two possibilities for achieving the right level of explicitness in expressing rhetorical relations: explication through an independent connective without integration or integration through subordination, with the subordinating conjunct expressing the rhetorical relationship (Pelsmaekers, Braecke, & Geluykens, 1998).

Details

Greater production and quality of details by L2 writers were related to more language switches while writing (Lay, 1982), greater writing experience (Cumming, 1989), greater ESL proficiency (Cumming, 1989; Kamimura & Oi, 2001), writing in match condition (when language of writing and content were the same; Friedlander, 1990), and coherence (Khalil, 1989). In terms of story background information, L1 writers used more details than L2 writers (M. Lee, 2003).

Audience

L2 writers did not display the same kind or degree of sensitivity to audience as the L1 writers did (D. Johnson, 1992). More skilled L2 writers made reference to the audience, especially in terms of modifying their content and presenting stronger or weaker opinions, depending on the target reader. Less skilled L2 writers made little reference to audience (Victori, 1999).

Paraphrase

L1 writers used almost twice as much simple paraphrase as their L2 counterparts. L2 writers had a higher ratio of repetition to paraphrase than did L1 writers, indicating they may have a greater preference for repetition over paraphrase than do the L1 writers (Reynolds, 1995).

Position

Neither L1 nor L2 writers exhibited a definite preference in choosing a position (for vs. against) (Kamimura & Oi, 1998). However, there was a statistically significant difference between L1 and L2 writers with regard to taking a position; L1 writers were more decisive than L2 writers (Oi, 1999).

Main Idea

In terms of location of main idea, L1 and L2 texts were mostly identical or similar. Students perceived initial position of main idea as best, but were unsure about whether this originated in L1 or in L2 (Hirose, 2003).

Orientations

L1 writers did not write longer orientations than L2 writers. Advanced L2 writers did not write longer orientations than beginning L2 writers. Orientation length may have varied as a function of L2 writers' first language background (Scarcella, 1984).

Appeals

L1 writers used more logical appeals and fewer affective appeals than did L2 writers. Regarding the content of the appeals, the L2 writers were more emotionally oriented, whereas the L1 writers were more logically oriented (Kamimura & Oi, 1998).

Parallelism

There was no statistically significant difference in amount of parallelism in an L1 writer's first and second language writing. Parallelism was a rhetorical strategy that seemed to transfer from L1 to L2 (Khalil, 1999).

Discussion

Of the 35 categories in this chapter, the top three (cohesion, organizational/rhetorical pattern, and modes/aims) together accounted for more than 40% of the findings reported. In the cohesion category, lexical cohesion accounted for 32% of findings. In the organizational/rhetorical pattern category, studies focusing on Japanese subjects accounted for 56% of findings. In the modes/aims category, narration accounted for 46% of the findings. The cohesion category was composed of six subcategories, as was the organizational/rhetorical pattern. The modes/aims category had five. This suggests that a handful of issues with regard to textual issues in L2 composing have been looked at both in breadth and in depth.

Additionally, a very small fraction of individual findings reported here were supported by more than one study. There were 14 individual findings (4%) supported by two sources, two findings (0.5%) supported by three sources, and one (0.3%) supported by five.

The foregoing would seem to suggest that in inquiry into textual issues in L2 writers' texts there are few sustained programs of research. There are, however, some notable exceptions, for example Connor (Carrel & Connor, 1991; Connor, 1984; Schneider & Connor, 1990); Kamimura & Oi (Field & Oi, 1992; Kamimura & Oi, 1998, 2001); Khalil (Khalil, 1989, 1999); and Reynolds (Reynolds, 1995, 2005).

Written Text

Grammatical Issues

Introduction

The focus of this chapter, which draws from the findings of 63 reports of research, is second language written text, specifically grammatical issues. These issues are divided into six basic categories: parts of speech/ form classes, sentence elements, sentence processes, functional element classes, sentence qualities, and mechanics. The organizing principle for the ordering of these categories is most to least findings. The order of presentation of these categories and their subcategories is indicated in the chapter outline below.

Chapter 14 Outline

Parts of speech/form classes
    Verbs
            Modals
            Passives
            Tense
            Verb type
            Lexical verbs
            Verb form
            Verb frequency
            Aspect
    Conjunctions
    Pronouns
    Prepositions
    Adverbials
    Articles
    Adjectives
    Nouns
Sentence elements
    Words/lexis

Clauses
Syntactic complexity/maturity
T-units
Sentence processes
Person
Use of first and third person
Use of first person
Coordination
Subordination
Nominalization
Comparison
Agreement
Complementation
Collocation
Segmentation
Functional element classes
Hedges
Connectors
Intensifiers
Idioms
Discourse markers
Downtoners
Emphatics
Illocutionary markers
Overstatements
Softening devices
Subordinators
Sentence qualities
Accuracy
Complexity
Length
Structure
Fluency
Type
Mechanics
Spelling
Punctuation
Orthography
General
Abbreviations and symbols

Findings

Parts of Speech/Form Classes

Verbs

MODALS

L1 and L2 writers were heavily dependent on the use of modal verbs (K. Hyland & Milton, 1997). The overall use of modals increased as L2 writing ability level increased (Grant & Ginther, 2000). L1 and L2 writing were similar in modal usage, with *will, may*, and *would* always occurring among the most frequently used devices to indicate qualification and certainty. L1 and L2 writers made substantial use of epistemic modal verbs, particularly *will, would* and *may*; L2 writers appeared to depend far more heavily on these devices (K. Hyland & Milton, 1997). L1 writers preferred reserved modals (e.g. *might, perhaps, would probably*) whereas L2 writers preferred root modals (e.g. *should, must, had to*; Hu et al., 1982). L2 writers used modal verbs of necessity (e.g. *must*) more than L1 writers did; L2 writers used fewer instances of the predictive modal *would* than did L1 writers (Hinkel, 2002).

PASSIVES

L2 writers used more passives as they improved in writing ability (Ferris, 1994a; Grant & Ginther, 2000; Kameen, 1983). More skilled L2 writers used more passives than less skilled L2 writers did (Kameen, 1980). In one study, L2 writers used fewer passives than did L1 writers (Hinkel, 2002); however, in another study, L2 writers were reported to use more passives (Hinkel, 1997). It was also reported that L2 writers saw self-reference as a marker of self-assurance and individuality, which they did not feel when composing; thus, they preferred the anonymity of passive forms (K. Hyland, 2002).

TENSE

L2 texts frequently included verb tense errors (Bryant, 1984; Chandrasegaran, 1986; Hu et al., 1982; Khuwaileh & Al Shoumali, 2000; Meziani, 1984; S. Olsen, 1999), more verb tense errors than in L1 texts (Benson, et al., 1992; Khuwaileh & Al Shoumali, 2000), and fewer variations on present tense use (Reynolds, 2005). The use of present and past tense by L2 writers increased across ability levels (Grant & Ginther, 2000). L2 writers developed their use of appropriate tense over a 2-year period (McCarthey et al., 2005).

VERB TYPE

L2 writers used more private verbs (e.g. *think, feel, believe*; Hinkel, 2003) and relied heavily on private verbs to state their opinions in essays (Grant

& Ginther, 2000). L2 writing also included more public verbs (verbs that refer to actions that can be observed publicly and that are used to introduce indirect and reported statements, e.g. *agree*), expecting/tentative verbs (verbs that refer to future time and are often employed in tentative constructions that imply an element of uncertainty, e.g. *expect*), and *be-*copula (*be* as main verb) verbs (Hinkel, 2002, 2003).

LEXICAL VERBS

Neither L1 nor L2 writers made rich use of lexical (i.e. nonmodal) verbs: *think* and *know* in the L2 texts and *believe, seem,* and *think* in the L1 texts account for almost two-thirds of all forms (K. Hyland & Milton, 1997).

VERB FORM

L2 writers' grammar errors included inappropriate verb forms (Ghrib-Maamaouri, 2001). There was no difference in the use of verb forms and plural morphology in the writing of male and female L2 writers (Morris, 1998).

VERB FREQUENCY

L2 writing involved fewer words per verb (Lanauze & Snow, 1989) and fewer verb phrases per sentence (Huie & Yahya, 2003). Overall verb frequency increased across L2 proficiency levels (because text length increased; Grant & Ginther, 2000).

ASPECT

L2 writers used perfect and progressive aspect less than L1 writers did (Hinkel, 2002).

Conjunctions

There was a relationship between L2 proficiency level and the use of conjunctions: Writers with high and mid L2 proficiency used more conjunctions than those with low L2 proficiency. There was also a relationship between L2 writing ability and the use of conjunctions: L2 writers with high writing ability used fewer conjunctions than those with mid writing ability, and those with high and mid writing ability used a larger number of conjunctions than did those with low writing ability (Kiany & Nejad, 2001). Also, the use of conjunctions was positively correlated with holistic scores (Ferris, 1994a).

L1 writers used a significantly lower percentage of coordinate conjunctions (e.g. *and*) than did L2 writers, but a higher percentage of subordinate conjunction openers (e.g. *when*). L2 (Arabic) writers used significantly more coordinate conjunctions than writers from three other language backgrounds (Spanish, Chinese, and English). L2 (Chinese) writers used a higher number of subordinate conjunction openers than did the L2

(Spanish) and L2 (Arabic) writers. L2 (Chinese) and L1 (English) writers used significantly more subordinate conjunctions in comparison/contrast topics (Reid, 1992). L2 writers used more phrase-level (e.g. *or*) and sentence-level (e.g. *moreover*) conjunctions than did L1 writers (Hinkel, 2002).

Over time, L2 writers increased their use of conjunctions (Grant & Ginther, 2000), and the majority of L2 writers used fewer sentences beginning with coordinating conjunctions (*and, but, so*); thus, their written speech looked less like oral speech (Casanave, 1994).

Pronouns

L1 writers used a significantly lower percentage of pronouns than did L2 writers (Reid, 1992). L2 writing involved more pronominal noun phrases (Lanauze & Snow, 1989).

There was an increase in the use of first person pronouns across L2 proficiency levels (Grant & Ginther, 2000). L2 writers used more first person singular pronouns than did L1 writers (Wu & Rubin, 2000). L2 writers were far more likely to employ a first person pronoun with an epistemic verb (e.g. *know*) than were L1 writers, and this likelihood increased as proficiency declined (K. Hyland & Milton, 1997).

There was a decrease in the use of second person pronouns across proficiency levels (Grant & Ginther, 2000). L2 writers used fewer second person pronouns than their L1 peers (Reynolds, 2005). One of the most significant differences between higher- and lower-rated L2 texts was the use of second person pronouns. (Jarvis et al., 2003).

Self-referential pronouns and determiners made up 10% of L2 students' writing; *I* was most common, making up 60% of the total. Author pronouns (first person pronouns referring to the writer) in L2 students' writing were used mainly to state a discoursal goal and explain a methodological approach. Many L2 writers used self-mention to express personal benefits from a project and to frame a report. Very few L2 writers used personal pronouns associated with explicit cognitive verbs (e.g. *think*) (K. Hyland, 2002).

Interlingual (L1) errors (errors resulting from L1 interference) included incorrect use of impersonal *it* (Bryant, 1984). One of the most significant differences between higher- and lower-rated L2 texts was found with impersonal *it* (Jarvis et al., 2003). The frequency rates of assertive pronouns (e.g. *anyone, somebody*) in L2 writing significantly exceeded those in L1 essays (Hinkel, 2005).

Prepositions

For L2 writers, the overall use of prepositions increased as L2 writing ability level increased (Grant & Ginther, 2000), and the use of prepositions was positively correlated with holistic scores (Ferris, 1994b). L1 writers used a higher percentage of prepositions than did L2 writers (Reid, 1992); L2 writers averaged far more errors than L1 writers in use of prepositions (Benson et al., 1992). Errors involving prepositions were among the most frequently made by L2 writers (Meziani, 1984). Errors included those of omission or misuse of prepositions and ambiguity and vagueness of prepositions (Chandrasegaran, 1986). Language mixing was reported as a cause of error in the use of prepositions (S. Olsen, 1999).

Adverbials

L2 writers' number of adverbials increased with grade level (Yau & Belanger, 1985) and writing ability level (Grant & Ginther, 2000). The most significant differences between higher- and lower-rated L2 texts were found with adverbials and adverbial subordination (Jarvis et al., 2003). L1 writers exhibited a greater range and frequency of adverbials; however, both L1 and L2 writers were heavily dependent on a narrow range of adverbs (K. Hyland & Milton, 1997). L2 writers' texts included more manner adverbs, conjunctive adverbs, and adverb clauses of cause than did L1 writers' texts. L2 writers used fewer reduced adverb clauses than L1 writers did (Hinkel, 2002).

Articles

The use of articles increased as L2 writing level increased; L2 writers used a smaller number of indefinite articles and a larger number of definite articles (Grant & Ginther, 2000). Article errors—especially the omission of definite and indefinite articles (Bryant, 1984; Chandrasegaran, 1986)—were more frequent in L2 writing than in L1 writing (Meziani, 1984). L2 writers' article errors seemed to have resulted from hypercorrection, overgeneralization of grammar rules, and interference or transfer from L1 (Ghrib-Maamaouri, 2001).

Adjectives

The overall use of adjectives by L2 writers increased along with L2 writing level (Grant & Ginther, 2000). L2 texts included more predicate adjectives and adjective/verb modifiers and fewer reduced adjective clauses than L1 texts (Hinkel, 2002). L1 and L2 writing were positively correlated with regard to attributive adjective use (Leung, 1984).

Nouns

L2 writing involved fewer nouns than did L1 writing (Lanauze & Snow, 1989). The overall use of nouns increased as writing level (Grant & Ginther, 2000) and grade level (Yau & Belanger, 1985) increased. L2 writers used more interpretive nouns (nouns referring to cognitive inferential states that are a result of information, thought, and experience processing, e.g. *analysis*) and vague nouns (nouns whose meaning depends on the context in which they are used, e.g. *stuff*) than did L1 writers (Hinkel, 2002, 2003).

Sentence elements

Words/Lexis

L2 writers wrote fewer words (Clachar, 1999; Ferris, 1994b; Linnarud, 1986) overall, fewer words per verb (Lanauze & Snow, 1989), fewer words per clause (Ferris, 1994b), fewer words per T-unit (Reynolds, 1995), and fewer words per sentence (Benson et al., 1992) than did L1 writers. They repeated words more often (Linnarud, 1983; Reynolds, 2005) and used shorter words (Ferris, 1994b) and fewer and a lesser variety of two-syllable words (Huie & Yahya, 2003). L2 writers' main problems were inappropriateness, wordiness, and redundancy (Doushaq, 1986).

L2 writers exhibited a less diverse vocabulary (Butler-Nalin, 1984) and less lexical originality (lexical words exclusive to one writer; Linnarud, 1983), individuality (originality of lexis; Linnarud, 1986), sophistication (level of difficulty), variation (type–token ratio; Linnarud, 1983, 1986), and lexical choice (Hu et al., 1982). They used fewer lexical words (Hu et al., 1982; Linnarud, 1983), less lexicality (percentage of lexical words in a text), less lexical density (lexical items divided by number of words— the percentage of lexical words), and a less complex lexical network than did their L1 counterparts (Hu et al., 1982). L2 writers made more word choice errors (Sonomura, 1996) and errors in diction (Benson et al., 1992). L1 writers tended to avoid repetition of lexical items regardless of the length of the essay, whereas the L2 writers found such avoidance more difficult. Longer L2 essays had more errors and greater repetition of lexical items than L1 essays. The more original the lexis in the text, the higher the level of sophistication (Linnarud, 1986).

However, lexical density was similar for both L1 and L2 writers (contradiction noted), and it was reported that L2 writers could reach a native-like level of lexis (Linnarud, 1983). As L2 proficiency level increased, L2 writers wrote more (Grant & Ginther, 2000; Kamimura, 1996), longer, and more specific words and made more use of lexical features (Grant & Ginther, 2000).

More skilled writers L2 writers wrote more words per error-free T-unit (Lim, 1983) and longer T-units (more words per T-unit; Kameen, 1983) and had access to more lexical tools than did less skilled L2 writers (Ferris, 1994a). Male L2 writers paid less attention to guidelines with regard to vocabulary; female L2 writers took great pains to adhere to all of the guidelines (Morris, 1998).

L2 lexical choice errors were often a result of the use of bilingual dictionaries. Limited vocabulary knowledge led to language mixing (S. Olsen,

1999), but vocabulary was better for subjects who used more L1 (Lay, 1983).

L2 text quality was negatively related to percentage of lexical error—quality increased when error decreased—and positively related to lexical variation with and without error. However, neither lexical error nor lexical variation alone accounted for quality as well as they did together. Lexical density had little, if any, relationship to quality (Engber, 1995).

Limited vocabulary was the most cited difference between L1 and L2 writing (Silva, 1992). For L2 writers, a lack of appropriate lexical terms was also a main component of logic errors (Ghrib-Maamaouri, 2001). Percentage of unrepeated content words fluctuated, more showing greater command of vocabulary (Casanave, 1994). Lexical error was one of the most common types of error in L2 texts (Ghrib-Maamaouri, 2001; H. Kobayashi & Rinnert, 1992; Leung, 1984).

One of the most significant differences between higher- and lower-rated L2 texts was mean word length (Jarvis et al., 2003). Number of words per clause correlated significantly with quality of L2 writing (Kameen, 1983).

Clauses

For L2 writers, mean clause length (words per clause) correlated significantly with quality of writing (Kameen, 1983), increased with grade level (Yau & Belanger, 1985), and distinguished between the L1 and L2 writers (Ferris, 1994b). L2 writers used more clauses than L1 writers (Hu et al., 1982). Clauses per T-unit increased with grade level (Yau & Belanger, 1985). Number of clauses did not distinguish between more and less skilled L2 writers (Kameen, 1980). Also, L2 writers had more adverb clauses of cause that did L1 writers, but fewer reduced adjective clauses and reduced adverb clauses (Hinkel, 2002).

L2 writers' interlingual errors included the unidiomatic reversal of negative clauses and the misplacement of *I think* in clauses in which a judgment is made (Bryant, 1984). Over time, L2 writers' coordination of independent clauses increased or changed very little (Casanave, 1994). L2 writers were more likely to use sentences with a dependent clause containing the topical subject (Ferris, 1994b).

Syntactic Complexity/Maturity

There was a positive relationship between syntactic complexity/maturity and age (Yau & Belanger, 1984), grade level (Carlisle, 1989; Yau & Belanger, 1984), L2 writing ability level (Ferris, 1994a), experience in L2 learning (Yau & Belanger, 1984), and instructional context: it was greater for bilingual program students than for submersion program students (Carlisle, 1989). Syntactic maturity development in L2 writers was similar to that shown by L1 writers (Yau & Belanger, 1985). Age was a decisive factor in the production and greater use of L2 syntactic patterns, which developed more in the age period of 12–14 years (Torras & Celaya, 2001). Greater demands on syntactic resources were made by exposition than by narrative; all syntactic factors showed more complexity in the expository mode than in the narrative mode (Yau & Belanger, 1984).

T-units

L1 writers had longer T-units than L2 writers (M. Lee, 2003), and more skilled L2 writers produced longer T-units than did less skilled L2 writers (Kameen, 1980). L2 T-unit length was positively related to grade level (Yau & Belanger, 1985), language development (Lim, 1983), and text quality (Intaraprawat & Steffensen, 1995). Over time, most L2 writers wrote longer T-units (Casanave, 1994). L2 writing had fewer T-units than L1 writing (Lanauze & Snow, 1989). Error-free T-units were positively related to L2 writing ability, language development (Lim, 1983), and text quality (Flahive & Bailey, 1993).

Sentence Processes

Person

USE OF FIRST AND THIRD PERSON

When the perspective was shifted from the first person to the third person, low-proficiency L2 students' writing became poorer in quantity and quality, whereas the high-proficiency students' writing exhibited no decrease in quantity and a slight decline in quality. But when the perspective was shifted from the third person to the first person, the students' writing showed both quantitative and qualitative development, and development was more clearly observed in the stories of those with high L2 proficiency. Thus, the third person point of view did not negatively affect the writing performance of students with high proficiency, but the third person perspective constrained the composing processes of those with low proficiency (Kamimura & Oi, 2001).

It was reported that, when L2 writers wrote in the first person, they could identify with the protagonist and feel as if they were themselves participating in the story; in contrast, when they wrote in the third person, they had to detach themselves from the standpoint of the protagonist. Overall, writers with high L2 proficiency were able to compose a more developed story in both third person and first person; for those with low L2 proficiency, their composing difficulties seemed to be doubled when writing in L2 in the third person, since they had to face both linguistic and cognitive issues (Kamimura & Oi, 2001).

USE OF FIRST PERSON

There was no significant difference between L2 students' writing in L2 and L1 students' writing in L1 with regard to first person singular or plural pronouns. The L2 students used a higher frequency of first person plural pronouns in their L2 writing than did L1 students. L2 students writing in the L2 used a higher frequency of first person plural pronouns than when writing in their L1 (Wu & Rubin, 2000). Few L2 writers used first person when stating claims, but they did use first person when thanking others (K. Hyland, 2002).

Coordination

Age was a decisive factor in L2 writers' production and greater use of coordination, which developed more in the age period of 12–14 years (Torras & Celaya, 2001). However, it was also reported that amount of coordination did not increase with grade level (Yau & Belanger, 1985). Coordination of independent clauses increased or changed very little, but most students used fewer sentences beginning with coordinating conjunctions (e.g. *and, but, so*; Casanave, 1994).

L2 (Arabic) writers used more coordination with *and* than did L1 English writers and used coordination as a low-level or local rhetorical strategy rather than a global strategy for paragraph development (Fakhri, 1994). However, it was also reported that there were more coordinators in L1 (Arabic) writing than in L2 (English) writing (Khalil, 1999).

Subordination

As L2 proficiency level increased, L2 writers incorporated more subordination (Grant & Ginther, 2000). Age was also a decisive factor in the production and greater use of subordination (Torras & Celaya, 2001). The most significant differences between higher- and lower-rated L2 texts were found in adverbial subordination (Jarvis et al., 2003). L2 writers' errors in the use of subordination caused them problems in encoding relationships between rhetorical elements (Pelsmaekers et al., 1998).

Nominalization

The use of nominalizations in L2 texts was positively correlated with holistic scores (Ferris, 1994a). More skilled L2 writers used more nominalization than did their less skilled counterparts (Grant & Ginther, 2000). One of the most significant differences between higher- and lower-rated L2 texts was found in nominalization (Jarvis et al., 2003).

Comparison

Errors in comparison were more common for L2 than for L1 writers, but those due to idiomaticity were a similar proportion of the total in the both groups. Similar error patterns were found with the comparative pattern (e.g. *as* ADV/ADJ *as*; Sonomura, 1996).

Agreement

One of the most frequent errors in L2 writers' texts was agreement between subject and verb (S. Olsen, 1999), the successful use of which develops over time (McCarthey et al., 2005). However, one study found that L1 and L2 writers were similar with regard to subject–verb agreement (Benson et al., 1992).

Complementation

There was an increase across L2 proficiency levels in terms of overall complementation (Grant & Ginther, 2000). The most significant differences between higher and lower rated L2 texts were in complementation (Jarvis et al., 2003).

Collocation

L2 writers' texts had fewer collocations (Hinkel, 2002) and more collocation errors than those of L1 writers (Hu et al., 1982; Sonomura, 1996).

Segmentation

L2 children's errors in segmentation were not random, but were evidence of hypotheses students were making (Edelsky & Jilbert, 1985).

Functional Element Classes

Hedges

More skilled L2 writers' text had twice the proportion of correctly used hedges (terms that allow writers to express reservations about their assertions, e.g. *probably*) as those of less skilled L2 writers (Intaraprawat & Steffensen, 1995). Greater use of hedges in L2 texts may have been due to a combination of lower proficiency and lower levels of self-esteem and confidence (contradiction noted; Wu & Rubin, 2000).

Whereas the L2 academic texts written by Chinese, Japanese, Korean, and Indonesian speakers included epistemic hedges (e.g. *apparently*) at median rates significantly higher than those encountered in the essays of novice L1 writers, speakers of Arabic and Vietnamese employed significantly fewer of these textual features. For lexical hedges (e.g. *sort of*), the L2 writing of Japanese, Indonesian, Vietnamese, and Arabic speakers included significantly lower median rates of hedging than L1 prose, whereas the Chinese and Korean students' median rates of lexical hedges were largely similar to those in L1 prose. Fewer than half of all essays in any group contained possibility hedges (e.g. *perhaps*). L2 writers employed a limited range of hedging devices, largely associated with conversational discourse and casual spoken interaction. These findings were further supported by a prevalence of conversational intensifiers (e.g. *really*) and overstatements (exaggerations) in the L2 writing that are ubiquitous in informal speech but are rare in formal written prose (Hinkel, 2005).

Connectors

Connector (e.g. *however*) density (the number of connectors per number of finite clauses) discriminated between L2 and L1 writing; it correlated positively in L2 and negatively in L1. When the number of *that* clauses and relative clauses is subtracted, the discriminatory power increased—again, positively for L2 and negatively for L1 writing (that is, a greater density of connectors correlated with high scores in L2 writing, but a lower density correlated to high scores in L1 writing; Lintermann-Rygh, 1985). L2 writers used more connectors than did L1 writers; some connectors were overused and others were underused (Granger & Tyson, 1996). L2 writers' errors in the use of connectors caused them problems in encoding relationships between rhetorical elements (Pelsmaekers et al., 1998).

Intensifiers

The median frequency rates of the L2 writers on three types of intensifiers (universal pronouns [e.g. *all*], amplifiers [e.g. *absolutely*], and emphatics [e.g. *certainly*]) associated with exaggeration and inflation of the actual state of affairs significantly exceeded those of L1 novice writers. These findings were further supported by a prevalence of conversational intensifiers (e.g. *really*) in the L2 writing that are ubiquitous in informal speech but are rare in formal written prose (Hinkel, 2005).

Idioms

L2 text had fewer idiomatic phrases than L1 writers' texts (Hinkel, 2002). Although L2 writers' texts included error in idiom use (Chandrasegaran, 1986), grammatical errors were more common. Errors due to idiomaticity made up a similar proportion of total errors in both L1 and L2 texts (Sonomura, 1996).

Discourse Markers

L2 writers' texts were more likely to have sentences that began with discourse markers (e.g. *in conclusion*) and sentences with a dependent clause containing the topical subject than those of L1 writers (Ferris, 1994b).

Downtoners

L2 writers from two language groups—Arabic and Indonesian—used downtoners (e.g. *almost*) at median frequency rates similar to those encountered in L1 texts overall; essays from other language groups—Chinese, Japanese, Korean, and Vietnamese—included them significantly less frequently (Hinkel, 2005).

Emphatics

Good L2 essays had twice the number of emphatics (e.g. *undoubtedly*) as poor L2 essays had (Intaraprawat & Steffensen, 1995). L1 writers used more emphatic devices than did L2 writers (Kamimura & Oi, 1998).

Illocutionary Markers

In good and poor L2 essays, more errors occurred in low-frequency categories, such as illocutionary markers (which indicate the act the writer is performing, e.g. *to conclude*); good essays had three times as many illocutionary markers as poor ones (Intaraprawat & Steffensen, 1995).

Overstatements

There was a prevalence of overstatements (exaggerations) in L2 writing that are ubiquitous in informal speech but are rare in formal written prose (Hinkel, 2005).

Softening Devices

L2 writers' heavy dependence on softening devices (e.g. *maybe*) contrasted with their use of emphatic devices (Kamimura & Oi, 1998).

Subordinators

There was no statistically significant difference between numbers of subordinate conjunctions in L1 and L2 texts (Khalil, 1999).

Sentence Qualities

Accuracy

Accuracy (number of errors) and fluency (number of words) were highly correlated. L1 writers' accuracy was significantly higher than that of L2 writers (Tarone et al., 1993). In early and late starters (with regard to what age students began to study the L2), fluency developed faster and achieved higher levels than did accuracy. Early starters' development was more pronounced in accuracy than in fluency. Early starters made extensive use of memorized sequences or patterns in their writing, aiding accuracy scores, whereas late starters produced longer, more varied sentences, thus favoring fluency over accuracy (Torras & Celaya, 2001).

For L2 writers, grammatical errors were the most common and most difficult problems in L2 writing (Ghrib-Maamaouri, 2001; Leung, 1984). L2 writers made more grammatical errors than L1 writers (Sims & Guice, 1992; Sonomura, 1996). L2 writers' grammar errors included inappropriate verb forms, articles, noun forms, and prepositions and seemed to have resulted from hypercorrection, overgeneralization of grammar rules, and interference/transfer (Ghrib-Maamoauri, 2001).

Complexity

It was reported that L2 writers used simpler sentences (Hu et al., 1982; Huie & Yahya, 2003) with less depth (Hu et al., 1982); however, it was also reported that sentence complexity for L1 and L2 groups was similar (M. Lee, 2003). In one case, sentences written in L1 were more complex than sentences in L2 (Khuwaileh & Al Shoumali, 2000). And sentence complexity in writing was greater than that in speech for L2 learners (Wald, 1987).

For both early and late starters (in studying L2), fluency developed faster and achieved higher levels than did complexity. Particularly, in the area of complexity, the late starters developed more rapidly than the early starters. For the early starters, complexity was the area that seemed to develop least. When complexity is broken down to grammatical complexity and lexical complexity, there was significant improvement in lexical complexity for both early and late starters (Torras & Celaya, 2001).

Length

L2 writers' sentence length seemed to have resulted from exam stress, abandonment of messages that were too difficult, or a lack of instruction in writing (Ghrib-Maamaouri, 2001). L1 writers had more words per sentence than did L2 writers (Benson et al., 1992). L2 late starters produced longer sentences than L2 early starters (Torras & Celaya, 2001). In one instance, sentences written in L1 were longer than sentences written in L2 (Khuwaileh & Al Shoumali, 2000).

Structure

Sentence depth was greater for L1 than for L2 writers (Hu et al., 1982). Sentence structure was better for L2 writers who used more L1 (Lay, 1983). L2 writers' truncated/fragmented sentence constructions seemed to have resulted from exam stress, abandonment of messages that were too difficult, or a lack of training in writing (Ghrib-Maamaouri, 2001).

Fluency

For the early starter L2 learners, development was more pronounced in accuracy than in fluency. The early starters made extensive use of memorized sequences or patterns in their writing, aiding fluency and accuracy scores, whereas the late starters produced longer, more varied sentences, thus favoring fluency over accuracy (Torras & Celaya, 2001).

Type

L1 writers used more run-on and comma splice sentences (Benson et al., 1992), more "type 1" sentences (in which topical subject, grammatical subject, and initial sentence element coincide; Ferris, 1994b), and more *it*-cleft constructions (*It seems that . . .*) than did L2 writers (Hinkel, 2002, 2003). L2 writers' used more existential *there* constructions (*There is/are. . .*; Hinkel, 2003).

Mechanics

Spelling

For primary school learners, L2 spelling errors were evidence of hypotheses students were making (Edelsky & Jilbert, 1985), features of L2 orthography, L2 phonics generalizations (Edelsky, 1986), and L1 interference (Huie & Yahya, 2003).

For secondary school L2 students, there were differences between early and late learners' spelling in the occurrence of partials (conventionally spelled words that partially resemble the intended word, but more visually than semantically or phonologically; Wald, 1987). Language mixing errors (resulting when learners inserted elements from L1 into their interlanguage owing to lack of forms in L2) included spelling errors resulting from double consonants in the L2, incorrect use of letters associated with the L2, and the use of L1 adjective forms when writing in L2 (S. Olsen, 1999).

Adult L2 writers made more spelling errors than did L1 writers (Hu et al., 1982; Tesdell, 1984) and had more habitual errors than slips. The percentage of spelling errors among the speakers of languages that use the Roman alphabet was similar to the percentage of spelling errors among speakers of languages that do not (Tesdell, 1984).

Punctuation

In child L2 writers, errors in punctuation were not so much random as they were sensible, often evidence that the children were trying out hypotheses about the language in which they were writing (Edelsky, 1986; Edelsky & Jilbert, 1985). Early invented punctuation patterns focused on local units, such as the word or the line, whereas later invented patterns focused on textual issues (Edelsky, 1986).

One study of adults reported that L1 writers made more errors in punctuation than L2 writers (Hu et al., 1982). Another claimed that L1 basic and L2 writers were similar in their use of punctuation (Benson et al., 1992).

L2 writers' errors in the use of punctuation caused them problems in encoding relationships between rhetorical elements (Pelsmaekers et al., 1998). Male L2 writers paid less attention to guidelines with regard to punctuation; female L2 writers took great pains to adhere to all of the guidelines (Morris, 1998).

Orthography

Orthography errors, one of the most common L2 errors, frequently occurred as a result of generalizations (when learners used L1 previous knowledge to form L2 rules; S. Olsen, 1999).

General

Mechanical problems in L2 writing were based in interlingual and intralingual interference and inappropriate use of writing strategies (Ghrib-Maamaouri, 2001).

Abbreviations and Symbols

Abbreviations and symbols were used by L1 but not by L2 writers (Hu et al., 1982).

Discussion

There were clear differences in terms of the number of findings among the six major categories of grammatical issues in the L2 texts. Parts of speech/ form classes elements had the most (32%), with verbs alone accounting for 12% of all findings; followed by sentence elements (28%), with words/ lexis constituting 17% of all findings; sentence processes (12%); sentence qualities (11%); functional element classes (9%); and mechanics (7%). It is assumed that more findings in a particular area may reflect greater depth in the research of this area.

There were also differences in terms of number of subcategories per major category of grammatical issues in L2 texts. Functional element classes had the most with eleven (26%), followed by sentence processes with nine (21%), parts of speech/form classes with eight (19%), sentence qualities with six (14%), mechanics with five (12%), and sentence elements with four (9%). It is assumed that more subcategories for a particular category may reflect greater breadth in the research in that category.

It should also be noted that only a small fraction of the individual findings reported here were supported by more than one study. Only 16 findings (6%) were supported by evidence from two studies; only three (1%) were supported by evidence from three studies; and one (0.03%) was supported by six studies. All the other individual findings here were supported by only one study. There was a strong focus on analyses of students' errors in the research reported on in this chapter.

As in the other areas reviewed, the inquiry into grammatical issues in L2 writers' text has produced few sustained programs of research. Some notable exceptions, however, are Ferris (Ferris, 1994a, 1994b; Jarvis et al., 2003), Hinkel (Hinkel, 1997, 2002, 2003, 2005); and Reynolds (Reynolds, 1995, 2002, 2005).

Table 1 Alphabetical listing of studies cited in section III

Study author(s)	Year of publication	Number of subjects	Subjects' L1(s)	Subjects' L2(s)
Achiba & Kuromiya	1983	154	Japanese	English
Akyel	1994	78	Turkish	English
Albrechtsen	1997	1	Dutch	English
Aliakbari	2002	23	Persian	English
Allison	2005	8	Chinese; others unspecified	English
Angelova & Riazantseva	1999	4	Indonesian, Russian, Taiwanese	English
Armengol-Castells	2001	3	Catalan	English, Spanish
Arndt	1987	6	Chinese	English
Bartelt	1982	187	Navajo, Western Apache	English
Bartelt	1983	140	Navajo, Western Apache	English
Belcher & Hirvela	2005	6	Chinese, Japanese	English
Benson, Deming, Denzer, & Valeri-Gold	1992	112	Amharic, Arabic, Cambodian, Chinese, English, Farsi, French, Gola, Gujartic, Hindi, Japanese, Korean, Portuguese, Somali, Spanish, Tagalog, Thai, Tigringa, Vietnamese	English
Bermudez & Prater	1994	37	Spanish	English
Betancourt & Phinney	1988	60	Spanish	English
Blanton	2005	2	Amharic, Vietnamese	English
Bosher	1998	3	Cambodian, Lao, Vietnamese	English
Bouton	1995	130	Chinese, English, Hindi, Japanese, Korean	English
Bryant	1984	200	Japanese	English
Buckwalter & Lo	2002	1	Chinese	English

Continued overleaf

Table 1 (continued) Alphabetical listing of studies cited in section III

Study author(s)	Year of publication	Number of subjects	Subjects' L1(s)	Subjects' L2(s)
Bunton	1999	13	Cantonese, Mandarin	English
Butler-Nalin	1984	13	English; others not specified	English
Campbell	1990	30	Not specified	English
Canale, Frenette, & Belanger	1988	32	French	English
Carlisle	1989	63	Spanish	English
Carrell & Connor	1991	33	Chinese, German, Greek, Hebrew, Hindi, Italian, Japanese, Serbo-Croatian, Spanish, Urdu, Vietnamese	English
Carrell & Monroe	1993	87	Arabic, Bengali, Chinese, English, German, Japanese, Lao, Romanian, Spanish, Tagalog, Turkish, Vietnamese; others not specified	English
Carson, Carrell, Silberstein, Kroll, & Kuehn	1990	105	Chinese, Japanese	English
Carson & Kuehn	1992	48	Chinese	English
Casanave	1994	16	Japanese	English
Chandrasegaran	1986	10	Chinese, Malay	English
Chandrasegaran	2000	3	Not specified	English
Chenoweth & Hayes	2001	13	English	French, German
Choi	1986	9	English, Korean	English
Choi	1988	9	English, Korean	English
Christianson	1997	51	Japanese	English
Clachar	1999	13	Spanish	English
Connor	1984	4	English, Japanese, Spanish	English
Connor & Mayberry	1996	1	Finnish	English

Table I (continued) Alphabetical listing of studies cited in section III

Study author(s)	Year of publication	Number of subjects	Subjects' L1(s)	Subjects' L2(s)
Cronnell	1985	170	Spanish	English
Cumming	1989	23	French	English
Cumming	1990b	23	French	English
Cumming, Rebuffot, & Ledwell	1989	14	English	French
Doushaq	1986	96	Arabic	English
Edelsky	1982	9	Spanish	English
Edelsky	1986	9	Spanish	English
Edelsky & Jilbert	1985	26	Spanish	English
Elliot	1986	1	Arabic	English
Engber	1995	66	Arabic, Chinese, French, Indonesian, Italian, Japanese, Korean, Malay, Polish, Portuguese, Romanian, Russian, Spanish, Thai	English
Evensen	1990	9	Swedish	English
Fakhri	1994	60	Arabic, Chinese, Japanese, Spanish, Thai, Vietnamese	English
Ferenz	2005	6	Hebrew	English
Ferris	1994a	160	Arabic, Chinese, Japanese, Spanish	English
Ferris	1994b	60	English; others not specified	English
Ferris & Politzer	1981	60	Spanish	English
Field & Oi	1992	96	English, Cantonese	English
Flahive & Bailey	1993	40	Mandarin, Spanish, Vietnamese; 9 other languages not specified	English
Friedlander	1990	28	Chinese	English
Gentil	2005	3	French	English

Continued overleaf

Table 1 (continued) Alphabetical listing of studies cited in section III

Study author(s)	Year of publication	Number of subjects	Subjects' L1(s)	Subjects' L2(s)
Ghrib-Maamaouri	2001	25	Arabic, French	English
Gosden	1996	16	Japanese	English
Granger & Tyson	1996	Not specified	English, French	English
Grant & Ginther	2000	90	Not specified	English
Gungle & Taylor	1989	284	Arabic, Chinese, Malay, Portuguese, Spanish; other languages not specified	English
Hall, C.	1990	4	Chinese, French, Norwegian, Polish	English
Hawes & Thomas	1997	100	Malay	English
Hedgcock & Atkinson	1993	272	English, Indonesian, Japanese, Korean, Mandarin, Thai	English
Hinkel	1997	150	Chinese, English, Indonesian, Japanese, Korean	English
Hinkel	2001	895	Arabic, English, Indonesian, Japanese, Korean	English
Hinkel	2002	1,457	Arabic, Chinese, English, Indonesian, Japanese, Korean, Vietnamese	English
Hinkel	2003	1,083	Arabic, Chinese, English, Indonesian, Japanese, Korean	English
Hinkel	2005	745	Arabic, Chinese, English, Indonesian, Japanese, Korean, Vietnamese	English
Hirose	2003	15	Japanese	English
Hirose & Sasaki	1994	19	Japanese	English
Hu, Brown, & Brown	1982	101	Chinese, English	English
Hudelson	1989a	2	Spanish	English
Huie & Yahya	2003	396	English, Kanjoval, Spanish; others not specified	English
Hyland, K.	2002	64	Cantonese	English

Table 1 (continued) Alphabetical listing of studies cited in section III

Study author(s)	Year of publication	Number of subjects	Subjects' L1(s)	Subjects' L2(s)
Hyland, K.	2004a	240	Cantonese	English
Hyland & Milton	1997	920	Cantonese, English	English
Hyland & Tse	2005	465	Cantonese	English
Indrasuta	1988	60	English, Thai	English
Intaraprawat & Steffensen	1995	12	Chinese, Farsi, French, Hindi, Japanese, Korean, Spanish, Thai	English
Janopoulos	1986	79	Arabic, Chinese, Farsi, Hebrew, Hindi, Korean, Marathi, Spanish, Tamil, Telegu, Turkish; other Asian and European languages not specified	English
Jarvis, Grant, Bikowski, & Ferris	2003	338	Arabic, Chinese, Japanese, Spanish	English
Johns	1984	Not specified	Chinese	English
Johnson, D.	1992	35	Not specified	English
Johnson, P.	1992	40	English, Malay	English
Jones	1985	2	Portuguese, Spanish	English
Jones & Tetroe	1987	6	Spanish	English
Kameen	1980	50	Arabic, Chinese, Farsi, French, Hebrew, Ibo, Italian, Japanese, Lambya, Malay, Portuguese, Spanish, Thai, Urdu	English
Kameen	1983	50	Arabic, Chinese, Farsi, French, Hebrew, Ibo, Italian, Japanese, Lambya, Malay, Portuguese, Spanish, Thai, Urdu	English
Kamimura	1996	39	Japanese	English
Kamimura & Oi	1998	52	English, Japanese	English
Kamimura & Oi	2001	51	Japanese	English

Continued overleaf

Table 1 (continued) Alphabetical listing of studies cited in section III

Study author(s)	Year of publication	Number of subjects	Subjects' L1(s)	Subjects' L2(s)
Kelly	1986	9	Finnish, Indonesian, Italian, Polish, Sinhala, Spanish, Tagalog	English
Khalil	1989	20	Arabic	English
Khalil	1999	40	Arabic	English
Khuwaileh & Al Shoumali	2000	150	Arabic	English
Kiany & Nejad	2001	120	Farsi	English
Kobayashi, H.	1984	226	English, Japanese	English
Kobayashi & Rinnert	1992	48	Japanese	English
Kobayashi & Rinnert	2001	53	Japanese	English
Kubota	1998	46	Japanese	English
Lai	1986	82	Chinese	English
Lanauze & Snow	1989	38	Spanish	English
Lay	1982	4	Chinese	English
Lay	1983	5	Chinese	English
Lee, M.	2003	80	English, Chinese	English
Lee, S.-Y.	2005	270	Chinese	English
Leung	1984	40	Cantonese	English
Lim	1983	120	Not specified	English
Linnarud	1983	63	English, Swedish	English
Linnarud	1986	63	English, Swedish	English
Lintermann-Rygh	1985	24	Norwegian	English
Liu & Braine	2005	50	Chinese	English
Ma & Wen	1999	133	Chinese	English
Maier	1992	18	English, Japanese, Korean, Tahitian	English

Table I (continued) Alphabetical listing of studies cited in section III

Study author(s)	Year of publication	Number of subjects	Subjects' L1(s)	Subjects' L2(s)
Manchón, Roca, & Murphy	2000	3	Spanish	English
Mauranen	1996	Not specified	English, Finnish	English
Maxwell & Falick	1992	40	American Sign Language	English
McCarthey & Garcia	2005	11	Mandarin, Spanish	English
McCarthey, Guo, & Cummins	2005	5	Mandarin	English
Meziani	1984	50	Arabic	English
Mohan & Lo	1985	30	Chinese	English
Moragne e Silva	1989	1	Portuguese	English
Morris	1998	42	French	English
Norment	1986	30	Chinese	English
Oi	1999	65	English, Japanese	English
Olsen, S.	1999	39	Norwegian	English
Parkhurst	1990	17	English, Farsi, French, German, Greek, Hebrew, Hungarian, Italian, Korean	English
Pelsmaekers, Braecke, & Geluykens	1998	190	Dutch	English
Porte	1997	71	Spanish	English
Qi	1998	1	Chinese	English
Raimes	1985	8	Burmese, Chinese, Greek, Spanish	English
Raimes	1987	8	Chinese, Farsi, Haitian Creole, Spanish	English
Reid	1992	638	Arabic, Chinese, English, Spanish	English
Reynolds	1995	42	Arabic, Chinese, English, Japanese, Korean, Romance (not further specified)	English

Continued overleaf

Table I (continued) Alphabetical listing of studies cited in section III

Study author(s)	Year of publication	Number of subjects	Subjects' L1(s)	Subjects' L2(s)
Reynolds	2002	735	English, Spanish, Vietnamese; others not specified	English
Reynolds	2005	735	English, Spanish, Vietnamese; others not specified	English
Roca	1996	10	Spanish	English
Roca, Marin, & Murphy	2001	21	Spanish	English
Roca, Murphy, & Manchón	1999	19	Spanish	English
St. John	1987	30	Spanish	English
Sasaki	2000	12	Japanese	English
Sasaki	2004	11	Japanese	English
Sasaki & Hirose	1996	70	Japanese	English
Scarcella	1984	110	Japanese, Korean, Romance (not further specified), Taiwanese	English
Schneider & Connor	1990	40	Not specified	English
Shaw	1991	22	Arabic, Bengali, Chinese, Indonesian, Kanuri, Sinhala, Thai, Turkish, Urdu	English
Shih	1998	50	Chinese, Japanese, Korean, Tagalog, Vietnamese	English
Silva	1992	13	Arabic/French, Chinese, Japanese, Portuguese, Tamil, Turkish	English
Sims & Guice	1992	214	Chinese, English, Korean; others not specified	English
Skibniewski	1988	3	Polish	English
Skibniewski & Skibniewska	1986	21	Polish	English
Smith, V.	1994	6	German	English
Sonomura	1996	67	Hawaii Creole English; others not specified	English
Söter	1988	223	Arabic, English, Vietnamese	English
Spack	1997a	1	Japanese	English

Table I (continued) Alphabetical listing of studies cited in section III

Study author(s)	Year of publication	Number of subjects	Subjects' LI(s)	Subjects' L2(s)
Stalker & Stalker	1989	10	Arabic, Chinese, English, Greek	English
Sze	2002	1	Chinese	English
Takagaki	2003	3	Japanese	English
Tardy	2005a	2	Chinese, Thai	English
Tardy	2005b	4	Chinese, Japanese, Korean, Thai	English
Tarone, Downing, Cohen, Gillette, Murie, & Dailey	1993	129	Arabic, Cambodian, English, French, Hmong, Indonesian, Japanese, Korean, Lao, Spanish, Vietnamese	English
Tesdell	1984	56	Arabic, Chinese, Malay, Spanish	English
Torras & Celaya	2001	63	Not specified	English
Urzua	1987	4	Cambodian, Lao	English
Uzawa	1994	22	Japanese	English
Uzawa	1996	22	Japanese	English
Victori	1999	4	Spanish	English
Wald	1987	19	Spanish	English
Wang & Wen	2002	16	Chinese	English
Wikborg	1990	144	Swedish	English
Wong, A.	2005	4	Chinese	English
Wong, R.	1993	43	Chinese	English
Woodall	2002	28	English, Japanese, Spanish	English, Spanish, Japanese
Wu & Rubin	2000	80	English, Chinese	English
Yasuda	2004	3	Japanese	English

Continued overleaf

Table 1 (continued) Alphabetical listing of studies cited in section III

Study author(s)	Year of publication	Number of subjects	Subjects' L1 (s)	Subjects' L2(s)
Yau & Belanger	1984	60	Chinese	English
Yau & Belanger	1985	60	Chinese	English
Zainuddin & Moore	2003	4	Malay	English
Zamel	1982	8	Arabic, Greek, Italian, Japanese, Spanish	English
Zamel	1983	6	Chinese, Hebrew, Persian, Portuguese, Spanish	English
Zhang, M.	2000	107	Chinese	English
Zimmerman	2000	52	German	English

Table 2 Chronological listing of studies cited in section III

Study author(s)	Year of publication	Number of subjects	Subjects' L1 (s)	Subjects' L2(s)
Kameen	1980	50	Arabic, Chinese, Farsi, French, Hebrew, Ibo, Italian, Japanese, Lambya, Malay, Portuguese, Spanish, Thai, Urdu	English
Ferris & Politzer	1981	60	Spanish	English
Bartelt	1982	187	Navajo, Western Apache	English
Edelsky	1982	9	Spanish	English
Hu, Brown, & Brown	1982	101	Chinese, English	English
Lay	1982	4	Chinese	English
Zamel	1982	8	Arabic, Greek, Italian, Japanese, Spanish	English
Achiba & Kuromiya	1983	154	Japanese	English
Bartelt	1983	140	Navajo, Western Apache	English

Table 2 *(continued)* Chronological listing of studies cited in section III

Study author(s)	Year of publication	Number of subjects	Subjects' L1(s)	Subjects' L2(s)
Kameen	1983	50	Arabic, Chinese, Farsi, French, Hebrew, Ibo, Italian, Japanese, Lambya, Malay, Portuguese, Spanish, Thai, Urdu	English
Lay	1983	5	Chinese	English
Lim	1983	120	Not specified	English
Linnarud	1983	63	English, Swedish	English
Zamel	1983	6	Chinese, Hebrew, Persian, Portuguese, Spanish	English
Bryant	1984	200	Japanese	English
Butler-Nalin	1984	13	English; others not specified	English
Connor	1984	4	English, Japanese, Spanish	English
Johns	1984	Not specified	Chinese	English
Kobayashi, H.	1984	226	English, Japanese	English
Leung	1984	40	Cantonese	English
Meziani	1984	50	Arabic	English
Scarcella	1984	110	Japanese, Korean, Romance (not further specified), Taiwanese	English
Tesdell	1984	56	Arabic, Chinese, Malay, Spanish	English
Yau & Belanger	1984	60	Chinese	English
Cronnell	1985	170	Spanish	English
Edelsky & Jilbert	1985	26	Spanish	English
Jones	1985	2	Portuguese, Spanish	English
Lintermann-Rygh	1985	24	Norwegian	English
Mohan & Lo	1985	30	Chinese	English
Raimes	1985	8	Burmese, Chinese, Greek, Spanish	English

Continued overleaf

Table 2 (continued) Chronological listing of studies cited in section III

Study author(s)	Year of publication	Number of subjects	Subjects' LI(s)	Subjects' L2(s)
Yau & Belanger	1985	60	Chinese	English
Chandrasegaran	1986	10	Chinese, Malay	English
Choi	1986	9	English, Korean	English
Doushaq	1986	96	Arabic	English
Edelsky	1986	9	Spanish	English
Elliot	1986	1	Arabic	English
Janopoulous	1986	79	Arabic, Chinese, Farsi, Hebrew, Hindi, Korean, Marathi, Spanish, Tamil, Telegu, Turkish; other Asian and European languages not specified	English
Kelly	1986	9	Finnish, Indonesian, Italian, Polish, Sinhala, Spanish, Tagalog	English
Lai	1986	82	Chinese	English
Linnarud	1986	63	English, Swedish	English
Norment	1986	30	Chinese	English
Skibniewski & Skibniewska	1986	21	Polish	English
Arndt	1987	6	Chinese	English
Jones & Tetroe	1987	6	Spanish	English
Raimes	1987	8	Chinese, Farsi, Haitian Creole, Spanish	English
St. John	1987	30	Spanish	English
Urzua	1987	4	Cambodian, Lao	English
Wald	1987	19	Spanish	English
Betancourt & Phinney	1988	60	Spanish	English
Canale, Frenette, & Belanger	1988	32	French	English
Choi	1988	9	English, Korean	English

Table 2 *(continued)* Chronological listing of studies cited in section III

Study author(s)	Year of publication	Number of subjects	Subjects' L1(s)	Subjects' L2(s)
Indrasuta	1988	60	English, Thai	English
Skibniewski	1988	3	Polish	English
Söter	1988	223	Arabic, English, Vietnamese	English
Carlisle	1989	63	Spanish	English
Cumming	1989	23	French	English
Cumming, Rebuffot, & Ledwell	1989	14	English	French
Gungle & Taylor	1989	284	Arabic, Chinese, Malay, Portuguese, Spanish; other languages not specified	English
Hudelson	1989a	2	Spanish	English
Khalil	1989	20	Arabic	English
Lanauze & Snow	1989	38	Spanish	English
Moragne e Silva	1989	1	Portuguese	English
Stalker & Stalker	1989	10	Arabic, Chinese, English, Greek	English
Campbell	1990	30	Not specified	English
Carson, Carrell, Silberstein, Kroll, & Kuehn	1990	105	Chinese, Japanese	English
Cumming	1990b	23	French	English
Evensen	1990	9	Swedish	English
Friedlander	1990	28	Chinese	English
Hall, C	1990	4	Chinese, French, Norwegian, Polish	English
Parkhurst	1990	17	English, Farsi, French, German, Greek, Hebrew, Hungarian, Italian, Korean	English
Schneider & Connor	1990	40	Not specified	English

Continued overleaf

Table 2 (continued) Chronological listing of studies cited in section III

Study author(s)	Year of publication	Number of subjects	Subjects' L1(s)	Subjects' L2(s)
Wikborg	1990	144	Swedish	English
Carrell & Connor	1991	33	Chinese, German, Greek, Hebrew, Hindi, Italian, Japanese, Serbo-Croatian, Spanish, Urdu, Vietnamese	English
Shaw	1991	22	Arabic, Bengali, Chinese, Indonesian, Kanuri, Sinhala, Thai, Turkish, Urdu	English
Benson, Deming, Denzer, & Valeri-Gold	1992	112	Amharic, Arabic, Cambodian, Chinese, English, Farsi, French, Gola, Gujartic, Hindi, Japanese, Korean, Portuguese, Somali, Spanish, Tagalog, Thai, Tigringa, Vietnamese	English
Carson & Kuehn	1992	48	Chinese	English
Field & Oi	1992	96	English, Cantonese	English
Johnson, D.	1992	35	Not specified	English
Johnson, P.	1992	40	English, Malay	English
Kobayashi & Rinnert	1992	48	Japanese	English
Maier	1992	18	English, Japanese, Korean, Tahitian	English
Maxwell & Falick	1992	40	American Sign Language	English
Reid	1992	638	Arabic, Chinese, English, Spanish	English
Silva	1992	13	Arabic/French, Chinese, Japanese, Portuguese, Tamil, Turkish	English
Sims & Guice	1992	214	Chinese, English, Korean; others not specified	English
Carrell & Monroe	1993	87	Arabic, Bengali, Chinese, English, German, Japanese, Lao, Romanian, Spanish, Tagalog, Turkish, Vietnamese; others not specified	English

Table 2 (continued) Chronological listing of studies cited in section III

Study author(s)	Year of publication	Number of subjects	Subjects' L1(s)	Subjects' L2(s)
Flahive & Bailey	1993	40	Mandarin, Spanish, Vietnamese; 9 other languages not specified	English
Hedgcock & Atkinson	1993	272	English, Indonesian, Japanese, Korean, Mandarin, Thai	English
Tarone, Downing, Cohen, Gillette, Murie, & Dailey	1993	129	Arabic, Cambodian, English, French, Hmong, Indonesian, Japanese, Korean, Lao, Spanish, Vietnamese	English
Wong, R.	1993	43	Chinese	English
Akyel	1994	78	Turkish	English
Bermudez & Prater	1994	37	Spanish	English
Casanave	1994	16	Japanese	English
Fakhri	1994	60	Arabic, Chinese, Japanese, Spanish, Thai, Vietnamese	English
Ferris	1994a	160	Arabic, Chinese, Japanese, Spanish	English
Ferris	1994b	60	English; others not specified	English
Hirose & Sasaki	1994	19	Japanese	English
Smith, V.	1994	6	German	English
Uzawa	1994	22	Japanese	English
Bouton	1995	130	Chinese, English, Hindi, Japanese, Korean	English
Engber	1995	66	Arabic, Chinese, French, Indonesian, Italian, Japanese, Korean, Malay, Polish, Portuguese, Romanian, Russian, Spanish, Thai	English
Intaraprawat & Steffensen	1995	12	Chinese, Farsi, French, Hindi, Japanese, Korean, Spanish, Thai	English

Continued overleaf

Table 2 (continued) Chronological listing of studies cited in section III

Study author(s)	Year of publication	Number of subjects	Subjects' L1(s)	Subjects' L2(s)
Reynolds	1995	42	Arabic, Chinese, English, Japanese, Korean, Romance (not further specified)	English
Connor & Mayberry	1996	1	Finnish	English
Gosden	1996	16	Japanese	English
Granger & Tyson	1996	Not specified	English, French	English
Kamimura	1996	39	Japanese	English
Mauranen	1996	Not specified	English, Finnish	English
Roca	1996	10	Spanish	English
Sasaki & Hirose	1996	70	Japanese	English
Sonomura	1996	67	Hawaii Creole English; others not specified	English
Uzawa	1996	22	Japanese	English
Albrechtsen	1997	1	Dutch	English
Christianson	1997	51	Japanese	English
Hawes & Thomas	1997	100	Malay	English
Hinkel	1997	150	Chinese, English, Indonesian, Japanese, Korean	English
Hyland & Milton	1997	920	Cantonese, English	English
Porte	1997	71	Spanish	English
Spack	1997a	1	Japanese	English
Bosher	1998	3	Cambodian, Lao, Vietnamese	English
Kamimura & Oi	1998	52	English, Japanese	English
Kubota	1998	46	Japanese	English
Morris	1998	42	French	English
Pelsmaekers, Braecke, & Geluykens	1998	190	Dutch	English

Table 2 (continued) Chronological listing of studies cited in section III

Study author(s)	Year of publication	Number of subjects	Subjects' L1(s)	Subjects' L2(s)
Qi	1998	1	Chinese	English
Shih	1998	50	Chinese, Japanese, Korean, Tagalog, Vietnamese	English
Angelova & Riazantseva	1999	4	Indonesian, Russian, Taiwanese	English
Bunton	1999	13	Cantonese, Mandarin	English
Clachar	1999	13	Spanish	English
Khalil	1999	40	Arabic	English
Ma & Wen	1999	133	Chinese	English
Oi	1999	65	English, Japanese	English
Olsen, S.	1999	39	Norwegian	English
Roca, Murphy, & Manchón	1999	19	Spanish	English
Victori	1999	4	Spanish	English
Chandrasegaran	2000	3	Not specified	English
Grant & Ginther	2000	90	Not specified	English
Khuwaileh & Al Shoumali	2000	150	Arabic	English
Manchón, Roca, & Murphy	2000	3	Spanish	English
Sasaki	2000	12	Japanese	English
Wu & Rubin	2000	80	English, Chinese	English
Zhang, M.	2000	107	Chinese	English
Zimmerman	2000	52	German	English
Armengol-Castells	2001	3	Catalan	English, Spanish
Chenoweth & Hayes	2001	13	English	French, German
Ghrib-Maamaouri	2001	25	Arabic, French	English

Continued overleaf

Table 2 (continued) Chronological listing of studies cited in section III

Study author(s)	Year of publication	Number of subjects	Subjects' L1 (s)	Subjects' L2(s)
Hinkel	2001	895	Arabic, English, Indonesian, Japanese, Korean	English
Kamimura & Oi	2001	51	Japanese	English
Kiany & Nejad	2001	120	Farsi	English
Kobayashi & Rinnert	2001	53	Japanese	English
Roca, Marin, & Murphy	2001	21	Spanish	English
Torras & Celaya	2001	63	Not specified	English
Aliakbari	2002	23	Persian	English
Buckwalter & Lo	2002	1	Chinese	English
Hinkel	2002	1,457	Arabic, Chinese, English, Indonesian, Japanese, Korean, Vietnamese	English
Hyland, K.	2002	64	Cantonese	English
Reynolds	2002	735	English, Spanish, Vietnamese; others not specified	English
Sze	2002	1	Chinese	English
Wang & Wen	2002	16	Chinese	English
Woodall	2002	28	English, Japanese, Spanish	English, Spanish, Japanese
Hinkel	2003	1,083	Arabic, Chinese, English, Indonesian, Japanese, Korean	English
Hirose	2003	15	Japanese	English
Huie & Yahya	2003	396	English, Kanjoval, Spanish; others not specified	English
Jarvis, Grant, Bikowski, & Ferris	2003	338	Arabic, Chinese, Spanish, Japanese	English
Lee, M.	2003	80	English, Chinese	English

Table 2 (continued) Chronological listing of studies cited in section III

Study author(s)	Year of publication	Number of subjects	Subjects' L1(s)	Subjects' L2(s)
Takagaki	2003	3	Japanese	English
Zainuddin & Moore	2003	4	Malay	English
Hyland, K.	2004a	240	Cantonese	English
Sasaki	2004	11	Japanese	English
Yasuda	2004	3	Japanese	English
Allison	2005	8	Chinese; others unspecified	English
Belcher & Hirvela	2005	6	Chinese, Japanese	English
Blanton	2005	2	Amharic, Vietnamese	English
Ferenz	2005	6	Hebrew	English
Gentil	2005	3	French	English
Hinkel	2005	745	Arabic, Chinese, English, Indonesian, Japanese, Korean, Vietnamese	English
Hyland & Tse	2005	465	Cantonese	English
Lee, S.-Y.	2005	270	Chinese	English
Liu & Braine	2005	50	Chinese	English
McCarthey & Garcia	2005	11	Mandarin, Spanish	English
McCarthey, Guo, & Cummins	2005	5	Mandarin	English
Reynolds	2005	735	English, Spanish, Vietnamese; others not specified	English
Tardy	2005a	2	Chinese, Thai	English
Tardy	2005b	4	Chinese, Japanese, Korean, Thai	English
Wong, A.	2005	4	Chinese	English

Afterword

Future directions

We have attempted in this book not merely to produce an organized and annotated bibliography of the research on L2 writing in North America over the past 25 years but to contextualize that research through our understandings of the major trends and developments that the research documents. Our purpose in preparing the book was to consolidate knowledge about L2 writing, not to set an agenda for future research. The previous chapters in this book have, we hope, helped to consolidate that knowledge as well as to identify key themes, issues, and findings arising from it. But, in reviewing the landscape of inquiry about L2 writing over the past 25 years, certain trends have inevitably emerged just as new concerns have appeared. Some matters have come more clearly into focus, such as the variety of contexts in which L2 writing is taught and learned, the accumulated wisdom about ways in which teachers respond to L2 students' writing, or the fact that more proficient writers seem to do more of almost everything when they write than their less proficient counterparts do. Other matters are conspicuous by their relative absence, such as the relatively few descriptions of L2 writing development and instruction in settlement or business contexts; of teachers' usual practices for classroom interaction in L2 writing courses; or of the many psychological dimensions of composing in a second language (a particular focus of scholarship on L2 writing in Europe). Where considerable knowledge about L2 writing has accumulated, it invites systematic research syntheses of empirical research findings, as in Ortega's (2003) or Wolfe-Quintero, Inagaki, and Kim's (1998) syntheses of empirical findings about measures of L2 text features or Ferris' (2003) or L. Goldstein's (2005) reviews of research on responding to L2 students' written compositions. Where knowledge is evidently lacking, it invites new studies. In these ways, new directions for research are progressively emerging and will undoubtedly continue to do so in the future.

One way of considering the totality of research on L2 writing to date is from the vantage point of etic and emic perspectives, proposed by Pike

(1967). As anthropological researchers might ask, does the research on L2 writing tell us about local, insider (emic) as well as external, outsider (etic) perspectives on human phenomena and cultures? In a sense, neither viewpoint has been firmly established. Most inquiry on L2 writing has, with good intentions, sought to describe, evaluate, or influence the emic viewpoint of students who are learning to write in a second language. But the perspective adopted in research and educational practices has often been from the outsiders' etic perspective (of interested teachers or researchers who are not themselves members of the cultures concerned, cf. Atkinson & Ramanathan, 1995). Moreover, there are few etic frameworks that could serve to explain the astonishing variability worldwide that exists in respect to writing in second languages. One notable exception is Hornberger's (2003) continua of biliteracy. Her theory, however, serves primarily to demarcate the range of factors in people's personal development through their lifespan, sociolinguistic contexts, and features of their first and second languages. These elements illuminate and also complexify the concept of biliteracy but they do not explain how biliterate development happens, can be assessed systemically, or should be supported pedagogically.

There is certainly a need for future research to continue to describe and elucidate local contexts for learning and teaching L2 writing. This has been the trend of most research in the past decade. But there is a pressing need to consolidate and understand inquiry from local contexts within a programmatic, emic perspective. The syntheses in the present book make a small step in this direction. But large, conceptual issues remain. What factors determine the contexts in which L2 writing is taught and learned, constituting their uniqueness as well as their commonalities? What theories inform, or should inform, pedagogical and assessment practices for L2 writing, contributing to more appropriate, just, or effective educational policies? How do people actually learn all of the multifaceted, complex things required to write in a second language? What, if any, unique composing processes, discourse interactions, and text forms come into play in new forms of multimedia communications, such as blogs, chat or messaging systems, or collaborative, electronic writing groups—a type of context that research prior to 2005 barely considered, but that from the present vantage point is obviously a growing phenomenon with unique manifestations for L2 writers? Answers to some of these questions may come from future comparative, longitudinal, or multimethod research. Research on a large-scale, cross-case, long-term basis may reveal things that scarcely appear in the small-scale, case study approaches that have dominated L2 writing inquiry up to now. In turn, the prevailing focus on adult learners of English writing in academic contexts has overshadowed the many other languages, learner groups, and contexts of L2 writing internationally. So casting research on L2 writing globally, into various languages, across different student populations at different ages, and into diverse educational contexts is certainly worthwhile and necessary. But vigorous, unique, or large-scale projects may not in themselves resolve issues or bring new understanding. Principles and theories are needed too to make sense of these matters and to inform policies that do them justice. The emic requires explanation in reference to the etic. Such an extraordinary amount of research has investigated and documented local contexts for learning and teaching L2 writing since 1980 that we now have a distinct sense of the scope of these activities. But we still lack firm insights into the etic principles that govern or explain these phenomena. Spaces between the general and local also remain to be circumscribed. For example, L2 writing curricula are often defined in reference to curriculum standards or language proficiency tests, or both. But few analyses have sought to link these curriculum or policy elements to ordinary practices for teaching, learning, and societal interactions. Indeed, one future trend must surely be to produce more studies of L2 writing that evaluate relations between fundamental issues, such as learning or teaching, and the social contexts, educational policies, and intergroup behaviors that underpin them.

References

Abedi, J., Hofstetter, C., & Lord, C. (2004). Assessment accommodations for English language learners: Implications for policy-based empirical research. *Review of Educational Research, 74*, 1, 1–28.

Achiba, M., & Kuromiya, Y. (1983). Rhetorical patterns extant in the English composition of Japanese students. *Japan Association of Language Teachers Journal, 5*, 1–13.

ACTFL (American Council on the Teaching of Foreign Languages). (1986). *ACTFL Proficiency Guidelines*. Hastings-on-Hudson, NY: Authors.

Adamson, H. D. (1990). ESL students' use of academic skills in content courses. *English for Specific Purposes, 9*, 67–87.

Adamson, H. D. (1993). *Academic competence: Theory and classroom practice: Preparing ESL students for content courses*. New York: Longman.

Adger, C., & Peyton, J. (1999). Enhancing the education of immigrant students in secondary school: Structural challenges and directions. In C. Faltis & P. Wolfe (Eds.), *So much to say: Adolescents, bilingualism, and ESL in the secondary school* (pp. 205–224). New York: Teachers College Press.

Ahmad, U. (1997). Research article introductions in Malay: Rhetoric in an emerging research community. In A. Duszak (Ed.), *Culture and styles of academic discourse* (pp. 273–303). New York: Mouton de Gruyter.

Akyel, A. (1994). First language use in EFL writing: Planning in Turkish vs. planning in English. *International Journal of Applied Linguistics, 4*, 169–196.

Albrechtsen, D. (1997). One writer, two languages: A case study of a 15-year-old student's writing process in Dutch and English. *International Journal of Applied Linguistics, 7*, 223–250.

Alderson, J. C. (2005a). *Diagnosing foreign language proficiency*. London: Continuum.

Alderson, J. C. (Ed.). (2005b). Language assessment in Europe. Special issue of *Language Testing, 22*, 3.

Alderson, J. C., & Banerjee, J. (2002). State of the art review: Language testing and assessment (Part 2). *Language Teaching, 35*, 79–113.

Alderson, J. C., & Hamp-Lyons, L. (1996). TOEFL preparation courses: A study of washback. *TESOL Quarterly, 13*, 280–297.

Alderson, J. C., & Huhta, A. (2005). The development of a suite of computer-based diagnostic tests based on the Common European Framework. *Language Testing, 22*, 301–320.

Aliakbari, M. (2002). Writing in a foreign language: A writing problem or a language problem? *PAAL, 6*, 157–168.

Aljaafreh, A., & Lantolf, J. (1994). Negative feedback as regulation and second language learning in the zone of proximal development. *Modern Language Journal, 78*, 465–483.

Allison, D. (1996). Pragmatist discourse and English for academic purposes. *English for Specific Purposes, 15*, 85–103.

Allison, D. (2005). Authority and accommodation in higher degree research proposals. *Hong Kong Journal of Applied Linguistics, 8*, 155–180.

Allison, D., & Wu, S. M. (2002). Investigating writing development in an academic English language curriculum. In J. Flowerdew (Ed.), *Academic discourse* (pp. 253–267). London: Longman.

Ammon, P. (1985). Helping children learn to write in ESL: Some observations and some hypotheses. In S. Freedman (Ed.), *The acquisition of written language: Response and revision* (pp. 65–84). Norwood, NJ: Ablex.

Anderson, G., & Irvine, P. (1993). Informing critical literacy with ethnography. In C. Lankshear & P. McLaren (Eds.), *Critical literacy: Politics, praxis and the postmodern* (pp. 81–104). Albany, NY: SUNY Press.

Angelil-Carter, S. (1997). Second language acquisition of spoken and written English: Acquiring the skeptron. *TESOL Quarterly, 31*, 263–287.

Angelil-Carter, S. (2000). *Stolen language? Plagiarism in language*. Reading, MA: Pearson.

Angelova, M., & Riazantseva, A. (1999). "If you don't tell me, how can I know?": A case study of four international students learning to write the U.S. way. *Written Communication, 16*, 491–525.

Archibald, A. (1994). *The acquisition of discourse proficiency: A study of the ability of German school students to produce written texts in English as a foreign language*. Frankfurt: Peter Lang.

Armengol-Castells, L. (2001). Text-generating strategies of three multilingual writers: A protocol-based study. *Language Awareness, 10*, 91–106.

Arndt, V. (1987). Six writers in search of texts: A protocol based study of L1 and L2 writing. *ELT Journal, 41*, 257–267.

Ashwell, T. (2000). Patterns of teacher response to student writing in a multiple-draft composition classroom: Is content feedback followed by form feedback the best method? *Journal of Second Language Writing, 9*, 227–258.

Atkinson, D. (1997). A critical approach to critical thinking in TESOL. *TESOL Quarterly, 31*, 71–94.

Atkinson, D. (2003a). L2 writing in the post-process era: Introduction. *Journal of Second Language Writing, 12*, 3–15.

Atkinson, D. (2003b). Writing and culture in the post-process era. *Journal of Second Language Writing, 12*, 49–63.

Atkinson, D. (2004). Contrasting rhetorics/contrasting cultures: Why contrastive rhetoric needs a better conceptualization of culture. *Journal of English for Academic Purposes, 3*, 277–289.

Atkinson, D., & Ramanathan, V. (1995). Cultures of writing: An ethnographic comparison of L1 and L2 university writing/language programs. *TESOL Quarterly, 29*, 539–568.

Au, K. (1993). *Literacy instruction in multicultural settings*. Fort Worth, TX: Harcourt-Brace.

Auerbach, E. (1989). Toward a social-contextual approach to family literacy. *Harvard Educational Review, 59*, 165–181.

Auerbach, E. (1992). *Making meaning, making change: Participatory curriculum development for adult ESL literacy*. Washington, DC: Center for Applied Linguistics and Delta Systems.

Auerbach, E. (1993). Re-examining English Only in the ESL classroom. *TESOL Quarterly, 27*, 9–32.

Auerbach, E., & Burgess, D. (1985). The hidden curriculum of survival ESL. *TESOL Quarterly, 19*, 475–495.

August, D., & Hakuta, K. (Eds.). (1997). *Improving schooling for language minority children: A research agenda.* Washington, DC: National Academy Press.

Bachman, L. (1990). *Fundamental considerations in language testing.* Oxford: Oxford University Press.

Bachman, L. (2000). Modern language testing at the turn of the century: Assuring that what we count counts. *Language Testing, 17*, 1, 1–42.

Bachman, L., & Palmer, A. (1989). The construct validation of self-ratings of communicative language ability. *Language Testing, 6*, 14–29.

Bachman, L., & Palmer, A. (1996). *Language testing in practice.* Oxford, UK: Oxford University Press.

Bailey, K. (1999). *Washback in language testing.* TOEFL Monograph No. 15. Princeton, NJ: Educational Testing Service.

Baldauf, R. (1986). Linguistic constraints on participation in psychology. *The American Psychologist, 41*, 220–224.

Baldauf, R., & Jernudd, B. (1983). Language of publications as a variable in scientific communication. *Australian Review of Applied Linguistics, 6*, 97–108.

Ballard, B., & Clanchy, J. (1991). Assessment by misconception: Cultural influences and intellectual traditions. In L. Hamp-Lyons (Ed.), *Assessing second language writing in academic contexts* (pp. 19–36). Norwood, NJ: Ablex.

Bardovi-Harlig, K., & Bofman, T. (1989). Attainment of syntactic and morphological accuracy by advanced language learners. *Studies in Second Language Acquisition, 11*, 17–34.

Barks, D., & Watts, P. (2001). Textual borrowing strategies for graduate-level ESL writers. In D. Belcher & A. Hirvela (Eds.), *Linking literacies: Perspectives on L2 reading–writing connections* (pp. 246–267). Ann Arbor: University of Michigan Press.

Bartelt, H. G. (1982). Rhetorical redundancy in Apachean English inter-language. In *Essays in Native American English* (pp. 157–172). San Antonio, TX: Trinity University.

Bartelt, H. G. (1983). Transfer and variability of rhetorical redundancy in Apachean English interlanguage. In S. M. Gass & L. Selinker (Eds.), *Language transfer in language learning* (pp. 297–305). Rowley, MA: Newbury House.

Bascia, N., Cumming, A., Datnow, A., Leithwood, K., & Livingstone, D. (Eds.). (2005). *International handbook of educational policy.* Dordrecht, The Netherlands: Springer.

Basturkmen, H., & Lewis, M. (2002). Learner perspectives of success in an EAP writing course. *Assessing Writing, 8*, 31–46.

Beer, A. (2000). Diplomats in the basement: Graduate engineering students and intercultural communication. In P. Dias & A. Paré (Eds.), *Transitions: Writing in academic and workplace settings* (pp. 61–88). Cresskill, NJ: Hampton Press.

Belcher, D. (1989). How professors initiate nonnative speakers into their disciplinary discourse communities. *Texas Papers in Foreign Language Education, 1*, 204–225.

Belcher, D. (1991). Nonnative writing in a corporate setting. *The Technical Writing Teacher, 18*, 104–115.

Belcher, D. (1994). The apprenticeship approach to advanced academic literacy: Graduate students and their mentors. *English for Specific Purposes, 13*, 23–34.

Belcher, D. (1995). Writing critically across the curriculum. In D. Belcher & G. Braine (Eds.), *Academic writing in second language* (pp. 135–154). Norwood, NJ: Ablex.

Belcher, D. (1997). An argument for nonadversarial argumentation: On the relevance of the feminist critique of academic discourse to L2 writing pedagogy. *Journal of Second Language Writing, 6*, 1–21.

Belcher, D. (1999). Authentic interaction in a virtual classroom: Leveling the playing field in a graduate seminar. *Computers and Composition, 16,* 253–267.

Belcher, D. (2001). Does second language writing theory have gender? In T. Silva, & P. Matsuda (Eds.), *On second language writing* (pp. 59–71). Mahwah, NJ: Erlbaum.

Belcher, D. (2004). Trends in teaching English for Specific Purposes. *Annual Review of Applied Linguistics, 24,* 165–186.

Belcher, D., & Connor, U. (Eds.). (2001). *Reflections on multiliterate lives.* Buffalo, NY: Multilingual Matters.

Belcher, D., & Hirvela, A. (Eds.). (2001). *Linking literacies: Perspectives on L2 reading–writing connections.* Ann Arbor: University of Michigan Press.

Belcher, D., & Hirvela, A. (2005). Writing the qualitative dissertation: What motivates and sustains commitment to a fuzzy genre? *Journal of English for Academic Purposes, 4,* 187–205.

Bell, J. (1995). The relationship between L1 and L2 literacy: Some complicating factors. *TESOL Quarterly, 29,* 687–704.

Bell, J. (1997). Shifting frames, shifting stories. In C. Casanave & S. Schecter (Eds.), *On becoming a language educator: Personal essays on professional development* (pp. 133–143). Mahwah, NJ: Erlbaum.

Bell, J. (2002). Narrative inquiry: More than just telling stories. *TESOL Quarterly, 36,* 207–213.

Benesch, S. (Ed.). (1988). *Ending remediation: Linking ESL and content in higher education.* Washington, DC: TESOL.

Benesch, S. (1993). ESL, ideology, and the politics of pragmatism. *TESOL Quarterly, 27,* 705–717.

Benesch, S. (1995). Genres and processes in sociocultural context. *Journal of Second Language Writing, 4,* 191–195.

Benesch, S. (1996). Needs analysis and curriculum development in EAP: An example of a critical approach. *TESOL Quarterly, 30,* 723–738.

Benesch, S. (1998). Anorexia: A feminist EAP curriculum. In T. Smoke (Ed.), *Adult ESL: Politics, pedagogy, and participation in classroom and community programs* (pp. 101–114). Mahwah, NJ: Erlbaum.

Benesch, S. (1999). Rights analysis: Studying power relations in an academic setting. *English for Specific Purposes, 18,* 313–327.

Benesch, S. (2001). *Critical English for academic purposes: Theory, politics, and practice.* Mahwah, NJ: Erlbaum.

Benson, B., Deming, M., Denzer, D., & Valeri-Gold, M. (1992). A combined basic writing/English as a second language class: Melting pot or mishmash? *Journal of Basic Writing, 11,* 58–74.

Berg, E. (1999). The effects of trained peer response on ESL students' revision types and writing quality. *Journal of Second Language Writing, 8,* 215–241.

Berkenkotter, C., & Huckin, T. (1995). *Genre knowledge in disciplinary communication: Cognition/culture/power.* Hillsdale, NJ: Erlbaum.

Bermudez, A., & Prater, D. (1994). Examining the effects of gender and second language proficiency on Hispanic writers' persuasive discourse. *Bilingual Research Journal, 18,* 47–62.

Bernstein, S. (2004). Teaching and learning in Texas: Accountability testing, language, race, and place. *Journal of Basic Writing, 23,* 4–24.

Besnier, N. (1993). Literacy and feelings: The encoding of affect in Nukulaelae letters. In B. Street (Ed.), *Cross-cultural approaches to literacy* (pp. 62–86). Cambridge, UK: Cambridge University Press.

Betancourt, F., & Phinney, M. (1988). Sources of writing block in bilingual writers. *Written Communication, 5,* 461–479.

Bhatia, V. K. (1993). *Analyzing genre: Language use in professional settings.* London: Longman.

Bialystok, E. (1998). Coming of age in applied linguistics. *Language Learning, 48,* 497–518.

Biber, D., Conrad, S., Reppen, R., Byrd, P., & Helt, M. (2002). Speaking and writing in the university: A multidimensional comparison. *TESOL Quarterly, 36,* 9–48.

Blalock, S. (1997). Negotiating authority through one-to-one collaboration in the multicultural writing center. In C. Severino, J. Guerra, & J. Butler (Eds.), *Writing in multicultural settings: Research and scholarship in composition* (pp. 79–93). New York: Modern Language Association.

Blanton, L. (1995). Elephants and paradigms. *College ESL, 5,* 1-21.

Blanton, L. (1998). *Varied voices: On language and literacy learning.* Boston: Heinle & Heinle.

Blanton, L. (2002). Seeing the invisible: Situating L2 literacy acquisition in child–teacher interaction. *Journal of Second Language Writing, 11,* 295–310.

Blanton, L. (2005). Student, interrupted: A tale of two would-be writers. *Journal of Second Language Writing, 14,* 105–121.

Blanton, L., & Kroll, B. (Eds.) (2002). *ESL composition tales: Reflections on teaching.* Ann Arbor: University of Michigan Press.

Bloch, C., & Alexander, N. (2003). A luta continua!: The relevance of the continua of biliteracy to South African multilingual schools. In N. Hornberger (Ed.), *Continua of biliteracy: An ecological framework for educational policy, research, and practice in multilingual settings* (pp. 91–121). Clevedon, UK: Multilingual Matters.

Bloch, J. (2001). Plagiarism and the ESL student: From printed to electronic texts. In D. Belcher & A. Hirvela (Eds.), *Linking literacies: Perspectives on L2 reading–writing connections* (pp. 209–228). Ann Arbor: University of Michigan Press.

Bloch, J. (2002). Student/teacher interaction via email: The social context of Internet discourse. *Journal of Second Language Writing, 11,* 117–134.

Bloch, J. (2004). Second language cyber rhetoric: A study of Chinese L2 writers in an online USENET group. *Language Learning and Technology, 8,* 66–82.

Bloch, J., & Brutt-Griffler, J. (2001). Implementing CommonSpace in the ESL composition classroom. In D. Belcher & A. Hirvela (Eds.), *Linking literacies: Perspectives on L2 reading–writing connections* (pp. 309–333). Ann Arbor: University of Michigan Press.

Bosher, S. (1998). The composing processes of three Southeast Asian writers at the post-secondary level: An exploratory study. *Journal of Second Language Writing, 7,* 205–241.

Bosher, S., & Rowenkamp, J. (1992). *Language proficiency and academic success: The refugee/immigrant in higher education* (Eric Document ED 353 914).

Bosher, S., & Rowenkamp, J. (1998). The refugee/immigrant in higher education: The role of educational background. *College ESL, 8,* 23–42.

Bosher, S., & Smalkoski, K. (2002). From needs analysis to curriculum development: Designing a course in health-care communication for immigrant students in the USA. *English for Specific Purposes, 21,* 59–79.

Bouton, L. (1995). A cross-cultural analysis of the structure and content of letters of reference. *Studies in Second Language Acquisition, 17,* 211–244.

Boyd, M. (1992). Immigrant women: Language, socio-economic inequalities, and policy issues. In B. Burnaby & A. Cumming (Eds.), *Socio-political aspects of ESL* (pp. 141–159). Toronto: OISE Press.

Braddock, R., Lloyd-Jones, R., & Schoer, L. (1963). *Research in written composition.* Urbana, IL: National Council of Teachers of English.

Braine, G. (1989). Writing in science and technology: An analysis of assignments from ten undergraduate courses. *English for Specific Purposes, 8,* 3–15.

Braine, G. (1995). Writing in the natural sciences and engineering. In D. Belcher & G. Braine (Eds.), *Academic writing in a second language: Essays on research and pedagogy* (pp. 113–135). Norwood, NJ: Ablex.

Braine, G. (1996). ESL students in first-year writing courses: ESL versus mainstream classes. *Journal of Second Language Writing, 5*, 91–107.

Braine, G. (1999a). From the periphery to the center: One teacher's journey. In G. Braine (Ed.), *Non-native educators in English language teaching* (pp. 15–27). Mahwah, NJ: Erlbaum.

Braine, G. (Ed.). (1999b). *Non-native educators in English language teaching.* Mahwah, NJ: Erlbaum.

Braine, G. (2001). A study of English as a Foreign Language (EFL) writers on a Local Area Network (LAN) and in traditional classes. *Computers and Composition, 18,* 275–292.

Braine, G. (2002). Academic literacy and the nonnative speaker graduate student. *Journal of English for Academic Purposes, 1,* 59–68.

Braine, G. (2005). The challenge of academic publishing: A Hong Kong perspective. *TESOL Quarterly, 39,* 707–716.

Brauer, G. (2000). Product, process, and the writer within: History of a paradigm shift. In G. Brauer (Ed.), *Writing across languages* (pp. 15–22). Stamford, CT: Ablex.

Braxley, K. (2005). Mastering academic English: International graduate students' use of dialogue and speech genres to meet the writing demands of graduate school. In J. Hall, G. Vitanova, & L. Marchenkova (Eds.), *Dialogue with Bakhtin on second and foreign language learning* (pp. 11–32). Mahwah, NJ: Lawrence Erlbaum.

Bridgeman, B., & Carlson, S. (1983). *Survey of academic writing tasks required of graduate and undergraduate students.* TOEFL Research Report 15. Princeton, NJ: Educational Testing Service.

Bridgeman, B., & Carlson, S. (1984). Survey of academic writing tasks. *Written Communication, 1,* 247–280.

Brindley, G. (1998a). Describing language development? Rating scales and second language acquisition. In L. Bachman & A. Cohen (Eds.), *Interfaces between second language acquisition and language testing research* (pp. 112–140). Cambridge, UK: Cambridge University Press.

Brindley, G. (1998b). Outcomes-based assessment and reporting in language learning programmes: A review of the issues. *Language Testing, 15,* 45–85.

Brindley, G. (2000). Assessment in the Adult Migrant Education Program. In G. Brindley (Ed.), *Studies in immigrant English language assessment,* vol. 1 (pp. 1–43). Sydney, Australia: NCELTR Publications, Macquarie University.

Brindley, G. (2001). Investigating rater consistency in competency-based language assessment. In G. Brindley & C. Burrows (Eds.), *Studies in immigrant English language assessment,* vol. 2 (pp. 59–80). Sydney, Australia: NCELTR Publications, Macquarie University.

Brindley, G., & Wigglesworth, G. (Eds.). (1997). *Access: Issues in language test design and delivery.* Sydney, Australia: NCELTR Publications, Macquarie University.

Brinton, D., Snow, M., & Wesche, M. (1989). *Content-based second language instruction.* Boston: Heinle & Heinle.

Brock, M., & Walters, L. (1993). *Teaching composition around the Pacific rim.* Clevedon, UK: Multilingual Matters.

Brown, A. (2005). Self-assessment of writing in independent language learning programs: The value of annotated samples. *Assessing Writing, 10,* 174–191.

Brown, J. D. (1991). Do English and ESL faculties rate writing samples differently? *TESOL Quarterly, 25,* 587–603.

Bruce, S., & Rafoth, B. (Eds.). (2004). *ESL writers: A guide for writing center tutors.* Portsmouth, NH: Boynton/Cook Heinemann.

Bryant, W. H. (1984). Typical errors made in English by Japanese ESL students. *JALT Journal, 6,* 1–18.

Buckwalter, J., & Lo, Y. (2002). Emergent literacy in Chinese and English. *Journal of Second Language Writing, 11*, 269–293.

Buijs, G. (Ed.). (1993). *Migrant women: Crossing boundaries and changing identities.* Oxford: Berg Publishers.

Bunton, D. (1999). The use of higher level metatext in Ph.D. theses. *English for Specific Purposes, 18*, S41–S56.

Burnaby, B. (1992). Official language training for adult immigrants in Canada: Features and issues. In B. Burnaby & A. Cumming (Eds.), *Sociopolitical aspects of ESL in Canada* (pp. 3–34). Toronto: OISE Press.

Burnaby, B., & Cumming, A. (Eds.). (1992). *Sociopolitical aspects of ESL in Canada.* Toronto: OISE Press.

Burns, A., & Hood, S. (Eds.). (1995). *Teachers' voices: Exploring course design in a changing curriculum.* Sydney, Australia: NCELTR Publications, Macquarie University.

Burrough-Boenisch, J. (2003). Shapers of published NNS research articles. *Journal of Second Language Writing, 12*, 224–243.

Burrows, C. (2001). Searching for washback: The impact of assessment in the Certificate in Spoken and Written English. In G. Brindley & C. Burrows (Eds.), *Studies in immigrant English language assessment*, vol. 2 (pp. 95–184). Sydney, Australia: NCELTR Publications, Macquarie University.

Butler-Nalin, K. (1984). Revising patterns in students' writing. In A. Applebee (Ed.), *Contexts for learning to write* (pp. 121–133). Norwood, NJ: Ablex.

Byrd, P., & Nelson, G. (1995). NNS performance on writing proficiency exams: Focus on students who failed. *Journal of Second Language Writing, 4*, 273–285.

Byrd, P., & Reid, J. (Eds.). (1998). *Grammar in the composition classroom: Essays on teaching ESL for college-bound students.* Boston: Heinle & Heinle.

Cadman, K. (1997). Thesis writing for international students: A question of identity? *English for Specific Purposes, 16*, 3–14.

Cadman, K. (2002). English for Academic Possibilities: The research proposal as a contested site in postgraduate genre pedagogy. *Journal of English for Academic Purposes, 1*, 85–104.

Cameron, R. (1998). A language-focused needs analysis for ESL-speaking nursing students in class and clinic. *Foreign Language Annals, 31*, 203–218.

Campbell, C. (1990). Writing with others' words: Using background reading text in academic compositions. In B. Kroll (Ed.), *Second language writing: Research insights for the classroom* (pp. 211–230). New York: Cambridge University Press.

Canagarajah, S. (1993a). American textbooks and Tamil students: Discerning ideological tensions in the ESL classroom. *Language, Culture and Curriculum, 6*, 143–156.

Canagarajah, S. (1993b). Comment on Ann Raimes's "Out of the woods: Emerging traditions in the teaching of writing": Up the garden path: Second language writing approaches, local knowledge, and pluralism. *TESOL Quarterly, 27*, 301–306.

Canagarajah, S. (1993c). Critical ethnography of a Sri Lankan classroom: Ambiguities in student opposition to reproduction through ESOL. *TESOL Quarterly, 27*, 601–626.

Canagarajah, S. (1996). "Nondiscursive" requirements in academic publishing, material resources of periphery scholars, and the politics of knowledge production. *Written Communication, 13*, 435–472.

Canagarajah, S. (1999). *Resisting linguistic imperialism in English teaching.* Oxford, UK: Oxford University Press.

Canagarajah, S. (2001a). Addressing issues of power and difference in ESL academic writing. In J. Flowerdew & M. Peacock (Eds.), *Research perspectives on English for academic purposes* (pp. 117–131). New York: Cambridge University Press.

Canagarajah, S. (2001b). The fortunate traveler: Shuttling between communities and literacies by economy class. In D. Belcher & U. Connor (Eds.), *Reflections on multiliterate lives*. Buffalo, NY: Multilingual Press.

Canagarajah, S. (2002a). *Critical academic writing and multilingual students*. Ann Arbor: University of Michigan Press.

Canagarajah, S. (2002b). *The geopolitics of academic writing and knowledge production*. Pittsburgh, PA: University of Pittsburgh Press.

Canagarajah, S. (2002c). Multilingual writers and the academic community: Towards a critical relationship. *Journal of English for Academic Purposes, 1*, 29–44.

Canagarajah, S. (2004). Multilingual writers and the struggle for voice in academic discourse. In A. Pavlenko & A. Blackledge. (Eds.), *Negotiation of identities in multilingual contexts* (pp. 266–289). Clevedon: Multilingual Matters.

Canale, M., Frenette, N., & Belanger, M. (1988). Evaluation of minority student writing in first and second languages. In J. Fine (Ed.), *Second language discourse: A textbook of current research* (pp. 147–165). Norwood, NJ: Ablex.

Candlin, C. (Ed.). (2002). *Research and practice in professional discourse*. Hong Kong: City University of Hong Kong Press.

Canseco, G., & Byrd, P. (1989). Writing required in graduate courses in business administration. *TESOL Quarterly, 23*, 305–316.

Cantoni-Harvey, G. (1987). *Teaching ESL in the content areas*. Reading, MA: Addison-Wesley.

Cardelle, M., & Corno, L. (1981). Effects on second language learning of variations in written feedback on homework assignments. *TESOL Quarterly, 15*, 251–261.

Carlisle, R. (1989). The writing of Anglo and Hispanic elementary school students in bilingual, submersion, and regular programs. *Studies in Second Language Acquisition, 11*, 257–280.

Carrasquillo, A., & Rodriguez, V. (1996). *Language minority students in the mainstream classroom*. Clevedon, UK: Multilingual Matters.

Carrell, P., & Connor, U. (1991). Reading and writing descriptive and persuasive texts. *Modern Language Journal, 75*, 314–324.

Carrell, P., & Monroe, L. (1993). Learning styles and composition. *Modern Language Journal, 77*, 148–162.

Carroll, J. B. (1975). *The teaching of French as a foreign language in eight countries*. New York: John Wiley & Sons.

Carson, J. (1992). Becoming biliterate: First language influences. *Journal of Second Language Writing, 1*, 37–60.

Carson, J. (1998). Cultural backgrounds: What should we know about multilingual students? *TESOL Quarterly, 32*, 735–740.

Carson, J. (2001). A task analysis of reading and writing in academic contexts. In D. Belcher & A. Hirvela (Eds.), *Linking literacies: Perspectives on L2 reading–writing connections* (pp. 48–83). Ann Arbor: University of Michigan Press.

Carson, J., Carrell, P., Silberstein, S., Kroll, B., & Kuehn, P. (1990). Reading–writing relationships in first and second language. *TESOL Quarterly, 24*, 245–266.

Carson, J., Chase, N., & Gibson, S. (1993). *Academic demands of the undergraduate curriculum: What students need*: Final Report to the Fund for the Improvement of Post-Secondary Education. Atlanta: Center for the Study of Adult Literacy, Georgia State University.

Carson, J., Chase, N., Gibson, S., & Hargrove, M. (1992). Literacy demands of the undergraduate curriculum. *Reading Research and Instruction, 31*, 25–50.

Carson, J., & Kuehn, P. (1992). Evidence of transfer and loss in developing second language writers. *Language Learning, 42*, 157–182.

Carson, J., & Leki, I. (Eds.) (1993). *Reading in the composition classroom: Second language perspectives*. Boston: Heinle & Heinle.

Carson, J., & Nelson, G. (1994). Writing groups: Cross-cultural issues. *Journal of Second Language Writing, 3,* 17–30.

Carson, J., & Nelson, G. (with Danison, N., & Gajdusek, L.). (1995). Social dimensions of second-language writing instruction: Peer response groups as cultural context. In D. Rubin (Ed.), *Composing social identity in written language* (pp. 89–109). Mahwah, NJ: Lawrence Erlbaum.

Carson, J., & Nelson, G. (1996). Chinese students' perceptions of ESL peer response group interaction. *Journal of Second Language Writing, 5,* 1–19.

Casanave, C. (1992). Cultural diversity and socialization: A case study of a Hispanic woman in a doctoral program in sociology. In D. Murray (Ed.), *Diversity as resource: Redefining cultural literacy* (pp. 148–180). Washington, DC: TESOL.

Casanave, C. (1994). Language development in students' journals. *Journal of Second Language Writing, 3,* 179–201.

Casanave, C. (1995). Local interactions: Constructing contexts for composing in a graduate sociology program. In D. Belcher & G. Braine (Eds.), *Academic writing in a second language* (pp. 83–110). Norwood, NJ: Ablex.

Casanave, C. (1998). Transitions: The balancing act of bilingual academics. *Journal of Second Language Writing, 7,* 175–203.

Casanave, C. (2002). *Writing games.* Mahwah, NJ: Erlbaum.

Casanave, C. (2003). Looking ahead to more sociopolitically-oriented case study research in L2 writing scholarship (But should it be called "post-process?"). *Journal of Second Language Writing, 12,* 85–102.

Casanave, C. (2004). *Controversies in second language writing: Dilemmas and decisions in research and instruction.* Ann Arbor: University of Michigan Press.

Casanave, C., & Hubbard, P. (1992). The writing assignments and writing problems of doctoral students: Faculty perceptions, pedagogical issues and needed research. *English for Specific Purposes, 11,* 33–49.

Casanave, C. P., McCornick, A. J., & Hiraki, S. (1993). Conversations by E-mail: A study of the interactive writing experiences of a Japanese deaf student and two English teachers. *SFC Journal of Language and Communication, 2,* 145–175.

Casanave, C., & Schecter, S. (Eds.). (1997). *On becoming a language educator: Personal essays on professional development.* Mahwah, NJ: Erlbaum.

Casanave, C., & Vandrick, S. (Eds.). (2003). *Writing for scholarly publication: Behind the scenes in language education.* Mahwah, NJ: Erlbaum.

Centre for Canadian Language Benchmarks. (2000). *Canadian language benchmarks.* Ottawa: Authors.

Chamberlin, C. (1997). ESL students' perceptions of the university classroom in the United States. *College ESL, 7,* 1–19.

Chamot, A. U., & O'Malley, J. M. (1987). The cognitive academic language learning approach: A bridge to the mainstream. *TESOL Quarterly, 21,* 227–249.

Chandler, J. (2003). The efficacy of various kinds of error feedback for improvement in the accuracy and fluency of L2 student writing. *Journal of Second Language Writing, 12,* 267–296.

Chandrasegaran, A. (1986). An exploratory study of ESL students' revision and self-correction skills. *RELC Journal, 17,* 26–40.

Chandrasegaran, A. (2000). An analysis of obliqueness in student writing. *Regional English Language Centre Journal, 31,* 23–44.

Chandrasoma, R., Thomson, C., & Pennycook, A. (2004). Beyond plagiarism: Transgressive and nontransgressive intertextuality. *Journal of Language, Identity, and Education, 3,* 171–194.

Chang, Y., & Swales, J. (1999). Informal elements in English academic writing: Threats or opportunities for non-native speakers? In C. Candlin & K. Hyland (Eds.), *Writing: Texts, processes, and practices* (pp. 145–167). London: Longman.

Chapelle, C. (1999). Validity in language assessment. *Annual Review of Applied Linguistics, 19*, 254–272.

Charge, N., & Taylor, L. (1997). Recent developments in IELTS. *ELT Journal, 51*, 374–380.

Chastain, K. (1990). Characteristics of graded and ungraded compositions. *Modern Language Journal, 74*, 10–14.

Chaudron, C. (1988). *Second language classrooms: Research on teaching and learning.* New York: Cambridge University Press.

Cheng, L., Myles, J., & Curtis, A. (2004). Targeting language support for non-native English-speaking graduate students at a Canadian university. *TESL Canada Journal, 21*, 50–71.

Cheng, W., & Warren, M. (2005). Peer assessment of language proficiency. *Language Testing, 22*, 93–121.

Chenoweth, N. A., & Hayes, J. R. (2001). Fluency in writing: Generating text in L1 and L2. *Written Communication, 18*, 80–98.

Chiang, Y.-S., & Schmida, M. (1999). Language identity and language ownership: Linguistic conflicts of first-year university writing students. In L. Harklau, M. Siegal, & K. Losey (Eds.), *Generation 1.5 meets college composition* (pp. 81–96). Mahwah, NJ: Erlbaum.

Cho, S. (2004). Challenges of entering discourse communities through publishing in English: Perspectives of non-native speaking doctoral students in the United States of America. *Journal of Language, Identity, and Education, 3*, 47–72.

Choi, Y. (1986). A study of coherence in Korean speakers' argumentative writing in English. *Studies in the Linguistic Sciences, 16*, 2, 67–94.

Choi, Y. (1988). Text structure of Korean speakers' argumentative essays in English. *World Englishes, 7*, 2, 129–142.

Christianson, K. (1997). Dictionary use by EFL writers: What really happens. *Journal of Second Language Writing, 6*, 23–43.

Christie, F. (1999). Genre theory and ESL teaching: A systemic functional perspective. *TESOL Quarterly, 33*, 759–763.

Christison, M., & Krahnke, K. (1986). Student perceptions of academic language study. *TESOL Quarterly, 20*, 61–78.

Clachar, A. (1999). It's not just cognition: The effect of emotion on multiple-level discourse processing in second-language writing. *Language Sciences, 21*, 31–60.

Clachar, A. (2000). Opposition and accommodation: An examination of Turkish teachers' attitudes toward Western approaches to the teaching of writing. *Research in the Teaching of English, 35*, 66–100.

Clair, N. (1995). Mainstream classroom teachers and ESL students. *TESOL Quarterly, 29*, 189–196.

Clapham, C., & Alderson, J. C. (Eds.). (1996). *Constructing and trialing the IELTS test.* IELTS Research Report No. 3. Cambridge, UK: Cambridge Local Examinations Syndicate.

Clark, E. (1995). How did you learn to write in English when you haven't been taught in English?: The language experience approach in a dual language program. *Bilingual Research Journal, 19*, 611–627.

Cmejrkova, S., & Danes, F. (1997). Academic writing and cultural identity: The case of Czech academic writing. In A. Duszak (Ed.), *Culture and styles of academic discourse* (pp. 41–61). New York: Mouton de Gruyter.

Cohen, A. (1987). Student processing of feedback on their compositions. In A. Wenden & J. Rubin (Eds.), *Learner strategies in language learning* (pp. 57–69). Englewood Cliffs, NJ: Prentice-Hall.

Cohen, A., & Cavalcanti, M. (1990). Feedback on written compositions: Teacher and student verbal reports. In B. Kroll (Ed.), *Second language writing: Research insights for the classroom* (pp. 155–177). Cambridge, UK: Cambridge University Press.

Collier, V. (1987). Age and rate of acquisition of second languages for academic purposes. *TESOL Quarterly, 21*, 617–641.

Collier, V. (1989). How long? A synthesis of research on academic achievement in a second language. *TESOL Quarterly, 23*, 509–531.

Collier, V. (1995). *Promoting academic success for ESL students.* Jersey City, NJ: NJTESOL-BE.

Collier, V., & Thomas, W. P. (1989). How quickly can immigrants become proficient in school English? *Journal of Educational Issues of Minority Students, 5*, 26–38.

Collignon, F. (1993). Reading for composing: Connecting processes to advancing ESL literacies. In J. Carson & I. Leki (Eds.), *Reading in the composition classroom: Second language perspectives* (pp. 258–273). Boston: Heinle & Heinle.

Connor, U. (1984). A study of cohesion and coherence in English as a Second Language students' writing. *Papers in Linguistics, 17*, 301–316.

Connor, U. (1987). Research frontiers in writing analysis. *TESOL Quarterly, 21*, 677–696.

Connor, U. (1988). A contrastive study of persuasive business correspondence: American and Japanese. In S. Bruno (Ed.), *Global implications for business* (pp. 57–72). Houston, TX: University of Houston—Clear Lake.

Connor, U. (1990). Linguistic/rhetorical measures for international persuasive student writing. *Research in the Teaching of English, 24*, 67–87.

Connor, U. (1996). *Contrastive rhetoric: Cross-cultural aspects of second-language writing.* New York: Cambridge University Press.

Connor, U. (1999). Learning to write academic prose in a second language: A literacy autobiography. In G. Braine (Ed.), *Non-native educators in English language teaching* (pp. 29–42). Mahwah, NJ: Erlbaum.

Connor, U. (2002). New directions in contrastive rhetoric. *TESOL Quarterly, 36*, 493–510.

Connor, U. (2004). Intercultural rhetoric research: Beyond texts. *Journal of English for Academic Purposes, 3*, 291–304.

Connor, U. (2005). Response to Kubota & Lehner. *Journal of Second Language Writing, 14*, 132–136.

Connor, U., & Asenavage, K. (1994). Peer response groups in ESL writing classes: How much impact on revision? *Journal of Second Language Writing, 3*, 257–276.

Connor, U., & Carrell, P. (1993). The interpretation of tasks by writers and readers in holistically rated direct assessment of writing. In J. Carson & I. Leki (Eds.), *Reading in the composition classroom* (pp. 141–160). Boston: Heinle & Heinle.

Connor, U., & Farmer, M. (1990). The teaching of topical structure analysis as a revision strategy for ESL writers. In B. Kroll (Ed.), *Second language writing: Research insights for the classroom* (pp. 126–139). New York: Cambridge University Press.

Connor, U., & Kramer, M. (1995). Writing from sources: Case studies of graduate students in business management. In D. Belcher & G. Braine (Eds.), *Academic writing in a second language: Essays on research and pedagogy* (pp. 155–182). Norwood, NJ: Ablex.

Connor, U., & Mayberry, S. (1996). Learning discipline-specific academic writing: A case study of a Finnish graduate student in the United States. In E. Ventola & A. Mauranen (Eds.), *Academic writing: Intercultural and textual issues* (pp. 231–253). Amsterdam: John Benjamins.

Connor-Linton, J. (1995a). Cross-cultural comparisons of writing standards: American ESL and Japanese EFL. *World Englishes, 14*, 99–115.

Connor-Linton, J. (1995b). Looking behind the curtain: What do L2 composition ratings really mean? *TESOL Quarterly, 29*, 762–765.

Conrad, S., & Goldstein, L. (1999). ESL student revision after teacher-written comments: Text, contexts, and individuals. *Journal of Second Language Writing, 8*, 147–179.

Cooley, L., & Lewkowicz, J. (1997). Developing awareness of the rhetorical and linguistic conventions of writing a thesis in English: Addressing the needs of EFL/ESL postgraduate students. In A. Duszak (Ed.), *Culture and styles of academic discourse* (pp. 113–129). New York: Mouton de Gruyter.

Cope, B., & Kalantzis, M. (Eds.). (2000). *Multiliteracies: Literacy learning and the design of social futures.* London: Routledge.

Council of Europe. (2001). *Common European framework of reference for languages: Learning, teaching, assessment.* Cambridge, UK: Cambridge University Press.

Crandall, J. (1987). *ESL through content-area instruction: Mathematics, science, and social studies.* New York: Prentice-Hall.

Crandall, J. (1993). Professionalism and professionalization of adult ESL literacy. *TESOL Quarterly, 27,* 497–515.

Cresswell, A. (2000). Self-monitoring in student writing: Developing learner responsibility. *ELT Journal, 54,* 235–244.

Crisco, V. (2004). Rethinking language and culture on the institutional borderland. *Journal of Basic Writing, 23,* 39–63.

Cronnell, B. (1985). Language influences in the English writing of third- and sixth-grade Mexican-American students. *Journal of Educational Research, 8,* 168–173.

Crusan, D. (2002). An assessment of ESL writing placement assessment. *Assessing Writing, 8,* 17–30.

Cumming, A. (1985). Responding to the writing of ESL students. *Highway One, 8,* 58–78.

Cumming, A. (1986). Intentional learning as a principle for ESL writing instruction: A case study. In P. Lightbown & S. Firth (Eds.), *TESL Canada Journal,* Special Issue 1, 69–83.

Cumming, A. (1989). Writing expertise and second language proficiency. *Language Learning, 39,* 81–141.

Cumming, A. (1990a). Expertise in evaluating second language compositions. *Language Testing, 7,* 31–51.

Cumming, A. (1990b). Metalinguistic and ideational thinking in second language composing. *Written Communication, 7,* 482–511.

Cumming, A. (1991). Uses of biliteracy among Indo-Canadian women learning language and literacy. *Canadian Modern Language Review/La Revue canadienne des langues vivantes, 47,* 697–707.

Cumming, A. (1992). Instructional routines in ESL composition teaching. *Journal of Second Language Writing, 1,* 17–35.

Cumming, A. (1993). Teachers' curriculum planning and accommodations of innovations: Three case studies of adult ESL instruction. *TESL Canada Journal, 11,* 30–52.

Cumming, A. (1994). Does language assessment facilitate recent immigrants' participation in Canadian society? *TESL Canada Journal, 11,* 117–133.

Cumming, A. (1997). The testing of second-language writing. In D. Corson (Series Ed.) & C. Clapham (Volume Ed.), *Language assessment,* Vol. 7 of *Encyclopedia of language and education* (pp. 51–63). Dordrecht, Netherlands: Kluwer.

Cumming, A. (1998). Theoretical perspectives on writing. In W. Grabe (Ed.), *Annual Review of Applied Linguistics, 18. Foundations of second language teaching* (pp. 61–78). New York: Cambridge University Press.

Cumming, A. (2001a). The difficulty of standards, for example in L2 writing. In T. Silva & P. Matsuda (Eds.), *On second language writing* (pp. 209–229). Mahwah, NJ: Erlbaum.

Cumming, A. (2001b). Learning to write in a second language: Two decades of research. In R. Manchon (Ed.), *Writing in the L2 classroom: Issues in research and pedagogy,* Special Issue of *International Journal of English Studies, 1, 2,* 1–23.

Cumming, A. (2001c). ESL/EFL writing instructors' practices for assessment: General or specific purposes? *Language Testing, 18*, 207–224.

Cumming, A. (2003). Experienced ESL/EFL writing instructors' conceptualization of their teaching: Curriculum options and implications. In B. Kroll (Ed.), *Exploring the dynamics of second language writing* (pp. 71–92). New York: Cambridge University Press.

Cumming, A. (2004). Broadening, deepening, and consolidating. *Language Assessment Quarterly, 1*, 5–18.

Cumming, A. (Ed.). (2006). *Goals for academic writing: ESL students and their instructors*. Amsterdam: John Benjamins.

Cumming, A. (2007). New directions in testing English language proficiency for university entrance. In J. Cummins & C. Davison (Eds.), *International handbook of English language teaching* (pp. 473–485). New York: Springer.

Cumming, A., Busch, M., & Zhou, A. (2002). Investigating learners' goals in the context of adult second-language writing. In G. Rijlaarsdam (Series Ed.) & S. Ransdell & M. Barbier (Vol. Eds.), *Studies in writing, Volume 11: New directions for research in L2 writing* (pp. 189–208). Dordrecht, Netherlands: Kluwer.

Cumming, A., & Gill, J. (1991). Learning ESL literacy among Indo-Canadian women. *Language, Culture and Curriculum, 4*, 181–200.

Cumming, A., & Gill, J. (1992). Motivation or accessibility? Factors permitting Indo-Canadian women to pursue ESL literacy instruction. In B. Burnaby & A. Cumming (Eds.), *Sociopolitical aspects of ESL* (pp. 241–252). Toronto: OISE Press.

Cumming, A., Grant, L., Mulcahy-Ernt, P., & Powers, D. (2004). A teacher-verification study of speaking and writing prototype tasks for a new TOEFL. *Language Testing, 21*, 159–197.

Cumming, A., Kantor, R., Baba, K., Erdosy, U., Eouanzoui, K., & James, M. (2005). Differences in written discourse in independent and integrated prototype tasks for next generation TOEFL. *Assessing Writing, 10*, 5–43.

Cumming, A., Kantor, R., & Powers, D. (2001). *Scoring TOEFL essays and TOEFL 2000 prototype tasks: An investigation into raters' decision making and development of a preliminary analytic framework*. TOEFL Monograph No. 22. Princeton, NJ: Educational Testing Service.

Cumming, A., Kantor, R., & Powers, D. (2002). Decision making while rating ESL/EFL writing tasks: A descriptive framework. *Modern Language Journal, 86*, 67–96.

Cumming, A., Kantor, R., Powers, D., Santos, T., & Taylor, C. (2000). *TOEFL 2000 writing framework: A working paper*. TOEFL Monograph No. 18. Princeton, NJ: Educational Testing Service.

Cumming, A., & Mellow, D. (1996). An investigation into the validity of written indicators of second language proficiency. In A. Cumming & R. Berwick (Eds.), *Validation in language testing* (pp. 72–93). Clevedon, UK: Multilingual Matters.

Cumming, A., Rebuffot, J., & Ledwell, M. (1989). Reading and summarizing challenging texts in first and second languages. *Reading and Writing: An Interdisciplinary Journal, 2*, 201–219.

Cumming, A., & Riazi, A. (2000). Building models of adult second-language writing instruction. *Learning and Instruction, 10*, 55–71.

Cumming, A., & So, S. (1996). Tutoring second language text revision: Does the approach to instruction or the language of communication make a difference? *Journal of Second Language Writing, 5*, 197–226.

Cummins, J. (1986). Language proficiency and academic achievement. In E. Bialystok (Ed.), *Bilingualism in education: Aspects of theory, research and practice* (pp. 138–161). New York: Longman.

Cummins, J. (2001). *Negotiating identities: Education for empowerment in a diverse society*. Los Angeles: California Association for Bilingual Education.

Cummins, J., & Davison, C. (Eds.) (2007). *International handbook of English language teaching*. New York: Springer.

Cummins, J., & Sayers, D. (1995). *Brave new schools: Challenging cultural illiteracy*. Toronto: OISE Press/University of Toronto Press.

Currie, P. (1993). Entering a disciplinary community: Conceptual activities required to write for one introductory university course. *Journal of Second Language Writing, 2*, 101–117.

Currie, P. (1998). Staying out of trouble: Apparent plagiarism and academic survival. *Journal of Second Language Writing, 7*, 1–18.

Currie, P. (2001). On the question of power and control. In T. Silva & P. K. Matsuda (Eds.), *On second language writing* (pp. 29–38). Mahwah, NJ: Erlbaum.

Currie, P., & Cray, E. (2004). ESL literacy: Language practice or social practice? *Journal of Second Language Writing, 13*, 111–132.

Curry, M., & Lillis, T. (2004). Multilingual scholars and the imperative to publish in English: Negotiating interests, demands, and rewards. *TESOL Quarterly, 38*, 663–688.

Darling-Hammond, L., Ancess, J., & Falk, B. (1995). *Authentic assessment in action: Studies of schools and students at work*. New York: Teachers College Press.

Dávila de Silva, A. (2004). Emergent Spanish writing of a second grader in a whole-language classroom. In B. Pérez (Ed.), *Sociocultural contexts of language and literacy* (2nd ed., pp. 247–274). Mahwah, NJ: Erlbaum.

Day, E. (2002). *Identity and the young English language learner*. Clevedon, UK: Multilingual Matters.

Deckert, G. (1993). Perspectives on plagiarism from ESL students in Hong Kong. *Journal of Second Language Writing, 2*, 131–148.

de Guerrero, M., & Villamil, O. (1994). Social-cognitive dimensions of interaction in L2 peer revision. *Modern Language Journal, 78*, 484–496.

de Guerrero, M., & Villamil, O. (2000). Activating the ZPD: Mutual scaffolding in L2 peer revision. *Modern Language Journal, 84*, 51–68.

de Haan, P., & van Esch, K. (2005). The development of writing in English and Spanish as foreign languages. *Assessing Writing, 10*, 100–116.

Delgado-Gaitan, C. (1987). Mexican adult literacy: New directions for immigrants. In S. Goldman & H. Trueba (Eds.), *Becoming literate in English as a Second Language* (pp. 9–33). Norwood, NJ: Ablex.

Dennett, J. (1988). Not to say is better than to say (a Japanese proverb): How rhetorical structure reflects cultural context in Japanese-English technical writing. *IEEE Transactions on Professional Communication, 31*, 116–119.

Derwing, T., DeCorby, E., Ichikawa, J., & Jamieson, K. (1999). Some factors that affect the success of ESL high school students. *Canadian Modern Language Review/ La Revue canadienne des langues vivantes, 55*, 532–547.

Derwing, T., & Ho, L. (1991). Canada's forgotten literacy learners. In L. Walker & C. Chambers (Eds.), *Curriculum Canada X: The literacy curriculum in Canada in the 1990's* (pp. 14–21). Lethbridge, Canada: University of Lethbridge.

DeVillar, R., & Jiang, B. (2001). Building a community of adult ESL learners. In J. Murphy & P. Byrd (Eds.), *Understanding the courses we teach: Local perspectives on English language teaching* (pp. 135–154). Ann Arbor: University of Michigan Press.

Dewey, J. (1916, republished 1966). *Democracy and education*. New York: Macmillan.

Dias, P., Freedman, A., Medway, P., & Paré, A. (Eds.). (1999). *Worlds apart: Acting and writing in academic and workplace contexts*. Mahwah, NJ: Lawrence Erlbaum.

Dias, P., & Paré, A. (Eds.). (2000). *Transitions: Writing in academic and workplace settings*. Cresskill, NJ: Hampton Press.

Diaz, S., Moll, L., & Mehan, H. (1986). Sociocultural resources in instruction: A context-specific approach. In Bilingual Education Office (Ed.), *Beyond language: Social and cultural factors in schooling language minority students* (pp. 187–230). Los Angeles: California State University, Evaluation, Dissemination and Assessment Center.

Dickson, P., & Cumming, A. (Eds.) (1996) *Profiles of language education in 25 countries*. Slough, UK: National Foundation for Educational Research.

Diederich, P. B. (1974). *Measuring growth in English*. Urbana, IL: National Council of Teachers of English.

Divoky, D. (1988). The model minority goes to school. *Phi Delta Kappan, 70,* 219–222.

Donato, R.,& McCormick, D. (1994). A sociocultural perspective on language learning strategies: The role of mediation. *Modern Language Journal, 78,* 453–464.

Dong, Y. (1996). Learning how to use citations for knowledge transformation: Nonnative doctoral students' dissertation writing in science. *Research in the Teaching of English, 30,* 428–457.

Dong, Y. (1998). From writing in their native language to writing in English: What ESL students bring to our writing classrooms. *College ESL, 8,* 87–105.

Dong, Y. (1999). The need to understand ESL students' native language writing experiences. *Teaching English in the Two Year College* (March), 277–285.

Doushaq, M. (1986). An investigation into stylistic errors of Arab students learning English for academic purpose. *English for Specific Purposes, 5,* 27–39.

Dubin, F., & Kuhlman, N. (Eds.). (1992). *Cross-culture literacy: Global perspectives on reading and writing*. Englewood Cliffs, NJ: Prentice-Hall.

Duff, P. (2001). Language, literacy, content, and (pop) culture: Challenges for ESL students in mainstream courses. *Canadian Modern Language Review/La Revue canadienne des langues vivantes, 58,* 103–132.

Duff, P. (2002). The discursive co-construction of knowledge, identity and difference. *Applied Linguistics, 23,* 289–322.

Duff, P., Wong, P., & Early, M. (2000). Learning language for work and life: The linguistic socialization of immigrant Canadians seeking careers in healthcare. *Canadian Modern Language Review/La Revue canadienne des langues vivantes, 57,* 9–57.

Duffy, J. (2004). Letters from the Fair City: A rhetorical conception of literacy. *College Composition and Communication, 56,* 223–250.

Durgunoglu, A. (1998). Acquiring literacy in English and Spanish in the United States. In A. Durgunoglu & L. Verhoeven (Eds.), *Literacy development in a multilingual context* (pp. 135–145). Mahwah, NJ: Erlbaum.

Durgunoglu, A., Mir, M., & Arino-Martin, S. (2002). The relationships between bilingual children's reading and writing in their two languages. In G. Rijlaarsdam (Series Ed.) & S. Ransdell & M. Barbier (Vol. Eds.), *Studies in writing, Volume 11: New directions for research in L2 writing* (pp. 81–100). Dordrecht, Netherlands: Kluwer.

Duszak, A. (1997a). Cross cultural academic communication: A discourse-community view. In A. Duszak (Ed.), *Culture and styles of academic discourse* (pp. 11–39). New York: Mouton de Gruyter.

Duszak, A. (Ed.). (1997b). *Culture and styles of academic discourse*. New York: Mouton de Gruyter.

Early, M. (1989). A snapshot of ESL students' integration patterns. *TESL Canada Journal/Revue TESL du Canada, 7,* 52–60.

Early, M. (1990). From task to text: A case study of ESL students' development of expository discourse. *TESL Talk, 20,* 111–125.

Early, M. (1992). Aspects of becoming an academically successful ESL student. In B.

Burnaby & A. Cumming (Eds.), *Sociopolitical aspects of ESL education in Canada* (pp. 265–275). Toronto: OISE Press.

Early, M. (2001). Language and content in social practice: A case study. *Canadian Modern Language Review, 58,* 156–179.

Edelsky, C. (1982). Writing in a bilingual program: The relation of L1 and L2 texts. *TESOL Quarterly, 16,* 211–228.

Edelsky, C. (1986). *Writing in a bilingual program: Habia una vez.* Norwood, NJ: Ablex.

Edelsky, C. (1989). Bilingual children's writing: Fact and fiction. In D. Johnson & D. Roen (Eds.), *Richness in writing: Empowering ESL students* (pp. 165–176). New York: Longman.

Edelsky, C. (1996). *With literacy and justice for all.* Bristol, PA: Taylor & Francis.

Edelsky, C., & Jilbert, K. (1985). Bilingual children and writing: Lessons for all of us. *Volta Review, 87,* 57–72.

Ekbatani, G., & Pierson, H. (Eds.). (2000). *Learner-directed assessment in ESL.* Mahwah, NJ: Erlbaum.

Elley, W. B. (1994). Acquiring literacy in a second language: The effect of book-based programs. In A. Cumming (Ed.), *Bilingual performance in reading and writing* (pp. 331–366). Amsterdam: John Benjamins.

Elliott, M. (1986). Nasr's development as a writer in his second language: The first six months. *Annual Review of Applied Linguistics, 9,* 120–153.

Ellis, R. (2003). *Task-based language learning and teaching.* Oxford, UK: Oxford University Press.

Emig, J. (1971). *The composing process of twelfth graders.* Urbana, IL: National Council of Teachers of English.

Engber, C. (1995). The relationship of lexical proficiency to the quality of ESL compositions. *Journal of Second Language Writing, 4,* 139–155.

Enginarlar, H. (1993). Student response to teacher feedback in EFL writing. *System, 21,* 193–204.

Epp, L., Stawychny, M., Bonham, A., & Cumming, A. (2002). *Benchmarking the English language demands of the nursing profession across Canada.* Winnipeg, Canada: Red River Community College. Report submitted to the Centre for Canadian Language Benchmarks. Available from http://www.language.ca.

Erbaugh, M. (1990). Taking advantage of China's literary tradition in teaching Chinese students. *Modern Language Journal, 74,* 15–27.

Erdosy, U. (2001). The influence of prior experience on the construction of scoring criteria for ESL composition: A case study. In R. Manchon (Ed.), *Writing in the L2 classroom: Issues in research and pedagogy,* Special Issue of *International Journal of English Studies, 1,* 2, 175–196. University of Murcia, Spain.

Evensen, L. (1990). Pointers to superstructure in student writing. In U. M. Connor & A. Johns (Eds.), *Coherence in writing: Research and pedagogical perspectives* (pp. 169–183). Alexandria, VA: TESOL.

Fakhri, A. (1994). Text organization and transfer: The case of Arab ESL learners. *IRAL, 32,* 78–86.

Fairclough, N. (1989). *Language and power.* London: Longman.

Fairclough, N. (1995). *Critical discourse analysis.* London: Longman.

Faltis, C., & Wolfe, P. (Eds.). (1999). *So much to say: Adolescents, bilingualism, and ESL in the secondary school.* New York: Teachers College Press.

Fathman, A., & Whalley, E. (1990). Teacher response to student writing: Focus on form versus content. In B. Kroll (Ed.) *Second language writing: Research insights for the classroom* (pp. 178–190). Cambridge, UK: Cambridge University Press.

Fazio, L. (2001). The effect of corrections and commentaries on the journal writing accuracy of minority- and majority-language students. *Journal of Second Language Writing, 10,* 235–249.

Feez, S. (1998). *Text-based syllabus design*. Sydney, Australia: National Centre for English Language Teaching and Research, Macquarie University.

Ferdman, B. (1990). Literacy and cultural identity. *Harvard Educational Review, 60,* 181–204.

Ferenz, O. (2005). EFL writers' social networks: Impact on advanced academic literacy development. *Journal of English for Academic Purposes, 4,* 339–351.

Ferguson, P. (1998). The politics of adult ESL literacy: Becoming politically visible. In T. Smoke (Ed.), *Adult ESL: Politics, pedagogy, and participation in classroom and community programs* (pp. 3–15). Mahwah, NJ: Erlbaum.

Ferris, D. (1994a). Lexical and syntactic features of ESL writing by students at different levels of L2 proficiency. *TESOL Quarterly, 28,* 414–420.

Ferris, D. (1994b). Rhetorical strategies in student persuasive writing: Differences between native and non-native English speakers. *Research in the Teaching of English, 28,* 45–65.

Ferris, D. (1995). Student reactions to teacher response in multiple-draft composition classrooms. *TESOL Quarterly, 29,* 33–53.

Ferris, D. (1997). The influence of teacher commentary on student revision. *TESOL Quarterly, 31,* 315–339.

Ferris, D. (1999a). The case for grammar correction in L2 writing classes: A response to Truscott (1996). *Journal of Second Language Writing, 8,* 1–10.

Ferris, D. (1999b). One size does not fit all: Response and revision issues for immigrant student writers. In L. Harklau, K. Losey, & M. Siegal, (Eds.), *Generation 1.5 meets college composition* (pp. 143–157). Mahwah, NJ: Erlbaum.

Ferris, D. (2001). Teaching "Writing for Proficiency" in summer school: Lessons from a foxhole. In J. Murphy & P. Byrd (Eds.), *Understanding the courses we teach: Local perspectives on English language teaching* (pp. 328–345). Ann Arbor: University of Michigan Press.

Ferris, D. (2002). *Treatment of error in second language student writing*. Ann Arbor: University of Michigan Press.

Ferris, D. (2003). *Response to student writing: Implications for second language students*. Mahwah, NJ: Erlbaum.

Ferris, D., & Hedgcock, J. (2005). *Teaching ESL composition: Purpose, process, and practice* (2nd ed.). Mahwah, NJ: Erlbaum.

Ferris, D., Pezone, S., Tade, C., & Tinti, S. (1997). Teacher commentary on student writing: Descriptions and implications. *Journal of Second Language Writing, 6,* 155–182.

Ferris, D., & Roberts, B. (2001). Error feedback in L2 writing classes: How explicit does it need to be? *Journal of Second Language Writing, 10,* 185–212.

Ferris, M., & Politzer, R. L. (1981). Effects of early and delayed second language acquisition: English composition skills of Spanish-speaking junior high school students. *TESOL Quarterly, 15,* 263–274.

Field, Y., & Oi, Y. (1992). A comparison of internal conjunctive cohesion in the English essay writing of Cantonese speakers and native speakers of English. *Regional English Language Centre Journal, 23,* 15–28.

Fishman, S., & McCarthy, L. (2001). An ESL writer and her discipline-based professor: Making progress even when goals don't match. *Written Communication, 18,* 181–228.

Flahive, D., & Bailey, N. (1993). Exploring reading/writing relationships in adult second language learners. In J. Carson & I. Leki (Eds.), *Reading in the composition class: Second language perspectives* (pp. 128–140). Boston: Heinle & Heinle.

Flowerdew, J. (1999a). Problems in writing for scholarly publication in English: The case of Hong Kong. *Journal of Second Language Writing, 8,* 243–264.

Flowerdew, J. (1999b). Writing for scholarly publication in English: The case of Hong Kong. *Journal of Second Language Writing, 8*, 123–145.

Flowerdew, J. (2000). Discourse community, legitimate peripheral participation, and the nonnative-English-speaking scholar. *TESOL Quarterly, 34*, 127–150.

Flowerdew, J. (2001). Attitudes of journal editors to nonnative speaker contributions. *TESOL Quarterly, 35*, 121–150.

Flowerdew, L. (2000). Using a genre-based framework to teach organizational structure in academic writing. *ELT Journal, 54*, 369–378.

Flowerdew, L. (2003). A combined corpus and systemic-functional analysis of the problem–solution pattern in a student and professional corpus of technical writing. *TESOL Quarterly, 37*, 3, 489–511.

Foltz, P., Kintsch, W., & Landauer, T. (1998). Analysis of text coherence using latent semantic analysis. *Discourse Processes, 25*, 285–307.

Foster, D., & Russell, D. (Eds.). (2002). *Writing and learning in cross-national perspective: Transitions from secondary to higher education.* Urbana, IL: NCTE.

Fox, H. (1994). *Listening to the world: Cultural issues in academic writing.* Urbana, IL: NCTE.

Francis, N. (2000). An examination of written expression in bilingual students' "non-academic" language: Assessment of sense of story structure and interlinguistic transfer. *International Journal of Applied Linguistics, 10*, 187–219.

Franco, M. (1996). Designing a writing component for teen courses at a Brazilian language institute. In K. Graves (Ed.), *Teachers as course developers* (pp. 119–150). Cambridge, UK: Cambridge University Press.

Franken, M., & Haslett, S. (2002). When and why talking can make writing harder. In G. Rijlaarsdam (Series Ed.) & S. Ransdell & M. Barbier (Vol. Eds.), *Studies in writing, Volume 11: New directions for research in L2 writing* (pp. 209–229). Dordrecht, Netherlands: Kluwer.

Frantzen, D. (1995). The effects of grammar supplementation on written accuracy in an intermediate Spanish content course. *Modern Language Journal, 79*, 329–344.

Frase, L., Faletti, J., Ginther, A., & Grant, L. (1999). *Computer analysis of the TOEFL Test of Written English.* TOEFL Research Report No. 64. Princeton, NJ: Educational Testing Service.

Freedman, A., & Medway, P. (Eds.). (1994). *Learning and teaching genre.* Portsmouth, NH: Heinemann.

Freeman, Y., & Freeman, D. (1989). Whole language approaches to writing with secondary students of English as a second language. In D. Johnson & D. Roen (Eds.), *Richness in writing: Empowering ESL students* (pp. 177–192). New York: Longman.

Freeman, Y., & Freeman, D. (1992). *Whole language for second language learners.* Portsmouth, NH: Heinemann.

Freire, P. (1970). *Pedagogy of the oppressed.* New York: Continuum.

Friedlander, A. (1990). Composing in English: Effects of a first language on writing in English as a second language. In B. Kroll (Ed.), *Second language writing: Research insights for the classroom* (pp. 109–125). New York: Cambridge University Press.

Frodesen, J. (1995). Negotiating the syllabus: A learning-centred, interactive approach to ESL graduate writing course design. In D. Belcher & G. Braine (Eds.), *Academic writing in a second language: Essays on research and pedagogy* (pp. 331–350). Norwood, NJ: Ablex.

Frodesen, J., & Holten, C. (2003). Grammar and the ESL writing class. In B. Kroll (Ed.), *Exploring the dynamics of second language writing* (pp. 141–161). New York: Cambridge University Press.

Frodesen, J., & Starna, N. (1999). Distinguishing incipient and functional bilingual writers: Assessment and instructional insights gained through second-language writer profiles. In L. Harklau, K. Losey, & M. Siegal (Eds.), *Generation 1.5 meets college composition* (pp. 61–79). Mahwah, NJ: Erlbaum.

Fu, D. (1995). *My trouble is my English*. Portsmouth, NH: Boynton/Cook.

Garcia, O. (1999). Educating Latino high school students with little formal schooling. In C. Faltis & P. Wolfe (Eds.), *So much to say: Adolescents, bilingualism, and ESL in the secondary school* (pp. 61–82). New York: Teachers College Press.

Gee, J. (1996). *Social linguistics and literacies: Ideology in discourses* (2nd ed.). London: Taylor & Francis.

Gee, J. (2005). *An introduction to discourse analysis: Theory and method*. New York: Routledge.

Genishi, C., Stires, S., & Yung-Chan, D. (2001). Writing in an integrated curriculum: Prekindergarten English language learners as symbol makers. *Elementary School Journal, 101*, 399–416.

Gentil, G. (2005). Commitments to academic biliteracy. Case studies of Francophone university writers. *Written Communication, 22*, 421–471.

Geva, E., & Wade-Woolley, L. (1998). Component processes in becoming English–Hebrew biliterate. In A. Durgunoglu & L. Verhoeven (Eds.), *Literacy development in a multilingual context: Cross-cultural perspectives* (pp. 85–110). Mahwah, NJ: Erlbaum.

Ghrib-Maamouri, E. (2001). Thinking and writing in EFL: Cutting off Medusa's head. *ITL Review of Applied Linguistics, 133/144*, 243–269.

Gibbons, P. (1993). *Learning to learn in a second language*. Portsmouth, NH: Heinemann.

Gibbs, W. (1995). Trends in scientific communication: Lost science in the third world. *Scientific American* (August) 92–99.

Gillespie, M. K. (2000). Research in writing: Implications for adult literacy education. In J. Comings, B. Garner, & C. Smith (Eds.), *Annual review of adult learning and literacy*, Vol. 2 (pp. 63–110). San Francisco: Jossey-Bass.

Ginther, A., & Grant, L. (1996). *A review of the academic needs of native English-speaking college students in the United States*. TOEFL Monograph Report 1. Princeton, NJ: Educational Testing Service.

Goldstein, L. (2001). For Kyla: What does the research say about responding to ESL writers. In T. Silva & P. Matsuda (Eds.), *On second language writing* (pp. 73–89). Mahwah, NJ: Erlbaum.

Goldstein, L. (2005). *Teacher written commentary in second language writing classrooms*. Ann Arbor: University of Michigan Press.

Goldstein, L., & Conrad, S. (1990). Student input and negotiation of meaning in ESL writing conferences. *TESOL Quarterly, 24*, 443–460.

Goldstein, T. (1996). *Two languages at work: Bilingual life on the production floor*. New York: Mouton de Gruyter.

Goodlad, J. (1984). *A place called school: Prospects for the future*. New York: McGraw-Hill.

Goodman, Y. (1984). *A two year case study observing the development of third and fourth grade Native American children's writing processes*. Tucson, AZ: University of Arizona.

Gosden, H. (1992). Research writing and NNSs: From the editors. *Journal of Second Language Writing, 1*, 123–139.

Gosden, H. (1995). Success in research article writing and revision: A social-constructionist perspective. *English for Specific Purposes, 14*, 37–57.

Gosden, H. (1996). Verbal reports of Japanese novices' research writing practices in English. *Journal of Second Language Writing, 5*, 109–128.

Gosden, H. (2003). "Why not give us the full story?": Functions of referees' comments in peer reviews of scientific research papers. *Journal of English for Academic Purposes, 2*, 87–101.

Grabe, W. (2001). Notes toward a theory of second language writing. In T. Silva & P. Matsuda (Eds.), *On second language writing* (pp. 39–57). Mahwah, NJ: Erlbaum.

Grabe, W. (2003). Reading and writing relations: Second language perspectives on research and practice. In B. Kroll (Ed.), *Exploring the dynamics of second language writing* (pp. 242–262). New York: Cambridge University Press.

Grabe, W., & Kaplan, W. (1996). *Theory and practice of writing: An applied linguistic perspective.* Harlow, UK: Longman.

Granger, S., & Tyson, S. (1996). Connector usage in the English essay writing of native and non-native EFL speakers in English. *World Englishes, 15,* 17–27.

Grant, L., & Ginther, L. (2000). Using computer-tagged linguistic features to describe L2 writing differences. *Journal of Second Language Writing, 9,* 123–145.

Green, A. (2005). EAP study recommendations and score gains on the IELTS Academic Writing test. *Assessing Writing, 10,* 44–60.

Greenberg, K. (1986). The development and validation of the TOEFL writing test: A discussion of TOEFL Research Reports 15 and 19. *TESOL Quarterly, 20,* 531–544.

Gregoire, G., Derderian, F., & LeLorier, J. (1995). Selecting the language of the publications included in a meta-analysis: Is there a tower of Babel bias? *Journal of Clinical Epidemiology, 48,* 159–163.

Guerra, J. C. (1996). "It is as if my story repeats itself." Life, language, and literacy in a Chicago comunidad. *Education and Urban Society, 29,* 35–53.

Guerra, J. C. (1998). *Close to home: Oral and literate practices in a transnational Mexicano community.* New York: Teachers College Press.

Gungle, B., & Taylor, V. (1989). Writing apprehension and second language writers. In D. Johnson & D. Roen (Eds.), *Richness in writing: Empowering ESL students* (pp. 235–245). New York: Longman.

Gutierrez, K. (1992). A comparison of instructional contexts in writing process classrooms with Latino children. *Education and Urban Society, 24,* 244–262.

Gutierrez, K. (1994). How talk, context, and script shape contexts for learning: A cross-case comparison of journal sharing. *Linguistics and Education, 5,* 335–365.

Hale, G., Taylor, C., Bridgeman, B., Carson, J., Kroll, B., & Kantor, R. (1996). *A study of writing tasks assigned in academic degree programs.* TOEFL Research Report 54. Princeton, NJ: Educational Testing Service.

Hall, C. (1990). Managing the complexity of revising across languages. *TESOL Quarterly, 24,* 43–60.

Hall, E. (1991). Variations in composing behaviors of academic ESL writers in test and non-test situations. *TESL Canada Journal, 8,* 9–33.

Halliday, M. A. K., & Hasan, R. (1985). *Language, context, and text: Aspects of language in a social-semiotic perspective.* Geelong, Australia: Deakin University Press.

Halliday, M. A. K., & Matthiessen, C. (2004). *An introduction to functional grammar* (3rd ed.). London: Cassell.

Hamilton, M., Barton, D., & Ivanic, R. (Eds.). (1994). *Worlds of literacy.* Clevedon, UK: Multingual Matters.

Hammond, J. (1987). An overview of the genre-based approach to the teaching of writing in Australia. *Australian Review of Applied Linguistics, 10,* 163–181.

Hammond, J., & Macken-Horarik, M. (1999). Critical literacy: Challenges and questions for ESL classrooms. *TESOL Quarterly, 33,* 528–544.

Hamp-Lyons, L. (1986). No new lamps for old yet, please. *TESOL Quarterly, 20,* 790–796.

Hamp-Lyons, L. (Ed.) (1991). *Assessing second language writing in academic contexts.* Norwood, NJ: Ablex.

Hamp-Lyons, L. (2007). The impact of testing practices on teaching: Ideologies and alternatives. In J. Cummins & C. Davison (Eds.), *International handbook of English language teaching* (pp. 487–504). New York: Springer.

Hamp-Lyons, L., & Condon, W. (2000). *Assessing the portfolio: Practice, theory and research*. Cresskill, NJ: Hampton Press.

Hamp-Lyons, L., & Henning, G. (1991). Communicative writing profiles: An investigation of the transferability of a multiple-trait scoring instrument across ESL writing assessment contexts. *Language Learning, 41*, 337–373.

Hamp-Lyons, L., & Kroll, B. (1997). *TOEFL 2000–writing: Composition, community, and assessment*. TOEFL Monograph Report No. 5. Princeton, NJ: Educational Testing Service.

Hamp-Lyons, L., & Mathias, S. (1994). Examining expert judgments of task difficulty on essay tests. *Journal of Second Language Writing, 3*, 49–68.

Han, J. W., & Ernst-Slavit, G. (1999). Come join the literacy club: One Chinese ESL child's literacy experience in a 1st grade classroom. *Journal of Research in Childhood Education, 13*, 144–154.

Hansen, J. (2000). Interactional conflicts among audience, purpose, and content knowledge in the acquisition of academic literacy in an EAP course. *Written Communication, 17*, 27–52.

Hardman, J. (1999). A community of learners: Cambodians in an adult ESL classroom. *Language Teaching Research, 3*, 145–166.

Harklau, L. (1994a). ESL versus mainstream classes: Contrasting L2 learning environments. *TESOL Quarterly, 28*, 241–272.

Harklau, L. (1994b). Tracking and linguistic minority students: Consequences of ability grouping for second language learners. *Linguistics and Education, 6*, 217–244.

Harklau, L. (1999a). The ESL learning environment in secondary school. In C. Faltis & P. Wolfe (Eds.), *So much to say: Adolescents, bilingualism, and ESL in the secondary school* (pp. 42–60). New York: Teachers College Press.

Harklau, L. (1999b). Representing culture in the ESL writing classroom. In E. Hinkel (Ed.), *Culture in language teaching and learning* (pp. 109–130). New York: Cambridge University Press.

Harklau, L. (2000). From the "good kids" to the "worst": Representations of English language learners across educational settings. *TESOL Quarterly, 34*, 35–67.

Harklau, L. (2001). From high school to college: Student perspectives on literacy practices. *Journal of Literacy Research, 33*, 33–70.

Harklau, L. (2002). The role of writing in classroom second language acquisition. *Journal of Second Language Writing, 11*, 329–350.

Harklau, L. (2003). Representational practices and multi-modal communication in US high schools: Implications for adolescent immigrants. In R. Bayley & S. Schecter (Eds.), *Language socialization in bilingual and multilingual societies* (pp. 83–97). Buffalo, NY: Multilingual Matters.

Harklau, L. (2007). The adolescent English language learner: Identities lost and found. *The International Handbook of English language teaching*. In J. Cummins & C. Davison (Eds.), *The International Handbook of English language teaching* (pp. 559–573). Norwell, MA: Springer.

Harklau, L., Losey, K., & Siegal, M. (Eds.). (1999). *Generation 1.5 meets college composition*. Mahwah, NJ: Erlbaum.

Harley, B. (1989). Functional grammar in French immersion: A classroom experiment. *Applied Linguistics, 10*, 331–359.

Harley, B., Allen, P., Cummins, J., & Swain, M. (Eds.). (1990). *The development of second language proficiency*. Cambridge, UK: Cambridge University Press.

Harper, H., Peirce, B., & Burnaby, B. (1996). English-in-the-workplace for garment workers: A feminist project? *Gender and Education, 8*, 5–19.

Harris, M. (1997). Cultural conflicts in the writing center: Expectations and assumptions of ESL students. In C. Severino, J. Guerra, & J. Butler (Eds.), *Writing in multicultural settings: Research and scholarship in composition* (pp. 220–233). New York: Modern Language Association.

Harris, M., & Silva, T. (1993). Tutoring ESL students: Issues and options. *College Composition and Communication, 44*, 525–537.

Hartley, T. (1994). Generations of literacy among women in a bilingual community. In D. Barton, M. Hamilton, & R. Ivanic (Eds.), *Worlds of literacy* (pp. 29–40). Philadelphia: Multilingual Matters.

Hartman, B., & Tarone, E. (1999). Preparation for college writing: Teachers talk about writing instruction for Southeast Asian students in secondary school. In L. Harklau, K. Losey, & M. Siegal, (Eds.), *Generation 1.5 meets college composition* (pp. 99–118). Mahwah, NJ: Erlbaum.

Harwood, N., & Hadley, G. (2004). Demystifying institutional practices: Critical pragmatism and the teaching of academic writing. *English for Specific Purposes, 23*, 355–377.

Haswell, R. H. (1988). Error and change in college student writing. *Written Communication, 5*, 479–499.

Haswell, R. (1998). Searching for Kiyoko: Bettering mandatory ESL writing placement. *Journal of Second Language Writing, 7*, 133–174.

Hawes, T., & Thomas, S. (1997). Problems in thematisation in student writing. *RELC Journal, 28*, 35–55.

Hawkey, R., & Barker, F. (2004). Developing a common scale for the assessment of writing. *Assessing Writing, 9*, 122–159.

Hawkins, M. (2005). Becoming a student: Identity work and academic literacies in early schooling. *TESOL Quarterly, 39*, 59–82.

Hayes, E. (1989). Hispanic adults and ESL programs: Barriers to participation. *TESOL Quarterly, 23*, 47–61.

Hedgcock, J., & Atkinson, D. (1993). Differing reading–writing relationships in L1 and L2 literacy development. *TESOL Quarterly, 27*, 329–333.

Hedgcock, J., & Lefkowitz, N. (1992). Collaborative oral/aural revision in foreign language writing instruction. *Journal of Second Language Writing, 1*, 255–276.

Hedgcock, J., & Lefkowitz, N. (1994). Feedback on feedback: Assessing learner receptivity to teacher response in L2 composing. *Journal of Second Language Writing, 3*, 141–163.

Hedgcock, J., & Lefkowitz, N. (1996). Some input on input: Two analyses of student response to expert feedback in L2 writing. *Modern Language Journal, 80*, 287–308.

Hedge, T. (1988). *Writing.* Oxford, UK: Oxford University Press.

Heller, M. (2001). Gender and public space in a bilingual school. In A. Pavlenko, A. Blackledge, I. Piller, & M. Teutsch-Dwyer (Eds.), *Multilingualism, second language learning, and gender* (pp. 257–282). New York: Mouton de Gruyter.

Helms-Park, R., & Stapleton, P. (2003). Questioning the importance of individualized voice in undergraduate L2 argumentative writing: An empirical study with pedagogical implications. *Journal of Second Language Writing, 12*, 247–265.

Hillocks, G. (1986). *Research on written composition: New directions for teaching.* Urbana, IL: National Conference on Research in English/ERIC Clearinghouse on Reading and Communication Skills.

Hinkel, E. (1997). Indirectness in L1 and L2 academic writing. *Journal of Pragmatics, 27*, 361–386.

Hinkel, E. (2001). Matters of cohesion in L2 academic texts. *Applied Language Learning, 12*, 111–132.

Hinkel, E. (2002). *Second language writers' texts: Linguistic and rhetorical features.* Mahwah, NJ: Erlbaum.

Hinkel, E. (2003). Simplicity without elegance: Features of sentences in L1 and L2 academic texts. *TESOL Quarterly, 37*, 275–301.

Hinkel, E. (2005). Hedging, inflating, and persuading in L2 academic writing. *Applied Language Learning, 15*, 29–53.

Hirose, K. (2003). Comparing L1 and L2 organizational patterns in the argumentative writing of Japanese EFL students. *Journal of Second Language Writing, 12,* 181–209.

Hirose, K., & Sasaki, M. (1994). Explanatory variables for Japanese students' expository writing in English: An exploratory study. *Journal of Second Language Writing, 3,* 203–229.

Hirvela, A. (2001). Incorporating reading into EAP writing courses. In J. Flowerdew (Ed.), *Research perspectives on English for academic purposes* (pp. 330–346). New York: Cambridge University Press.

Hirvela, A. (2004). *Connecting reading and writing in second language writing instruction.* Ann Arbor: University of Michigan Press.

Hirvela, A. (2005). Computer-based reading and writing across the curriculum: Two case studies of L2 writers. *Computers and Composition, 22,* 337–356.

Hirvela, A., & Belcher, D. (2001). Coming back to voice: The multiple voices and identities of mature multilingual writers. *Journal of Second Language Writing, 10,* 83–106.

Hirvela, A., & Sweetland, Y. (2005). Two case studies of L2 writers' experiences across learning-directed portfolio contexts. *Assessing Writing, 10,* 192–213.

Hoffman, A. (1998). An exploratory study of goal setting and the nature of articulated goals in second language writing development. *New Zealand Studies in Applied Linguistics, 4,* 33–48.

Holmes, V., & Moulton, M. (1995). A contrarian view of dialogue journals: The case of a reluctant participant. *Journal of Second Language Writing, 4,* 223–251.

Homburg, T. J. (1984). Holistic evaluation of ESL compositions: Can it be validated objectively? *TESOL Quarterly, 18,* 87–107.

Hood, S., & Knightley, S. (1991). *Literacy development: A longitudinal study.* Sydney, Australia: New South Wales Adult Migrant English Service.

Hornberger, N. (1989). Continua of biliteracy. *Review of Educational Research, 59,* 271–296.

Hornberger, N. (Ed.). (2003). *Continua of biliteracy: An ecological framework for educational policy, research, and practice in multilingual settings.* Clevedon, UK: Multilingual Matters.

Hornberger, N., & Skilton-Sylvester, E. (2000). Revising the continua of biliteracy: International and critical perspectives. *Language and Education, 14,* 96–122.

Horowitz, D. (1986a). Process, not product: Less than meets the eye. *TESOL Quarterly, 20,* 141–144.

Horowitz, D. (1986b). What professor actually require: Academic tasks for the ESL classroom. *TESOL Quarterly, 20,* 445–462.

Hu, Z., Brown, D., & Brown, L. B. (1982). Some linguistic differences in the written English of Chinese and Australian students. *Language Learning and Communication, 1,* 39–49.

Huckin, T., & Olsen, L. (1984). The need for professionally oriented ESL instruction in the United States. *TESOL Quarterly, 18,* 273–294.

Hudelson, S. (1984). Kan yu ret an rayt en Ingles: Children become literate in English as a second language. *TESOL Quarterly, 18,* 221–238.

Hudelson, S. (1986). ESL children's writing: What we've learned, what we're learning. In P. Rigg & D. S. Enright (Eds.), *Children and ESL: Integrating perspectives* (pp. 25–54). Washington, DC: TESOL.

Hudelson, S. (1989a). A tale of two children: Individual differences in ESL children's writing. In D. Johnson & D. Roen (Eds.), *Richness in writing: Empowering ESL students* (pp. 84–99). New York: Longman.

Hudelson, S. (1989b). *Write on: Children writing in ESL.* Englewood Cliffs, NJ: Prentice Hall Regents.

Hughey, J. B., Wormuth, D. R., Hartfield, V. F., & Jacobs, H. L. (1983). *Teaching ESL composition: Principles and techniques.* Rowley, MA: Newbury House.

Huie, K., & Yahya, N. (2003). Learning to write in the primary grades: Experiences of English language learners and mainstream students. *TESOL Journal, 12,* 25–38.

Hunter, J. (1997). Multiple perceptions: Social identity in a multilingual elementary classroom. *TESOL Quarterly, 31,* 603–611.

Huss, R. (1995). Young children becoming literate in English as a second language. *TESOL Quarterly, 29,* 767–774.

Hutchinson, T., & Waters, A. (1987). *English for specific purposes: A learning-centred approach.* New York: Cambridge University Press.

Hyland, F. (1998). The impact of teacher-written feedback on individual writers. *Journal of Second Language Writing, 7,* 255–286.

Hyland, F. (2000). ESL writers and feedback: Giving more autonomy to students. *Language Teaching Research, 4,* 33–54.

Hyland, F. (2001). Dealing with plagiarism when giving feedback. *ELT Journal, 55,* 375–381.

Hyland, F. (2003). Focusing on form: Student engagement with teacher feedback. *System, 31,* 217–230.

Hyland, F., & Hyland, K. (2001). Sugaring the pill: Praise and criticism in written feedback. *Journal of Second Language Writing, 10,* 185–212.

Hyland, K. (2002). Authority and invisibility: Authorial identity in academic writing. *Journal of Pragmatics, 34,* 1091–1112.

Hyland, K. (2003a). Genre-based pedagogies: A social response to process. *Journal of Second Language Writing, 12,* 17–29.

Hyland, K. (2003b). *Teaching second language writing.* New York: Cambridge University Press.

Hyland, K. (2004a). Disciplinary interactions: Metadiscourse in L2 postgraduate writing. *Journal of Second Language Writing, 13,* 133–151.

Hyland, K. (2004b). *Genre and second language writing.* Ann Arbor: University of Michigan Press.

Hyland, K., & Hyland, F. (Eds.). (2006). *Feedback on ESL writing: Contexts and issues.* New York: Cambridge University Press.

Hyland, K., & Milton, J. (1997). Qualification and certainty in L1 and L2 students' writing. *Journal of Second Language Writing, 6,* 183–205.

Hyland, K., & Tse, P. (2005). Hooking the reader: A corpus study of evaluative 'that' in abstracts. *English for Specific Purposes, 24,* 123–139.

Hyon, S. (1996). Genre in three traditions: Implications for ESL. *TESOL Quarterly, 30,* 693–722.

Ibrahim, A. M. (1999). Becoming black: Rap and hip hop, race, gender, identity, and the politics of ESL learning. *TESOL Quarterly, 33,* 349–369.

Indrasuta, C. (1988). Narrative styles in the writing of Thai and American students. In A. Purves (Ed.), *Writing across languages: Issues in contrastive rhetoric* (pp. 206–227). Newbury Park, CA: Sage.

Intaraprawat, P., & Steffensen, M. (1995). The use of metadiscourse in good and poor ESL essays. *Journal of Second Language Writing, 4,* 253–272.

Ishikawa, S. (1995). Objective measurement of low-proficiency EFL narrative writing. *Journal of Second Language Writing, 4,* 51–69.

Ivanic, R., & Camps, D. (2001). I am how I sound: Voice as self-representation in L2 writing. *Journal of Second Language Writing, 10,* 3–33.

Jackson, J. (2002). The L2 case discussion in business: An ethnographic investigation. In J. Flowerdew (Ed.), *Academic discourse* (pp. 268–286). London: Longman.

Jacobs, G. (1987). First experiences with peer feedback on compositions: Student and teacher reaction. *System, 15,* 325–333.

Jacobs, G., Curtis, A., Braine, G., & Huang, S. (1998). Feedback on student writing: Taking the middle path. *Journal of Second Language Writing, 7*, 307–317.

Jacobs, H., Zinkgraf, S., Wormuth, D., Hartfiel, V., & Hughey, J. (1981). *Testing ESL composition: A practical approach*. Rowley, MA: Newbury House.

Jacobs, S. (1982). *Composing and coherence: The writing of eleven pre-medical students*. Washington, DC: Center for Applied Linguistics.

Jacoby, S., Leech, D., & Holten, C. (1995). A genre-based developmental writing course for undergraduate ESL science majors. In D. Belcher & G. Braine (Eds.), *Academic writing in a second language: Essays on research and pedagogy* (pp. 351–373). Norwood, NJ: Ablex.

James, K. (1984). The writing of theses by speakers of English as a foreign language: The results of a case study. *Common Ground, 117*, 99–113.

Janopoulos, M. (1986). The relationship of pleasure reading and second language writing proficiency. *TESOL Quarterly, 20*, 763–768.

Janopoulos, M. (1992). University faculty tolerance of NS and NNS writing errors: A comparison. *Journal of Second Language Writing, 1*, 109–121.

Janopoulos, M. (1995). Writing across the curriculum, writing proficiency exams, and the NNS college student. *Journal of Second Language Writing, 4*, 43–50.

Jarvis, S. (2002). Short texts, best-fitting curves and new measures of lexical diversity. *Language Testing, 19*, 57–84.

Jarvis, S., Grant, L., Bikowski, D., & Ferris, D. (2003). Exploring multiple profiles of highly rated learner compositions. *Journal of Second Language Writing, 12*, 377–403.

Jenkins, S., & Hinds, J. (1987). Business letter writing: English, French, and Japanese. *TESOL Quarterly, 21*, 327–349.

Jenkins, S., Jordan, M., & Weiland, P. (1993). The role of writing in graduate engineering education: A survey of faculty beliefs and practices. *English for Specific Purposes, 12*, 51–67.

Jimenez, R. (2000). Literacy and the identity development of Latina/o students. *American Educational Research Journal, 37*, 971–1000.

Johns, A. (1981). Necessary English: A faculty survey. *TESOL Quarterly, 15*, 51–57.

Johns, A. (1984). Textual cohesion and the Chinese speaker of English. *Language Learning and Communication, 3*, 69–73.

Johns, A. (1991a). Faculty assessment of ESL student literacy skills: Implications for writing assessment. In L. Hamp-Lyons (Ed.), *Assessing second language writing in academic contexts* (pp. 167–179). Norwood, NJ: Ablex.

Johns, A. (1991b). Interpreting an English competency examination: The frustration of an ESL science student. *Written Communication, 8*, 379–401.

Johns, A. (1992). Toward developing a cultural repertoire: A case study of a Lao college freshman. In D. Murray (Ed.), *Diversity as resource: Redefining cultural literacy* (pp. 183–201). Washington, DC: TESOL.

Johns, A. (1993). Reading and writing tasks in English for academic purposes classes: Products, processes, and resources. In J. Carson & I. Leki (Eds.), *Reading in the composition classroom: Second language perspectives* (pp. 274–289). Boston, MA: Heinle & Heinle.

Johns, A. (1995). Genre and pedagogical purposes. *Journal of Second Language Writing, 4*, 181–191.

Johns, A. (1997). *Text, role, and context*. New York: Cambridge University Press.

Johns, A. (2003a). Academic writing: A European perspective. *Journal of Second Language Writing, 12*, 313–316.

Johns, A. (2003b). Genre and ESL/EFL composition instruction. In B. Kroll (Ed.), *Exploring the dynamics of second language writing* (pp. 195–217). New York: Cambridge University Press.

Johnson, D. (1992). Interpersonal involvement in discourse: Gender variation in L2 writers' complimenting strategies. *Journal of Second Language Writing, 1,* 195–215.

Johnson, P. (1992). Cohesion and coherence in compositions in Malay and English. *Regional English Language Centre Journal, 23,* 1–27.

Johnson, R. K. (Ed.). (1989). *The second language curriculum.* New York: Cambridge University Press.

Jones, S. (1985). Problems with monitor use in second language composing. In M. Rose (Ed.), *When a writer can't write: Studies in writer's block and other composing process problems* (pp. 96–118). New York: Guilford.

Jones, S., & Tetroe, J. (1987). Composing in a second language. In A. Matsuhashi (Ed.), *Writing in real time* (pp. 34–57). Norwood, NJ: Ablex.

Joseph, P., Bravmann, S., Windschitle, M., Mikel, E., & Green, N. (2000). *Cultures of curriculum.* Mahwah, NJ: Erlbaum.

Kachru, B. (Ed.). (1992). *The other tongue.* Urbana: University of Illinois Press.

Kachru, Y. (1995). Contrastive rhetoric in World Englishes. *English Today, 41,* 21–31.

Kagan, S. (1986). Cooperative learning and sociocultural factors in schooling. In Bilingual Education Office (Ed.), *Beyond language: Social and cultural factors in schooling language minority students* (pp. 187–230). Los Angeles: California State University.

Kameen, P. (1980). Syntactic skill and ESL writing quality. *ON TESOL '79: The learner in focus: Selected papers from the 13th annual convention of TESOL,* 343–350.

Kameen, P. (1983). Syntactic skill and ESL writing quality. In A. Freedman, I. Pringle, & J. Yalden (Eds.), *Learning to write: First language/second language* (pp. 162–170). London: Longman.

Kamimura, T. (1996). Composing in Japanese as a first language and English as a foreign language: A study of narrative writing. *Regional English Language Centre Journal, 27,* 47–69.

Kamimura, T., & Oi, K. (1998). Argumentative strategies in American and Japanese English. *World Englishes, 17,* 307–323.

Kamimura, T., & Oi, K. (2001). The effects of different points of view on the story production of Japanese EFL students. *Foreign Language Annals, 34,* 118–130.

Kanno, Y., & Applebaum, S. D. (1995). ESL students speak up: Their stories of how we are doing. *TESL Canada Journal/Revue TESL du Canada, 12,* 32–49.

Kaplan, R. (1966). Cultural thought patterns in inter-cultural education. *Language Learning, 16,* 1–20.

Kaplan, R. (1993). The hegemony of English in science and technology. *Journal of Multilingual and Multicultural Development, 14,* 151–172.

Kaplan, R. (Ed.). (1995). *The teaching of writing in the Pacific basin.* Special Issue of *Journal of Asian Pacific Communication, 6,* 1/2.

Kaplan, R. (2000). Response to "On the future of second language writing." *Journal of Second Language Writing, 9,* 311–314.

Kaplan, R. (2001). English—the accidental language of science? In U. Ammon (Ed.), *The dominance of English as a language of science: Effects on other languages and language communities* (pp. 3–26). New York: Mouton de Gruyter.

Katz, M. (2000). Workplace language teaching and the intercultural construction of ideologies of competence. *Canadian Modern Language Review/La Revue canadienne des langues vivantes, 57,* 144–172.

Katznelson, H., Perpignan, H., & Rubin, B. (2001). What develops *along with* the development of second language writing? Exploring the "by-products." *Journal of Second Language Writing, 10,* 141–159.

Kells, M. (2002). Linguistic contact zones in the college writing classroom: An examination of ethnolinguistic identity and language attitudes. *Written Communication, 19,* 5–43.

Kelly, P. (1986). How do ESL writers compose? *Australian Review of Applied Linguistics, 9*, 94–119.

Kepner, C. G. (1991). An experiment in the relationship of types of written feedback to the development of second-language writing skills. *Modern Language Journal, 75*, 305–313.

Kerfoot, C. (1993). Participatory education in a South African context: Contradictions and challenges. *TESOL Quarterly, 27*, 431–447.

Kern, R. (2000). *Literacy and language teaching.* Oxford, UK: Oxford University Press.

Kern, R., & Schultz, J. (1992). The effects of composition instruction on intermediate level French students' writing performance: Some preliminary findings. *Modern Language Journal, 76*, 1–13.

Kern, R., & Warschauer, M. (Eds.) (2000). *Network-based language teaching: Concepts and practice.* Cambridge, UK: Cambridge University Press.

Khalil, A. (1989). A study of cohesion and coherence in Arab EFL college students' writing. *System, 17*, 359–371.

Khalil, A. (1999). The role of cross-linguistic influence in Palestinian EFL students' English compositions. *INTERFACE. Journal of Applied Linguistics, 13*, 99–112.

Khuwaileh, A. A., & Al Shoumali, A. (2000). Writing errors: A study of the writing ability of Arab learners of academic English and Arabic at university. *Language Culture and Curriculum, 13*, 174–183.

Kiany, G. R., & Nejad, M. K. (2001). On the relationship between English proficiency, writing ability, and the use of conjunctions in Iranian EFL learners' compositions. *ITL Review of Applied Linguistics, 133/134*, 227–241.

King, K., & Hornberger, N. (2005). Literacies in families and communities. In N. Bascia, A. Cumming, A. Datnow, K. Leithwood, & D. Livingstone (Eds.), *International Handbook of Educational Policy*, Vol. 2 (pp. 715–734). Dordrecht, The Netherlands: Springer.

Kitagawa, M. (1989). Letting ourselves be taught. In D. Johnson & D. Roen (Eds.), *Richness in writing: Empowering ESL students* (pp. 70–83). New York: Longman.

Klassen, C. (1991). Bilingual language use by low-education Latin American newcomers. In D. Barton & R. Ivanic (Eds.), *Writing in the community* (pp. 35–57). Thousand Oaks, CA: Sage.

Klassen, C. (1992). Obstacles to learning: The account of low-education Latin American adults. In B. Burnaby & A. Cumming (Eds.), *Sociopolitical aspects of ESL.* Toronto: OISE Press.

Klassen, C., & Burnaby, B. (1993). "Those who know": Views on literacy among adult immigrants in Canada. *TESOL Quarterly, 27*, 377–397.

Kobayashi, H. (1984). Rhetorical patterns in English and Japanese. *TESOL Quarterly, 18*, 737–738.

Kobayashi, H., & Rinnert, C. (1992). Effects of first language on second language writing: Translation versus direct composition. *Language Learning, 42*, 183–215.

Kobayashi, H., & Rinnert, C. (1996). Factors affecting composition evaluation in an EFL context: Cultural rhetorical pattern and readers' background. *Language Learning, 46*, 397–437.

Kobayashi, H., & Rinnert, C. (2001). Factors relating to EFL writers' discourse level revision skills. In R. M. Manchón (Ed.), *Writing in the L2 classroom: Issues in research and pedagogy.* Special Issue of *International Journal of English Studies, 1, 2*, 71–102.

Kobayashi, H., & Rinnert, C. (2002). High school student perceptions of first language literacy instruction: Implications for second language writing. *Journal of Second Language Writing, 11*, 91–116.

Kobayashi, T. (1992). Native and nonnative reactions to ESL compositions. *TESOL Quarterly, 26*, 81–112.

Koelsch, N., & Trumbull, (1996). Portfolios: Bridging cultural and linguistic worlds. In R. Calfee & P. Perfumo (Eds.), *Writing portfolios in the classroom: Policy and practice, promise and peril* (pp. 261–284). Mahwah, NJ: Erlbaum.

Kondo-Brown, K. (2002). A FACETS analysis of rater bias in measuring Japanese second language writing performance. *Language Testing, 19*, 3–31.

Kong, A., & Pearson, P. D. (2003). The road to participation: The construction of a literacy practice in a learning community of linguistically diverse learners. *Research in the Teaching of English, 38*, 85–124.

Kramsch, C., & Lam, W. (1999). Textual identities: The importance of being non-native. In G. Braine (Ed.), *Non-native educators in English language teaching* (pp. 57–72). Mahwah, NJ: Erlbaum.

Krashen, S. (1984). *Writing: Research, theory, and application.* Oxford: Pergamon Press.

Kreeft, J., Shuy, R., Staton, J., Reed, L., & Morroy, R. (1984). *Dialogue writing: Analysis of student–teacher interactive writing in the learning of English as a second language.* Washington, DC: Center for Applied Linguistics.

Kroll, B. (1979). A survey of writing needs of foreign and American college freshmen. *ELT Journal, 33*, 219–226.

Kroll, B. (1998). Assessing writing abilities. *Annual Review of Applied Linguistics, 18*, 219–240.

Kroll, B. (Ed.). (2003). *Exploring the dynamics of second language writing.* New York: Cambridge University Press.

Kroll, B., & Reid, J. (1994). Guidelines for designing writing prompts: Clarifications, caveats, and cautions. *Journal of Second Language Writing, 3*, 231–255.

Kubota, R. (1997). A reevaluation of the uniqueness of Japanese written discourse. *Written Communication, 14*, 460–480.

Kubota, R. (1998). An investigation of L1–L2 transfer in writing among Japanese university students: Implications for contrastive rhetoric. *Journal of Second Language Writing, 7*, 69–100.

Kubota, R. (1999). Japanese culture constructed by discourses: Implications for Applied Linguistics research and ELT. *TESOL Quarterly, 33*, 9–35.

Kubota, R. (2003). New approaches to gender, class, and race in second language writing. *Journal of Second Language Writing, 12*, 31–47.

Kubota, R., & Lehner, A. (2004). Toward critical contrastive rhetoric. *Journal of Second Language Writing, 13*, 7–27.

Kuhn, T. (1962). *The structure of scientific revolutions.* Chicago: University of Chicago Press.

Kulick, D., & Stroud, C. (1993). Conceptions and uses of literacy in a Papua New Guinean village. In B. Street (Ed.), *Cross-cultural approaches to literacy* (pp. 30–61). Cambridge, UK: Cambridge University Press.

Kunnan, A. (Ed.). (1998). *Validation in language assessment.* Mahwah, NJ: Erlbaum.

Kunnan, A. (Ed.). (2000). *Fairness and validation in language assessment.* Cambridge, UK: Cambridge University Press.

Kutz, E., Groden, S., & Zamel, V. (1993). *The discovery of competence: Teaching and learning with diverse student writers.* Portsmouth, NH: Boynton/Cook.

Lado, R. (1961). *Language testing: The construction and use of foreign language tests.* London: Longman.

Lado, R. (1964). *Language teaching: A scientific approach.* New York: McGraw-Hill.

Lai, P. (1986). The revision processes of first year students at the National University of Singapore. *RELC Journal, 17*, 71–84.

Lalande, J. (1982). Reducing composition errors: An experiment. *Modern Language Journal, 66*, 140–149.

Lam, W. S. E. (2000). L2 literacy and the design of the self: A case study of a teenager writing on the internet. *TESOL Quarterly, 34,* 457–482.

Lanauze, M., & Snow, C. (1989). The relation between first- and second-language writing skills: Evidence from Puerto Rican elementary school children in bilingual programs. *Linguistics and Education, 1,* 323–339.

Land, R., & Whitley, C. (1989). Evaluating second language essays in regular composition classes: Towards a pluralistic U.S. rhetoric. In D. Johnson & D. Roen (Eds.), *Richness in writing: Empowering ESL students* (pp. 284–293). New York: Longman.

Larsen-Freeman, D. (1978). An ESL index of development. *TESOL Quarterly, 12,* 439–448.

Larsen-Freeman, D., & Strom, V. (1977). The construction of a second language acquisition index of development. *Language Learning, 27,* 123–134.

Laufer, B. (1991). The development of L2 lexis in the expression of the advanced learner. *Modern Language Journal, 75,* 440–448.

Laufer, B., & Nation, P. (1995). Vocabulary size and use: Lexical richness in L2 written composition. *Applied Linguistics, 16,* 307–322.

Lay, N. (1982). Composing processes of adult ESL learners: A case study. *TESOL Quarterly, 16,* 406–407.

Lay, N. (1983). Native language and the composing process. In M. S. B. Kwalick & V. Slaughter (Eds.), *New York writes* (pp. 17–21). New York: City University of New York.

Lay, N., Carro, G., Tien, S., Niemann, T., & Leong, S. (1999). Connections: High school to college. In L. Harklau, K. Losey, & M. Siegal (Eds.), *Generation 1.5 meets college composition* (pp. 175–190). Mahwah, NJ: Erlbaum.

Lea, M., & Street, B. (1998). Student writing in higher education: An academic literacies approach. *Studies in Higher Education, 23,* 157–172.

Lee, H. (2004). A comparative study of ESL writers' performance in a paper-based and a computer-delivered writing test. *Assessing Writing, 9,* 4–26.

Lee, M. (2003). Discourse structure and rhetoric of English narratives: Differences between native English and Chinese non-native English writers. *Text, 23,* 347–368.

Lee, S. J. (1997). The road to college: Hmong American women's pursuit of higher education. *Harvard Educational Review, 67,* 803–827.

Lee, S. J. (2001). More than "model minorities" or "delinquents": A look at Hmong American high school students. *Harvard Educational Review, 71,* 505–528.

Lee, S.-Y. (2005). Facilitating and inhibiting factors in English as a foreign language writing performance: A model testing with structural equation modeling. *Language Learning, 55,* 335–374.

Leibowitz, B. (2005). Learning in an additional language in a multilingual society: A South African case study on university-level writing. *TESOL Quarterly, 39,* 661–681.

Leki, I. (1990). Coaching from the margins: Issues in written response. In B. Kroll (Ed.) *Second language writing: Research insights for the classroom* (pp. 57–68). Cambridge, UK: Cambridge University Press.

Leki, I. (1991a). The preferences of ESL students for error correction in college-level writing classes. *Foreign Language Annals, 24,* 203–218.

Leki, I. (1991b). Twenty-five years of contrastive rhetoric: Text analysis and writing pedagogies. *TESOL Quarterly, 25,* 123–143.

Leki, I. (1992). *Understanding ESL writers: A guide for teachers.* Portsmouth, NH: Boynton/Cook, Heineman.

Leki, I. (1995a). Coping strategies of ESL students in writing tasks across the curriculum. *TESOL Quarterly, 29,* 235–260.

Leki, I. (1995b). Good writing: I know it when I see it. In D. Belcher & G. Braine, (Eds.), *Academic writing in a second language* (pp. 23–46). Norwood, NJ: Ablex.

Leki, I. (1999). "Pretty much I screwed up": Ill-served needs of a permanent resident. In L. Harklau, K. Losey, & M. Siegal (Eds.), *Generation 1.5 meets college composition: Issues in the teaching of writing to U.S. educated learners of ESL* (pp. 17–43). Mahwah, NJ: Erlbaum.

Leki, I. (Ed.). (2001a). *Academic writing programs.* Alexandria, VA: TESOL.

Leki, I. (2001b). Hearing voices: L2 students' experiences in L2 writing courses. In T. Silva & P. Matsuda (Eds.), *On second language writing* (pp. 17–28). Mahwah, NJ: Erlbaum.

Leki, I. (2001c). "A narrow thinking system": Nonnative-English speaking students in group projects across the curriculum. *TESOL Quarterly, 35,* 39–67.

Leki, I. (2003a). Coda: Pushing L2 writing research. *Journal of Second Language Writing, 12,* 103–105.

Leki, I. (2003b). Living through college literacy: Nursing in a second language. *Written Communication, 20,* 81–98.

Leki, I. (2004). Meaning and development of academic literacy in a second language. In B. Huot, C. Bazerman, & B. Stroble (Eds.), *Multi-literacies for the 21st century* (pp. 115–128). Cresswood, NJ: Hampton Press.

Leki, I. (2006). "You cannot ignore": Graduate L2 students' experience of and responses to written feedback practices. In K. Hyland & F. Hyland (Eds.), *Feedback in second language writing: Contexts and issues* (pp. 266–285). New York: Cambridge University Press.

Leki, I. (2007). *Undergraduates in a second language: Challenges and complexities of academic literacy development.* Mahwah, NJ: Erlbaum.

Leki, I., & Carson, J. (1994). Students' perceptions of EAP writing instruction and writing needs across the disciplines. *TESOL Quarterly, 28,* 81–101.

Leki, I., & Carson, J. (1997). "Completely different worlds": EAP and the writing experiences of ESL students in university courses. *TESOL Quarterly, 31,* 39–69.

Lepetit, D., & Cichocki, W. (2002). Teaching language to future health professionals: A needs assessment study. *Modern Language Journal, 86,* 384–396.

Leung, L. (1984). The relationship between first and second language writing. *Language Learning and Communication, 3,* 187–202.

Li, G. (2002). *"East is east, west is west"? Home literacy, culture, and schooling.* New York: Peter Lang.

Li, X.-M. (1996). *"Good writing" in cross-cultural context.* Albany, NY: SUNY Press.

Li, X.-M. (1999). Writing from the vantage point of an outside/insider. In G. Braine (Ed.), *Non-native educators in English language teaching.* Mahwah, NJ: Erlbaum.

Li, Y. (2005). Multidimensional enculturation: The case of an EFL Chinese doctoral student. *Journal of Asian Pacific Communication, 15,* 153–170.

Liebman, J. (1988). Contrastive rhetoric: Students as ethnographers. *Journal of Basic Writing, 7,* 6–27.

Liebman-Kleine, J. (1986). In defense of teaching process in ESL composition. *TESOL Quarterly, 20,* 783–788.

Lillis, T., & Curry, M. (2006). Professional academic writing by multilingual scholars: Interactions with literacy brokers in the production of English-medium texts. *Written Communication, 23,* 3–35.

Lim, H. (1983). The development of syntax in the writing of university ESL students. *TESOL Quarterly, 17,* 313–314.

Linnarud, M. (1983). On lexis: The Swedish learner and the native speaker compared. *Cross-language Analysis and Second Language Acquisition, 10,* 249–261.

Linnarud, M. (1986). *Lexis in composition: A performance analysis of Swedish learners' written English.* Malmo, Sweden: Liber Forlag.

Lintermann-Rygh, I. (1985). Connector density: An indicator of essay quality? *Text*, 5, 347–357.

Little, D. (2005). The Common European Framework and the European Language Portfolio: Involving learners and their judgments in the assessment process. *Language Testing*, 22, 321–336.

Liu, M., & Braine, G. (2005). Cohesive features in argumentative writing produced by Chinese undergraduates. *System*, 33, 4, 623–636.

Liu, J., & Hansen, J. (2002). *Peer response in second language writing classrooms*. Ann Arbor: University of Michigan Press.

Llewelyn, S. (1995) Topics, text types and grammar: Making the links. In A. Burns & S. Hood (Eds.), *Teachers' voices: Exploring course design in a changing curriculum* (pp. 67–74). Sydney, Australia: NCELTR Publications, Macquarie University.

Lo Bianco, J. (2000). Multiliteracies and multilingualism. In B. Cope & M. Kalantzis (Eds.), *Multiliteracies: Literacy learning and the design of social futures* (pp. 92–105). London: Routledge.

LoCastro, V., & Masuko, M. (2002). Plagiarism and academic writing of learners of English. *Hermes, Journal of Linguistics*, 28, 11–38.

Lockhart, C., & Ng, P. (1995). Analyzing talk in ESL peer response groups: Stances, functions, and content. *Language Learning*, 45, 605–655.

Long, S. (1998). Learning to get along: Language acquisition and literacy development in a new cultural setting. *Research in the Teaching of English*, 33, 8–47.

Losey, K. (1997). *Listen to the silences: Mexican American interaction in the composition classroom and the community*. Norwood, NJ: Ablex.

Lucas, T. (1992). Diversity among individuals: Eight students making sense of classroom journal writing. In D. Murray (Ed.), *Diversity as resource: Redefining cultural literacy* (pp. 202–232). Washington, DC: TESOL.

Lucas, T., Henze, R., & Donato, R. (1990). Promoting the success of Latino language-minority students: An exploratory study of six high schools. *Harvard Educational Review*, 60, 315–340.

Luke, A. (2005). Evidence-based state literacy policy: A critical alternative. In N. Bascia, A. Cumming, A. Datnow, K. Leithwood, & D. Livingstone (Eds.), *International Handbook of Educational Policy*, Vol. 2 (pp. 661–675). Dordrecht, The Netherlands: Springer.

Lumley, T. (2002). Assessment criteria in a large-scale writing test: What do they really mean to the raters? *Language Testing*, 19, 246–276.

Lumley, T. (2005). *Assessing second language writing: The rater's perspective*. Frankfurt: Peter Lang.

Lvovich, N. (2003). Sociocultural identity and academic writing: A second language learner profile. *Teaching English in the Two-Year College*, 31, 179–247.

Lynch, B., & Davidson, F. (1994). Criterion-referenced language test development: Linking curricula, teachers, and tests. *TESOL Quarterly*, 28, 727–743.

Ma, G., & Wen, Q. (1999). The relationship of second language learners' linguistic variables to second language writing ability. *Foreign Language Teaching and Research*, 4, 34–39.

Maguire, M. (1997). Shared and negotiated territories: The socio-cultural embeddedness of children's acts of meaning. In A. Pollard, D. Thiessen, & A. Filer (Eds.), *Children and their curriculum: The perspectives of primary and elementary school children* (pp. 51–80). Washington, DC: Falmer Press.

Maguire, M., & Graves, B. (2001). Speaking personalities in primary school children's L2 writing. *TESOL Quarterly*, 35, 561–593.

Maier, P. (1992). Politeness strategies in business letters by native and non-native English speakers. *English for Specific Purposes*, 11, 189–205.

Makino, T. (1993). Learner self-correction in EFL written compositions. *ELT Journal, 47*, 337–341.

Malicky, G., & Derwing, T. (1993). Literacy learning of adults in a bilingual ESL classroom. *Alberta Journal of Educational Research, 39*, 393–406.

Manchón, R. M., Roca, J., & Murphy, E. (2000). An approximation to the study of backtracking in L2 writing. *Learning and Instruction, 10*, 13–35.

Mangelsdorf, K. (1992). Peer reviews in the ESL composition classroom: What do students think? *ELT Journal, 46*, 158–172.

Mangelsdorf, K., & Schlumberger, A. (1992). ESL student response stances in a peer-review task. *Journal of Second Language Writing, 1*, 235–254.

Manton, J. (1998). The relationship between knowing our students' real needs and effective teaching. In T. Smoke (Ed.), *Adult ESL: Politics, pedagogy, and participation in classroom and community programs* (pp. 41–54). Mahwah, NJ: Lawrence Erlbaum.

Manyak, P. (2001). Participation, hybridity, and carnival: A situated analysis of a dynamic literacy practice in a primary-grade English immersion class. *Journal of Literacy Research, 33*, 423–465.

Markee, N. (1997). *Managing curricular innovation.* New York: Cambridge University Press.

Martin, J. R. (1992). *English text: System and structure.* Amsterdam: John Benjamins.

Martin-Jones, M., & Bhatt, A. (1998). Literacies in the lives of young Gujarati speakers in Leicester. In A. Durgunoglu & L. Verhoeven (Eds.), *Literacy development in a multilingual context: Cross-cultural perspectives* (pp. 37–50). Mahwah, NJ: Erlbaum.

Martin-Jones, M., & Jones, K. (Eds.) (2000). *Multilingual literacies: Reading and writing different worlds.* Amsterdam: John Benjamins.

Masny, D., & Ghahremani-Ghajar, S. (1999). Weaving multiple literacies: Somali children and their teachers in the context of school culture. *Language, Culture and Curriculum, 12*, 72–93.

Matalene, C. (1985). Contrastive rhetoric: An American writing teacher in China. *College English, 47*, 789–807.

Matsuda, P. K. (1998). Situating ESL writing in a cross-disciplinary context. *Written Communication, 15*, 99–121.

Matsuda, P. K. (1999). Composition studies and ESL writing: A disciplinary division of labor. *College Composition and Communication, 50*, 699–721.

Matsuda, P. K. (2001). Voice in Japanese written discourse: Implications for second language writing. *Journal of Second Language Writing, 10*, 35–53.

Matsuda, P. K. (2002). Negotiation of identity and power in a Japanese on-line discourse community. *Computers and Composition, 19*, 39–55.

Matsuda, P. K. (2003a). Basic writing and second language writers: Toward an inclusive definition. *Journal of Basic Writing, 22*, 67–89.

Matsuda, P. K. (2003b). Coming to voice: Publishing as a graduate student. In C. Casanave & S. Vandrick (Eds.), *Writing for scholarly publication: Behind the scenes in language education* (pp. 39–51). Mahwah, NJ: Erlbaum.

Matsuda, P. K. (2003c). Process and post-process: A discursive history. *Journal of Second Language Writing, 12*, 65–83.

Matsuda, P. K. (2003d). Second language writing in the twentieth century: A situated historical perspective. In B. Kroll (Ed.), *Exploring the dynamics of second language writing* (pp. 15–34). New York: Cambridge University Press.

Matsuda, P. K., Canagarajah, S., Harklau, L., Hyland, K., & Warschauer, M. (2003). Changing currents in second language writing research: A colloquium. *Journal of Second Language Writing, 12*, 151–179.

Matsuda, P., Cox, M., Jordan, J., & Ortmeier-Hooper, C. (Eds.). (2006). *Second language writing in the composition classroom: A critical sourcebook.* Boston: Bedford/ St. Martin's.

Matsuda, P., Ortmeier-Hooper, C., & You, X. (Eds.). (2006). *The politics of second language writing: In search of the promised land.* West Lafayette, IN: Parlor Press.

Matsumoto, K. (1995). Research paper writing strategies of professional Japanese EFL writers. *TESL Canada Journal/Revue TESL du Canada, 13,* 17–27.

Mauranen, A. (1996). Discourse competence: Evidence from thematic development in native and non-native texts. In E. Ventola & A. Mauranen (Eds.), *Academic writing: Intercultural and textual issues* (pp. 195–230). Amsterdam: John Benjamins.

Maxwell, M., & Falick, T. (1992). Cohesion and quality in deaf and hearing children's written English. *Sign Language Studies, 77,* 345–372.

McCarthey, S. (2002). *Students' identities and literacy learning.* Newark, DE: International Reading Association and National Reading Conference.

McCarthey, S., & Garcia, G. (2005). English language learners' writing practices and attitudes. *Written Communication, 22,* 36–75.

McCarthey, S., Garcia, G., Lopez-Velasquez, A., Lin, S., & Guo, Y. (2004). Understanding writing contexts for English language learners. *Research in the Teaching of English, 38,* 351–394.

McCarthey, S., Guo, Y., & Cummins, S. (2005). Understanding changes in elementary Mandarin students' L1 and L2 writing. *Journal of Second Language Writing, 14,* 71–104.

McGroarty, M. (1992). Second language instruction in the workplace. *Annual Review of Applied Linguistics, 13,* 86–108.

McGroarty, M., & Scott, S. (1993). Reading, writing, and roles in U.S. adult literacy textbooks. *TESOL Quarterly, 27,* 563–573.

McGroarty, M., & Zhu, W. (1997). Triangulation in classroom research: A study of peer revision. *Language Learning, 47,* 1–43.

McKay, P. (2000). On ESL standards for school-age learners. *Language Testing, 17,* 185–214.

McKay, P. (2007). The standards movement and ELT for school-aged learners. In J. Cummins & C. Davison (Eds.), *International handbook of English language teaching* (pp. 439–456). New York: Springer.

McKay, S. (1993). *Agendas for second language literacy.* Cambridge, UK: Cambridge University Press.

McKay, S., & Weinstein-Shr, G. (1993). English literacy in the U.S.: National policies, personal consequences. *TESOL Quarterly, 27,* 399–419.

McKay, S., & Wong, S. (1996). Multiple discourses, multiple identities: Investment and agency in second-language learning among Chinese adolescent immigrant students. *Harvard Educational Review, 66,* 577–608.

McKenna, E. (1987). Preparing foreign students to enter discourse communities in the U.S. *English for Specific Purposes, 6,* 187–202.

McQuillan, G. (1994). Let them speak for themselves: ESL students on multiculturalism. *College ESL, 4,* 26–38.

Medgyes, P., & Kaplan, R. (1992). Discourse in a foreign language: The example of Hungarian scholars. *International Journal of the Sociology of Language, 98,* 67–100.

Mendonca, C., & Johnson, K. (1994). Peer review negotiations: Revision activities in ESL writing instruction. *TESOL Quarterly, 28,* 745–769.

Mendelsohn, D., & Cumming, A. (1987). Professors' ratings of language use and rhetorical organization in ESL compositions. *TESL Canada Journal, 5,* 11–26.

Meziani, A. (1984). Moroccan learners' English errors: A pilot study. *International Review of Applied Linguistics, 22,* 297–310.

Milanovic, M., Saville, N., & Shen, S. (1996). A study of the decision-making behaviour of composition markers. In M. Milanovic & N. Saville (Eds.), *Performance testing, cognition and assessment* (pp. 92–114). Cambridge, UK: Cambridge University Press.

Miller, J. (2000). Language use, identity, and social interaction: Migrant students in Australia. *Research on Language and Social Interaction, 33,* 69–100.

Miller, J., & Seller, W. (1985). *Curriculum: Perspectives and practice.* New York: Longman.

Mlynarczyk, R. (1998). *Conversations of the mind.* Mahwah, NJ: Erlbaum.

Mohan, B. (1986). *Language and content.* Reading, MA: Addison-Wesley.

Mohan, B., & Lo, W. (1985). Academic writing and Chinese students: Transfer and developmental factors. *TESOL Quarterly, 19,* 515–534.

Mohan, B., & Slater, T. (2005). The evaluation of causal discourse and language as a resource for meaning. In J. Foley (Ed.), *Language, education and discourse: Functional approaches* (pp. 171–187). London: Continuum.

Moje, E., Collazo, T., Carillo, R., and Marx, R. (2000). "Maestro, what is 'quality'?": Language, literacy, and discourse in project-based science. *Journal of Research in Science Teaching, 38,* 469–498.

Moll, L. (1989). Teaching second language students: A Vygotskian perspective. In D. Johnson & S. Roen (Eds.), *Richness in writing* (pp. 55–69). New York: Longman.

Moll, L., & Diaz, S. (1987). Change as the goal of educational research. *Anthropology and Education Quarterly, 18,* 300–311.

Moll, L., Saez, R., & Dworkin, J. (2001). Exploring biliteracy: Two student case examples of writing as a social practice. *Elementary School Journal, 101,* 435–449.

Moragne e Silva, M. (1989). A study of composing in a first and a second language. *Texas Papers in Foreign Language Education, 1,* 132–151.

Morgan, B. (1998). *The ESL classroom: Teaching, critical practice, and community development.* Toronto: University of Toronto Press.

Moriarty, P. (1998). Learning to be legal: Unintended meanings for adult schools. In T. Smoke (Ed.), *Adult ESL: Politics, pedagogy, and participation in classroom and community programs* (pp. 17–39). Mahwah, NJ: Erlbaum.

Morita, N. (2004). Negotiating participation and identity in second language academic communities. *TESOL Quarterly, 38,* 573–603.

Morris, L. A. (1998). Differences in men's and women's ESL writing at the junior college level: Consequences for research on feedback. *The Canadian Modern Language Review, 55,* 219–238.

Moulton, M. R., & Holmes, V. L. (1994). Writing in a multilingual classroom: Using dialogue journals to ease transitions. *College ESL, 4,* 12–25.

Muchinsky, D., & Tangren, N. (1999). Immigrant student performance in an academic intensive English program. In L. Harklau, K. Losey, & M. Siegal (Eds.), *Generation 1.5 meets college composition* (pp. 211–234). Mahwah, NJ: Erlbaum.

Muchiri, M., Mulamba, N., Myers, G., & Ndoloi, D. (1995). Importing composition: Teaching and researching academic writing beyond North America. *College Composition and Communication, 46,* 175–198.

Myers, G. (1988). The social construction of science and the teaching of English: An example of research. In P. Robinson (Ed.), *Academic writing: Process and product* (pp. 143–150). London: Modern English Publications/British Council.

Myles, J., & Cheng, L. (2003). The social and cultural life of non-native English speaking international graduate students at a Canadian university. *Journal of English for Academic Purposes, 2,* 247–263.

Nassaji, H., & Cumming, A. (2000). What's in a ZPD? A case study of a young ESL student and teacher interacting through dialogue journals. *Language Teaching Research, 4,* 95–121.

Nelson, G. (1998). Categorizing, classifying, labeling: A fundamental cognitive process. *TESOL Quarterly, 32,* 727–735.

Nelson, G., & Carson, J. (1998). ESL students' perceptions of effectiveness in peer response groups. *Journal of Second Language Writing, 7,* 113–131.

Nelson, G., & Murphy, J. (1992). An L2 writing group: Task and social dimensions. *Journal of Second Language Writing, 1,* 171–193.

Nelson, G., & Murphy, J. (1993). Peer response groups: Do L2 writers use peer comments in revising their drafts? *TESOL Quarterly, 27,* 135–142.

Nero, S. (2000). The changing faces of English: A Caribbean perspective. *TESOL Quarterly, 34,* 483–510.

New, E. (1999). Computer-aided writing in French as a foreign language: A qualitative and quantitative look at the process of revision. *Modern Language Journal, 83,* 80–97.

New London Group. (1996). A pedagogy of multiliteracies: Designing social futures. *Harvard Educational Review, 66,* 60–92.

Newman, M., Trenchs-Parera, M., & Pujol, M. (2003). Core academic literacy principles versus culture-specific practices: A multi-case study of academic achievement. *English for Specific Purposes, 22,* 45–71.

New South Wales Adult Migrant English Service. (1995). *Certificates in Spoken and Written English* (2nd ed.) Sydney, Australia: Authors.

Norment, N. (1986). Organizational structures of Chinese subjects writing in Chinese and ESL. *Journal of the Chinese Language Teachers Association, 21,* 49–72.

Norris, J., & Ortega, L. (Eds.) (2006). *Synthesizing research on language learning and teaching.* Amsterdam: John Benjamins.

North, B. (2000). *The development of a Common Framework Scale of language proficiency.* Frankfurt: Peter Lang.

Norton, B. (1997). Language, identity, and the ownership of English. *TESOL Quarterly, 31,* 409–429.

Norton, B. (1998). Using journals in second language research and teaching. In T. Smoke (Ed.), *Adult ESL: Politics, pedagogy, and participation in classroom and community programs* (pp. 55–71). Mahwah, NJ: Erlbaum.

Norton, B. (2000). *Identity and language learning: Gender, ethnicity and educational change.* New York: Pearson Education.

Norton, B., & Vanderheyden, K. (2004). Comic book culture and second language learners. In B. Norton & K. Toohey (Eds.), *Critical pedagogy and language learning* (pp. 201–222). New York: Cambridge University Press.

Nunan, D. (1988). *The learner-centred curriculum.* Cambridge, UK: Cambridge University Press.

Oi, K. (1999). Comparison of argumentative styles: Japanese college students vs. American college students – An analysis using the Toulmin Model. *Japan Association of College English Teachers Bulletin, 30,* 85–102.

Olsen, L. (1997). *Made in America: Immigrant students in our public schools.* New York: New Press.

Olsen, L., & Huckin, T. (1983). *Principles of communication for science and technology.* New York: McGraw Hill.

Olsen, S. (1999). Errors and compensatory strategies: A study of grammar and vocabulary in texts written by Norwegian learners of English. *System, 27,* 191–205.

Orellana, M., Reynolds, J., Dorner, L., & Meza, M. (2003). In other words: Translating and "para-phrasing" as a family literacy practice in immigrant households. *Reading Research Quarterly, 38,* 12–34.

Ortega, L. (2003). Syntactic complexity measures and their relationship to L2 proficiency: A research synthesis of college-level L2 writing. *Applied Linguistics, 24,* 492–518.

Ostler, S. (1980). A survey of academic needs for advanced ESL. *TESOL Quarterly, 14*, 489–502.

Pally, M., Katznelson, H., Perpignan, H., & Rubin, B. (2002). What is learned in sustained-content writing classes along with writing? *Journal of Basic Writing, 21*, 90–115.

Paltridge, B. (1997). *Genres, frames, and writing in research settings*. Amsterdam: John Benjamins.

Paltridge, B. (2001). *Genre and the language learning classroom*. Ann Arbor: University of Michigan Press.

Panetta, C. (2001). *Contrastive rhetoric revisited and redefined*. Mahwah, NJ: Erlbaum.

Parkhurst, C. (1990). The composition process of science writers. *English for Specific Purposes, 9*, 169–180.

Parks, S. (2000). Professional writing and the role of incidental collaboration: Evidence from a medical setting. *Journal of Second Language Writing, 9*, 101–122.

Parks, S. (2001). Moving from school to the workplace: Disciplinary innovation, border crossings, and the reshaping of a written genre. *Applied Linguistics, 22*, 405–438.

Parks, S., Huot, D., Hamers, J., & Lemonnier, F. (2005). "History of theatre" websites: A brief history of the writing process in a high school ESL language arts class. *Journal of Second Language Writing, 14*, 233–258.

Parks, S., & Maguire, M. (1999). Coping with on-the-job writing in ESL: A constructivist-semiotic perspective. *Language Learning, 49*, 143–175.

Parry, K. (1991). Building vocabulary through academic reading. *TESOL Quarterly, 25*, 629–653.

Parry, K., & Su, X. (Eds.). (1998). *Culture, literacy, and learning English*. Portsmouth, NH: Boynton/Cook.

Patthey-Chavez, G., & Clare, L. (1996). Task, talk, and text: The influence of instructional conversation on transitional bilingual writers. *Written Communication, 13*, 515–563.

Patthey-Chavez, G., & Ferris, D. (1997). Writing conferences and the weaving of multi-voiced texts in college composition. *Research in the Teaching of English, 31*, 51–90.

Paulus, T. (1999). The effect of peer and teacher feedback on student writing. *Journal of Second Language Writing, 8*, 265–289.

Pavlenko, A. (2001a). "How am I to become a woman in an American vein?": Transformations of gender performance in second language learning. In A. Pavlenko, A. Blackledge, I. Piller, & M. Teutsch-Dwyer (Eds.), *Multilingualism, second language learning, and gender* (pp. 133–174). New York: Mouton de Gruyter.

Pavlenko, A. (2001b). "In the world of tradition, I was unimagined": Negotiation of identities in cross-cultural autobiographies. *The International Journal of Bilingualism, 5*, 317–344.

Pavlenko, A. (2001c). Language learning memoirs as a gendered genre. *Applied Linguistics, 22*, 213–240.

Pavlenko, A., & Blackledge, A. (Eds.). (2004). *Negotiation of identities in multilingual contexts*. Clevedon, UK: Multilingual Matters.

Pearson, S. (1983). The challenge of Mai Chung: Teaching technical writing to the foreign-born professional in industry. *TESOL Quarterly, 17*, 383–399.

Pecorari, D. (2001). Plagiarism and international students: How the English-speaking university responds. In D. Belcher & A. Hirvela (Eds.), *Linking literacies: Perspectives on L2 reading-writing connections* (pp. 229–245). Ann Arbor: University of Michigan Press.

Pecorari, D. (2003). Good and original: Plagiarism and patchwriting in academic second-language writing. *Journal of Second Language Writing, 12*, 317–345.

Peirce, B. N. (1997). Language, identity, and the ownership of English. *TESOL Quarterly, 31,* 409–429.

Peirce, B., Harper, H., & Burnaby, B. (1993). Workplace ESL at Levi Strauss: Dropouts speak out. *TESL Canada Journal, 10,* 9–30.

Pelsmaekers, K., Braecke, C., & Geluykens, R. (1998). Rhetorical relations and subordination in L2 writing. In A. Sánchez-Macarro & R. Carter (Eds.), *Linguistic choice across genres: Variation in spoken and written English* (pp. 191–213). Amsterdam: John Benjamins.

Pennington, M. (1993). A critical examination of word processing effects in relation to L2 writers. *Journal of Second Language Writing, 2,* 227–255.

Pennington, M. (1996). *The computer and the non-native writer: A natural partnership.* Cresskill, NJ: Hampton Press.

Pennington, M., Brock, M., & Yue, F. (1996). Explaining Hong Kong students' response to process writing: An exploration of causes and outcomes. *Journal of Second Language Writing, 5,* 227–252.

Pennington, M., Costa, V., So, S., Shing, J., Hirose, K., & Niedzielski, K. (1997). The teaching of English-as-a-Second-Language writing in the Asia-Pacific region: A cross-country comparison. *Regional English Language Centre Journal, 28,* 120–143.

Pennycook, A. (1994a). The complex contexts of plagiarism: A reply to Deckert. *Journal of Second Language Writing, 3,* 277–284.

Pennycook, A. (1994b). *The cultural politics of English as an international language.* London: Longman.

Pennycook, A. (1996a). Borrowing others' words: Text, ownership, memory, and plagiarism. *TESOL Quarterly, 30,* 201–230.

Pennycook, A. (1996b). TESOL and critical literacies: Modern, Post, or Neo? *TESOL Quarterly, 30,* 163–171.

Pennycook, A. (1997). Vulgar pragmatism, critical pragmatism, and EAP. *English for Specific Purposes, 16,* 253–269.

Pennycook, A. (Ed.). (1999). Critical approaches to TESOL. Special issue of *TESOL Quarterly, 33.*

Pennycook, A. (2001). *Critical applied linguistics: A critical introduction.* Mahwah, NJ: Erlbaum.

Perez, B. (2004a). *Becoming biliterate: A study of two-way bilingual immersion education.* Mahwah, NJ: Erlbaum.

Perez, B. (Ed.). (2004b). *Sociocultural contexts of language and literacy* (2nd ed.) Mahwah, NJ: Erlbaum.

Perkins, K. (1980). Using objective methods of attained writing proficiency to discriminate among holistic evaluations. *TESOL Quarterly, 14,* 61–69.

Perrotta, B. (1994). Writing development and second language acquisition in young children. *Childhood Education, 70,* 237–241.

Perrucci, R., & Hu, H. (1995). Satisfaction with social and educational experiences among international graduate students. *Research in Higher Education, 36,* 491–508.

Peyton, J. (1990). Beginning at the beginning: First grade ESL students learn to write. In A. Padilla, H. Fairchild, & C. Valades (Eds.), *Bilingual education issues and strategies* (pp. 195–218). Newbury Park, CA: Sage.

Peyton, J. (1993). The development of beginning writers: Six student profiles. In J. K. Peyton & J. Staton (Eds.), *Dialogue journals in the multilingual classroom: Building language fluency and writing skills through written interaction* (pp. 47–99). Norwood, NJ: Ablex.

Peyton, J., & Staton, J. (Eds.) (1993). *Dialogue journals in the multilingual classroom: Building fluency and writing skills through written interaction.* Norwood, NJ: Ablex.

Phillipson, R. (1992). *Linguistic imperialism.* Oxford, UK: Oxford University Press.

Phillipson, R., & Skutnabb-Kangas, T. (2000). Englishisation: One dimension of globalisation. *AILA Review, 13*, 19–36.

Pike, K. (1967). *Language in relation to a unified theory of the structure of human behavior* (2nd ed.) Paris: Mouton.

Platt, E. (1993). Vocational/VESL teacher collaboration: Some substantive issues. *English for Specific Purposes, 12*, 139–157.

Platt, E., & Troudi, S. (1997). Mary and her teachers: A Grebo-speaking child's place in the mainstream classroom. *Modern Language Journal, 81*, 28–49.

Polio, C. (1997). Measures of linguistic accuracy in second language writing research. *Language Learning 47*, 101–143.

Polio, C. (2003). Research on second language writing: An overview of what we investigate and how. In B. Kroll (Ed.), *Exploring the dynamics of second language writing* (pp. 35–65). New York: Cambridge University Press.

Polio, C., Fleck, C., & Leder, N. (1998). "If only I had more time": ESL learners' changes in linguistic accuracy on essay revisions. *Journal of Second Language Writing, 7*, 43–68.

Porte, G. (1997). The etiology of poor second language writing: The influence of perceived teacher preferences on second language revision strategies. *Journal of Second Language Writing, 6*, 61–78.

Porto, M. (2001). Cooperative writing response groups and self-evaluation. *ELT Journal, 55*, 38–46.

Powers, D., Burstein, J., Chodrow, M., Fowles, M., & Kukich, K. (2002). Comparing the validity of automated and human scoring of essays. *Journal of Educational Computing Research, 26*, 407–425.

Powers, J., & Nelson, J. (1995). L2 writers and the writing center: A national survey of writing center conferencing at graduate institutions. *Journal of Second Language Writing, 4*, 113–138.

Prior, P. (1991). Contextualizing writing and response in a graduate seminar. *Written Communication, 8*, 267–310.

Prior, P. (1995). Redefining the task: An ethnographic examination of writing and response in graduate seminars. In D. Belcher & G. Braine (Eds.), *Academic writing in a second language: Essays on research and pedagogy* (pp. 47–82). Norwood, NJ: Ablex.

Prior, P. (1998). *Writing/disciplinarity: A sociohistoric account of literate activity in the academy*. Mahwah, NJ: Erlbaum.

Purves, A. (1986). Rhetorical communities, the international students and basic writing. *Journal of Basic Writing, 5*, 38–51.

Purves, A. (Ed.). (1988). *Writing across languages and cultures: Issues in contrastive rhetoric*. Newbury Park, CA: Sage.

Qi, D. (1998). An inquiry into language-switching in second language composing processes. *The Canadian Modern Language Review, 54*, 413–435.

Qi, D., & Lapkin, S. (2001). Exploring the role of noticing in a three-stage second language writing task. *Journal of Second Language Writing, 10*, 277–303.

Quian, S. (1995). Ethical problems: Authorship, ghost writing, ghost translation and copy-editing? *European Science Editing, 54*, 9–11.

Quintero, E. (2002). A problem-posing approach to using native language writing in English literacy instruction. In G. Rijlaarsdam (Series Ed.) & S. Ransdell & M. Barbier (Vol. Eds.), *Studies in writing, Volume 11: New directions for research in L2 writing* (pp. 231–244). Dordrecht, The Netherlands: Kluwer.

Radecki, P., & Swales, J. (1988). ESL students' reaction to written comments on their written work. *System, 16*, 355–365.

Raimes, A. (1985). What unskilled writers do as they write: A classroom study of composing. *TESOL Quarterly, 19*, 229–258.

Raimes, A. (1987). Language proficiency, writing ability, and composing strategies: A study of ESL college student writers. *Language Learning, 37,* 439–468.

Raimes, A. (1990). The TOEFL test of written English: Causes for concern. *TESOL Quarterly, 24,* 427–442.

Raimes, A. (1991). Out of the woods: Emerging traditions in the teaching of writing. *TESOL Quarterly, 25,* 407–430.

Raimes, A. (1998). Teaching writing. *Annual Review of Applied Linguistics, 18,* 142–167.

Ramanathan, V. (2002). *The politics of TESOL education.* New York: Routledge Falmer.

Ramanathan, V. (2003). Written textual production and consumption (WTPC) in vernacular and English-medium settings in Gujarat, India. *Journal of Second Language Writing, 12,* 125–150.

Ramanathan, V. (2004). *The English–vernacular divide: Postcolonial language politics and practice.* Clevedon, UK: Multilingual Matters.

Ramanathan, V., & Atkinson, D. (1999). Individualism, academic writing, and ESL writers. *Journal of Second Language Writing, 8,* 45–75.

Ramanathan, V., & Kaplan, R. (1996). Audience and voice in current L1 composition texts: Some implications for ESL student writers. *Journal of Second Language Writing, 5,* 21–34.

Rampton, B. (1995). *Crossing: Language and ethnicity among adolescents.* London: Longman.

Ransdell, S., Lavelle, B., & Levy, C. M. (2002). The effects of training a good working memory strategy on L1 and L2 writing. In G. Rijlaarsdam (Series Ed.) & S. Ransdell & M. Barbier (Vol. Eds.), *Studies in writing, Volume 11: New directions for research in L2 writing* (pp. 133–144). Dordrecht, The Netherlands: Kluwer.

Raymond, P., & Parks, S. (2002). Transitions: Orienting to reading and writing assignments in EAP and MBA contexts. *Canadian Modern Language Review/La Revue canadienne des langues vivantes, 59,* 152–180.

Rea-Dickins, P. (2001). Mirror, mirror on the wall: Identifying processes of classroom assessment. *Language Testing, 18,* 429–462.

Reder, S. (1987). Comparative aspects of functional literacy development: Three ethnic American communities. In D. Wagner (Ed.), *The future of literacy in a changing world* (pp. 250–270). New York: Pergamon Press.

Reichelt, M. (1999). Toward a comprehensive view of L2 writing: Foreign language writing in the U.S. *Journal of Second Language Writing, 8,* 181–204.

Reichelt, M. (2001). A critical review of foreign language writing research on pedagogical practices. *Modern Language Journal, 85,* 578–598.

Reichelt, M. (2003). Defining "Good writing": A cross-cultural perspective. *Composition Studies, 31,* 99–126.

Reichelt, M. (2005). English-language writing instruction in Poland. *Journal of Second Language Writing, 14,* 215–232.

Reid, J. (1992). A computer text analysis of four cohesion devices in English discourse by native and nonnative writers. *Journal of Second Language Writing, 1,* 79–107.

Reid, J. (1993). *Teaching ESL writing.* Englewood Cliffs, NJ: Regents/Prentice Hall.

Reid, J. (1994). Responding to ESL students' texts: The myths of appropriation. *TESOL Quarterly, 28,* 273–92.

Reid, J. (2001). Advanced EAP writing and curriculum design: What do we need to know? In T. Silva & P. Matsuda (Eds.) *On second language writing* (pp. 143–160). Mahwah, NJ: Erlbaum.

Reyes, M. (1992). Challenging venerable assumptions: Literacy instruction for linguistically different students. *Harvard Educational Review, 62,* 427–486.

Reynolds, D. (1995). Repetition in nonnative speaker writing: More than quantity. *Studies in Second Language Acquisition, 17,* 185–209.

Reynolds, D. (2001). Writing research questions for K–12 English-language learners: A neglected topic. *TESOL Research Interest Section Newsletter, 8,* 4–5.

Reynolds, D. (2002). Learning to make things happen: Causality in the writing of middle-grade English language learners. *Journal of Second Language Writing, 11,* 311–328.

Reynolds, D. (2005). Linguistic correlates of second language literacy development: Evidence from middle-grade learner essays. *Journal of Second Language Writing, 14,* 19–45.

Riazi, A. (1997). Acquiring disciplinary literacy: A social-cognitive analysis of text production and learning among Iranian graduate students of education. *Journal of Second Language Writing, 6,* 105–137.

Riazi, A., Lessard-Clouston, M., & Cumming, A. (1996). Observing ESL writing instruction: A case study of four teachers. *Journal of Intensive English Studies, 10,* 19–30.

Rifken, B., & Roberts, F. (1995). Error gravity: A critical review of research design. *Language Learning, 45,* 511–537.

Rigg, P. (1985). Petra: Learning to read at 45. *Journal of Education, 167,* 129–143.

Rigg, P., & Allen V. (Eds.). (1989). *When they don't all speak English: Integrating the ESL student into the regular classroom.* Urbana, IL: National Council of Teachers of English.

Riley, P. (1996). "Look in thy heart and write": Students' representations of writing and learning to write in a foreign language. In E. Ventola & A. Mauranen (Eds.), *Academic writing: intercultural and textual issues* (pp. 115–135). Amsterdam: John Benjamins.

Rinnert, C., & Kobayashi, H. (2001). Differing perceptions of EFL writing among readers in Japan. *Modern Language Journal, 85,* 189–209.

Robb, T., Ross, S., & Shortreed, I. (1986). Salience of feedback on error and its effect on ESL writing quality. *TESOL Quarterly, 20,* 83–93.

Robson, B. (1981). *Alternatives in ESL and literacy: Ban Vinai.* Washington, DC: Center for Applied Linguistics.

Roca, J. (1996). Linearization strategies in EFL writing: Some observations. *Lenguaje y Textos, 8,* 191–208.

Roca, J., Marin, J., & Murphy, L. (2001). A temporal analysis of formulation processes in L1 and L2 writing. *Language Learning, 51,* 497–538.

Roca, J., Murphy, L., & Manchón, R. (1999). The use of restructuring strategies in EFL writing: A study of Spanish learners of English as a foreign language. *Journal of Second Language Writing, 8,* 13–44.

Rockhill, K. (1987). Gender, language and the politics of literacy. *The British Journal of Sociology of Education, 8,* 153–167.

Rockhill, K. (1991). Literacy as threat/desire: Longing to be SOMEBODY. In J. Gaskell & A. McLaren (Eds.), *Women and education* (2nd ed., pp. 333–349). Calgary, AB: Detselig Enterprises.

Rodby, J. (1999). Contingent literacy: The social construction of writing for nonnative English-speaking college freshman. In L. Harklau, K. Losey, & M. Siegal (Eds.), *Generation 1.5 meets college composition* (pp. 45–60). Mahwah, NJ: Erlbaum.

Roessingh, H. (1999). Adjunct support for high school ESL learners in mainstream English classes: Ensuring success. *TESL Canada Journal, 17,* 72–86.

Rosenfeld, M., Leung, S., & Oltman, P. (2001). *The reading, writing, speaking, and listening tasks important for academic success at the undergraduate and graduate levels.* TOEFL Monograph 21. Princeton, NJ: Educational Testing Service.

Rosenthal, J. (2000). ESL students in the mainstream: Observations from content area faculty. In L. Kasper (Ed.), *Content based college ESL instruction* (pp. 71–90). Mahwah, NJ: Erlbaum.

Rothschild, D., & Klingenberg, F. (1990). Self and peer evaluation of writing in the intensive ESL classroom. *TESL Canada Journal, 8*, 52–65.

Ruetten, M. (1994). Evaluating ESL students' performance on proficiency exams. *Journal of Second Language Writing, 3*, 85–96.

Russell, P., & Yoo, J. (2001). Learner investment in second language writing. In X. Bonch-Bruevich, W. Crawford, J. Hellermann, C. Higgins, & H. Nguyen (Eds.), *The past, present, and future of second language research: Selected proceedings of the 2000 Second Language Research Forum* (pp. 181–196). Somerville, MA: Cascadilla.

St. John, M. (1987). Writing processes of Spanish scientists publishing in English. *English for Specific Purposes, 6*, 113–120.

Saito, H. (1994). Teachers' practices and students' preferences for feedback on second language writing: A case study of adult ESL learners. *TESL Canada Journal/Revue TESL du Canada, 11*, 46–70.

Sakyi, A. (2001). Validation of holistic scoring for ESL writing assessment: A study of how raters evaluate ESL compositions on a holistic scale. In A. Kunnan (Ed.), *Fairness and validation in language assessment* (pp. 130–153). Cambridge, UK: Cambridge University Press.

Samraj, B. (1994). Coping with a complex environment: Writing in a school of natural resources. In R. Khoo (Ed.), *LSP: Problems and prospects* (pp. 127–143). Singapore: Regional English Language Centre.

Samway, K. (1993). "This is hard, isn't it?": Children evaluating writing. *TESOL Quarterly, 27*, 233–257.

Santos, T. (1988). Professors' reactions to the academic writing of nonnative-speaking students. *TESOL Quarterly, 22*, 69–90.

Santos, T. (1992). Ideology in composition: L1 and ESL. *Journal of Second Language Writing, 1*, 1–15.

Santos, T. (2001). The place of politics in second language writing. In T. Silva & P. Matsuda (Eds.), *On second language writing* (pp. 173–190). Mahwah, NJ: Erlbaum.

Sapp, D. (2002). Towards an international and intercultural understanding of plagiarism and academic dishonesty in composition: Reflections from the People's Republic of China. *Issues in Writing, 13*, 58–79.

Sasaki, M. (2000). Toward an empirical model of EFL writing processes: An exploratory study. *Journal of Second Language Writing, 9*, 259–291.

Sasaki, M. (2004). A multiple-data analysis of the 3.5-year development of EFL student writers. *Language Learning, 54*, 525–582.

Sasaki, M., & Hirose, K. (1996). Explanatory variables for EFL students' expository writing. *Language Learning, 46*, 137–174.

Saville-Troike, M. (1984). What really matters in second language learning for academic achievement? *TESOL Quarterly, 18*, 199–219.

Saxena, M. (1994). Literacies among Panjabis in Southall. In M. Hamilton, D. Barton, & R. Ivanic (Eds.), *Worlds of literacy* (pp. 195–214). Clevedon, UK: Multilingual Matters.

Scarcella, R. (1984). How writers orient their readers in expository essays: A comparative study of native and non-native English writers. *TESOL Quarterly, 18*, 671–688.

Scarcella, R. (1990). *Teaching language minority students in the multicultural classroom*. Englewood Cliffs, NJ: Regents/Prentice Hall.

Schechter, S., & Harklau, L. (1991). *Annotated bibliography on writing in a non-native language*. Technical Report 51. Berkeley, CA: Center for the Study of Writing, University of California.

Schleppegrell, M., & Colombi, M. C. (Eds.) (2002). *Developing advanced literacy in first and second languages*. Mahwah, NJ: Erlbaum.

Schmidt, M. A. (2000). Teachers' attitudes toward ESL students and programs. In S. Wade (Ed.), *Inclusive education: A casebook and readings for prospective and practicing teachers* (pp. 121–128). Mahwah, NJ: Erlbaum.

Schneider, M., & Connor, U. (1990). Analyzing topical structure in ESL essays: Not all topics are equal. *Studies in Second Language Acquisition, 12*, 411–427.

Schneider, M., & Fujishima, N. (1995). When practice doesn't make perfect. The case of an ESL graduate student. In D. Belcher & G. Braine (Eds.), *Academic writing in a second language: Essays on research and pedagogy* (pp. 3–22). Norwood, NJ: Ablex.

Schoonen, R. (2005). Generalizability of writing scores: An application of structural equation modeling. *Language Testing, 22*, 1–30.

Schoonen, R., Vergeer, M., & Eiting, M. (1997). The assessment of writing ability: Expert readers versus lay readers. *Language Testing, 14*, 157–184.

Scollon, R. (1995). Plagiarism and ideology: Identity in intercultural discourse. *Language and Society, 24*, 1–28.

Selinker, L., Tarone, E., & Hanzeli, V. (Eds.). (1981). *English for academic and technical purposes*. Rowley, MA: Newbury House.

Selinker, L., Todd-Trimble, M., & Trimble, L. (1978). Rhetorical function-shifts in EST discourse. *TESOL Quarterly, 12*, 311–320.

Semke, H. (1984). The effects of the red pen. *Foreign Language Annals, 17*, 195–202.

Severino, C. (1993). The sociopolitical implications of response to second language and second dialect writing. *Journal of Second Language Writing, 2*, 181–201.

Shaw, P. (1991). Science research students' composing processes. *English for Specific Purposes, 10*, 189–206.

Shen, F. (1989). The classroom and the wider culture: Identity as key to learning English composition. *College Composition and Communication, 40*, 459–465.

Sheppard, K. (1994). *Content-ESL across the USA: A technical report*. Washington, DC: Center for Applied Linguistics.

Shermis, M., & Burstein, J. (Eds.) (2003). *Automated essay scoring: A cross-disciplinary perspective*. Mahwah, NJ: Erlbaum.

Shi, L. (1998). Effects of prewriting discussions on adult ESL students' compositions. *Journal of Second Language Writing, 7*, 319–345.

Shi, L. (2001). Native and nonnative-speaking EFL teachers' evaluation of Chinese students' English writing. *Language Testing, 18*, 303–325.

Shi, L. (2002). How Western-trained Chinese TESOL professionals publish in their home environment. *TESOL Quarterly, 36*, 625–634.

Shi, L. (2003). Writing in two cultures: Chinese professors return from the West. *Canadian Modern Language Review/La Revue canadienne des langues vivantes, 59*, 369–391.

Shi, L., & Beckett, G. (2002). Japanese exchange students' writing experiences in a Canadian university. *TESL Canada Journal, 20*, 38–56.

Shi, L., & Cumming, A. (1995). Teachers' conceptions of second language writing instruction: Five case studies. *Journal of Second Language Writing, 4*, 87–111.

Shih, M. (1986). Content-based approaches to teaching academic writing. *TESOL Quarterly, 20*, 617–648.

Shih, M. (1998). ESL writers' grammar editing strategies. *College ESL, 8*, 64–86.

Shih, M. (2001). A course in grammar-editing for ESL writers. In J. Murphy & P. Byrd (Eds.), *Understanding the courses we teach: Local perspectives on English language teaching* (pp. 346–363). Ann Arbor: University of Michigan Press.

Shohamy, E. (2001). *The power of tests: A critical perspective on the uses of language tests*. New York: Pearson Education.

Shohamy, E., Gordon, C., & Kraemer, R. (1992). The effect of raters' background and training on the reliability of direct writing tests. *Modern Language Journal, 76,* 27–33.

Short, D. (1997). Reading and 'riting and . . . social studies: Research on integrated language and content in secondary classrooms. In M. A. Snow & D. M. Brinton (Eds.), *The content-based classroom* (pp. 213–232). White Plains, NY: Addison-Wesley Longman.

Short, D. (1999). Integrating language and content for effective sheltered English programs. In C. Faltis & P. Wolfe (Eds.), *So much to say: Adolescents, bilingualism, and ESL in secondary school* (pp. 105–137). New York: Teachers College Press.

Silva, T. (1990). Second language composition instruction: Developments, issues, and directions in ESL. In B. Kroll (Ed.), *Second language writing: Research insights for the classroom* (pp. 11–23). New York: Cambridge University Press.

Silva, T. (1992). L1 vs. L2 writing: ESL graduate students' perceptions. *TESL Canada Journal, 10,* 27–47.

Silva, T. (1993). Toward an understanding of the distinct nature of L2 writing: The ESL research and its implications. *TESOL Quarterly, 27,* 657–677.

Silva, T. (1994). An examination of writing program administrators' options for placement of ESL students in first year writing classes. *Writing Program Administration, 18,* 37–43.

Silva, T. (1997). On the ethical treatment of ESL writers. *TESOL Quarterly, 31,* 359–363.

Silva, T., & Brice, C. (2004). Research in teaching writing. *Annual Review of Applied Linguistics, 24,* 70–106.

Silva, T., Brice, C., & Reichelt, M. (1999). *Annotated bibliography of scholarship in second language writing: 1993–1997.* Stamford, CT: Ablex.

Silva, T., & Leki, I. (2004). Family matters: The influence of applied linguistics and composition studies on second language writing studies—past, present, and future. *Modern Language Journal, 88,* 1–13.

Silva, T., Leki, I., & Carson, J. (1997). Broadening the perspective of mainstream composition studies: Some thoughts from the disciplinary margins. *Written Communication, 14,* 3, 398–428.

Silva, T., & Matsuda, P. (2002). Writing. In N. Schmitt (Ed.), *An introduction to applied linguistics* (pp. 251–266). London: Arnold.

Silva, T., Reichelt, M., Chikuma, Y., Duval-Couetil, N., Mo, R., Velez-Rendon, G., & Wood, S. (2003). Second language writing up close and personal: Some success stories. In B. Kroll (Ed.), *Exploring the dynamics of second language writing* (pp. 93–114). New York: Cambridge University Press.

Sims, B., & Guice, S. (1992). Differences between business letters from native and nonnative speakers of English. *The Journal of Business Communication, 29,* 23–39.

Sionis, C. (1995). Communication strategies in the writing of scientific research articles by non-native users of English. *English for Specific Purposes, 14,* 99–113.

Skibniewski, L. (1988). The writing processes of foreign language learners in their native and foreign languages: Evidence from thinking-aloud and behavior protocols. *Studia Anglica Posnaniensia, 21,* 177–186.

Skibniewski, L., & Skibniewska, M. (1986). Experimental study: The writing processes of intermediate/advanced foreign language learners in their foreign and native languages. *Studia Anglica Posnaniensia, 19,* 142–163.

Skinner, B. F. (1954). The science of learning and the art of teaching. *Harvard Educational Review, 24,* 86–97.

Skutnabb-Kangas, T. (2000). *Linguistic genocide in education, or worldwide diversity and human rights?* Mahwah, NJ: Erlbaum.

Smagorinsky, P. (Ed.). (2006). *Research on composition: Multiple perspectives on two decades of change.* New York: Teachers College Press.

Smith, D. (2000). Rater judgments in the direct assessment of competency-based second language writing ability. In G. Brindley (Ed.), *Studies in immigrant English language assessment,* vol. 1 (pp. 159–189). Sydney, Australia: National Centre for English Language Teaching and Research, Macquarie University.

Smith, V. (1994). *Thinking in a foreign language: An investigation into essay writing and translation by L2 learners.* Tubingen: Narr.

Smoke, T. (1988). Using feedback from ESL students to enhance their success in college. In S. Benesch (Ed.), *Ending remediation: Linking ESL and content in higher education* (pp. 7–19). Washington, DC: TESOL.

Smoke, T. (1994). Writing as a means of learning. *College ESL, 4,* 1–11.

Smoke, T. (Ed.). (1998). *Adult ESL: Politics, pedagogy, and participation in classroom and community programs.* Mahwah, NJ: Erlbaum.

Snow, M., & Brinton, D. (Eds.). (1997). *The content-based classroom: Perspectives on integrating language and content.* New York: Longman.

Solsken, J., Willett, J., & Wilson-Keenan, J. (2000). Cultivating hybrid texts in multicultural classrooms: Promise and challenge. *Research in the Teaching of English, 35,* 179–212.

So-mui, F., & Mead, K. (2000). An analysis of English in the workplace: The communication needs of textile and clothing merchandisers. *English for Specific Purposes, 19,* 351–368.

Song, B., & August, B. (2002). Using portfolios to assess the writing of ESL students: A powerful alternative? *Journal of Second Language Writing, 11,* 49–72.

Song, B., & Caruso, I. (1996). Do English and ESL faculty differ in evaluating the essays of native English-speaking and ESL students? *Journal of Second Language Writing, 5,* 163–182.

Sonomura, M. (1996). *Idiomaticity in the basic writing of American English: Formulas and idioms in the writing of multilingual and creole-speaking community college students in Hawaii.* New York: Peter Lang.

Söter, A. (1988). The second language learner and cultural transfer in narration. In A. Purves (Ed.), *Writing across languages and cultures: Issues in contrastive rhetoric* (pp. 177–205). Newbury Park, CA: Sage.

Spaan, M. (1993). The effect of prompt in essay examinations. In D. Douglas & C. Chapelle (Eds.), *A new decade of language testing research* (pp. 98–122). Washington, DC: TESOL.

Spack, R. (1988). Initiating ESL students in the academic discourse community: How far should we go? *TESOL Quarterly, 22,* 29–51.

Spack, R. (1997a). The acquisition of academic literacy in a second language. *Written Communication, 14,* 3–62.

Spack, R. (1997b). The rhetorical construction of multilingual students. *TESOL Quarterly, 31,* 765–774.

Spener, D. (Ed.). (1994). *Adult biliteracy in the United States.* McHenry, IL: Delta Systems and Center for Applied Linguistics.

Spolsky, B. (1995). *Measured words: The development of objective language testing.* Oxford, UK: Oxford University Press.

Stalker, J. W., & Stalker, J. C. (1989). The acquisition of rhetorical strategies in introductory paragraphs in written academic English: A comparison of NNS and NSs. In S. Gass, C. Madden, D. Preston, & L. Selinker (Eds.), *Variations in second language acquisition, Volume 1: Discourse and pragmatics* (pp. 144–152). Clevedon, UK: Multilingual Matters.

Stanley, J. (1992). Coaching student writers to be effective peer evaluators. *Journal of Second Language Writing, 1,* 217–233.

Stansfield, C., & Ross, J. (1988). A long-term research agenda for the Test of Written English. *Language Testing, 5*, 160–186.

Stapleton, P. (2002). Critical thinking in Japanese L2 writing: Rethinking tired constructs. *ELT Journal, 56*, 250–257.

Starfield, S. (2002). "I'm a second language English speaker": Negotiating writer identity and authority in Sociology One. *Journal of Language, Identity, and Education, 1*, 121–140.

Stein, P. (1998). Reconfiguring the past and the present: Performing literacy histories in a Johannesburg classroom. *TESOL Quarterly, 32*, 517–528.

Stern, H. H., Allen, P., & Harley, B. (1992). *Issues and options in language teaching.* Oxford, UK: Oxford University Press.

Sternglass, M. (1997). *Time to know them.* Mahwah, NJ: Erlbaum.

Stewart, T., Rehorick, S., & Perry, B. (2001). Adapting the Canadian Language Benchmarks for writing assessment. *TESL Canada Journal, 18*, 48–64.

Storch, N. (2002). Patterns of interaction in ESL pair work. *Language Learning, 52*, 119–158.

Storch, N. (2005). Collaborative writing: Product, process, and students' reflections. *Journal of Second Language Writing, 14*, 153–173.

Storch, N., & Tapper, J. (1997). Student annotations: What NNS and NS university students say about their own writing. *Journal of Second Language Writing, 6*, 245–264.

Storch, N., & Tapper, J. (2002). A useful kind of interaction? Evaluations by university students of feedback on written assignments. *Australian Review of Applied Linguistics, 25*, 147–167.

Stoynoff, S., & Chapelle, C. (2005). *ESOL tests and testing.* Alexandria, VA: TESOL.

Street, B. (1984). *Literacy in theory and practice.* Cambridge, UK: Cambridge University Press.

Street, B. (Ed.). (1993). *Cross-cultural approaches to literacy.* New York: Cambridge University Press.

Street, B. (Ed.). (2001). *Literacy and development: Ethnographic perspectives.* New York: Routledge.

Street, B. (2005). Recent applications of New Literacy Studies in educational contexts. *Research in the Teaching of English, 39*, 417–423.

Sullivan, K., & Lindgren, E. (2002). Self-assessment in autonomous computer-aided second language writing. *ELT Journal, 56*, 669–679.

Susser, B. (1994). Process approaches in ESL/EFL writing instruction. *Journal of Second Language Writing, 3*, 31–47.

Susser, B. (1998). EFL's othering of Japan: Orientalism in English language teaching. *JALT Journal, 20*, 49–82.

Sutherland-Smith, W. (2004). Pandora's box: Academic perceptions of student plagiarism in writing. *Journal of English for Academic Purposes, 5*, 83–95.

Svendsen, C., & Krebs, K. (1984). Identifying English for the job: Examples from health care occupations. *English for Specific Purposes, 3*, 153–164.

Swain, M., & Lapkin, S. (1995). Problems in output and the cognitive processes they generate: A step towards second language learning. *Applied Linguistics, 16*, 371–391.

Swain, M., & Lapkin, S. (1998). Interaction and second language learning: Two adolescent French immersion students working together. *Modern Language Journal, 83*, 320–338.

Swales, J. (1990a). *Genre analysis: English in academic and research settings.* New York: Cambridge University Press.

Swales, J. (1990b). Nonnative speaker graduate engineering students and their introductions: Global coherence and local management. In U. Connor & A. Johns

(Eds.), *Coherence in writing: Research and pedagogical perspectives* (pp. 189–206). Alexandria, VA: TESOL.

Swales, J. (1997). English as Tyrannosaurus rex. *World Englishes, 16*, 373–382.

Swales, J., & Feak, C. B. (1994). *English in today's research world: A writing guide.* Ann Arbor: University of Michigan Press.

Swales, J., & Lindemann, S. (2002). Teaching the literature review to international graduate students. In A. Johns (Ed.), *Genre in the classroom* (pp. 105–120). Mahwah, NJ: Lawrence Erlbaum.

Swales, J., & Luebs, M. (2002). Genre analysis and the advanced second language writer. In E. Barton & G. Stygall (Eds.), *Discourse studies in composition* (pp. 135–154). Cresskill, NJ: Hampton Press.

Sweedler-Brown, C. (1993). ESL essay evaluation: The influence of sentence-level and rhetorical features. *Journal of Second Language Writing, 2*, 3–17.

Sze, C. (2002). A case study of the revision process of a reluctant ESL student writer. *TESL Canada Journal, 19*, 21–36.

Takagaki, T. (2003). The revision patterns and intentions in L1 and L2 by Japanese writers: A case study. *TESL Canada Journal/Revue TESL du Canada, 21*, 22–38.

Tang, G., & Tithecott, J. (1999). Peer response in ESL writing. *TESL Canada Journal/Revue TESL du Canada, 16*, 20–38.

Tannacito, D. (1995). *A guide to writing English as a second or foreign language: An annotated bibliography of research and pedagogy.* Alexandria, VA: TESOL.

Tardy, C. (2004). The role of English in scientific communication: Lingua franca or Tyrannosaurus rex? *Journal of English for Academic Purposes, 3*, 247–269.

Tardy, C. (2005a). Expressions of disciplinarity and individuality in a multimodal genre. *Computers and Compositions, 22*, 319–336.

Tardy, C. (2005b). "It's like a story": Rhetorical knowledge development in advanced academic literacy. *Journal of English for Academic Purposes, 4*, 325–338.

Tardy, C. (2006). Researching first and second language genre learning: A comparative review and a look ahead. *Journal of Second Language Writing, 15*, 79–101.

Tarnopolsky, O. (2000). Writing English as a foreign language: A report from Ukraine. *Journal of Second Language Writing, 9*, 209–226.

Tarone, E., Downing, B., Cohen, A., Gillette, S., Murie, R., & Dailey, B. (1993). The writing of Southeast Asian-American students in secondary school and university. *Journal of Second Language Writing, 2*, 149–172.

Taylor, C., Kirsch, I., Jamieson, J., & Eignor, D. (1999). Examining the relationship between computer familiarity and performance on computer-based language tasks. *Language Learning, 49*, 219–274.

Tedick, D., & Mathison, D. (1995). Holistic scoring in ESL writing assessment: What does an analysis of rhetorical features reveal? In D. Belcher & G. Braine (Eds.) *Academic writing in a second language* (pp. 205–230). Norwood, NJ: Ablex.

Tesdell, L. S. (1984). ESL spelling errors. *TESOL Quarterly, 18*, 333–4.

TESOL (Teachers of English to Speakers of Other Languages). (2001). *Scenarios for ESL standards-based assessment.* Alexandria, VA: Authors.

Thatcher, B. (2000). L2 professional writing in a US and South American context. *Journal of Second Language Writing, 9*, 41–69.

Thesen, L. (1997). Voices, discourse, and transition: In search of new categories in EAP. *TESOL Quarterly, 31*, 487–511.

Thonus, T. (2002). Tutor and student assessments of academic writing tutorials: What is "success"? *Assessing Writing, 8*, 110–137.

Thonus, T. (2003). Serving generation 1.5 learners in the university writing center. *TESOL Journal, 12*, 17–24.

Thonus, T. (2004). What are the differences? Tutor interactions with first- and second-language writers. *Journal of Second Language Writing, 13*, 227–242.

Tollefson, J. W. (1986). Functional competencies in the U.S. Refugee Program: Theoretical and practical problems. *TESOL Quarterly, 20*, 649–664.

Tollefson, J. W. (1989). *Alien winds: The re-education of America's Indochinese refugees.* New York: Praeger.

Toohey, K. (1998). "Breaking them up, taking them away": ESL students in Grade 1. *TESOL Quarterly, 32*, 61–84.

Toohey, K. (2000). *Learning English in schools: Identity, social relations, and classroom practice.* Clevedon: Multilingual Matters.

Toohey, K., & Day, E. (1999). Language learning: The importance of access to community. *TESL Canada Journal, 17*, 40–53.

Torras, M. R., & Celaya, M. L. (2001). Age-related differences in the development of written production. An empirical study of EFL school learners. In R. M. Manchón (Ed.), *Writing in the L2 classroom: Issues in research and pedagogy.* Special Issue of *International Journal of English Studies, 1*, 2, 103–126.

Townsend, J., & Fu, D. (1998). A Chinese boy's joyful initiation into American literacy. *Language Arts, 75*, 193–201.

Trimbur, J. (1994). Taking the social turn: Teaching writing post-process. *College Composition and Communication, 45*, 108–118.

Trueba, H. (1987). Organizing classroom instruction in specific sociocultural contexts: Teaching Mexican youth to write in English. In S. Goldman & H. Trueba (Eds.), *Becoming literate in English as a second language* (pp. 235–252). Norwood, NJ: Ablex.

Truscott, J. (1996). The case against grammar correction in L2 writing classes. *Language Learning, 46*, 327–369.

Tsui, A., & Ng, M. (2000). Do secondary L2 writers benefit from peer comments? *Journal of Second Language Writing, 9*, 147–170.

Tucker, A. (1995). *Decoding ESL: International students in the American college classroom.* Portsmouth, NH: Boynton/Cook.

Turner, C., & Upshur, J. (2002). Rating scales derived from student samples: Effects of the scale maker and the student sample on scale content and student scores. *TESOL Quarterly, 36*, 49–70.

Tyler, R. (1949). *Basic principles of curriculum and instruction.* Chicago: University of Chicago Press.

Tyndall, B., & Kenyon, D. (1996). Validation of a new holistic rating scale using Rasch Multi-faceted analysis. In A. Cumming & R. Berwick (Eds.), *Validation in language testing* (pp. 39–57). Clevedon, UK: Multilingual Matters.

Urzua, C. (1986). A child's story. In P. Rigg & D. S. Enright (Eds.), *Children and ESL: Integrating perspectives* (pp. 93–112). Washington, DC: TESOL.

Urzua, C. (1987). "You stopped too soon": Second language children composing and revising. *TESOL Quarterly, 21*, 279–304.

Uzawa, K. (1994). Translation, L1 writing, and L2 writing of Japanese ESL learners. *Journal of CAAL, 16*, 119–134.

Uzawa, K. (1996). Second language learners' process of L1 writing, L2 writing, and translation from L1 into L2. *Journal of Second Language Writing, 5*, 271–294.

Valdes, G. (1996). *Con respeto: Bridging the distances between culturally diverse families and schools.* New York: Teachers College Press.

Valdes, G. (1999). Incipient bilingualism and the development of English language writing abilities in the secondary school. In C. Faltis & P. Wolfe (Eds.), *So much to say: Adolescents, bilingualism, and ESL in the secondary school* (pp. 138–175). New York: Teachers College Press.

Valdes, G. (2000). Nonnative English speakers: Language bigotry in English mainstream classrooms. *ADE Bulletin, 124*, 12–17.

Valdes, G. (2001). *Learning and not learning English: Latino students in American schools.* New York: Teachers College Press.

Valdes, G. (2004). The teaching of academic language to minority second language learners. In A. Ball & S. Freedman (Eds.), *Bakhtinian perspectives on language, literacy, and learning* (pp. 66–98). New York: Cambridge University Press.

Valdes, G., Haro, P., & Echevarriarza, M. (1992). The development of writing abilities in a foreign language: Contributions toward a general theory of L2 writing. *Modern Language Journal, 76,* 333–352.

Valdes, G., & Sanders, P. A. (1998). Latino ESL students and the development of writing abilities. In C. R. Cooper & L. Odell (Eds.), *Evaluating writing* (pp. 249–278). Urbana, IL: National Council of Teachers of English.

Vandrick, S. (1994). Feminist pedagogy and ESL. *College ESL, 4,* 69–92.

Vandrick, S. (1995). Privileged ESL university students. *TESOL Quarterly, 29,* 375–381.

Vandrick, S. (1997). The role of hidden identities in the postsecondary ESL classroom. *TESOL Quarterly, 31,* 153–157.

Vann, R., Lorenz, F., & Meyer, D. (1991). Error gravity: Faculty response to errors in the written discourse of nonnative speakers of English. In L. Hamp-Lyons (Ed.), *Assessing second language writing in academic contexts* (pp. 181–195). Norwood, NJ: Ablex.

Vann, R., Meyer, D., & Lorenz, F. (1984). Error gravity: A study of faculty opinion of ESL errors. *TESOL Quarterly, 18,* 427–440.

Vasquez, O. (1992). A Mexicano perspective: Reading the world in a multicultural setting. In D. Murray (Ed.), *Diversity as resource: Redefining cultural literacy* (pp. 113–134). Washington, DC: TESOL.

Vaughn, C. (1991). Holistic assessment: What goes on in the raters' minds? In L. Hamp-Lyons (Ed.), *Assessing second language writing in academic contexts* (pp. 111–125). Norwood, NJ: Ablex.

Victori, M. (1999). An analysis of writing knowledge in EFL composing: A case study of two effective and two less effective writers. *System, 27,* 537–555.

Villalva, K. (2006). Hidden literacies and inquiry approaches of bilingual high school writers. *Written Communication, 23,* 91–129.

Villamil, O., & de Guerrero, M. (1996). Peer revision in the L2 classroom: Social-cognitive activities, mediating strategies, and aspects of social behavior. *Journal of Second Language Writing, 5,* 51–75.

Volk, D., & de Acosta, M. (2003). Reinventing texts and contexts: Syncretic literacy events in young Puerto Rican children's homes. *Research in the Teaching of English, 38,* 8–48.

Vollmer, G. (2000). Praise and stigma: Teachers' constructions of the "typical ESL student." *Journal of Intercultural Studies, 21,* 53–66.

Wald, B. (1987). The development of writing skills among Hispanic high school students. In S. Goldman & H. Trueba (Eds.), *Becoming literate in English as a second language* (pp. 155–185). Norwood, NJ: Ablex.

Wallace, C. (1997). IELTS: Global implications of curriculum and materials design. *ELT Journal, 51,* 370–373.

Walqui, A. (2000). *Access and engagement: Program design and instructional approaches for immigrant students in secondary school.* Washington, DC: Center for Applied Linguistics.

Walsh, C. (1994). Engaging students in learning: Literacy, language, and knowledge production with Latino adolescents. In D. Spener (Ed.), *Adult biliteracy in the United States* (pp. 211–237). Washington, DC: Center for Applied Linguistics.

Wang, W., & Wen, Q. (2002). L1 use in the L2 composing process: An exploratory study of 16 Chinese EFL writers. *Journal of Second Language Writing, 11,* 225–246.

Warden, C. (2000). EFL business writing behaviors in differing feedback environments. *Language Learning, 50,* 573–616.

Warschauer, M. (1999). *Electronic literacies: Language, culture, and power in online education.* Mahwah, NJ: Erlbaum.

Waters, A. (1996). *A review of research into needs in English for academic purposes of relevance to the North American higher education context.* TOEFL Monograph 6. Princeton, NJ: Educational Testing Service.

Watt, D., & Roessingh, H. (1994). ESL dropout: The myth of educational equity. *Alberta Journal of Educational Research, 40,* 283–296.

Watt, D., & Roessingh, H. (2001). The dynamics of ESL drop-out: Plus ça change. *Canadian Modern Language Review/La Revue canadienne des langues vivantes, 58,* 203–222.

Watt, D., Roessingh, H., & Bosetti, L. (1996). Success and failure: Stories of ESL students' educational and cultural adjustment to high school. *Urban Education, 31,* 199–221.

Way, D. P., Joiner, E. G., & Seaman, M. A. (2000). Writing in the secondary foreign language classroom: The effects of prompts and tasks on novice learners of French. *The Modern Language Journal, 84,* 171–184.

Weigle, S. (1994). Effects of training on raters of ESL compositions. *Language Testing, 11,* 197–223.

Weigle, S. (1998). Using FACETS to model rater training effects. *Language Testing, 15,* 263–287.

Weigle, S. (2002). *Assessing writing.* Cambridge, UK: Cambridge University Press.

Weigle, S. (2004). Integrating reading and writing in a competency test for non-native speakers of English. *Assessing Writing, 9,* 27–55.

Weigle, S., Boldt, H., & Valsecchi, M. (2003). Effects of task and rater background in the evaluation of ESL student writing. *TESOL Quarterly, 37,* 345–354.

Weigle, S., & Nelson, G. (2004). Novice tutors and their ESL tutees: Three case studies of tutor roles and perceptions of tutorial success. *Journal of Second Language Writing, 13,* 203–225.

Weinstein, G. (1984). Literacy and second language acquisition: Issues and perspectives. *TESOL Quarterly, 18,* 471–484.

Weinstein-Shr, G. (1993). Literacy and social process: A community in transition. In B. Street (Ed.), *Cross-cultural approaches to literacy* (pp. 272–293). Cambridge, UK: Cambridge University Press.

Weir, C., & Milanovic, M. (2003). *Continuity and innovation: Revising the Cambridge Proficiency in English examination: 1913–2002.* Cambridge, UK: Cambridge University Press.

Weissberg, B. (1993). The graduate seminar: Another research-process genre. *English for Specific Purposes, 12,* 23–35.

Weissberg, B. (1994). Speaking of writing: Some functions of talk in the ESL composition class. *Journal of Second Language Writing, 3,* 121–139.

Weissberg, B. (2000). Developmental relationships in the acquisition of English syntax: Writing vs speech. *Learning and Instruction, 10,* 37–53.

Welaratna, U. (1992). A Khmer perspective: Connections between Khmer students' behavior, history, and culture. In D. Murray (Ed.), *Diversity as resource: Redefining cultural literacy* (pp. 135–147). Washington, DC: TESOL.

Westerbrook, L., & Bergquist-Moody. (1996). A whole-language approach to mainstreaming. In J. Clegg (Ed.), *Mainstreaming ESL: Case studies in integrating ESL students into the mainstream curriculum* (pp. 65–93). Clevedon, UK: Multilingual Matters.

Widdowson, H. (1983). *Learning purpose and language use.* Oxford, UK: Oxford University Press.

Wikborg, E. (1990). Types of coherence breaks in Swedish student writing: Misleading paragraph division. In U. M. Connor & A. Johns (Eds.), *Coherence in writing: Research and pedagogical perspectives* (pp. 131–149). Alexandria, VA: TESOL.

Willett, J. (1995). Becoming first graders in an L2: An ethnographic study of L2 socialization. *TESOL Quarterly, 29*, 473–503.

Williams, J. (1995). ESL composition program administration in the United States. *Journal of Second Language Writing, 4*, 157–179.

Williams, J. (2002). Undergraduate second language writers in the writing center. *Journal of Basic Writing, 21*, 73–91.

Williams, J. (2004). Tutoring and revision: Second language writers in the writing center. *Journal of Second Language Writing, 13*, 173–201.

Williams, J., & Severino, C. (2004). The writing center and second language writers. *Journal of Second Language Writing, 13*, 165–172.

Wilson-Keena, J., Willett, J., & Solsken, J. (2001). Families as curriculum partners in an urban elementary inclusion classroom. In J. Murphy & P. Byrd (Eds.), *Understanding the courses we teach: Local perspectives on English language teaching* (pp. 92–114). Ann Arbor: University of Michigan Press.

Winer, L. (1992). "Spinach to chocolate": Changing awareness and attitudes in ESL writing teachers. *TESOL Quarterly, 26*, 57–80.

Wolfe-Quintero, K., Inagaki, S., & Kim, H.-Y. (1998). *Second language development in writing: Measures of fluency, accuracy and complexity.* Honolulu: University of Hawai'i at Manoa.

Wolfe-Quintero, K., & Segade, G. (1999). University support for second-language writers across the curriculum. In L. Harklau, K. Losey, & M. Siegal (Eds.), *Generation 1.5 meets college composition* (pp. 191–209). Mahwah, NJ: Erlbaum.

Wong, A. (2005). Writers' mental representations of the intended audience and of the rhetorical purpose for writing and the strategies that they employed when they composed. *System, 33*, 29–47.

Wong, R. (1993). Strategies for construction of meaning: Chinese students in Singapore writing in English and Chinese. *Language, Culture, and Curriculum, 6*, 291–301.

Woodall, B. (2002). Language-switching: Using the first language while writing in a second language. *Journal of Second Language Writing, 11*, 7–28.

Wu, S.-Y., & Rubin, D. (2000). Evaluating the impact of collectivism and individualism on argumentative writing by Chinese and North American college students. *Research in the Teaching of English, 35*, 148–178.

Xu, H. (1999). Young Chinese ESL children's home literacy experiences. *Reading Horizons, 40*, 47–64.

Yakhontova, T. (2002). Selling or telling? Towards understanding cultural variation in research genres. In J. Flowerdew (Ed.), *Academic discourse* (pp. 216–232). London: Longman.

Yamada, K. (2003). What prevents ESL/EFL writers from avoiding plagiarism?: Analyses of 10 North American college websites. *System, 31*, 247–258.

Yang, L., & Shi, L. (2003). Exploring six MBA students' summary writing by introspection. *Journal of English for Academic Purposes, 2*, 165–192.

Yasuda, S. (2004). Revising strategies in ESL academic writing: A case study of Japanese postgraduate student writers. *Journal of Asian Pacific Communication, 14*, 91–112.

Yates, R., & Kenkel, J. (2002). Responding to sentence-level errors in writing. *Journal of Second Language Writing, 11*, 29–47.

Yau, M., & Belanger, J. (1984). The influence of mode on the syntactic complexity of EFL students at three grade levels. *TESL Canada Journal, 2*, 65–76.

Yau, M., & Belanger, J. (1985). Syntactic development in the writing of ESL students. *English Quarterly, 18*, 107–118.

Yeh, S. (1998). Empowering education: Teaching argumentative writing to cultural minority middle-school students. *Research in the Teaching of English*, 33, 49–83.

Yoon, H., & Hirvela, A. (2004). ESL student attitudes toward corpus use in L2 writing. *Journal of Second Language Writing*, 13, 257–283.

You, X. (2004a). New directions in EFL writing: A report from China. *Journal of Second Language Writing*, 13, 253–256.

You, X. (2004b). "The choice made from no choice": English writing instruction in a Chinese university. *Journal of Second Language Writing*, 13, 97–110.

Young, R., & Miller, E. (2004). Learning as changing participation: Discourse roles in ESL writing conferences. *Modern Language Journal*, 88, 519–535.

Youngs, C., & Youngs, G. (2001). Predictors of mainstream teachers' attitudes toward ESL students. *TESOL Quarterly*, 35, 97–120.

Zainuddin, H., & Moore, R. A. (2003). Audience awareness in L1 and L2 composing of bilingual writers. *TESL-EJ*, 7, 1–18. Retrieved June 21, 2005, from http://www-writing.berkeley.edu/TESL-EJ/ej25/a2.html

Zamel, V. (1976). Teaching composition in the ESL classroom: What we can learn from research in the teaching of English. *TESOL Quarterly*, 10, 67–76.

Zamel, V. (1982). Writing: The process of discovering meaning. *TESOL Quarterly*, 16, 195–209.

Zamel, V. (1983). The composing processes of advanced ESL students: Six case studies. *TESOL Quarterly*, 17, 165–187.

Zamel, V. (1985). Responding to student writing. *TESOL Quarterly*, 19, 79–101.

Zamel, V. (1987). Recent research on writing pedagogy. *TESOL Quarterly*, 21, 697–715.

Zamel, V. (1990). Through students' eyes: The experiences of three ESL writers. *Journal of Basic Writing*, 9, 83–97.

Zamel, V. (1992). Writing one's way into reading. *TESOL Quarterly*, 26, 463–485.

Zamel, V. (1995). Strangers in academia. *College Composition and Communication*, 46, 506–521.

Zhang, M. (2000). Cohesive features in the expository writing of undergraduates in two Chinese universities. *Regional English Language Centre Journal*, 31, 61–95.

Zhang, S. (1995). Reexamining the affective advantage of peer feedback in the ESL writing class. *Journal of Second Language Writing*, 4, 209–222.

Zhu, W. (2001). Interaction and feedback in mixed peer response groups. *Journal of Second Language Writing*, 10, 251–276.

Zhu, W. (2004). Faculty views on the importance of writing, the nature of academic writing, and teaching and responding to writing in the disciplines. *Journal of Second Language Writing*, 13, 29–48.

Zimmermann, R. (2000). L2 writing: Subprocesses, a model of formulating and empirical findings. *Learning and Instruction*, 10, 73–99.

Zwick, R., & Thayer, D. (1995). *A comparison of the performance of graduate and undergraduate school applicants on the Test of Written English*. TOEFL Research Report No. 50. Princeton, NJ: Educational Testing Service.

Zydek-Bednarczuk, U. (1997). Language culture, language awareness, and writing curricula in Polish schools. In A. Duszak (Ed.), *Culture and styles of academic discourse* (pp. 89–101). New York: Mouton de Gruyter.

Index